Belfast Studies in Language, Culture and Politics
General Editors: John M. Kirk and Dónall P. Ó Baoill

1: *Language and Politics: Northern Ireland, the Republic of Ireland, and Scotland* published 2000 ISBN 0 85389 791 3

2: *Language Links: the Languages of Scotland and Ireland* published 2001 ISBN 0 85389 795 6

3: *Linguistic Politics: Language Policies for Northern Ireland, the Republic of Ireland, and Scotland* published 2001 ISBN 0 85389 815 4

4: *Travellers and their Language* published 2002 ISBN 0 85389 832 4

5: Simone Zwickl, Language Attitudes, *Ethnic Identity and Dialect Use across the Northern Ireland Border: Armagh and Monaghan* published 2002 ISBN 0 85389 834 0

6: *Language Planning and Education: Linguistic Issues in Northern Ireland, the Republic of Ireland, and Scotland* published 2002 ISBN 0 85389 835 9

7: Edna Longley, Eamonn Hughes and Des O'Rawe (eds.) *Ireland (Ulster) Scotland: Concepts, Contexts, Comparisons* published 2003 ISBN 0 85389 844 8

8: Maolcholaim Scott and Roíse Ní Bhaoill (eds.) *Gaelic-Medium Education Provision: Northern Ireland, the Republic of Ireland, Scotland and the Isle of Man* published 2003 ISBN 0 85389 847 2

9: Dónall Ó Riagáin (ed.) *Language and Law in Northern Ireland* published 2003 ISBN 0 85389 848 0

10: *Towards our Goals in Broadcasting, the Press, the Performing Arts and the Economy: Minority Languages in Northern Ireland, the Republic of Ireland, and Scotland* published 2003 ISBN 0 85389 856 1

11: J. Derrick McClure (ed.) *Doonsin' Emerauds: New Scrieves anent Scots an Gaelic / New Studies on Scots and Gaelic* published 2004 ISBN 0 85389 860 X

12: Neal Alexander, Shane Murphy and Anne Oakman (eds.) *To the Other Shore: Cross-currents in Irish and Scottish Studies* published 2004 ISBN 0 85389 863 4

13: *Legislation, Literature and Sociolinguistics: Northern Ireland, the Republic of Ireland, and Scotland* published 2005 ISBN 0 85389 874 X

14: Shane Alcobia-Murphy, Johanna Archbold, John Gibney and Carole Jones (eds.) *Beyond the Anchoring Grounds: More Cross-currents in Irish and Scottish Studies* published 2006 ISBN 0 85389 885 5

15: Dónall Ó Riagáin (ed.) *Voces Diversae: Lesser-Used Language Education in Europe* published 2006 ISBN 0 85389 886 3

16: William Lamb *Scottish Gaelic Speech and Writing: Register Variation in an Endangered Language* published 2007 ISBN 0 85389 895 2

17: Alasdair MacCaluim *Reversing Language Shift: The Social Identity and Role of Scottish Gaelic Learners* published 2007 ISBN 0 85389 897 9

18: Seán Mac Corraidh *Teaching through the Medium of the Irish Language: Beliefs and Practices of Immersion Teachers in Irish-medium Primary Schools in Belfast* published 2007 ISBN 0 85389 898 7

19: *Language and Economic Development: Northern Ireland, the Republic of Ireland, and Scotland* published 2007 ISBN 0 85389 910 X

Reversing Language Shift:
The Social Identity and Role of Adult Learners of Scottish Gaelic

Alasdair MacCaluim

Cló Ollscoil na Banríona
Belfast 2007

First published in 2007
Cló Ollscoil na Banríona
Queen's University Belfast
Belfast, BT7 1NN

Belfast Studies in Language, Culture and Politics
www.bslcp.com

© Cló Ollscoil na Banríona and Alasdair MacCaluim

The publication of this volume has been made possible through the financial support of Bòrd na Gàidhlig.

British Library Cataloguing-in-Publication Data
A catalogue record for this book is available from the British Library.

ISBN 0 85389 897 9

Typeset by Nigel Craig and John Kirk in Granjon
Cover artwork by Kate MacDonald
Cover design by Colin Young
Printing by the Cromwell Press, Trowbridge

CONTENTS

1	Introduction	1
2	Gaelic and Reversing Language Shift Theory	7
3	The Gaelic Learning Infrastructure	20
4	The Social Identity of Gaelic Learners	76
5	The Gaelic Learners' Survey	108
6	Conclusions	228
	References	234
	Appendix 1: the Gaelic Learners' Survey Questionnaire	251
	Appendix 2: Learners' Views on Native Speakers	266
	Index	273

Publisher Disclaimer
The publisher has used its best endeavours to ensure that the URLs for external websites referred to in this book are correct at the time of going to press. However, the publisher has no responsibility for the websites and can make no guarantee that a site will remain live or that the content is or will remain appropriate.

Dedication

Tha an leabhar seo mar chuimhneachan air an dà ghaisgeach as motha ann an eachdraidh na h-Alba:

M' athair, Bill MacCaluim (1947-2005) agus Stuart Adamson, neach-ciùil (1958-2001)

Leviĝu, proletar' de l' tero
leviĝu, sklavoj de malsat'!
La Vero tondras en kratero,
sekvos finofara bat'.
La paseon plene ni forviŝos,
amasoj, marŝu, kresku ni!
La mond' en fundament' ŝanĝiĝos,
ne nul', sed ĉio estu ni!

Por batal', por la lasta
unuiĝu nia front'
internacia estos
la tuta homa mond'!

(La Internacio)

Acknowledgements

I would like to gratefully acknowledge the help and support of the following people during the production of my PhD thesis on which this book is based: Peadar Morgan and the staff of Clì Gàidhlig, Boyd Robertson, Davyth Hicks, Will Lamb, Ailean Caimbeul, Mairead NicIomhair, Gordon McCoy, Eddy Cavin, and everybody who helped me with questionnaire distribution. I would like to extend particular thanks to my PhD supervisors Ronald Black, Roibeard Ó Maolalaigh, Professor Kenneth MacKinnon and Professor William Gillies. I am also very grateful for the financial support which I received from the University of Edinburgh, the Catherine McCaig Trust and Comunn na Gàidhlig which enabled my studies.

I would like to gratefully acknowledge the help and support of the following people during the production of this book: Siùsaidh Hardy and Eilidh Shaw at Clì Gàidhlig, the Scottish Executive Gaelic Unit, Peadar Morgan, Alison Lang, Marc Mac an Fhilidh, Jenny MacCaluim, Ciorstaidh Mairead NicCaluim and Maureen McCallum.

In particular I would like to thank John Kirk, my publisher at Cló Ollscoil na Banríona, without whom the publicaton of this volume would not have been possible, Wilson McLeod for commenting so beneficially on drafts of the entire manuscript, and Bòrd na Gàidhlig for funding the publication of this book.

"What does seem peculiar, in view of the manifest vitality and innovativeness of Welsh-speaking Wales, is the constant lament that the end of the language is in sight. Perhaps I am fortunate in that, not having been brought up in a community in which Welsh was the dominant language, I cannot share the sense of despair felt by those who were brought up in such communities and who contemplate their erosion with something akin to panic. I am more aware of advances. [...] A great deal of the panic and despair stems, not so much from the erosion of the language in many of its former strongholds as from the realisation that the way of life associated with the language in those strongholds has passed away. I did not know that way of life, and so its passing leaves me unmoved. Indeed, it could be argued that the association of Welsh with a vanishing way of life was detrimental to the language, and that its continuance is dependent on its ability to anchor itself in modernity, an ability to which it has, to some extent, shown." (Davies 1993: 117)

"Bhiodh e fìor a ràdh nach tig an seann saoghal Gaidhealach air ais mar a bha e agus is ma dh'fhaodte gur e sin nàdar a' chaochlaidh. 'S e bhiodh truagh ged-thà, mura tigeadh dad ann a dheigheadh na àite. Tha mi toilichte a ràdh gu bheil caochladh choimhearsnachdan a' nochdadh air feadh na dùthcha anns an latha a th' ann. Nam bheachd-sa, chan eil aon nas luachmhoire na tè eile. Tha a h-àite aig gach tè." (NicFhionghuin 2001)

List of Tables

1.	Fishman's Graded Intergenerational Disruption Scale	9
2.	Students studying Gaelic by year	32
3.	Sex of all respondents	112
4.	Sex of entire CLI membership	113
5.	Age of all respondents	115
6.	Age of respondents in Scotland excluding university students	116
7.	Distribution of Gaelic learners by country of residence	117
8.	Location of all respondents in UK by country of residence	117
9.	Place of upbringing of respondents in the UK but outwith Scotland	117
10.	Place of upbringing of respondents outwith the UK	118
11.	Place of upbringing of respondents resident in Scotland	118
12.	Place of residence of CLI members in Scotland by local authority area	119
13.	Place of residence of CLI members in Scotland by pre-1996 region	120
14.	Residence in the Highlands or Lowlands: respondents in Scotland	121
15.	Upbringing in the Highlands or Lowlands: respondents in Scotland	121
16.	Upbringing or residence in the Highlands: respondents in Scotland	122
17.	Level of qualification: respondents in Scotland	122
18.	Level of qualification: respondents in Scotland vs. 1991 Census	123
19.	Level of qualification: respondents in UK outwith Scotland	123
20.	Level of qualification: respondents outwith UK	124
21.	Socio-economic status: respondents in Scotland	124
22.	Socio-economic status: respondents in UK outwith Scotland	125
23.	Economic position: Scottish and UK respondents vs. Scottish Census data	125
24.	Social Class based on occupation: [Registrar General's Social Class]	126
25.	Social Class based on occupation: Scottish respondents currently in employment	126
26.	Social Class based on occupation: all Scottish respondents	126
27.	Social Class based on occupation: respondents in UK outwith Scotland	127
28.	Social Class based on occupation: respondents outwith UK in employment	127
29.	Political affiliation: respondents in Scotland	129
30.	Political preference: respondents in Scotland vs. opinion polls	130
31.	Political preference: respondents in Scotland vs. opinion poll	130
32.	Political affiliation: respondents in UK outwith Scotland	131
33.	Voting intentions: respondents in UK outwith Scotland	131
34.	Political affiliation of respondents outwith UK	132
35.	Self-identification on a left-right spectrum: respondents in Scotland	132
36.	Self-identification on a left-right spectrum: respondents in rest of UK	133
37.	Self-identification on a left-right spectrum of respondents in the rest of the world	133
38.	National identity of respondents in Scotland	134
39.	National identity of respondents in rest of UK	135

40.	National identity of respondents outwith UK	135
41.	Identities of Scottish respondents	136
42.	Identification with Gael identity by level of fluency in spoken Gaelic: respondents in Scotland	137
43.	Identification with Gael identity by place of upbringing: respondents in Scotland	137
44.	Identification with Gael identity by place of residence: respondents in Scotland	138
45.	Identification with Gaelic speaker identity by level of fluency in spoken Gaelic: respondents in Scotland	138
46.	Identification with Highland identity: respondents in Scotland	139
47.	Identification with Island identity: respondents in Scotland	139
48.	Identities of UK respondents outwith Scotland	140
49.	Identities of respondents outwith UK	141
50.	Ability to speak languages other than Gaelic and English: all respondents	143
51.	Languages spoken: respondents with languages other than Gaelic and English	143
52.	Languages of which respondents in Scotland have knowledge	143
53.	Languages of which respondents in the rest of the UK have knowledge	144
54.	Languages of which respondents outwith the UK have knowledge	144
55.	Membership of non-Gaelic interest / pressure groups	145
56.	Nature of membership groups: respondents in Scotland	146
57.	Religious affiliation: all respondents	147
58.	Association with religious groups / denominations	148
59.	Involvement with religious groups / denominations: all respondents	148
60.	Frequency of religious group involvement: all respondents	148
61.	Ability of parents to speak Gaelic: all respondents	149
62.	Ability of grandparents to speak Gaelic: all respondents	149
63.	Learners of Gaelic: CLI respondents:	151
64.	Status of learners of Gaelic: CLI respondents:	151
65.	Ability in Gaelic: CLI respondents Scotland	152
66.	Ability in Gaelic: respondents in Scotland	152
67.	Ability in Gaelic: respondents in the UK outwith Scotland	153
68.	Ability in Gaelic: respondents in the rest of the world	153
69.	Level of target fluency: respondents in Scotland	153
70.	Level of target fluency: respondents in the UK outwith Scotland and the rest of world	154
71.	Expectancy of reaching target fluency: all respondents	154
72.	Formal qualifications in Gaelic: all respondents	155
73.	Length of time learning Gaelic: all respondents	156
74.	Pace and level of ability: respondents in Scotland and rest of UK	157
75.	Motivation for learning: respondents in Scotland	158
76.	Hobbies / interests influencing respondents to learn Gaelic	160

77.	Main reasons for learning Gaelic	161
78.	Other reasons for learning Gaelic	163
79.	The desire to reclaim Gaelic as a reason for learning	164
80.	Motivation for learning: respondents in the UK outwith Scotland	165
81.	Motivation for learning: respondents in rest of the world	167
82.	Importance of learning motivation: respondents in Scotland	168
83.	Importance of learning motivation: respondents in rest of UK	169
84.	Importance of learning motivation: respondents outwith the UK	170
85.	Ability to receive Radio nan Gaidheal: respondents in Scotland	172
86.	Time spent listening to Gaelic radio: respondents in Scotland	172
87.	Reception of Gaelic television: respondents in Scotland	173
88.	Time spent watching Gaelic television: respondents in Scotland	173
89.	Gaelic publications read: UK respondents	174
90.	Number of publications: all respondents	174
91.	Publications read by level of ability in reading Gaelic	175
92.	Participation in Gaelic-related events: respondents in Scotland	176
93.	Participation in Gaelic-related activities: respondents in Scotland	177
94.	Participation in Gaelic-related events: fluent/advanced respondents in Scotland	178
95.	Participation in Gaelic related activities: fluent advanced respondents in Scotland	178
96.	Participation in Gaelic related events: UK respondents outwith Scotland	179
97.	Participation in Gaelic related activities: UK respondents outwith Scotland	179
98.	Participation in Gaelic related events: respondents outwith UK	180
99.	Participation in Gaelic related activities: respondents outwith UK	180
100.	Gaelic abilities of respondents as returned for the 1991 Census	185
101.	Gaelic abilities of respondents as recorded in the 1991 Census	186
102.	Abilities in Gaelic as recorded in the 1991 Census	186
103.	Level of fluency in Gaelic as recorded in the 1991 Census	186
104.	Gaelic abilities of respondents to be returned in 2001 Census	187
105.	Communicative skills in Gaelic to be returned in 2001 Census	187
106.	Abilities in Gaelic to be returned in 2001 Census	188
107.	Gaelic related organisations: respondents in Scotland	189
108.	Organisations of which respondents are members	189
109.	Gaelic related organisations: respondents in UK outwith Scotland	189
110.	Organisations of which respondents in UK outwith Scotland are members	190
111.	Membership of Gaelic related organisations: respondents outwith UK	190
112.	Organisations of which respondents outwith UK are members	190
113.	Number of people in household: respondents in Scotland	191
114.	Gaelic spoken in the home: respondents in Scotland	191
115.	Speakers of Gaelic at home: respondents in Scotland	191
116.	Children: Scottish respondents	192

117.	Uptake of Gaelic-medium pre-school education	192
118.	Uptake of Gaelic-medium education: respondents with children of school age	193
119.	Uptake of Gaelic-medium education: respondents with children who have left school	194
120.	Possible future uptake of Gaelic-medium education	195
121.	Definition of the term *Gael*: all respondents	196
122.	Opinions on Gaelic as a national language: respondents in Scotland	197
123.	Opinions on Gaelic development: respondents in Scotland	199
124.	Opinions on linguistic issues: respondents in Scotland	201
125.	Opinions on Gaelic: respondents in Scotland	202
126.	Opinions on Gaelic: respondents in Scotland	203
127.	Opinions on Gaelic: respondents in Scotland	204
128.	Opinions on Gaelic issues: respondents in UK outwith Scotland	207
129.	Opinions on Gaelic issues: respondents outwith UK	209
130.	Opinions about difficulty of learning Gaelic: all respondents	211
131.	Reasons for difficulty of learning Gaelic: all respondents	212
132.	Views on the need of publicity for Gaelic	218
133.	Views on the need to teach about Gaelic in Schools	219
134.	Views on the need for new approach to Gaelic	221
135.	Views on Gaelic being "more than a means of communication"	225

List of figures

1.	Self-identification on a left-right spectrum: Scottish respondents	133
2.	Self-identification on a left-right spectrum: respondents in rest of UK	133
3.	Self-identification on a left-right spectrum: respondents outwith the UK	134
4.	Time spent learning Gaelic: respondents in Scotland	155
5.	Time spent learning Gaelic: respondents in rest of UK	156
6.	Time spent learning Gaelic: respondents in rest of world	156
7.	Number of publications read: respondents in Scotland	174

Foreword

Colin H. Williams

I am delighted to have been asked to write a foreword to this important study dealing with the contribution of adult learners to the reproduction of the Gaelic language. This volume is not only indicative of a growing awareness of the significance of adult learners to the health of any language, but also of the realization by language policy formulators of the supreme importance of understanding the interplay of key pillars which support minority language reproduction. It goes without saying that tolerance, goodwill and popular support are probably the most important 'soft' factors determining the nature of any language revitalization effort. But the support of the public and private sector, together with appropriate legislation, is also vital if the linguistic and communicative skills acquired during the educational experiences are to bear fruit.

There are, therefore, three ways in which this book can be read with profit. The first is as an insightful overview of what we know about the role of adult Gaelic learners in contributing to Reversing Language Shift efforts. The second is as a poignant reminder of how little real evidence is available to inform Gaelic language planners and policy advisers in their challenging task of revitalizing the language. The third is as a personal statement of commitment, professional determination and dedication to make things happen, so as to ameliorate several of the dangers identified here. For no matter how much we relate language planning to aggregate structural features, the process itself is surely dependent upon the decisions, life choices and shared values of so many committed individuals who collectively can bring about some degree of social change.

The main strength of the analysis which Alasdair MacCaluim presents is his 'opening up' of the world of the learners who constitute a sizeable and significant dimension of the contemporary Scottish Gaelic experience. In my view he provides a very good synthesis of their contribution based upon an empirical investigation of key aspects of Gaelic in social context. Naturally enough, he has a feel for the topic and a strong sympathy for the myriad feelings, doubts and joys which learners experience as they seek to move from raw beginners of learning Gaelic to 'insiders' and participants within Gaelic culture. But such enthusiasm does not stop him from being critical of the limited opportunities for learners and native speakers alike to engage in meaningful discourses. Neither does he shrink from examining and evaluating several of the difficulties which native speakers entertain when sustaining a conversation with learners, who may be fluent, but who do not fit the social type expectations of many native speakers as to what constitutes a legitimate 'Gael'. This is itself a value-laden term which he does well to unpack and relocate as central to the dualism of opening and closing which characterises the conventional Gaelic-speaking networks. But though I do not doubt that many learners can testify to unfortunate experiences, there is also room to praise the dedicated teachers, the gifted and inspiring speakers and the patient and, at times, heroic individuals who have sustained the language cause, often within the most disheartening of circumstances. The learner experience, of course, depends heavily on the foundation laid by prominent native-speaking Gaels, and it is encouraging to note that at long last several of their pioneering methods and techniques are not only being acknowledged, but also subjected to systematic evaluation so as to improve upon them.

With one eye on the learner and the other on the Scottish authorities, the author provides a detailed overview of the poor, if improving, infrastructure which exists to support learners. Here we are presented with a careful reconstruction of the current context, adopting a holistic, sympathetic yet critical, stance toward the many short-term and limited initiatives sponsored by government agencies. Lack of appropriate planning, funding and commitment characterises such actions; influenced too often by expedience rather than a thoroughgoing understanding and determined will to realise the potential of Gaelic in modern society. Based upon the evidence he has gathered, Alasdair MacCaluim is able to suggest practical policy measures for a variety of structural improvements with regard to teacher training, the development of teaching materials and a far greater use of IT and innovation within the media. He also offers an insightful treatment of the complex social identity of new speakers, which brings out the nuanced, often ambiguous, position of the learner within social networks. The Gaelic Learners' Survey, which is the heart of the volume, reveals a great deal of frustration and potential growth in the numbers of speakers. Sympathetic readers will immediately think of the way in which participant observation, learner's journals and diaries, consistent evaluation of Gaelic pedagogy and systematic analysis of time-series data could enrich these findings and draw out many of the insights given. But the truth is that so few of these additional sources of information have been available within a Gaelic context. However, there are currently encouraging signs of increased co-operation between government agencies, academic researchers and several voluntary movements to provide such data.

The book is limited to examples taken from contemporary Scotland, but the inclusion of discussions and insights related to language revitalization are pointers to much wider horizons. A careful reading of the results and the recommendations will enrich the comparative analysis of second language adult learning, especially within the so-called 'lesser-used languages of Europe' policy community. These are interesting, exciting and, it must be said, hugely frustrating times for that community. For at one level the development of regional autonomy in Catalonia, the Basque Country, Galicia, together with selected aspects of devolution within the UK, augurs well for a strengthened European Network of Language Planning Agencies. Its commitment to several of the themes of this book, namely education, particularly adult education, language transmission within the family, community development and language initiatives, not to mention the broader issues of political empowerment and appropriate, sustainable economic development, promises to strengthen the interventionist role of language planning as a tool for social engineering. However, there is a certain irony in that so much action and rhetoric is to be found at the superstructural level while at the base level both the territorial/sociolinguistic networks and the community vitality which have sustained such languages, albeit intermittently, are under severe threat.

Nevertheless, the research results presented here can be taken as a vital contribution to our understanding of the role of learners within Gaelic RLS efforts. The interpretation is replete with key messages, which deserve to be diffused within both the academic and the policy community and most importantly, of course, within the tutor's and learner's network. The informed set of realisable recommendations for policy development call for remedial action now. It is my hope that the sympathetic treatment offered here will not only alert us to Gaelic's precarious present, but also quicken our resolve to teach the language to both young and adult in formal and informal settings; and, having taught and learned it, to resolve to use it in as many situations as is feasible, for to paraphrase the opening quote of this volume "wanting to speak a language is the best possible reason for learning one".

Colin H. Williams
Language Policy and Planning Research Unit
School of Welsh
Cardiff University

1: Introduction

> Wanting to read a book is the best possible reason for writing one.
> (Davies 1993: 2)

Adult Learners of Scottish Gaelic: An Introduction

In the past twenty years, adult learners of Scottish Gaelic have become an increasingly visible component of the Gaelic speech community. This period has seen a steadily increasing level of interest in learning Gaelic and in the numbers of Gaelic learners. This trend of growth can be charted through a number of indicators such as the number of members of the national association for Gaelic learners and the viewing figures for the learners' television series *Speaking Our Language* (Comataidh Craolaidh Gàidhlig 1994: 8).

Some idea of the number of adult learners can be gained from research conducted in 1995 which found that there were then around 8,000 Gaelic learners in Scotland (Galloway 1995b). While few Gaelic learners reach fluency in the language at present (Robertson 2001a), more learners are becoming fluent in the language than ever before, largely due to the advent of a number of Gaelic immersion courses. It is also likely that a larger number of people may be interested in learning than are currently actively learning, as is suggested, for example, by the fact that over 30,000 people contacted the television series *Speaking our Language* for information about learning Gaelic (Johnstone 1994: 54). More recently, an opinion poll of a representative sample of the Scottish public conducted for the BBC on attitudes to Gaelic showed that 16% of respondents would consider learning the language in the future, with a further 16% responding 'maybe' (BBC 2003). Figures such as these become all the more significant when it is taken into account that the most recent national Census found that numbers of Gaelic speakers have fallen to under 60,000 (GROS 2005).

Recent decades have seen a steady fall in the numbers of native Gaelic speakers in Scotland and a rapid weakening of the use of the language in the few geographical communities in which it could still be said to be the community language. Parallel to this process, however, has been a growing movement to stem this decline and to maintain and increase the use of Gaelic. Due to the small and decreasing numbers of native Gaelic speakers, adult learners of Gaelic are increasingly seen by Gaelic development organisations and by the Gaelic community in general to have a key role to play in this effort to revitalise the language: to reverse language shift (RLS [Fishman 1991]).[1]

The view that adult learners could play a significant part in reversing Gaelic-English language shift can be seen, for example, in a report by the national Gaelic development agency Comunn na Gàidhlig which stated that "learners form an increasingly important sector of the Gaelic diaspora. Properly catered for, their role in the development of the language cannot be underestimated" (CnaG 1992: 68). In one of the strongest expressions of this view, Gordon Brown MP stated that "sixty five thousand is a critically small speech community. If we want to hear Gaelic spoken after the Millennium, new entrants will be needed. It is axiomatic that learners will

---

[1] Fishman's concept of Reversing Language Shift will be used throughout this study in preference to ill-defined and biologically based terminology such as language revival or revitalisation.

save the language" (*The Herald* 1999). Such a view was authoritatively restated by the Ministerial Advisory Group on Gaelic, which stated that "Gaelic is going to depend heavily on new adult speakers over the next 30 years at least" (Ministerial Advisory Group on Gaelic 2002: 51).

Gaelic Learners in Reversing Language Shift

At the beginning of the twenty-first century, Gaelic finds itself in a very weak position. Language shift from Gaelic to English has reached a very advanced stage. This can be seen in terms of the declining numbers of Gaelic speakers, in the low level of intergenerational transmission of the language and the weakening of Gaelic as a community language in the Western Isles.

According to the 2001 Census, there were 58,700 Gaelic speakers, some 1.2% of the Scottish population (GROS 2005). This marks a decrease from 65,978 or 1.4% of the population in the 1991 Census. This means that there was an average loss of around 700 Gaelic speakers each year between 1991 and 2001 (MacKinnon 2003). The numbers of children in Gaelic-medium education are far from being able to compensate numerically for this loss at present (MacKinnon 2003).[2] Census data also indicates only just over half of those able to speak Gaelic (53%) are able to read and write the language (GROS 2005).

The distribution of Gaelic speakers by age-group shows that Gaelic is strongest amongst older age-groups and weakest amongst younger people. As compared with the 1991 Cenusus, the 2001 Census demonstrated a slight upturn in the Gaelic speakers in the 5–15 age group (GROS 2005; MacKinnon 2003). However, this was not matched in the main Gàidhealtachd of the Outer Hebrides where numbers of young Gaelic speakers have continued to decline and the weakness of Gaelic in pre-school ages nationwide suggests that education rather than intergenerational transmission within the family has been responsible for the reported increases (GROS 2005).

The decline of Gaelic amongst younger age groups is now so advanced that, as McLeod has pointed out, it has now become difficult to find people under the age of 25 who speak Gaelic as a true first language or mother tongue. Those younger people who are able to speak Gaelic tend to be less proficient in Gaelic than in English and to speak Gaelic which is English-influenced and without a breadth of vocabulary or idiom (McLeod 2000: 6; Lamb 2001).

Gaelic has shown signs of substantial weakening as a community language in recent times. By 2001, the only place where Gaelic speakers formed a majority of the population were the Outer Hebrides, and parts of north of Skye (GROS 2005, MacKinnon 2006b: 1). Even within these areas, the position of Gaelic was far weaker within the main towns of Portree, Balivanich and Stornoway than it was in the rural hinterland.

So far has the situation now progressed that only 27.6% of Gaelic speakers were living in parishes where Gaelic speakers were in a local majority by 2001 and there was only one parish, the parish of Barvas in Lewis, where over 70% of the population were Gaelic speakers (MacKinnon 2006b). This parish contains only 3.9% of all Gaelic speakers. As MacKinnon has shown, the declining percentages of Gaelic-speakers in strongly Gaelic-speaking communities has been due not only to a decrease

---

[2] Figures for numbers of pupils in Gaelic-medium education available at www.cnag.org.uk/stats

intergenerational transmission, but also due to an increase in migration to and from these communities (MacKinnon 2006b: 1).

The percentage of young people able to speak Gaelic in the Outer Hebrides has shown a dramatic decline in the past three decades with the 2001 Census showing that only 42% of those under 25 were Gaelic speakers (McLeod 2003a). The proportion of children in Gaelic-medium education is also low in the Outer Hebrides with only 23.15% of primary school children, 494 pupils altogether, currently being educated through Gaelic (Comhairle nan Eilean Siar 2006). Research has shown a significant and rapid decline in the range of domains in which Gaelic is used in the traditional Gaelic-speaking communities (MacKinnon 1998d, 2000, 2006a, 2006b; NicAoidh 2006; Western Isles Language Planning Project 2005).

In the Lowlands and the areas of the Highlands where Gaelic is not the community language, areas in which a majority of Gaelic speakers now live, Census data and research suggest that the language is weaker both in terms of usage and intergenerational transmission than in the island Gaelic-speaking communities (MacKinnon 1998d, 2000, 2006b: 2; McLeod 2005; GROS 2005).

The retreat of Gaelic with the family has been marked in recent times. In 1991, only one Gaelic speaker in three lived in a family in which all members could speak Gaelic (MacKinnon 1999: 1). By 2001, this figure had reduced to one Gaelic speaker in five (MacKinnon 2006b: 2). Nationally, taking together all types of family where all adults can speak Gaelic, only 49.1% of their children were likely to do so too (MacKinnon 2006b: 2). There are regional variations within this picture with intergenerational transmission being weaker outwith the Outer Hebrides and Skye and Lochalsh.

In the 2001 Census, the 1,437 families with two Gaelic-speaking parents in the Outer Hebrides comprised only 45% of all households with Gaelic-speaking adults in the area and they were transmitting Gaelic to only 76.5% of their children. The 1,209 families in the area where one of a couple was a Gaelic speaker were transmitting Gaelic to only 36.9% of their children and the 307 lone parent families with a Gaelic-speaking parent were transmitting the language to only 50.5% of their children (MacKinnon 2006b: 2).

Outwith the Highlands, intergenerational transmission is far weaker. In this area, the 767 families with two Gaelic-speaking parents only comprised 11.5% of families containing a Gaelic speaker and had only transmitted the language to 54.3% of their children. For the 4,336 families where one of a couple was a Gaelic speaker, only 10.8% of their children were also Gaelic speakers and of the 1001 lone parent families with a Gaelic speaking parent, only 24.9% of children were Gaelic speakers.

Research has further shown a trend towards decline in the level of usage of the language in the family even in families where intergenerational transmission has taken place (NicAoidh 2006; Western Isles Language Planning Project 2005). Language shift has progressed so far in Gàidhealtachd areas that MacKinnon has concluded that "we are now at the point of last chance to retain majority Gaelic-speaking local communities" (2006b: 1).

In his influential books, *Reversing Language Shift* (1991) and *Can Endangered Languages be Saved?* (2001), Fishman has argued that adult learners have a very important role to play in reversing language shift in the case of languages such as Scottish Gaelic where intergenerational transmission is at a very low level and is in rapid decline. It is necessary that new speakers of the endangered language be created in order to maintain numbers of speakers and to re-establish intergenerational transmission.

For Fishman, the starting point in this process must be adult learners. When a language's intergenerational transmission has largely broken down and when its community use is faltering, RLS efforts must focus on bringing about the conditions in which the endangered language will be acquired by significant numbers of young adults who will in turn ensure the intergenerational transmission of the language to their offspring as a mother tongue.

That young adults should be prioritised in RLS efforts is of crucial importance according to Fishman. Teaching children through the medium of Xish as a second language, such as through Gaelic-medium education in Scotland, is very unlikely to lead to any significant degree of intergenerational transmission of Xish unless it is accompanied by a range of other interventions directed toward achieving RLS (1991: chapter 13).[3] Fishman has argued that "school must be preceded (or at least accompanied) by adult language learning of the threatened language as a second language, by instruction in parenting via Xish, and then by substantial child acquisition of it as a first language *even before the pupils-to-be show up at school*" (2001: 15). Only adults of child-bearing age can contribute directly to the intergenerational transmission of Xish. McLeod has illustrated this point with regard to Scotland, arguing that "Gaelic-medium education tends to mean simply teaching Gaelic to primary school children; it does not serve as the fuse to any kind of linguistic chain reaction" (McLeod 2002a: 285).

While adults of childbearing age reaching fluency in Xish have the potential to directly influence RLS through intergenerational transmission, all adult learners can have a more indirect influence on RLS through their involvement in the Xish community. For example, learners can add to the numbers of those speaking, reading writing and teaching Xish, producing and consuming Xish goods and services, and lobbying for Xish (MacCaluim 2006). Learners can also expand the level of social diversity and experience represented within the language community.

In the field of employment, adult learners have a crucial part to play as is often difficult to find suitably qualified Xish speaking staff. This has certainly been the case in Scotland where there have been persistent difficulties in filling teaching and other Gaelic posts (Galloway 1995a, Gaelic Medium Teachers' Action Group 2005). This is significant for RLS as Galloway has pointed out that an overwhelming majority of Gaelic-essential jobs are related to the promotion of the language and that the degree of success in recruiting for these posts is therefore closely linked to the wellbeing of the language (Galloway 1995a: 56).

In light of the above discussion, it is clear that adult Gaelic learners have a central role to play in reversing language shift in Scotland. The remainder of this study will be based on this basic premise. Throughout this study, the question of to what extent learners are currently able to fulfil a central role in RLS will be investigated.

Aims and Outline of this Study

It has been seen that adult learners must necessarily play a central role in RLS efforts if reversing language shift is to take part in Scotland and that learners are viewed by many commentators as being potential language saviours. The question which this study aims to investigate is whether Gaelic learners are, in fact, occupying a central role within RLS efforts and within the Gaelic speech community in general or

---

[3] The term *Xish* is used by Fishman to denote any endangered language.

whether they occupy a more peripheral position. This will be done through four chapters, each of which addresses a separate area relevant to Gaelic learning and learners and RLS. It is also intended that this study should serve as a general overview of the contemporary experience of learning Gaelic and the Gaelic learning scene.

Chapter 2 is entitled "Gaelic and Reversing Language Shift Theory" and discusses the present situation of Gaelic and attempts to maintain and develop the language in terms of Fishman's RLS theory, looking in particular at the implications of this for adult learners.

Chapter 3, "The Gaelic Learning Infrastructure", investigates the infrastructure for learning Gaelic in the context of RLS, looking in particular at its effectiveness in attracting Gaelic learners and bringing them to fluency, and making recommendations as to how this infrastructure might be improved. By doing so, this chapter will assess whether the current learning infrastructure is sufficient to ensure that learners become fluent in sufficient numbers to play a central role in RLS in terms of adding to the numbers of fluent speakers and in terms of intergenerational transmission.

Regardless of the numbers of Gaelic learners, however, the role which learners will actually be able to play in RLS and in the Gaelic speech community in general depends to a large extent on the position, if any, which they are perceived to have within this speech community by native Gaelic speakers, by the general public and by policy makers. Such subjects are investigated in chapter four: *The Social Identity of Gaelic Learners*. This chapter explores the social identity of learners, looking at the relationship between learners and both native speakers and non-speakers of Gaelic, investigating the social position which Gaelic learners occupy within Gaeldom and relating this issue to the broader one of RLS. Through discussing these issues, the chapter will investigate whether Gaelic learners are central or peripheral to the Gaelic speech community in a social sense as opposed to the numerical sense investigated in chapter three.

Many of the key issues raised in chapters three and four are revisited in more detail in chapter five, The Gaelic Learners' Survey, which reports and discusses the findings of a questionnaire survey of a large representative sample of Gaelic learners. The main areas investigated through the Gaelic Learners' Survey are: (1) the social background of Gaelic learners, (2) the motivation of learners, (3) the impact of learners on Gaelic affairs and on regenerating the language, and (4) the learners' views regarding the language, these all being matters of significance to RLS. This chapter is intended to provide a broad overview of a representative sample of learners in addition to investigating a range of issues with relevance to RLS.

The findings of the chapters are summarised and recommendations and conclusions drawn in a final conclusion chapter. It should be noted that this book is based on a PhD study of Gaelic learners (MacCaluim 2002) and has been expanded and updated to bring the story of Gaelic learners up to date [May 2006].

Two appendices are also included. The Gaelic Learners' Survey questionnaire forms Appendix 1. Appendix 2 contains a range of Gaelic learners' views on native speakers as gathered from the survey regarding Gaelic learners. This has been included in order to provide further illustration of points made in chapter three with regard to the social identity of Gaelic learners.

Adult Gaelic Learners: A Definition

As adult learners of Gaelic are the subject of this study, the term 'adult learner' must be defined. Although frequently used, the term 'Gaelic learner' is far more ambiguous than might at first appear and is able to convey any one of several different meanings. Most usually the expression is used to refer to someone who is either currently actively learning Gaelic or who has learned Gaelic to fluency. Semi-speakers, lapsed native speakers and passive bilinguals who are (re-)learning the language might also be called 'Gaelic learners', though they might also be considered to come within the category of 'native speakers'.

In common parlance, the active learning of the language is not always implied by the term 'Gaelic learner', as people who have made a failed attempt to learn Gaelic at some time in the past might often still find themselves being referred to in this way. This can also be the case for people who have learned a handful of words or stock phrases in Gaelic without seeking broader fluency. Supporters of the language who have not actually learned the language might also at times find themselves being classified as learners. It is also worth noting at this point that the designation 'native speaker' too carries some ambiguities. This will be examined at greater length in chapter four, the Social Identity of Gaelic Learners.

In this study, the expression 'Gaelic learner' or 'learner' will be used to describe anyone who is either learning or has learned Gaelic as an adult, including re-learners of the language. The term 'adult' will be taken to mean anyone aged 16 or over. The fact that the term 'learner' can be used both for people who are in the process of learning Gaelic and those who have learned the language to fluency can be a cause of confusion. Care will therefore be taken to distinguish between these different senses of the word 'learner' where this distinction may be of significance.

2: Gaelic and Reversing Language Shift Theory

> A well nigh complete reliance on the school and other higher order 'props'. (Fishman on Gaelic revitalisation initiatives 1991: 380)

Fishman's Theory of Reversing Language Shift

In his *Reversing Language Shift* (1991), which has been has been very influential both in academia and amongst minority language activists, Fishman established a series of key principles for bringing about RLS and devised a scale for the classification of the position of endangered languages – the Graded Intergenerational Disruption Scale for Threatened Languages (GIDS). Fishman's theory has subsequently been clarified and refined (Fishman 2001). Unlike commonly used terms such as 'revival', 'renaissance' and 'language death', Fishman's concept of RLS avoids the dangers of biological terminology. By providing a scale against which RLS efforts can be measured, Fishman also avoids the subjectivity which surrounds frequently used but ill-defined terms such as language 'revitalisation'. For this reason, the RLS theory provides a useful framework within which the situation of Gaelic can be measured.

In order to investigate the position of the adult learner in terms of the goal of RLS, this section will provide an introduction to Fishman's principles and will then briefly apply them to the present situation of Gaelic and to RLS efforts on behalf of Gaelic.

The basic principles of Fishman's model for RLS are easily summarised. The first is that there should be prior ideological clarification amongst pro-RLSers on key issues relating to the promotion of the language even before active language development efforts begin (1991: 10, 394). Before efforts are undertaken to reverse language shift, there should be careful consideration of the goals, prospects and circumstances of the prospective RLS movement by pro-RLSers (1991: 10). Without such prior discussion and clarification, differences in terms of aims, tactics and levels of commitment within the RLS movement can cause ongoing tension and splits over fundamental questions of principle. As Fishman has argued, "it is hard enough to row against the current; it is virtually impossible to do so without knowing where one would like to get to and why" (1991: 394). He warns that "without prior, honest clarification of both goals and doubts, circumstances and possibilities, the likelihood of future ruptures and difficulties is literally built-in" to the RLS movement (1991: 11).

The second principle is that RLS is a form of language planning and that to be successful in achieving this goal, pro-RLSers must engage in strategic planning for the language involving concrete, realisable goals based on step-by-step action. It is not sufficient to take what Fishman describes as the "let's try everything we possibly can and perhaps something will work" approach as this is highly unlikely to be effective (1991: 1).

Given the limitations in terms of money, numbers, time and political support which confront pro-RLS movements, prioritisation must take place in RLS efforts if they are to be successful. According to Fishman, the family-home-neighbourhood-community nexus is of the utmost importance in RLS. All language development efforts should aim to maintain or strengthen the use and intergenerational transmission of the endangered language in the family and immediate neighbourhood/community. Possible RLS measures should be prioritised according to their effectiveness in furthering this aim (1991: 67). Pro-RLSers should only target higher-order spheres such as the media and government once substantial progress has been made in the family and community/neighbourhood or if it can be proven that such progress would result from this targeting. Prioritisation of RLS measures should be guided by research and by learning from international examples.

For Fishman, the principle of 'first things first' is a key part of prioritisation. It is not only important that the correct RLS-efforts are undertaken, but that they are undertaken in the correct order (1991: 67). As Fishman says, "the right thing to do is the right thing only if it is done at the right time and in the right sequence with other things" (2001: 8). The GIDS scale described below provides guidance in helping to decide the priority and ordering of RLS measures.

In addition to stressing the importance of planning and prioritisation efforts, Fishman has also argued that self-reliance is a crucial principle of RLS. This is particularly the case in the earlier stages of RLS in which the home-family-community-neighbourhood axis is the main focus of effort (1991: 111). Creating secure domains for the use of the threatened language in these sectors is absolutely central to RLS and can best be done on a small scale by self-help effort by members of the language community itself. While outside agencies can be of help at all stages of RLS, the main players at this intimate, personal and small-scale level are necessarily members of the minority language community.

The idea of self-reliance in initial RLS efforts is also closely linked to the 'first things first' principle. Fishman advocates initial concentration on the 'home front', the home-school-community-neighbourhood constellation, where self-help is paramount before devoting scarce resources on the higher order spheres such as the mass media or higher level government and administration (1991: 5). This is for two reasons.

Firstly, measures taken at a high level are very unlikely to be successful in RLS terms if they do not build upon efforts to promote the language in the family and community. In other words, while high-level initiatives such as minority language television can help reinforce intergenerational transmission and community language use where they already exist, they can only play a very small and indirect part in helping to bring about intergenerational transmission and community language use where they do not.

Secondly, in order to bring about greater support from the state or from other high-level authorities, it is important that speakers of the endangered language show, through their self-help efforts, an active demand and need for such support. Quite simply, "if Xmen do not labor on behalf of Xish [...] no one will do it (or pay someone else to do it) for them, or even believe that Xmen themselves really believe that it is worth doing" (1991: 98).[4]

In order to analyse further the principles on which planning and prioritisation for RLS should be based, Fishman's GIDS scale for endangered language will now be investigated. The GIDS scale is simply a graded scale for the measurement of sociolinguistic disruption with respect to language communities and networks (Fishman 1991: 87). On the scale there are eight points, with higher numbers implying greater disruption. The higher the GIDS rating of a language, the lower the intergenerational continuity and maintenance prospects of a language community or network. Where a language has a high score on the GIDS, this almost always implies disruption in the preceding stages of the scale too (Fishman 1991: 87).

---

[4] The terms *Xish* and *Xmen/Xians* are used by Fishman to denote an endangered language and the group traditionally associated with that particular language. Similarly, *Yish* donates the language to which language shift is occurring from *Xish*. Fishman initially used the term *Xmen* but in more recent work has changed this to *Xians* so as to be non-sexist.

Table 1: Fishman's Graded Intergenerational Disruption Scale
[*the scale should be read from the bottom up*]
(Based on Fishman 1991: 87-114, 395. Text in bold by Fishman, *explanation in italics by present author*.)

1. **Education, work sphere, mass media and governmental operations at higher and nationwide levels.**
   - *Some use of Xish in higher level educational, occupational, governmental and media efforts (but without the additional safety provided by political independence).*

2. **Local/regional mass media and governmental services.**
   - *Some use of Xish in lower governmental services and mass media but not in the higher spheres of either. To reach this stage and to transcend it, Xians must show demand for and lobby for such services.*

3. **The local/regional (i.e non-neighbourhood) work sphere both among Xians and Yians.**
   - *Use of Xish in the lower work sphere (outside of the Xish neighbourhood/community) involving interaction between Xians and Yians. To reach this stage, Xish must be used by the workforce in workplaces controlled by Xians and efforts made by Xish speakers to obtain services through Xish from enterprises/services controlled by Yians.*

4. **Xish in lower education that meets the requirements of compulsory education law**
   - *Schools teaching through Xish (mainly in order to reinforce Xish as a first language). Schools can have a greater or lesser degree of Xish content/control:*
   - **4a. Schools in lieu of compulsory education, offering some instruction via Xish, but substantially under Yish curricular control.**
   - **4b. X-medium schools in lieu of compulsory education and substantially under Xish curricular and staffing control.**

II. RLS to transcend diglossia, subsequent to its attainment

5. **Schools for literacy acquisition, for the old and for the young, and not in lieu of compulsory education.**
   - *Xish literacy rates are generally low. To transcend this stage, self-help driven literacy efforts are necessary to enable increased communication and reduced isolation between and within Xish communities through correspondence, newsletters, internet, email, etc.*

6. **The intergenerational and demographically concentrated home-family-neighbourhood: the basis of mother tongue transmission.**
   - *Xish is weak or faltering at the home/family community level. To transcend this stage, a wide range of community and family efforts are required to bring about the attainment or maintenance of intergenerational informal use of the language and to bring about the demographic concentration and reinforcement of Xish through community/neighbourhood institutions.*

7. **Cultural interaction in Xish primarily involving the community-based older generation.**
   - *Most users of Xish are a socially integrated and ethnolinguistically active population but they are beyond childbearing age. Intergenerational transmission of Xish has largely not taken place from this generation to the next. To transcend this stage, these older Xish speakers should be encouraged to take part in Xish activities which will encourage the acquisition and use of Xish amongst younger people.*

8. **Reconstructing Xish and adult acquisition of XSL.**
   - *Xish is spoken or understood by only a few isolated elderly people or is no longer spoken or understood at all. To transcend this stage, Xish must be reconstructed from work with remaining speakers/semi-speakers/passive bilinguals of the language or from written or recorded sources and then taught to adults.*

I. RLS to attain diglossia (assuming prior ideological clarification)

The eight GIDS categories are separated into two separate groups by Fishman: the lower levels from stages 8–5 and the higher levels from 4–1. In the lower levels, the basic aim is to achieve and maintain intergenerational transmission and language use within the community. Of these, stage 6, the maintenance or establishment of families and communities/neighbourhoods speaking the threatened language is the most crucial and is described by Fishman as the crux or fulcrum stage in RLS. Stages 8 to 5 are the 'DIY stages' of RLS where self-help efforts by the threatened language community are of prime importance. Only once stable diglossia has been attained at this level should focus begin to shift to stages 4–1 on the GIDS scale, where efforts centre on the expansion of the use of the language in higher level domains.

While a 'first things first' approach is advocated by Fishman, this does not mean that each pro-RLS movement must start at stage 8 and pass through each intervening step (1991: 109, 2001: 465, 467). Rather, "it means that pro-RLS efforts should carefully gauge what stage they are at (in a particular location or neighborhood) and to undertake to repair lower, foundational stages before moving ahead to more advanced ones" (Fishman 1991: 109). The scale, in other words, aims to act as a diagnostic tool to help RLSers establish focus and priorities for their efforts (Fishman 2001: 465).

While Fishman argues that lower stages (i.e. the stages with higher GIDS scores) should be normally be tackled before concentrating on higher stages, this does not rule out efforts aimed at more than one stage at the same time. He argues that "linkages must be sought and instituted from above as well as below, so that additional and attractive functions [of Xish] can propel RLS and motivate those attracted to it" (2001: 467). Multi-stage RLS efforts are not contra-indicated as long as the lower stages of RLS continue to be targeted and as long as there is a significant linkage (a linkage that is actually demonstrated rather than merely assumed to exist) between efforts at the higher stage and the supporting of the 'fulcrum' stage of intergenerational transmission and community use of the language (2001: 467).

Having looked at Fishman's RLS theory in general, the place of adult Xish learners in RLS, the main focus of this study, will now be investigated. As has already been seen, Fishman divides the GIDS scale into the lower order spheres (stages 8–5) and the higher order spheres (stages 4–1). The lower order spheres are concerned mainly with contributing to the intergenerational transmission and neighbourhood/community use of Xish whereas the higher order spheres are concerned mainly with broadening the scope of the functions of Xish (1991: 380).

It is clear that adult Xish learners can play a role in both the lower and higher spheres of the GIDS scale, whether this be through, for example, filling the role of senior Xish speaking civil servants or broadcasters at stage 1, serving as Xish teachers at stage 4, raising Xish speaking children at stage 6, or helping to recreate and teach the language at stage 8. Learners can help RLS efforts in any number of ways ranging from being providers or consumers of services and goods through the medium of Xish to adding to the numbers of speakers and lobbyists for the language.

While adult learners are significant at all points on the GIDS scale, however, they have a particularly important role to play in the stages of RLS leading up to and including stage 6: the intergenerational transmission of Xish within the family as a mother tongue and the creation/maintenance of an Xish speaking community/neighbourhood. In GIDS stage 8, where languages (such as Cornish or Manx) must be reconstructed, the responsibility for RLS necessarily falls solely upon learners of the language. Learners are also of key importance in stages 7 and 6. In the former, Xish speakers form a socially integrated group but are mostly beyond childbearing age with intergenerational transmission largely not having taken place. In the latter stage, intergenerational transmission is attained in the family and reinforced with a demographically concentrated and institutionally supported community or neighbourhood.

The importance of adult learners of Xish to GIDS stage 6 and 7 cannot be overestimated. To transcend level 7 and to reach stage 6, it is necessary that younger speakers of Xish be created. For Fishman, the starting point in this process must necessarily be adult learners as young native Xish speakers are very few in such a situation. RLS efforts at stage 7 must focus on bringing about the conditions in which Xish will be acquired by significant numbers of young adults who will in turn ensure the intergenerational transmission of the language to their offspring as a mother tongue.

In practice, very few RLS movements have prioritised adult learners.[5] Rather, preschool and primary education have been taken as the point of departure for most RLS efforts (Fishman 1991: 368). As was seen in the introduction, Fishman is very critical of this approach, arguing that teaching children through the medium of Xish as a second language is very unlikely to create children who are fluent and confident in the language over a wide range of domains and registers, who will use the language outside the school setting and who will maintain the use of the language into adulthood and parenthood. Xish medium education on its own is, therefore, unlikely to lead to any significant degree of intergenerational transmission of Xish (1991: chapter 13). Fishman has argued that 'school must be preceded (or at least accompanied) by adult language learning of the threatened language as a second language, by instruction in parenting via Xish, and then by substantial child acquisition of it as a first language *even before the pupils-to-be show up at school*" (2001: 15). At levels 7 and 6, therefore, young Xish adult learners (and where applicable, young Xish mother-tongue speakers) are crucial in bringing about intergenerational transmission of Xish. Such Xish speakers also have a role to play in Xish community/neighbourhood development in general.

While young adults must be the primary targets for Xish learning, learners who learn Xish after childbearing age can also play a lesser role in RLS through involvement in Xish community/neighbourhood development. Learners of all ages can also help to reverse what Fishman has identified as a type of 'brain-drain' effect amongst threatened language communities. As a result of language shift, certain social classes and groupings can become underrepresented within the Xish speaking community as a result of differential levels of language shift taking place within different sections of Xish society (1991: 61). Xish learners can aid RLS through helping to reverse this 'brain-drain' by reinstating or expanding the level of social diversity and adding to the skills base represented within the Xish speaking community.

Before applying the above theory to the case of Gaelic, it should be noted that some criticisms of and amendments to Fishman's RLS theory have been put forward (e.g. Hornberger and King 2001: 184; Johnstone 1994: 21; MacKinnon 1995: 523). These criticisms have tended to be relatively minor and have, in the main, been related to the GIDS scale, touching upon points such as the boundaries between GIDS stages and the relative importance of these stages. More fundamental criticisms

---

[5] The example of Basque being a notable exception. See for example Azkue and Perales 2005.

of GIDS have tended to be based on a misinterpretation of the nature of the GIDS scale, seeing the use of a scale as being a deterministic approach having implications of evolutionary inevitability (e.g. Ó Riagáin 2001). Williams (1992) has also criticised Fishman's model, arguing that it is based on a consensual view of society, paying insufficient attention to power, struggle and conflict. As Fishman himself points out, however, the GIDS scale is best viewed as a diagnostic tool and a "heuristic theoretical stance, rather than a fully proven verity" (2001: 465, 1991: 396).

Regardless of any criticisms of GIDS, there can be little argument against the proposition that intergenerational transmission and community/neighbourhood use of Xish should be seen to be the centre of RLS efforts or against Fishman's overriding principles of planning, prioritisation and self-help. Rather, it is somewhat surprising that Fishman has been the first commentator to put these principles in writing. For all of the above reasons, therefore, it can be argued that Fishman's theory of RLS provides a suitable benchmark against which the situation of Gaelic and Gaelic RLS efforts can be measured.

Gaelic and Fishman's RLS Theory

Having investigated RLS theory in general, this must now be applied to the situation of Gaelic. Firstly, the present situation of Gaelic will be discussed in terms of the GIDS scale. Secondly, recent language maintenance and development efforts in general will be assessed in terms of Fishman's RLS theory. This will set the scene for the discussion of the position of adult learners of Gaelic throughout the remainder of this study.

On the GIDS scale, the stage most closely corresponding to the position of the community use and intergenerational transmission of Gaelic nationally is stage 7. As was seen in the introduction, intergenerational transmission has been in significant decline in the Outer Hebrides and in other areas where significant percentages of the population are Gaelic speakers, with the result that language shift has rapidly been occurring from GIDS stage 6 to stage 7 in the remaining Gaelic communities. As can also be seen from the description of the present situation of Gaelic above, stage 7 could also be said to obtain in the remainder of Scotland, with the language being even weaker in terms of intergenerational transmission and community use.

While the position of Gaelic in all parts of Scotland approximates to GIDS stage 7, the very different situation of the language in different parts of Scotland illustrates that there can be much diversity within this stage. In addition to isolated Gaelic speakers and learners in rural parts of the Lowlands and anglicised rural parts of the Highlands where there is neither a geographical Gaelic community nor a strong community of interest, stage 7 would also encompass island areas where Gaelic remains as the community language amongst the older generation and the Lowland cities and major Highland towns where there are many Gaelic speakers and relatively strong, though weakening, communities of interest.

As previously noted, Fishman has argued that higher (more disrupted) scores on the GIDS imply disruption at all or most of the preceding stages of GIDS, so that a language weak at stage 6, for example, would normally be even weaker in stages 5–1 (1991: 87). It would, therefore, be expected that Gaelic would be weak in stages 5–1. In Fishman's view, it would also be expected that Gaelic RLS efforts should focus primarily on achieving stage 6 on the GIDS scale and on measures in higher GIDS stages with a clear linkage to intergenerational transmission and community use of

Gaelic. It would further be expected that adult learners would be considered to be central to RLS efforts.

Indeed, Gaelic is generally as weak in GIDS stages 5–1 as it is at stages 6 and 7. At stage 5, for example, just over half of the Gaelic speakers identified in the 2001 Census were able to read and write the language. Gaelic could similarly be said to be very weak in terms of GIDS stage 3 or 2 as very few governmental, quasi-governmental or business services are available in Gaelic, even in areas where Gaelic is strong as a community language, with use of Gaelic being generally infrequent, limited and ad hoc rather than systematic (McLeod 2002a; Dunbar 2006: 12). Particularly notable has been the fact that Comhairle nan Eilean Siar, the local authority serving the Outer Hebrides, has "failed to take significant action to secure the language within its constituency area or to develop it as a working medium for its own operations" (McLeod 2002a: 292; see also Dunbar 2006: 12).

In stage 1, as in stage 2, Gaelic is very weak, with the language having a relatively limited presence in the Scottish Parliament and a very limited presence indeed in the Scottish Executive, local authorities, other higher public services and local and national print media (McLeod 2001a, McLeod 2002a).

While Gaelic is generally weak at the higher echelons of the GIDS scale, however, there are a range of language development initiatives based within these levels. In the first place, Gaelic-medium primary and secondary education is available in 61 primary and 20 secondary schools throughout Scotland, with 2068 primary and 315 secondary pupils receiving Gaelic-medium education in 2005–6 (Robertson 2006). Gaelic also has a significant presence in broadcasting with the existence of the Gaelic radio station BBC Radio nan Gaidheal and provision of a range of Gaelic television programmes, some funded by the BBC and others funded via a government financed Gaelic Broadcasting Fund of £8.5M per annum (Dunbar 2006: 7).

Scottish RLS Initiatives and Fishman's Theory

> Fàilte – Welcome to Scotland's Gaelic Renaissance.
> (Comunn na Gàidhlig cultural tourism brochure)
>
> Current Gaelic expenditure is all fur coat and no knickers.
> (Gaelic learner, Gaelic Learners' Survey)

Having discussed the present position of Gaelic in terms of the GIDS scale, efforts in Scotland to maintain and develop the language will now be discussed in terms of Fishman's principles. Following this brief overview of Gaelic development efforts in general, the remainder of this study will consider the issue of adult learners with particular reference to RLS.

Since the mid 1980s, a range of Gaelic development initiatives have been launched such as the establishment and expansion of Gaelic-medium education, the launch of Gaelic development agencies such as Comunn na Gàidhlig and an expansion of Gaelic radio and television.[6] These initiatives have lead to a perception both within the Gaelic community and the Scottish public in general that something of a Gaelic

---

[6] For more detailed descriptions of the development of Gaelic since the mid 1980s see for example Caimbeul 2000, Dunbar 2000, Dunbar 2006, Hutchinson 2005, MacKinnon 1991a, Johnstone 1994, Robastan 2006, Scottish Parliament Information Centre 2000, Scottish Parliament Information Centre 2004.

'revival' or 'renaissance' is taking place (Glaser 2007, S. Macdonald 1999, McEwan-Fujita 1997, McLeod 2002a, Oliver 2005, Rogerson and Gloyer 1995). While these initiatives have marked a significant increase in the level of financial support for Gaelic and have given the language a higher public profile, however, many weaknesses can be identified in terms of Fishman's principles. In the first place, there cannot be said to have been prior ideological clarification of the goals and tactics for RLS in Scotland (W. Gillies 1989b: 28).

The Gaelic development infrastructure has historically been fragmented and there has been little co-ordination or agreed policy or strategy uniting Gaelic development agencies (Taskforce on Public Funding of Gaelic 2000: 10). This has not aided the development of prior ideological clarification. Similarly, there has been a tendency in Gaelic development circles to view public acknowledgement and discussion of areas of disagreement as a sign of weakness and disunity as opposed to healthy debate necessary to achieving agreement and progress (Caimbeul 2000: 64).

One particularly important and potentially divisive issue has not been clarified, or indeed fully acknowledged or discussed by those involved in Gaelic development: the question to what extent (or whether) Gaelic should be promoted as a national language and to what extent (or whether) Gaelic should be promoted only as the language of the Highlands. Even within the Highlands there is the unresolved issue to what extent (or whether) Gaelic development initiatives should concentrate on the area as a whole or be geared primarily to communities such as Skye and the Western Isles where a significant percentage of residents are Gaelic speakers.

How this question is tackled by Gaelic agencies will be of central importance to the future of development of the language. Decisions on practical matters such as which services are available in Gaelic in different areas and where Gaelic employment is to be made available, and on symbolic issues such as the level of public visibility of the language nationally, will have a profound effect of the success or failure of RLS efforts. As will be discussed further below, this question is particularly relevant to Gaelic learners, as learners tend to be based in the Lowlands and as the level of public visibility is likely to have an impact on the numbers learning Gaelic.[7]

In addition to a lack of prior ideological clarification, Gaelic development efforts would also score poorly in terms of Fishman's principle that RLS initiatives should be based upon a language planning approach. As McLeod has argued, language development initiatives in Scotland have been "a 'renaissance' without planning" (McLeod 2002a). Within Gaelic development, little consideration has been given to language planning or policy and there has been little in the way of a strategic underpinning (McLeod 2002a, Dunbar 2006: 1). Initiatives have tended to be uncoordinated and ad hoc, driven neither by theory nor research (McLeod 2002a). Despite a large increase in public expenditure on Gaelic, little attention has been paid to ensuring that language development initiatives directly address the central question of increasing the intergenerational transmission and community use of the language (McLeod 2002a: 279).

In 1994, Johnstone pointed out in relation to research with practical application for the maintenance and development of Gaelic that: "the existing research-base covering developments in Scottish Gaelic is not extensive. Before a really clear and useful picture of findings from research can emerge, more funded research will be essential" (1994: 76). MacKinnon and McLeod have similarly pointed to a dearth of

---

[7] For further discussion of these issues, see MacCaluim forthcoming 2007, MacCaluim with McLeod 2001.

and need for Gaelic related research (MacKinnon 1997b, 1998b, 1998c, 1998d, 2006b; McLeod 2001a). These conclusions remain valid today. As research is of key importance to the formulation of effective language policy, this gap is a matter for concern (Cormack 2006: 211; MacKinnon 2006b; Robasdan 2006: 106, 108; Oliver 2005; Rothach 2006: 224). Likewise, very few of those involved professionally in Gaelic development have any specialist training or experience in language planning (Caimbeul 2000: 65, McLeod 2001a).

As a consequence of a lack of planning and research, Gaelic development initiatives have also largely failed to follow Fishman's 'first things first' principle. Rather than concentrating on the promotion of intergenerational transmission or the maintenance or creation of Gaelic-speaking communities, initiatives have overwhelmingly focussed on Gaelic-medium education and Gaelic broadcasting (McLeod 2001a). In 1991, Fishman himself said of Gaelic development initiatives that there was "a well nigh complete reliance on the school and other higher order 'props'" (1991: 380).

The growth of Gaelic-medium education in Scotland has been very significant and valuable. However, the Gaelic development movement in Scotland has failed to heed Fishman's warnings of the dangers of relying on education alone as the principal means of RLS as Gaelic-medium school education has been overwhelmingly stressed by Gaelic groups above all else as the main means of language maintenance (McLeod 2001a; Oliver 2006: 164). As Fishman has pointed out, it cannot be assumed that Gaelic-medium pupils from non-Gaelic speaking homes will become fully fluent and confident in a wide range of domains and registers and will use the language outside school and continue to use the language as adults and as parents.

GME has tended to be viewed in a vacuum and has not been accompanied by an emphasis and promotion of the use of Gaelic in the home or wider community (McLeod 2001a, 2002a: 285; Oliver 2006). Little or no attention has been paid by Gaelic development agencies to encouraging the intergenerational transmission of Gaelic within the family (MacKinnon 2006b: 3). Unlike in Wales and Ireland, for example, there have been no major information campaigns to explain to Gaelic-speaking parents why they should pass the language on to their children, how they can do this and how mixed-language couples can ensure intergenerational transmission.[8]

In the community, there are some valuable initiatives to encourage the use of Gaelic outwith the school such as classes for parents, the *Sradagan* (Gaelic youth clubs) and various trips and camps. Comunn na Gàidhlig also operates long-standing bilingual signage and Gaelic in the Community (*Gàidhlig sa Choimhearsnachd*) schemes providing financial assistance for community signage and language initiatives. More recently, the agency has purchased several sets of simultaneous translation equipment to enable the holding of community meetings in Gaelic.[9] Despite these significant projects, however, relatively little priority has been given to language initiatives at the community level and there have been no projects in Scotland as wide ranging as the Welsh *Mentrau Iaith* local language animation schemes.[10]

---

[8] For Irish examples, see www.teangafein.ie, Comhluadar and Foras na Gaeilge 2001. For a Welsh example, see: www.twfcymru.com.
[9] For more details of these initiatives, see www.cnag.org.uk.
[10] For more details of the Mentrau Iaith, see www.mentrau-iaith.com.

Along with GME, Gaelic broadcasting has been the key priority of Gaelic development efforts to date. The establishment and expansion of the Gaelic radio station BBC Radio nan Gaidheal has been of great significance to RLS, providing a range of information and entertainment tailored to the needs of the Gaelic community on the local and national levels and in building and maintaining a sense of group identity (Cormack 2006: 213). Such a radio service is in line with Fishman's advice to prioritise initiatives which will aid the strengthening of the Xish community and create domains for the language.

Gaelic television, however, does not as easily tie in with the 'first things first' principle. At present, an annual budget of £8.5M is devoted to the Gaelic Broadcasting Fund, most of which goes towards television. As such, television receives more funding than any other single aspect of Gaelic development.

Gaelic television has had the advantage of creating much Gaelic-related employment and producing quality television for Gaelic speakers. As will be discussed in detail later, Gaelic television is currently broadcast on mainstream channels carrying subtitles and has therefore also brought the language to the attention of hundreds of thousands of non-Gaelic speakers.

According to Fishman's theory, television would not be a priority for a language in a weak position such as Gaelic, for while it can help reinforce the language in existing Xish families and communities, it can play only a very small and indirect part in bringing about intergenerational transmission and in creating Xish communities where these do not already exist (Cormack 2006).

In the case of Gaelic broadcasting, the prioritisation of television by Gaelic agencies probably reflects less a belief that television is a key means of RLS than historical opportunism: the fact that the political climate in the early 1990s was such that only a relatively small amount of lobbying was sufficient to secure legislative changes that brought a significant increase in the public funding for Gaelic broadcasting and offered the possibility of establishing a full Gaelic television service (Caimbeul 2000).

While this is understandable, however, little has been done to investigate and maximise the potential which television can play as part of broader RLS efforts. For example, as discussed below, while Gaelic television is often assumed to aid RLS by 'raising the profile of the language', there has been little research into the relationship between the visibility of the language, attitudes towards the language and use, transmission and acquisition of the language (Cormack 2006: 211; McLeod 2002a: 289).

While Gaelic development efforts have tended to be centred on education and broadcasting, significant public money has also been devoted to the Gaelic arts and to economic development efforts with a Gaelic component (McLeod 2002a). Such areas theoretically have a close link to the stage 6 goals of strengthening community. Arts and cultural activities should provide domains in which Gaelic can be used and Gaelic economic development initiatives should provide Gaelic-speaking workplaces and economic sustainability for Gaelic-speaking families and communities. In practice, however, this has not tended to be the case in Scotland.

In the case of major 'Gaelic' arts and cultural activities and projects the level of Gaelic used is often tokenistic or minimal with projects frequently being aimed at largely English-monoglot audiences (Lang 2006, Lang and McLeod 2005, McLeod 2002b: 60). This is particularly the case with music as can be seen in fields such as Gaelic choirs, the Mòd and the Fèisean movement and also in projects involving the visual arts. Frequently a large percentage of performers and tutors participating in such groups and events are non-Gaelic speakers. Rather than creating a domain for the use of Gaelic, therefore, Gaelic arts projects have often proved alienative to Gaelic and RLS.

The outward orientation of the Gaelic arts sector can largely be attributed to the assumption that 'raising the profile of Gaelic' will in some way aid RLS (McLeod 2002b: 61). In practice, however, this approach has not been based on theory or research and it is uncertain to what extent that such arts activity will actually lead non-Gaelic speaking consumers to support or learn the language.

Like the 'Gaelic arts sector' or the 'Gaelic arts', there has been much discussion of the 'Gaelic sector' or the 'Gaelic economy'. As with the Gaelic arts sector, however, there are questions as to how far economic development initiatives relating to Gaelic and to Gaelic-speaking communities have served to promote RLS (McLeod 2002a: 287, 2002b, 2003b).

Several hundred Gaelic-essential jobs have been created, many in economically peripheral areas of the Highlands and Islands, through the expansion of the Gaelic development infrastructure in the form of Gaelic agencies, broadcasting, education, cultural initiatives and the related provision of Gaelic-medium goods and services (Galloway 1995a, Sproull and Ashcroft 1993, McLeod 2002b). This has led to the common use of the terms 'Gaelic sector' or 'Gaelic economy' (Sproull and Ashcroft 1993, Pedersen 2000, McLeod 2002b). While these developments have been very significant, however, there are some difficulties with the 'Gaelic economy' as currently conceptualised (McLeod 2001b, 2002b, 2003b).

Firstly, there is no guarantee that creating employment directly related to Gaelic development or Gaelic products and services will lead to the creation of Gaelic-speaking workplaces and thus create Gaelic domains within the community (McLeod 2002b: 60). In the field of Gaelic broadcasting for example, English is often the working language behind-the-scenes due to often monolingual English-speaking technical staff (Dunbar 2006: 8). As Caimbeul has pointed out, this scenario creates the danger that the language might be seen "as a passport to a job with no further commitment required by the learner or native speaker" (Caimbeul 2000: 65).

More serious for RLS is the fact that the discussion of the Gaelic economy has centred on jobs and goods and services directly related to Gaelic and has not sought to link Gaelic to issues of mainstream economic (and indeed social) development. In other words, minimal attention has been given by the relevant local authorities and economic development agencies to making Gaelic the language of workplaces other than those concerned directly with language development or to ensure that mainstream economic development initiatives in Gaelic speaking areas strengthen rather than weaken Gaelic (McLeod 2002b: 62-65; Rothach 2006: 222, 225). As McLeod has argued "Gaelic remains highly peripheral to the world of work and economic life, which remains an overwhelmingly English-language domain even in the most strongly Gaelic-speaking areas, and the recent growth of the Gaelic economy has done little to change this pattern" (2002b: 52).

The weaknesses of the 'Gaelic economy' also helps to illustrate another failing in terms of the Fishman criteria, namely a lack of the self-reliance which Fishman states should be a key tenet of RLS efforts. Gaelic jobs created within the 'Gaelic economy' have overwhelmingly been created directly or indirectly by public funding from local and central government and other public bodies such as Highland and Islands Enterprise with little or no self-sustaining, for-profit or not-for-profit co-operative enterprise existing (McLeod 2002b: 52; Dunbar 2000: 81; Dunbar 2006: 1). This lack of self-help is not only characteristic of the 'Gaelic economy' but of Gaelic development in general. Rather than being based on grass-roots, independent initiatives, Gaelic development efforts have overwhelmingly been focussed on securing government funding and government support (McLeod 2001a).

While Gaelic agencies such as Comunn na Gàidhlig have been very skilful in lobbying for public funding for valuable language initiatives, the nigh-complete dependence on public subsidy carries many risks. One consequence is that the Gaelic community often has little control of the key levers of Gaelic development policy (Dunbar 2000: 70). The dominance of public funding also means that language initiatives are vulnerable to changes in administrations and key personnel in local and national government and also in the state of the economy (Robasdan 2006: 103, 106). The freedom of Gaelic groups to lobby for the language is also threatened by their receipt of public funding (Dunbar 2000: 81).[11] The expansion in Gaelic development employment may also serve to co-opt and silence many of the most capable and opinionated Gaelic advocates (Dòmhnallach 2006).

Lobbying, like Gaelic development in general, has also been largely 'top-down'. Major advances for the language such as the creation of the Gaelic Television/Broadcasting Fund have been largely come about due to lobbying of key individuals by the Gaelic agencies themselves and have not been matched by consistent grass-roots efforts from within the Gaelic community in general (Caimbeul 2000, Dunbar 2000). There have been notably successful campaigns where the Gaelic agencies and Gaelic speakers at a grass-roots level have worked together on a co-ordinated basis (Caimbeul 2000). These have included the campaign for an expansion in Gaelic television in the late 1980s and early 1990s and more recently the campaign for a Gaelic language bill. In general, however, organised grass-roots activism has tended to be restricted to local issues such as local education provision rather than national issues. A measure of this is the lack of an independent Gaelic lobbying group. This situation is also risky as regards RLS. As Dunbar has pointed out: "why should we expect [politicians] to be more adventurous and bold that the Gaelic community itself?" (Dunbar 2000: 82).

To summarise, Gaelic development efforts in Scotland have to date proved very weak in terms of Fishman's rules for RLS. Gaelic development efforts have generally not been based on planning, research or theory, have lacked the foundation of prior ideological clarification and have relied largely on state support rather than self-help. Most importantly of all, there has been a failure to prioritise the crucial stage 6 on the GIDS scale. In particular, the most crucial area of all, intergenerational transmission, has been almost completely ignored.

It should be noted at this point that there have been some significant changes to the Gaelic development infrastructure in the new millennium which may result in the Gaelic development infrastructure becoming more effective in RLS terms. A Gaelic language board, Bòrd na Gàidhlig, has been established to develop Gaelic using a language planning model and has taken over the responsibility for the distribution of much of the Scottish Executive's budget for Gaelic. The Bòrd has also been charged with drawing up a national plan for Gaelic. The *Gaelic Language (Scotland) Act 2005*

---

[11] For example, Comunn na Gàidhlig were subject to severe criticism from a senior Western Isles Labour councillor and by the then Minister for Gaelic for opposing the Executive on a matter relating to Gaelic-medium education (Dunbar 2000: 84).

also gives Bòrd na Gàidhlig the power to compel devolved public bodies to draw up Gaelic language plans. These plans will be informed in turn by the national plan (Dunbar 2006: 18).

These measures are intended to create a more co-ordinated and strategic basis for Gaelic development. At the time of writing, however, it is too early to say how effective these changes will be as the Bòrd is a relatively new body, the national plan has not yet been published and no Gaelic plans have yet been drawn up by public bodies. The effectiveness of the new Gaelic development structures in RLS terms will depend upon matters such as the funding, membership and vision of Bòrd na Gàidhlig, their commitment to creating a more co-ordinated and planned approach to language development and to focus on intergenerational transmission (Dunbar 2006: 20; McLeod 2006b). It will also depend on how the Gaelic Language (Scotland) Act is interpreted by the Bòrd, Scottish Executive and by Scottish public bodies (McLeod 2006b).

Following this brief overview of RLS theory, the remainder of this study will look at Gaelic learners and learning in Scotland with reference to Fishman's principles. In terms of RLS theory, the creation of fluent adult learners in Scotland is necessary if language shift is to be reversed. For this to happen, learners would have to be considered to be a central part of RLS, and the Gaelic learning infrastructure would have to be able to bring a large number of learners, particularly young learners, to fluency and confidence in the language. Whether this is indeed the case will be a key issue investigated in the remainder of this study.

3: The Gaelic Learning Infrastructure

> A situation which is continually growing, though without direction or shape. (CLI newsletter, Spring 1984)

Introduction

The nature and quality of the facilities available for the learning of Gaelic are crucial factors in attempting to reverse language shift in Scotland, affecting as they do the number of Gaelic learners reaching fluency in the language. This chapter will describe the infrastructure for Gaelic learning, assessing its strengths and weaknesses and will chart changes in this area since the early 1990s, making suggestions for future improvements. Material investigated in this chapter will be supplemented by chapter five, "The Gaelic Learners' Survey", where the views of Gaelic learners on the Gaelic learning infrastructure will be discussed.

Literature Review

The only large-scale study of provision for Gaelic learners to date has been the 1992 *Feumalachdan Luchd-Ionnsachaidh / Provision for Gaelic Learners* report produced by the national Gaelic development agency Comunn na Gàidhlig (CnaG) and national Gaelic learners' association Comann an Luchd-Ionnsachaidh (CLI).[12] This was based on a national survey of Gaelic learners and tutors and comprehensively described the infrastructure for learners as of 1991, making recommendations for the future. The survey was completed by 760 learners and 128 tutors.

Feumalachdan identified several problems with the Gaelic learning infrastructure. In the first place, there was an over-reliance on evening classes with few other means of learning being available. There were no immersion courses, few work-based courses and only limited distance-learning facilities, for example. Classes tended to be 'one size fits all', with people at mixed levels of ability often being taught in composite classes and with the methods of teaching and areas of language taught failing to meet the specific needs or interests of all learners. Tutors tended to be volunteer native speakers with little or no formal training in language teaching, with the quality of teaching often being inadequate as a result. Other identified deficiencies included outdated or poor quality teaching materials and a lack of Gaelic broadcasting suitable for learners. A key conclusion was that "Provision for adult Gaelic learners is fragmented, lacks co-ordination and needs a more structured approach" (CnaG/CLI 1992: 65).

A similar conclusion was reached by the HM Inspectors of Schools report *Provision for Gaelic Education in Scotland,* which sought to describe and evaluate Gaelic education provision at all levels, including the adult learners' sector:

> There is a clear need for collaboration among Gaelic organisations, education authorities and institutions of further and higher education to ensure more effective and co-ordinated provision for adult learners [...] creation of a basic infrastructure is vital (Scottish Office 1994: 27).[13]

---

[12] This group has since changed its name to Clì Gàidhlig.
[13] A more recent report by Her Majesty's Inspectors of Education reiterated the need for expanded and improved facilities for Gaelic learners (HMIE 2005).

The results of these weaknesses identified in the Gaelic learning infrastructure can be seen through the results of a further two studies on Gaelic learners. A longitudinal study of a representative survey of learners by Wells suggested that traditional Gaelic learning methods such as evening classes were proving ineffective in bringing learners to fluency. Around half of his sample felt that they had made no progress in the language over a three-year period with another fifth believing that they had regressed and with the remainder being of the opinion that they had made only limited progress (1997: 25). The conclusion was:

> For adult learners wishing to break free of their English monolingualism the picture is bleak if the chosen route is via traditional methods of learning, for example night classes, or even short weekend or week-long courses. The longitudinal findings of this research [...] underline the lack of promise such routes offer [...] Clearly the status quo is untenable if a significant growth in the number of successful adult learners is to be achieved (Wells 1997: 25)

MacNeil and MacDonald's study of Gaelic learners also suggested that learners typically made very slow progress, with few people eventually becoming fluent (1997: 14).

To ensure that more learners reach fluency, *Feumalachdan* made the following main recommendations for the Gaelic learning infrastructure: a co-ordinated national strategy for Gaelic learners, a national development officer for adult learners, a national resource centre for Gaelic learners, provision for tutor training, the expansion of media commitment to Gaelic learners, establishment of Gaelic social groups, increased use of open learning and the encouragement of native speakers to take a more active role in the process of Gaelic learning (CnaG/CLI 1992: 67).

In addition to the wide-ranging studies of Gaelic learning identified above, there have been a number of more specialised works. MacNeil and MacDonald (1997) have studied the use of Gaelic television as a learning resource amongst a representative sample of learners, evaluating the actual and potential uses of this medium and making recommendations for future development.

Two studies have also been carried out into Gaelic immersion courses. A 1994 study by MacNeil and Beaton investigated the feasibility of establishing Gaelic immersion courses, exploring also the models and methods for immersion and intensive language teaching and learning. These issues were identified with particular reference to Gaelic related employment. A number of immersion courses were established in the years immediately following this report. A later study by Robertson (2001a) reviewed existing immersion provision and put forward recommendations for future development. The findings of these studies into immersion teaching and broadcasting will be described in more detail below.

Aims and Outline of this Chapter

This chapter will seek to provide an overview of the Gaelic learning infrastructure similar to that provided by the *Feumalachdan Luchd-Ionnsachaidh* report, seeking to describe the situation almost fifteen years on, assessing change in the intervening period and seeking to assess the effectiveness of today's Gaelic learners' infrastructure in RLS terms.

This study takes a broader view of the infrastructure of Gaelic than *Feumalachdan,* which was mainly concerned with provision made especially for Gaelic learners. This chapter investigates some areas not normally considered to be part of the adult learning infrastructure, such as school Gaelic learners' classes and Gaelic broadcasting. The rationale behind this expanded definition is to include areas which provide informal means of learning Gaelic or which help to attract new learners.

This chapter is divided into four main sections. The first will look at Gaelic learning and teaching, both formal and informal, including evening classes, weekend and summer courses, full time college and university courses, Gaelic as a secondary school subject, flexible learning opportunities, learning courses and materials, informal learning opportunities, and broadcasting and the internet as learning resources.

The following section looks at means of attracting Gaelic learners, considering the issue in general and also investigating the role of the school system and the broadcasting system in particular. The third section investigates organisations dedicated to Gaelic learning. The final section discusses progress made in the Gaelic learning infrastructure since 1992 and provides an overview of structural weaknesses, making recommendations for possible solutions. Where relevant, material from the Gaelic Learners' Survey will be used to illustrate matters in question.

Gaelic Learning and Teaching

Evening and Day Classes

Evening classes, normally organised by local authorities or colleges, remain the mainstay of Gaelic learning and are attended by most Gaelic learners at some point. 83% of respondents in the CnaG/CLI report were attending such classes for example. MacNeil and MacDonald's 1997 survey of learners also found that three-quarters of respondents had attended classes at some point (CnaG/CLI 1992: 13; MacNeil and MacDonald 1997). The Gaelic Learners' Survey similarly found that 83% of respondents were attending or had attended such classes.

Feumalachdan identified several problems with evening classes. There was an over-reliance on such classes with few other means of learning being available. Learners often found difficulty in finding Gaelic classes in their local area or at their level, this being in part due to a shortage of Gaelic tutors. Even where classes were available, not everybody surveyed found the evening class model suitable for their lifestyle, with many favouring more flexible learning opportunities. The quality of the learning experience was also often adversely affected by classes containing learners at very different levels of language learning and as a result of reliance on unqualified tutors.

The problems identified reflected a largely laissez-faire situation in the provision of evening classes for adult learners, with Gaelic classes being provided by a large number of colleges, local authorities, individuals and Gaelic organisations. A situation such as this makes the teaching of Gaelic to adults through evening classes difficult to co-ordinate or to plan strategically and also means that there are wide regional variations, with better provision being made for learners in some areas than in others.

The fact that classes are provided by a range of providers and that most classes are not working towards a certificate or qualification also means that there is nothing resembling a common curriculum for Gaelic learners and that there are no recognised levels of proficiency in the language for adult learners.

Since 1992 there have some advances relating to Gaelic evening classes. As detailed below, the development of some Gaelic immersion courses and other full time Gaelic courses and improved flexible learning opportunities have enabled some learners to escape the evening class circuit to become relatively fluent in a short space of time. There has also been an improvement in Gaelic teaching materials both for home and class use and in flexible learning facilities.

Perhaps more obvious than the improvements, however, have been the enduring problems. While the occasional weekend or one-day training seminars for tutors have been organised by bodies such as the Community Learning and Development Group for Gaelic (CLDG), there is still no organised support or systematic training structure for evening class teachers. As a result, tutors remain scarce and quality of tuition remains variable.[14] Classes are still often composite and often fail to cater for the needs of all the students, such as parents of children who want to learn phrases to use at home or learners who wish to gain qualifications such as Scottish Qualifications Authority modules or Higher exams, a problem identified in *Feumalachdan*. There are also large gaps between class terms in which few Gaelic classes run. Such factors mean that drop-out rates in classes are rather high.[15] The ad hoc and uncoordinated nature of evening class provision identified in the report also remains a concern.

One problem not mentioned in detail in *Feumalachdan* was that of the difficulty of finding classes at post-beginners level. Colleges and local authorities normally have limits for the number of students necessary to justify the running of a class meaning that numbers are very often insufficient to make classes at the intermediate or advanced stages viable.[16] This ironically means that it is often particularly difficult to identify suitable Gaelic classes in geographical Gaelic speaking communities as these tend to have small and scattered populations. Changes in the focus of local authority Community Education/Community Learning departments and funding cuts have also led to fewer Gaelic classes being available in many areas.

While there have not been major changes to evening classes themselves, however, there has been something of a change of philosophy. This has been a growing belief amongst Gaelic educationalists that the evening classes should only be one part of the Gaelic learning infrastructure along with other classes, courses and materials rather than being its very backbone. This is due to a growing recognition of the intrinsic limitations of the conventional evening class as a means of teaching Gaelic. This was reflected in the interviews conducted by the author with Peadar Morgan, then of CLI, with Margaret MacIver, then of Comunn na Gàidhlig, and Fionnlagh MacLeòid, director of Comhairle nan Sgoiltean Àraich (the Gaelic pre-school council), all of whom expressed the view that the era of the evening class had passed.[17] The current director of Clì Gàidhlig confirms that night classes alone cannot fulfil the needs of learners.[18] All were of the view that conventional evening classes had severe

---

[14] CLDRG was formerly known as the Community Education Review Group for Gaelic (CERG).

[15] Peadar Morgan, personal communication: interview, 22/04/98, Fionnlagh MacLeòid, personal communication: interview, 24/03/98.

[16] Siùsaidh Hardy, Clì Gàidhlig, personal communication: telephone interview, 9/05/2006.

[17] Peadar Morgan, op cit, Margaret MacIver, personal communication: interview, 21/04/98, Fionnlagh MacLeòid, op cit.

[18] Siùsaidh Hardy, personal communication: telephone interview, 9/05/2006.

limitations in terms of effectiveness in bringing learners to fluency. In addition to the inherent limitations of a two-hours per week class, the perceptions of the learners as to what can be achieved through evening classes are also often unrealistic. As MacLeòid has pointed out, learners attending classes often expect that they can become fluent mainly or wholly through attending a class once a week for a few years. Such overly optimistic expectations have, according to MacLeòid, resulted in many disappointed and disillusioned individuals and a very high drop-out rate for Gaelic classes with a majority of learners dropping out within two years.[19]

Conventional evening classes are insufficient for the needs of people who wish to become fluent quickly and at an early age in order to rear Gaelic-speaking children or to take advantage of increasing opportunities for Gaelic-related employment or Gaelic-medium further/higher education.

Limitations of evening classes can easily be illustrated when the amount of exposure to a language necessary to achieve fluency is considered. MacNeil and Beaton (1994) have estimated the length of time necessary for an adult to learn Gaelic on the basis of internationally recognised figures for other languages. To reach the Minimum Professional Levels in listening, speaking, reading and writing as laid down by the NATO Standardisation Agreement on Language Proficiency Tests would take an estimated 1125 hours. To reach the Full Professional Level would take almost 2000 hours (MacNeil and Beaton 1994: 54). Should they be relying mostly on evening classes, learners attending conventional 2 hour per week evening classes with terms of 10–20 weeks would, on this basis, take well over 15 years to reach the lower of these levels.

This very rough figure should also be considered in combination with the fact that classes are often difficult to find at the post-beginner stage and that few people would continue to attend classes for the necessary number of years even if a suitable graded series of classes existed.[20] As has been seen above in the discussion of studies by MacNeil and MacDonald (1997) and Wells (1997), the current largely evening-class based system of Gaelic learning has for the most part been largely unsuccessful in bringing learners to fluency.

Despite their failings, traditional Gaelic classes as detailed above still undoubtedly have a role to play in the Gaelic learning infrastructure, however. Due to family and work commitments, not all individuals can attend immersion or other intensive courses, for example. Although conventional evening classes alone may not be effective in bringing learners to fluency, they can nonetheless play a useful role within a broader learning programme supplemented with other means of learning, and they remain a relatively effective way of teaching the very basic levels of a language due to their relatively low cost and due to the personal contact with a tutor which they involve. Evening classes also have the potential to provide learners with information about other means to improve their language skills such as Gaelic broadcasting and publication, local Gaelic events and immersion and weekend courses.

Siùsaidh Hardy, director of Clì Gàidhlig, has also pointed out that evening classes will continue to be suitable for those 'hobbyist' learners who are attending classes for fun without seeking full fluency. Conversation based evening classes can also be used to supplement more intensive means of learning. As will be discussed below, evening classes can also play a part in delivering structured and progressive intensive Gaelic courses such as the Ulpan course.[21]

---

[19] Fionnlagh MacLeòid, op cit.
[20] Siùsaidh Hardy, Clì Gàidhlig, personal communication: telephone interview, 9/05/2006.
[21] Siùsaidh Hardy, personal communication: telephone interview, 9/05/2006.

There is nonetheless a growing recognition that evening classes should not be seen as a stand-alone method of learning Gaelic but rather should be accompanied by a range of intensive full-time, part-time and short courses, home based learning programmes, Gaelic social groups and greater informal opportunities to use the language. An ideal learner might start learning at an intensive Gaelic weekend course, continuing at weekly evening classes whilst attending a Gaelic social group and finally perhaps attending an immersion course, for example.

For such a model to be successful, however, there would need to be an expansion in the number and type of Gaelic learning opportunities available and a more structured approach to Gaelic learning provision. To what extent such provision has been forthcoming will be investigated throughout the course of this chapter as will suggestions as to how the present situation can be improved.

Summer and Weekend Courses

Alongside the evening class, the summer and weekend course is another mainstay of the traditional Gaelic learning infrastructure. The main venues for courses are the Gaelic college Sabhal Mòr Ostaig, Skye; Lews Castle College, Stornoway; and Ionad Chaluim Chile Ìle, Islay. Weekend courses are also held by CLI and by a small number of other providers in a variety of places. These are still relatively few and far between, however.

These courses have the advantage of being relatively intensive and of giving the learner a step forward in their language acquisition. More of the tutors in summer courses than in evening classes tend to be trained and experienced in Gaelic teaching. The main disadvantage of the summer school is the relatively high cost of attending, which militates against the participation of less well-off learners. Weekend courses, however, are usually less expensive. The main potential development in this area would be an expansion in the number and geographical distribution of weekend courses.

Intensive/Full-time Gaelic Courses

One significant development since 1992 has been the establishment of a number of full-time intensive courses aimed at bringing Gaelic learners to fluency in a short time. The first full-time Gaelic-medium further education courses, HNC/D courses in Business and Gàidhealtachd Studies, were established at Sabhal Mòr Ostaig in 1983 and were subsequently supplemented by a range of other courses for fluent speakers. Gaelic-medium courses aimed at fluent speakers were also been offered at Lews Castle College. While many fluent/near-fluent learners took advantage of these courses to improve their language skills, it was not until 1994 that a full time course specifically intended for non-fluent learners was established. This was Sabhal Mòr Ostaig's HNC in Gaelic and Communication, which was intended to bring the advanced student to fluency within a year (*CLI Newsletter*, September 1994: 8).

In 1995 the first immersion course aimed at beginners or near-beginners was begun in Fort William by Inverness College as a pilot project between the college and Comunn na Gàidhlig. This was a National Certificate level course. In the 1996–7 session further immersion courses were established at Clydebank College and by Inverness College, Inverness. In the later 1990s, there was an expansion in the number of immersion courses and the number of areas served, some operating within a

Further Education framework and others within a Higher Education degree framework. Students get between 550 and 700 hours of class contact per year through these courses (Robertson 2001a).

Provision within constituent colleges of the UHI Millennium Institute (UHIMI), the project to establish a University of the Highlands and Islands, has been particularly notable, with immersion courses having continually operated through Inverness and Lews Castle colleges and through Sabhal Mòr Ostaig since the late 1990s.

It was soon realised that while one-year immersion courses brought learners to a reasonable degree of proficiency, they were insufficient to bring learners to total fluency. For this reasons, second-year further education courses have been established for some of the immersion courses. In the period 1995–2001, numbers of students on Gaelic immersion courses rose from zero to around 150 (Robertson 2001a: 15).

While immersion courses have met with much success, a range of problems can also be identified in this sector. The first of these is the uncoordinated nature of development. At present there is no national framework or strategy for immersion courses and as the decision to establish or to continue an immersion course rests with individual colleges, some areas of the country are served better by immersion courses than others.

This lack of co-ordination nationally has also been seen in terms of a lack of standardisation of courses in terms of syllabuses and materials (Robertson 2001a). There are no dedicated learning and teaching resources specifically designed for immersion courses at present. This situation has meant that immersion course tutors have had to adapt or produce materials themselves.

There is similarly no national course structure or certification scheme designed specifically for Gaelic immersion courses, which has meant that the structure of courses has not been ideal for the purposes of promoting communicative competence in the language. To gain certification from the Scottish Qualifications Authority (SQA), each immersion course must contain a certain number of SQA modules. As there are currently insufficient modules designed for Gaelic learning to make up an immersion course on their own, a range of modules aimed at fluent Gaelic speakers and a range of translations of English language modules not directly linked to language learning are currently used within immersion courses (Robertson 2001a: 8). This situation has meant that immersion courses have not been able to bring learners to as a high a level of fluency as would be possible if a dedicated course structure and certification scheme existed.

The lack of co-ordination and standardisation of immersion courses on a national scale also extends to tuition. As noted elsewhere in this chapter, there is no Gaelic tutor training scheme. This has implications both for the quality and level of standardisation of teaching and for the future expansion of immersion courses. While the current Gaelic immersion course tutors tend to be highly trained and experienced, many coming from a background of Gaelic school teaching (Robertson 2001a), there are limited supplies of such tutors and structures for training in immersion teaching will be necessary to cope with expansion in this field.

Robertson has also identified a lack of co-ordination in terms of marketing of immersion courses. To date, marketing and publicity for immersion courses has been mostly undertaken by individual colleges. With the exception of a leaflet produced by Comunn na Gàidhlig in 1999, there has been no co-ordinated national marketing or branding of immersion courses (Robertson 2001: 6). To date, many of the colleges which have established or tried to establish an immersion course have arguably exhibited a lack of marketing skill, tending to market Gaelic courses as they would any other FE course and failing to recognise that potential immersion course students are often older, more middle class and educated to a higher degree than the average further education student and failing to market the courses intensively within Gaelic circles.

In addition to the lack of co-ordination, Robertson has also identified a difficulty in funding immersion courses and places on courses as a major weakness (2001a: 10). At present, no specific Gaelic-related funding is available for the Tertiary or Higher Education sectors. This differs from the primary and secondary and community education sectors where Scottish Executive funding is available under the Scheme of Specific Grants for Gaelic Education whereby three quarters of the cost of approved projects are paid by the Scottish Executive for up to five years in order to encourage local authorities to establish new Gaelic provision (Robertson 2001a).[22] Under current Scottish Further Education Funding Council arrangements, Gaelic immersion courses attract the same funding weighting factor as other language and communication courses, the lowest weighting factor: 0.73 per student. This does not take account of the intensive nature of the courses or the likelihood of small class sizes and means that large numbers of students are necessary if Gaelic courses are to be financially viable for colleges (Robertson 2001a: 10). Further and Higher Education funding arrangements for students also make it difficult in turn to achieve the class sizes necessary to run immersion courses as students with a higher education qualification or who have received a bursary for a further education course within the past five years are ineligible for bursary funding to cover further education courses (Robertson 2001a: 10).

The funding and marketing difficulties mentioned above have meant that many attempts to establish Gaelic immersion courses have failed and that many courses established have subsequently been discontinued such as courses in Aberdeen and Perth Colleges (Robertson 2001a: 2). Following an initial period of growth in the late 1990s which saw courses being mounted in 14 different locations throughout Scotland, there has been a stagnation and contraction in the sector, particularly in the Lowlands and outwith the UHI (Robertson 2001: 1). In 2000–1, immersion courses ran in the following colleges: North Highland, Clydebank, Jewel and Esk (Edinburgh), Falkirk, Inverness, Kilmarnock, Sabhal Mòr Ostaig (Skye) and Lews Castle (Lewis) (Robertson 2001a: 15). By 2006, courses were only being offered at Inverness College, Kilmarnock College, Stow College (Glasgow), Sabhal Mòr Ostaig, Lews Castle College, and Ionad Chaluim Chille Ilè.

As a result of these difficulties, numbers of students in immersion courses have shown only a very modest rate of growth, seemingly having stalled in the 100–150 bracket by 2001, a pattern of stagnation which remains to this day (Robertson 2001a: 10; Robasdan 2006: 107). As research has suggested that conventional non-intensive means of Gaelic learning are not effective in bringing learners to fluency, the slow rate of expansion of immersion courses is a matter for concern.

Also of concern in RLS terms is the average age of immersion course students which has tended to be relatively high. Robertson's study of 1999-2000 immersion course students found that 57% of students were over 30, for example, with few entering immersion courses directly from school (Robertson 2001a: 4).

---

[22] For more details of this scheme, see Taskforce on Public Funding of Gaelic 2000.

Despite the difficulties reported on the national scale, however, it should be noted that significant progress has been made within the UHIMI. The UHIMI project which comprises a number of colleges and research institutions working towards the establishment of a University for the Highlands and Islands, has developed Gaelic-medium degree courses and has facilitated the greater integration and standardisation of immersion courses at Highland colleges through the Gaelic and Related Studies programme. Under this scheme, BA (Hons) courses have been developed in Gaelic Language and Culture and Gaelic with North Atlantic Studies. These courses are offered at Sabhal Mòr Ostaig, Lews Castle College and Ionad Chaluim Chille Ilè.

The first year of each of these BA (Hons) courses comprises of one of two intensive courses. The first of these is the Cùrsa Comais, an immersion course for intermediate level learners, the second being the Gaelic and Communication course, an intensive course for advanced learners. These courses are at the Diploma of Higher Education level and approximate to HNC courses. The Cùrsa Comais is offered not only at Sabhal Mòr Ostaig and Lews Castle College, but also at Inverness College and Ionad Chaluim Chille Ilè. On completing these courses, students can either leave with a DipHE or work towards a BA (Hons) degree taught through the medium of Gaelic.[23]

While conventional Celtic degrees tend not to produce graduates who are fluent in Gaelic, the UHIMI courses give those wishing to study Gaelic this opportunity. As university degree courses, the UHI Gaelic courses are also likely to attract younger students than those currently attending the immersion courses. Through including the immersion teaching within the overall course, the courses also give those wanting to become fluent in Gaelic the opportunity to do so without having subsequently to pay to attend an immersion course.

Despite encouraging developments within the UHIMI, however, it is clear that the Gaelic immersion course sector is not currently living up to its potential. To improve the situation, a range of recommendations have been put forward by Robertson. These are a new and flexible course structure and certification scheme specifically for Gaelic immersion courses dedicated to bring students to the highest possible level of fluency in the shortest possible time, the production of dedicated teaching and learning materials designed specifically for immersion courses, a national marketing programme for immersion courses, and special funding arrangements for immersion courses to overcome the financial difficulties identified above (Robertson 2001a: 11, 12).

It is clear that an overall strategy for the development of immersion courses including such measures will be necessary to ensure that the number of courses expand, that they cover all areas of Scotland, and that development is in future more co-ordinated and more linked to broader RLS goals.

Five years after his report on immersion courses, Robertson has expressed frustration that the recommendations have not been implemented and has reiterated his call for a reform of funding to enable an expansion in the sector (Robasdan 2006: 107). He has further suggested that these should be adopted by Bòrd na Gàidhlig's national plan for Gaelic and suggests a target of 1,000 students per annum for immersion courses.

---

[23] Details from UHI Millennium Institute website: www.uhi.ac.uk.

Universities

While universities have taught Gaelic to learners for many decades, they are often neglected during discussion of provision for Gaelic learners. This omission reflects both the ambiguous position which the three university Celtic departments in Scotland occupy in the infrastructure for Gaelic learners and the broader debate surrounding the role of Celtic departments in Scotland.

The first Celtic chair in Scotland was established in Edinburgh in 1882, with further Celtic departments being founded in Glasgow at the beginning of the 1900s and in Aberdeen in 1916 (W. Gillies 1989b: 39). From the very beginning, Scottish Celtic departments have pursued varied objectives and wide subject matters (Stoddart 1895: 112; Gilllies 1989a). This can be seen from the very title of Edinburgh University's Chair of "Celtic Languages, History, Literature and Antiquities", which was expected to teach philology, literature and history in addition to Gaelic itself. Additionally, language maintenance as much as academic study was a motive for those supporting the establishment of the Edinburgh chair (Stoddart 1895: 112). This naturally led to great expectations from what was until the time of the Second World War a one-teacher department. The remit and expectations of the newer Celtic departments were similar.

The exact part which universities should play in teaching Gaelic to learners and in RLS in general has been a matter of ongoing debate both within and outwith academia as a result of the large and varied subject matter of the Celtic departments and their low levels of funding and staffing. A key issue has been how far it is the role of universities to teach modern Scottish Gaelic at introductory and intermediate level as opposed to more academic studies such as linguistics, dialectology, the medieval Celtic languages and the study of Gaelic language and literature at higher levels for more fluent speakers.

While universities have always taught Gaelic, the way in which this was traditionally done was not particularly suited to Gaelic learners. Courses were designed for native speakers. Thomson has argued that until the time of the Second World War, "there was almost an assumption that students would be fluent and literate in Gaelic and should explore other matters at university" (Thomson 1994: 291). It can, indeed, be argued that this situation continued for long after the war. While some Gaelic learners did study Celtic, such a course of study was difficult and unsuited for those mainly wishing to achieve fluency in Gaelic. Not only was the modern Gaelic component of the Celtic degree limited, but the older Gaelic studied was challenging even to native speakers and the teaching was conducted through English. In 1972, MacKinnon said of the situation that:

> In higher education Gaelic has typically been studied as part of 'Celtic'. The orientations of the Celtic departments of Edinburgh, Glasgow and Aberdeen Universities have been towards the study of Gaelic essentially as a literary language. Emphasis has been placed upon ancient literature and its comparison with the literature of other Celtic languages. The subject of the degree is 'Celtic' and not 'Gaelic' as such. Hence, the role of university studies in this field may have been alienative to Gaelic also. Even in Celtic departments, Gaelic has not been taught on par with other modern languages, but has been relegated to a subsidiary stage. Gaelic has been regarded as a study

whose affiliations are literary, archaeological, philological and historical. Thus Gaelic is not taught as a 'modern language'. (MacKinnon 1972: 135)

This situation has been gradually changing. As Gillies has pointed out, "Gaelic was hardly ever studied except by native speakers of the language: learners of the language have only become common in the last two or three decades" (W. Gillies 1989b: 39). This change was encouraged by the introduction of university ab initio Gaelic courses and the creation of structures by which students could begin learning the language in the first year and nevertheless earn an honours Celtic degree in four years.

The proportion of learners studying Celtic has increased due both to an increased public interest in Gaelic and to a decline in the number of native speakers. Gillies has identified many different groups amongst university learners: Gaelic semi-speakers, non-Gaelic-speaking Highlanders, Lowlanders feeling Gaelic to be an important part of their national identity and those interested in linguistics (W. Gillies 1989a: 19). More recently, students from England and outwith the UK, especially Germany and the USA, have been increasingly common.

Other advances for learners include the choice of specialising in either a modern Gaelic studies related option or a mediaeval Celtic option, which was introduced in Edinburgh University shortly after the appointment of Professor Gillies in 1979. Aberdeen University have introduced a Gaelic Studies honours course in which students are able to specialise in modern Scottish Gaelic and which aims to bring all students to fluency in any Gaelic language context by the end of their final honours year (Hunter 1995: 6). The University of Aberdeen also has a scheme whereby students studying a specified programme at Sabhal Mòr Ostaig may then proceed into the second year of a degree course in the department of Celtic.

In the 1990s, first-year Gaelic classes at Aberdeen and Glasgow universities were divided into three levels rather than two, with there being separate classes suitable for beginners, for those with a learners' exam qualification and for the more fluent speakers. Such a move ensures that the level of teaching is neither too high for those at an intermediate level nor too low for those more proficient in Gaelic. The emphasis on spoken Gaelic at all three university departments has also increased. Gaelic-medium teaching of Gaelic courses for fluent speakers and Gaelic-related honours options in all three universities is now common, this marking a great change from the early-mid 1990s when very little teaching was done through the medium of Gaelic.

As seen above, the 1990s have also seen the establishment of the UHI Millennium Institute project and the development of Gaelic-medium degrees. The establishment of the Board of Celtic Studies (Scotland) in 1989 has also enabled greater co-operation between the university Celtic departments.

Despite progress, there remain, however, some inherent limitations in universities from the point of view of bringing Gaelic learners to fluency. The first of these is that the remit of Celtic departments is far wider than merely bringing learners to fluency in written and spoken Gaelic. The fact that students must study a variety of subjects in their pre-honours years also significantly reduces the amount of time which can be spent on learning modern spoken/written Gaelic, which is only one of their subjects. Staffing also remains limited in the Celtic departments. A result of these factors is that many graduates of Gaelic/Celtic leave university without reaching fluency in Gaelic.

While it is reasonable to expect the traditional universities to provide a good grounding in speaking, reading and writing Gaelic and in specialised skills unavailable elsewhere, such as knowledge of Gaelic dialects, of writing Gaelic in a variety of registers or of translation, it is perhaps overambitious to expect them to bring beginners to complete fluency singlehandedly given the amount of practice necessary to achieve this end.[24]

Some suggestions can be made to overcome such difficulties, however. The first of these is Computer Assisted Language Learning (CALL). The availability of interactive Gaelic learning courses by computer would enable students to work at the language at their own pace and to spend as much or as little time as desired on the language. It would complement traditional teaching methods and would increase opportunities for learning without placing more demands on the staff of Celtic departments. The Board of Celtic Studies (Scotland) have undertaken a study into CALL which provides specifications that could be put into practice should financial support be found for such a project (McLeod 1998a). Such support has not been forthcoming to date, however, and it seems fairly unlikely that this project will now go ahead.

Also beneficial would be the increasing availability of Gaelic as a secondary school subject. This would be likely to increase the intake to Celtic departments and to increase the number of students with a reasonable grasp of Gaelic at entry level.

A more ambitious suggestion would be the introduction of an immersion course as a compulsory part of an honours degree in Celtic or Gaelic studies. One model would be the introduction of a three-month immersion course on the model of the highly intensive Welsh *Wlpan* immersion course in Lampeter for students to undertake prior to undertaking, or during, work for a Celtic degree. Desirable though this might be, however, as Hunter points out, this course would not be eligible for Scottish Executive student awards funding (Hunter 1995: 22).

For these reasons, a year-long immersion course might be suggested. This would bring Celtic more into line with other modern languages, where students studying for a degree must undertake a year in a country where the language which they are studying is spoken as part of an honours degree. The circumstances of Gaelic Scotland mean that a college Gaelic course rather than a stay in a Gaelic community would be more practical, with Sabhal Mòr Ostaig being the obvious location for such a course. Should such a course become a compulsory part of a Celtic honours degree then it is likely that Scottish Executive funding would become available for students for the extra year (Hunter 1995: 23). It might be the case, however, that alternative sources of funding would also have to be identified.

The advantages of such an immersion course would be that students would become more highly fluent in Gaelic. This would encourage more teaching through the medium of Gaelic and would enable universities to give students the language skills required in Gaelic-related employment such as teaching and journalism whilst not compromising the academic pedigree of the Celtic/Gaelic degree.

---

[24] This can be seen clearly from the hours of language instruction in language courses. A student studying Gaelic at Edinburgh University would spend approximately 450 hours receiving instruction in Gaelic over 4 years with the first year course involving roughly 100 hours of this (personal communication: email, Wilson McLeod, Department of Celtic and Scottish Studies, Edinburgh University 20.05.06). As seen above, it has been estimated that learning Gaelic to the Minimum Professional Levels in listening, speaking, reading and writing as laid down by the NATO Standardisation Agreement on Language Proficiency Tests would take an estimated 1125 hours. To reach the Full Professional Level would an estimated 2000 hours (MacNeil and Beaton 1994: 54).

The case for an intensive Gaelic course as part of the degree can also be made from the fact that some university students already currently choose to take a year out from their courses at the traditional universities to attend Sabhal Mòr Ostaig or to attend the college immediately after graduating in order to reach a greater level of fluency.

It might be added at this point that while the new Gaelic-medium degree courses at Sabhal Mòr Ostaig and Lews Castle College will attract many of those who might have previously studied in Glasgow, Aberdeen or Edinburgh, the three traditional Celtic departments will continue to appeal to those wishing to study a broader Celtic degree or to undertake joint honours degrees. Such joint honours courses are important, offering students the opportunity both to learn Gaelic and to study another academic field.

A final university issue requiring discussion is that of the relatively small number of students choosing Gaelic as a subject and the even smaller number continuing to study the language to honours level. In 2004–5 for example, there were only 200 first-year undergraduates studying Gaelic between the Universities of Aberdeen, Edinburgh and Glasgow, Sabhal Mòr Ostaig and Lews Castle College (Scottish Funding Council 2005: 5). It has been estimated that only around 15–20% of first-year students will continue Gaelic studies to completion of a degree, yielding an annual graduate total of at most 55–60 students per annum from Gaelic-based courses (Scottish Funding Council 2005: 5). The total of adult learners graduating in Celtic/Gaelic as fluent Gaelic speakers will be even lower than this, as the Scottish Funding Council figures also include native speakers and former GME school pupils graduating and do not take into account the fact that not all graduates will have reached fluency.

An organised publicity campaign for Gaelic as recommended below would be likely to increase the numbers of students, as would increased availability of Gaelic as a secondary school subject. Increased integration of publicity for university Celtic courses with publicity for other learners' courses at all levels would also be useful.

Gaelic as a Secondary School Subject

One area of Gaelic education which has received little discussion in debates about adult learners, Gaelic education and Gaelic development in general has been that of Gaelic as an optional secondary school subject.

Figures for the number of candidates sitting learners' exams show a relatively low total, which has remained fairly constant and has not exhibited the growth characteristic of Gaelic-medium education (Robertson 2002, 2003, 2004, 2005). In total, only 2,718 S1–S6 pupils in Scotland were studying Gaelic as a secondary subject for learners in the 2005–06 session. Only around 1.5% of secondary school pupils study Gaelic (McLeod 2004). The number of pupils choosing Gaelic as a subject for Standard and Higher grade exams was even lower as can be seen from Table 2 below. At present Gaelic learners' courses may only be chosen in a limited number of schools, only 36 in 2005–6 (Robertson 2006). At present, only 10 of Scotland's 32 local education authorities offer Gaelic as a subject in any of their secondary schools (Robertson 2006).[25] In the Lowlands, schools teaching Gaelic are few and far between (McLeod 2006b, Robertson 2006, Robasdan 2006: 29). Of the schools currently teaching Gaelic learners' courses, all but seven were in the Highland local authority areas of Comhairle nan Eilean Siar, Highland Council and Argyll and Bute (Robertson 2006).

Table 2: Students studying Gaelic by year

Year	S4	S5/6: Higher	S6: Advanced Higher/CSYS
2001–2	343	109	17
2001–2	379	133	30
2002–3	353	124	38
2004–5	361	125	9
2005–6	399	150	18

Opportunities to learn Gaelic in Scotland's Lowland cities are particularly limited (Robasdan 2006: 29). Gaelic cannot be studied at all in Dundee or Aberdeen at present, provision in Edinburgh is very limited and provision in Glasgow is virtually non-existent. In 2005–6, for example, only 13 learners were studying Gaelic in Edinburgh and 4 in Glasgow. This reflects a situation whereby Gaelic teachers are employed in schools to teach Gaelic-medium pupils and where any limited provision made for Gaelic learners is a spin off of this. A similar pattern can be seen in Stirling, Cumbernauld, Kilmarnock and Forfar (Robertson 2006).

While more schools offer Gaelic for learners in the Highlands than in the remainder of Scotland, the subject is by no means universally available. In the Comhairle nan Eilean Siar area Gaelic was available in all secondaries. In the Highland Council area, however, only 13 of 29 secondary schools offered Gaelic as a subject and in Argyll and Bute, only four of ten.

Even where Gaelic is available as a subject, numbers of pupils choosing this option have tended to be lower than might otherwise been the case due to the fact that pupils have often been made to choose between Gaelic and modern foreign languages such as French or have not had the opportunity to study Gaelic until second or third year (Smith 1968: 71; MacKinnon 1990: 148; Robertson 1999: 248, 2001: 13). Comunn na Gàidhlig have called on an end to the choice between Gaelic and foreign languages as part of an overall national policy on Gaelic education (CnaG 1997c: 7).

Many arguments can be put forward for the expansion of the teaching of Gaelic as an optional high school subject. Gaelic-medium education is not available in all areas, and not all parents choose such an option for their children even where it is available. As Comunn na Gàidhlig have argued:

> While Gaelic-medium education is granted the highest priority […] it is acknowledged that it may not be a viable option in all circumstances. It is therefore important that there should also be the option of learning Gaelic through conventional second language teaching (CnaG 1997c: 7).

The Gaelic Learners' Survey and other studies of Gaelic learners have consistently found that the age profile of learners is biased towards the middle-aged and the elderly, with very few in the strategically important 16-25 age group (CnaG/CLI 1992: 72; MacNeil and MacDonald 1997: 9). More widespread availability of Standard Grade and Higher Grade Gaelic classes would create a direct link between the school

---

[25] The number of schools offering Gaelic in each local authority in 2005–6 were: Highland Council – 13, Comhairle nan Eilean Siar – 11, Argyll and Bute – 4, Perth and Kinross – 2, Angus – 1, Glasgow – 1, East Ayrshire – 1, Edinburgh – 1, North Lanarkshire – 1, Stirling – 1 (Robertson 2006).

and Gaelic-medium further and higher education. It could be expected that this would lead to a greater number of school students going on to study Gaelic at university or Sabhal Mòr Ostaig and undertaking Gaelic related employment.[26]

The Gaelic Learners' Survey further identified lack of time, family commitments and cost as key difficulties in learning Gaelic. The choice to study Gaelic at secondary school would allow more students to begin learning Gaelic before the onset of such adult responsibilities and would, for some, act as a springboard to further study of the language.

It is also clear from the results of the Gaelic Learners' Survey and from *Feumalachdan* that many adult Gaelic learners regret that they were unable to study Gaelic at school. According to *Feumalachdan*, for example:

> Many were critical of the opportunities afforded to them in school (at both primary and secondary levels) to study Gaelic. Some expressed their feelings very strongly, with one saying that he felt 'cheated' by the failure of the education system to provide him with adequate opportunities in school to pursue his interest in the language (CnaG/CLI 1992: 8)

CLI have also recorded such feelings on the part of many of their members (*CLI Newsletter*, June 1994: 8). Increased availability of Gaelic as a subject would give many such individuals an opportunity to study the language at an earlier age.

There are many constraints to the expansion of secondary school Gaelic teaching. The most significant of these is the shortage of trained Gaelic teachers and the large number of subjects already contained on the school curriculum. It must also be remembered that Gaelic-medium subject teaching, Gaelic-medium primary education and other fields of Gaelic education and development are competing for a limited number of young, educated Gaelic speakers. To make too many demands for the teaching of Gaelic as a second language in secondary schools would be both counterproductive and difficult to achieve. A number of possible suggestions for expansion possible in the present situation have been put forward by Comunn na Gàidhlig and by Boyd Robertson, Head of Gaelic at Strathclyde University's Jordanhill teacher training campus (CnaG 1997c, 1997b, 1998; Robertson 1999: 255; Robasdan 2006: 108).

Robertson has recommended extending access to Gaelic as a subject through prioritising the availability of Gaelic as a subject in one secondary school in each of the main towns and cities due to the large population of these areas and due to the almost complete non-existence of Gaelic as a subject for learners in these areas (CnaG 1998: 4; MacIver 2001). He has identified Edinburgh, Aberdeen, Dundee, Stirling and Perth as such towns and cities and has further argued that provision should be made at two schools in Glasgow due to its size.[27] Such a policy would offer children in all of Scotland's major population centres the opportunity to study Gaelic whilst not placing too great a strain on the supply of teachers or on the finances of local authorities. This could be achieved either through pupils travelling to a particular school to study Gaelic or though employing itinerant Gaelic teachers. ICT links and open-learning could also be used. A Gaelic ICT Implementation Group appointed by

---

[26] Siùsaidh Hardy, Clì Gàidhlig, personal communication: telephone interview, 9/05/2006.
[27] Boyd Robertson, personal communication: interview, 2/10/98.

the Minister for Education is investigating the ways in which a virtual Gaelic-medium secondary school can be established using ICT to expand GM secondary provision. A pilot scheme involving teaching geography via video conferencing is currently being undertaken as part of the project. The expansion of such initiatives to cover provision for Gaelic learners would enable far more students to study Gaelic at school.[28]

Co-operation between local authorities, and particularly between Glasgow City and the authorities making up greater Glasgow, would also be desirable on this matter. Provision could be further expanded in future in line with supply of trained teachers and demand for the subject as part of an overall strategy for Gaelic education. Development of Gaelic for learners in the secondary school might also be facilitated by the expansion of secondary Gaelic-medium education which is currently resulting in Gaelic teachers being employed in a number of secondary schools where Gaelic provision was not previously made. The establishment of Scotland's first Gaelic secondary school in Glasgow in August 2006 could also provide an opportunity to expand provision for Gaelic learners in the city. It is not clear at the moment, however, whether local authorities will use such opportunities to expand Gaelic learners' provision.

Comunn na Gàidhlig's target for secondary education as set out in the *Secure Status for Gaelic* document provides a potential longer-term goal for Gaelic subject provision:

> Statutory provision should be put in place requiring all local authorities to provide instruction in the Gaelic language as a modern European language, through the medium of English, at all secondary schools in Scotland, upon a showing of reasonable demand. [...] 'Reasonable demand' for these purposes should be defined as "demand made on behalf of five or more pupils". (CnaG 1997b: 28)

Robertson recommends as a ten year aim that the number of high schools offering Gaelic provision should increase to 60 (Robasdan 2006: 36). Another longer-term aim should be to ensure that Gaelic is available as a subject in all secondary schools in the Highlands.

In his recommendations for a language policy for Scotland, Lo Bianco has similarly recommended that there should be a large-scale expansion in Gaelic subject teaching in addition to Gaelic-medium education, with all local authorities committing themselves to expanding Gaelic provision (2001: 81). McLeod has suggested that a basic provision of any local authority's Gaelic language plan under the *Gaelic Language (Scotland) Act* should be to ensure that at least one of its secondary schools offers Gaelic as subject (McLeod 2006b).

Comunn na Gàidhlig's report on a national policy for Gaelic education suggests that "Where practical difficulties arise, central government should support them [Local Authorities] in meeting this demand". This could be achieved thorough an expansion of specific grant funding for Gaelic education (1997c: 7).

---

[28] For further details of the Gaelic ICT Implementation Group and the Glasgow Gaelic secondary school, see the following Scottish Executive news releases:
http://www.scotland.gov.uk/News/Releases/2005/06/20173114
http://www.scotland.gov.uk/News/Releases/2004/05/5553
http://www.scotland.gov.uk/News/Releases/2005/07/01103921

Flexible Learning

Increased use of flexible learning for Gaelic learning was recommended by *Feumalachdan* (CnaG/CLI 1992: 68). Flexible learning courses, also known as open or distance learning courses, are normally courses conducted through the post or through open learning centres via written and audio materials and assessments. Some such courses also include occasional meetings between tutor and students.

Flexible learning has the advantage of allowing learners to learn Gaelic at times which suits them, being appropriate for those with family or work commitments which make conventional classes unworkable. It also offers access to learning opportunities for those living in areas where Gaelic classes are not available.

Conventional flexible learning courses have been offered by several colleges over the years. At present, Edinburgh's Telford College is by far the largest in terms of student numbers and numbers of courses offered. Telford currently offers SQA National Certificate Gaelic 1 and 2, a pre-Higher course and an SQA Higher (Learners) course.[29] The Gaelic 1 course is now available online and Gaelic 2 is also being developed to go online. There are presently around 90 students enrolled for flexible learning at the college.[30]

While flexible learning has advantages in terms of allowing learners to study at a convenient time, it nonetheless has some of the disadvantages of evening classes, particularly in terms of being non-intensive. Unlike classroom courses, conventional flexible learning is less interactive. Many of these disadvantages have been overcome through an innovative new flexible learning course from Sabhal Mòr Ostaig. The Gaelic Access Course (An Cùrsa Inntrigidh), which was introduced in 2000–01, uses modern technology in addition to more traditional learning methods to provide a more intensive course. The course consists of soundfiles or CDs, workbooks, weekly telephone tutorials and a number of optional weekend schools. The course also has a dedicated website and bulletin board for participants and regular progress assessments. The course has the advantage of allowing participants to work at their own pace but also enables students to meet and to co-operate so as to reduce isolation. It is expected that students should spend 8–10 hours on the course each week. Students completing An Cùrsa Inntrigidh achieve a relatively high level of fluency and confidence in spoken Gaelic and can also qualify for entry to the UHIMI Gaelic and Related Studies degree programme through the Cùrsa Comais intensive course mentioned above. In its first year of operation the access course attracted a healthy 40 participants and has now been so successful that over 500 students (may of them outwith Scotland) have now completed the course (Robertson 2001a: 15; Sabhal Mòr Ostaig 2005). There are currently three sections to the course and a fourth is now being developed to take students to a higher level of fluency. An accelerated stream has also been developed for those with some previous knowledge of the language or who wish to learn more quickly.[31]

The area of flexible learning is thus one where there has been a great deal of progress since 1992 and where further progress can be expected. The only factor which is likely to prevent rapid expansion in this sector is the relatively high cost of the Cùrsa Inntrigidh: studying parts 1–3 of the course would cost a student living in the UK £675.

---

[29] www.ed-coll.co.uk

[30] Katie Murray, Gaelic tutor, Edinburgh's Telford College, personal communications: email, 18.06.02 and 10.03.06.

[31] For more details of the course, see: http://www.smo.uhi.ac.uk/en/cursaichean/inntrigidh, http://www.smo.uhi.ac.uk/smo/naidheachd/fiosan/ci05_b.html

Gaelic Learning and Teaching Materials

Learners' materials have been another area in which there has been significant improvement since the early 1990s. *Feumalachdan* found that there was a general feeling among tutors that printed materials available were "hopelessly inadequate", being "out of date and unsuitable" with learners also being dissatisfied with the amount and quality of learning materials (CnaG/CLI 1992: 24, 65).

Many of the courses were perceived as too old-fashioned. One tutor stated, for example, that "many of the printed materials relate to a world that existed in Gaelic 40 years ago" (op. cit. 23). Some widely used courses such as *Gàidhlig Bheò*, *Gaelic Made Easy* and the original version of *Teach Yourself Gaelic* (Macdonald 1976, Paterson 1952, MacKinnon 1971), for example, use vocabulary and expressions which are highly old-fashioned and which relate to a type of agricultural lifestyle greatly at variance with modern urban and Highland life. McLeod for example talks of the "excessive rural bias and unhelpful stereotyping" of *Gàidhlig Bheò* (1998a: 11). Such tendencies were even more noted in earlier courses such as *Gaelic without Groans* and *Sàth* (Mackechnie 1962 [first published 1934], Ferguson n.d.).

Jones (1989) has argued that learners are more likely to continue learning if their learning materials are relevant to their lifestyles and has warned against the use of stereotypes in learning materials. She has identified sexism in many materials for Welsh learners. Sexism can be identified in some of the older Scottish materials too, most notably in *Gaelic is Fun* and in *Gàidhlig Bheò* (Ó Baoill 1991, Macdonald 1976).

In addition to containing stereotypes, most materials relied on a traditional, rather dry, grammar-based approach, with little weight being put on conversational Gaelic or on everyday expressions.[32] This meant that courses normally needed to be extensively supplemented with backup materials produced by the tutors if they were to be utilised in the class. While many people prefer a grammar-based approach to learning, there was a lack of an alternative for those preferring one based on functional, practical language based on everyday situations or for those wishing a mixture of both. With the exception of the book and audio tape-based *Can Seo* course for beginners and the book and video-based *Abair* course for advanced learners, there was also a lack of modern audio-visual backup materials such as videos and tapes (BBC 1979, MacSween 1990).

One urban learner commented on the deficiencies in the content of Gaelic teaching materials as follows in the *CLI Newsletter*, voicing concerns held by many learners (*CLI Newsletter* no. 5, 1994: 5):

> Previously I have found courses treated Gaelic too much as an academic endeavour (e.g. *Teach Yourself Gaelic* old book), too simplistic (e.g. *Can Seo*) or found it was not really teaching me Gaelic which was relevant to my own life (e.g. *Gàidhlig Bheò*). The last problem I found was a recurrent one. I have for many years wanted to learn Gaelic and have made a number of attempts but frequently found the courses were geared to teaching you vocabulary relevant especially to crofting etc. Whilst I understand that crofting is integral to the Gàidhealtachd my own personal situation is very different to this. I want to learn

---

[32] For a full discussion of different methodologies for language teaching with particular reference to Gaelic, see Fraser 1989: 62–91. For a review of older Gaelic learners' materials, see CLI's *Cuairt Litir Ionnsachaidh* 3 and 4, 1984–5.

Gaelic so that it is an integral part of my everyday life, but I live in an urban environment and want to be able to express my day-to-day experiences in Gaelic.

Since the early 1990s, a variety of new courses have been developed which have served a range of different needs and helped to solve some of the problems raised above. *Siuthad*, a structured course intended for use in evening classes with accompanying tapes, worksheets and teachers' notes, was produced in four parts between the late 1980s and late 1990s, with the different parts of the course corresponding roughly to Scotvec/SQA modules 1, 2, and 3 in Gaelic. The course presented Gaelic in a modern, all-Scotland context.

A new *Teach Yourself Gaelic* book with matching tapes was published in 1993 with greater emphasis on everyday language along with grammatical information (Robertson and Taylor 1993). The dialogues and the extensive background information provided about Gaelic subjects in the book are based around Gaelic-speaking areas and on city Gaeldom as they are today. 2001 saw the production of the relatively similar Routledge *Colloquial Scottish Gaelic* book with accompanying tapes which also places much emphasis on everyday language in addition to grammar (Spadaro and Graham 2001).

An ambitious multimedia course, *Speaking Our Language* (SOL), was commenced by Scottish Television in 1993. The SOL television programme ran for four series and contained a total of 72 programmes. Textbooks, videos, cassettes, a basic CD-ROM, a newsletter and an innovative teaching pack with worksheets and guidance for tutors accompanied this structured television series. The course also directly challenged stereotypes and sought to show the national relevance of Gaelic through showing Gaelic in a modern urban context. Like *Teach Yourself Gaelic*, SOL was based around everyday conversation. Unfortunately, the backup materials for this series are very expensive, a factor which may discourage people from buying them.[33]

1996 saw the production of the Hugo *Scottish Gaelic in Three Months* (Ó Maolalaigh and MacAonghuis 1996). This book, with accompanying cassettes, is based upon a more grammatical approach whilst also containing much everyday language. Dialogues are far more modern than those in older grammar-based courses with references made to Lowland as well as Highland places. Unfortunately, this book is now out of print, though it is still easy to locate copies. Older grammar reference books such as *Bun Chùrsa Gàidhlig* and *Cothrom Ionnsachaidh* also remain useful (Blacklaw 1978, Black 1992). The grammar book *Gràmar na Gàidhlig* for secondary schools is also a useful reference work for learners and a workbook has now been produced to accompany this (Byrne 2002, Caimbeul 2006).

One area which was largely unforeseen when *Feumalachdan* was published was the potential of computers for language learning. Development of computers since the mid-1990s has enabled technology to provide increasing opportunities for formal and informal learning. CD-ROMs are now extensively used for language courses, providing as they do the opportunity to combine the written and spoken work in an

---

[33] To buy the workbooks, videos and cassettes for series one of *Speaking Our Language* individually would cost around £68. To buy the materials for all four series would cost around £250. Prices based on Gaelic Books Council website www.gaelicbooks.net. The publishers Cànan have on occasion offered discounts but the prices for buying all the backup materials are still considerable.

interactive fashion and allowing learners to study whenever and wherever they wish. So far, one Gaelic learning CD-ROM for beginners has been produced as part of the *Speaking our Language* series and a further two have been produced by Eurotalk.[34] This sector remains very undeveloped for Gaelic in contrast with materials now available for many other modern languages.

In conclusion, although Gaelic teaching materials have improved since 1992, offering learners and tutors a greater choice, there are still some gaps in the materials available, particularly at the more advanced level and in the materials produced for tutors, and the situation could benefit from greater co-ordination in the provision of learning materials.[35] There is still a great need for more materials for use in Gaelic classes, and particularly for immersion courses.

Feumalachdan recommended that a national resource centre should be established to address the lack of appropriate learning/teaching resources for learners and to harness modern technology for Gaelic learning. Since the publication of the report, a national resource centre for Gaelic, Stòrlann Nàiseanta na Gàidhlig has been established. This centre, which was established in 1999, has not played an active role in the adult learners sector as yet, however. While the production of Gaelic adult learners materials is within the remit of the centre, the centre has to date concentrated almost exclusively on materials for Gaelic-medium school education as staffing levels remain low and the core funding of the centre is directed solely to the production of school materials. If the Stòrlann is to play an active role in the adult learners' sector in future, it is clear that specific funding for learners resources will have to be allocated in future.

Dictionaries

Feumalachdan Luchd-Ionnsachaidh found widespread dissatisfaction with Gaelic dictionaries amongst tutors and learners (CnaG/CLI 1992). Lack of grammatical information, of up-to-date vocabulary and of idioms were all singled out by respondents as were outdated orthography and the small scope of most dictionaries. The report concluded that "it is evident that there is a clear need for a Gaelic–English/English–Gaelic dictionary that contains modern terminology, has updated orthographic conventions, is affordable and user friendly" (1992: 26).

This conclusion reflected the fact that of the dictionaries available in 1992, many were outdated, a great majority of them having been published in the nineteenth or early twentieth centuries. For example, MacAlpine's *Pronouncing Gaelic-English Dictionary* was first published in 1832, MacBain's *Etymological Dictionary of the Gaelic Language* in 1896 and Dieckhoff's *Pronouncing Dictionary of Scottish Gaelic* in 1932 (MacAlpine 1971, MacBain 1982, Dieckhoff 1992).

Even the most comprehensive and commonly used dictionaries were outdated. Edward Dwelly's *Illustrated Gaelic to English Dictionary*, was first published in parts between 1901 and 1911. This dictionary was traditionally the most widely used Gaelic-English dictionary by both learners and native speakers as it is the largest and most comprehensive of its type with over 80,000 headwords. Dwelly lacks modern vocabulary, however, and due to its age makes it impossible for readers to tell which of the words are still in use and which have since passed out of use. The small print

---

[34] www.eurotalk.com
[35] Siùsaidh Hardy, Clì Gàidhlig, personal communication: telephone interview, 09.05.2006.

means that the dictionary is difficult to consult and the bulky nature of the book also makes it difficult for learners to carry around.

More outdated is MacLennan's Gaelic-English, English-Gaelic dictionary which was first published in 1925 and which is still on sale today despite being highly flawed (MacLennan 1979). The English-Gaelic side of the dictionary is based on Mackenzie's dictionary, first published in 1845, being intended as an aid to learning English for Gaelic speakers rather than vice versa, and even then "rather limited in its usefulness" due to over simple or simply incorrect definitions and due to containing a large number of archaic and obscure English head-words (Thompson 1992: 59).

The situation regarding Gaelic dictionaries improved to some extent in the decade preceding the *Feumalachdan* study. 1979 saw the publication of *Abair* (Gairm), a two-way pocket dictionary for learners by Renton and MacDonald complete with verbal nouns and the plurals and genitives of nouns (Renton and MacDonald 1979). As *Abair* only contains around 2,500 words, however, being far shorter than other bilingual pocket dictionaries such as the Collins Gem series, most learners of Gaelic quickly grow out of the dictionary as their language skills expand.

Thomson's *New English-Gaelic Dictionary* (Gairm) of 1981 which was updated in 1994 is larger with around 15,000 words. While being an advance from MacLennan's 1925 dictionary, Thomson's work is still not as comprehensive as might be expected of a modern dictionary and does not give genitives, plurals, verbal nouns or pronunciations. This means for example that Thomson's dictionary cannot be used to translate a simple sentence such as *I am reading the dictionary* into Gaelic. For these reasons, Thomson's work has to be used in conjunction with a Gaelic-English dictionary at all times. It also contains a variety of neologisms coined by the author, many of which have never become commonly used. There are further many inconsistencies in the dictionary with different spellings often being used for the same word at different places.

In 1992, Gaelic learners were poorly served by Gaelic dictionaries as most did not contain genitives, plurals, verbal nouns or other grammatical information vital for learning. Additionally, many words and expressions used each day by fluent speakers and frequently seen in print and heard on the radio had never been included in any Gaelic dictionary. Conversely, many archaic words very rarely heard were included in dictionaries still in use, providing a further cause of confusion for learners. The continued availability of a number of elderly and unsuitable dictionaries also provided an unnecessary source of confusion.

There have been improvements to Gaelic dictionaries in the period since the *Feumalachdan* study. Robert C. Owen's *Modern Gaelic-English Dictionary* (Gairm, 1993) was a significant improvement on previous Gaelic-English dictionaries. It is based on Thomson's work, but is more consistent and contains genitives, plurals, verbal nouns, comparatives of adjectives and other information essential for Gaelic learners. Many examples are given. It also contains verb tables and sections of place and personal names. Like Thomson's work on which it is based, however, the dictionary is somewhat limited in its content, containing under 10,000 entries.

1998 saw the publication of a new two-way pocket dictionary containing a large number of idioms, words for modern phenomena and words not previously seen in dictionaries. It has subsequently been re-issued featuring IPA pronunciation. This work, produced by Geddes and Grosset, is available at a reasonable price but like its predecessors does not contain genitives, plurals or verbal nouns, meaning as with the other dictionaries that it will normally have to be used in combination with another

(Buchanan and RLS 1998, 2004). At roughly 7,000 words on each side it is also rather small.

Other innovations since *Feumalachdan* include Sabhal Mòr Ostaig's *Stòr-dàta Briathrachais Gàidhlig / The Gaelic Terminology Database*, which gives Gaelic words for modern and technical terms (1993) and *Faclair na Pàrlamaid / Dictionary of Terms*, the Gaelic parliamentary dictionary produced by the Scottish Parliament, Scottish Executive and Comunn na Gàidhlig which provides parliamentary, governmental and political terminology (2001). These books are useful for those with a reasonable command of the language but are unsuitable for less advanced learners. The 1990s also saw the publication of Richard Cox's *Brìgh nam Facal* (1991), the first ever Gaelic-Gaelic dictionary. While it is intended for primary schools, it is also of use to learners, containing much grammatical information such as genitives, plurals and verbal nouns.

Despite some advances in the 1990s, Continued dissatisfaction with dictionaries was evidenced by the Gaelic Learners' Survey carried out for this survey which produced many comments about Gaelic dictionaries. Some of the comments were:

> I think it deplorable that for all the references to a Gaelic revival, no-one has seen fit to produce a cheapish modern dictionary (like, say Collins Gem) and that Acair are selling the two-way dictionary which, at base, is 150 years old. After all, where would one find a French or German dictionary compiled before the First World War, not to say the Crimean war?

> There is no comprehensive Gaelic dictionary. I frequently fail to trace published words in any of my six Gaelic dictionaries, including Dwelly. For 'Secure Status' a fully comprehensive dictionary is surely obligatory!

> I cannot read Gairm because it uses too many words which are not in my Gaelic dictionary. My main problem with reading Gaelic books is finding the words in my dictionary! A comprehensive pocket dictionary similar to the *Collins Gem* series would be a big help to learners.

Fortunately, however, the period since the millennium has been very significant in terms of lexicography. Two major Gaelic-English dictionaries have appeared, along with one major English–Gaelic dictionary and a bilingual dictionary for learners. Angus Watson's *Essential Gaelic-English Dictionary* (Birlinn 2001), while rather small in size at around 6,000 headwords, contains essential grammatical information for learners such as genitives, plurals and verbal nouns and examples of usage. It also contains irregular verb tables and is able to play something of the function of a thesaurus by giving cross-references between similar words. An even greater advance has been Colin Mark's *Gaelic-English Dictionary*, which is larger and more comprehensive, with essential grammatical information, examples of usage and extensive appendices on verbs, nouns, adjectives, adverbs, conjunctions, pronouns, prepositions, numerals and personal and place names (Mark 2004).

Angus Watson's comprehensive *Essential English–Gaelic Dictionary* was published in 2005, aimed particularly at the learner and containing many examples of usage.

While it is a great advance on all preceding English–Gaelic dictionaries, it does not contain genitives or plurals of nouns or verbal nouns, meaning that it has to be used in conjunction with a Gaelic-English dictionary. Like its Gaelic-English counterpart its number of headwords is also rather few.

Perhaps most significant of all for learners has been the production of the *Teach Yourself Gaelic Dictionary* (Robertson and MacDonald 2004). This compact two-way dictionary, which contains over 24,000 definitions, is comprehensive in scope and contains many examples, essential grammatical information such as genitives, plurals and verbal nouns and appendices of personal and placenames and basic grammar. Although designed primarily for learners, it is likely to be of use to fluent speakers too.

There can be no doubt that there has been an improvement in Gaelic dictionaries since the early 1990s and that suitable dictionaries now exist for learners. However, there are still some significant gaps in the market. These include a comprehensive two-way Gaelic dictionary containing a far larger number of words, a small and cheap but extensive two-way dictionary on the model of a Collins Gem and a comprehensive monolingual Gaelic dictionary. Gillies has also pointed to the need for a Gaelic thesaurus (W. Gillies 1994: 157).

In the long term, the range of Gaelic dictionaries available for learners and others is likely to increase as a result of The Dictionary of the Scottish Gaelic Language project which is an inter-university initiative by the Universities of Aberdeen, Edinburgh, Glasgow, Strathclyde and Sabhal Mòr Ostaig. Based on the model of the Dictionary of the Older Scottish Tongue and the Scottish National Dictionary, the project aims to produce a multi-volume historical Gaelic dictionary which will be published initially in an electronic format. As part of this project, a dictionary of the modern period will be produced. The dictionary database will also enable the production of a range of bilingual and monolingual dictionaries suitable for learners and other audiences.[36]

Informal Means of Learning

While class-based study is an essential part of learning, opportunities to hear and use Gaelic in more informal settings are also vital if a learner is to become fluent. At present many learners have few or no such opportunities. In their survey of Gaelic learners in Scotland, MacNeil and MacDonald found that 60% of their sample did not meet Gaelic speakers in their day-to-day environment. While a quarter of the sample tended to interact with up to three Gaelic speakers in the average day, "this constituted only a very patchy speech community in which to test out language learning, and develop it to communicative fluency" (MacNeil and MacDonald 1997: 12).

Similar problems of isolation were also noted by *Feumalachdan*, which concluded that weekend and summer courses were the only opportunity that most respondents had to practise their Gaelic outside the formal class, and which stated that "the main support facility required by students is the establishment of local groups which would help learners increase their fluency" (CnaG/CLI 1992: 58, 61, 68). It was further recommended that "native speakers should be encouraged to take a more active role in the process of Gaelic learning" (CnaG/CLI 1992: 58, 61, 68).

---

[36] For more details of the project, see www.faclair.ac.uk

At present there are a number of informal Gaelic groups for learners. These can be divided into two basic but overlapping types: self-help groups and social groups. The former are study groups and are often set up to help remedy the absence of Gaelic classes in a particular area. Gaelic social groups seek to bring people together for general Gaelic conversation. These are sometimes organised around specific events such as the Gaelic Walking Club which met for many years around central Scotland.

While *Feumalachdan* placed weight on the development of local Gaelic learners' groups, this remains a somewhat underdeveloped area. Groups are normally co-ordinated either by individuals or by local authority Community Education departments. As seen in the discussion of classes, these are areas where there is a lack of overall co-ordination and where such co-ordination would be hard to achieve. This is particularly the case for self-help groups, which are normally formed by individual learners simply because of a lack of alternative means of learning. While some groups such as the Cearcall Còmhraidh Dhùn Èideann (Edinburgh Conversation Circle) are long-established, many groups rely on the efforts of one or two individuals, meaning that they often do not last long.

Comunn na Gàidhlig attempted to inject more order into this situation through the creation of the short-lived post of Adult Learners' Development Officer, as recommended by the *Feumalachdan* report, who had the responsibility of helping to encourage Gaelic social groups. CLI too have been involved in the promotion of Gaelic clubs at various times. While important work has been done by these groups, however, it has been by its very nature limited. As Peadar Morgan, formerly Adult Learners' Development Officer and Director of CLI, has pointed out with regard to social groups, it is much easier to help establish informal Gaelic groups than to keep them going given their ad hoc and voluntary nature.[37] This is particularly the case when it is remembered that the task has mainly been undertaken nationally by one individual based in the Comunn na Gàidhlig or CLI office in Inverness, far from the majority of Gaelic learners.

Another problem identified by Morgan, one often encountered by those involved in the groups themselves, is the proper purpose and structure of the social group. Bringing together a group of people of various ages and backgrounds with little in common except an interest in Gaelic might not always be the recipe for an ideal evening. Organising successful groups is not always easy due to the mixture of informality and structure required. Another disadvantage with learners groups, whether for study or pleasure, is the fact that they are frequently only attended by non-fluent learners, which means that not all questions raised might be answered and that a large amount of English might be used.

Several suggestions might be made for improving the current situation. The first would be an increase in the number of individuals employed in supporting local Gaelic groups and in encouraging the participation of fluent speakers in them. This idea is developed in more detail below. Also useful would be the production of materials specifically intended for informal Gaelic groups – both study and social – as has been done in Wales by the Welsh learners' society *Cymdeithas yr Dysgwyr* (CYD). These could include guidelines about how to run social groups and how best to learn Gaelic through self-help groups. This could be done by the national Gaelic resource centre or by Clì Gàidhlig. Such materials are particularly significant given that

---

[37] Peadar Morgan, personal communication: interview, 22/04/98

informal Gaelic study groups seem set to become increasingly important, in the short term at least, due to lack of tutors and the absence of Gaelic classes in many areas.

A useful model for a successful Gaelic social group was *Abair Thusa,* a conversation group developed in Sleat, Skye by the Gaelic-related design company *Cànan.* These meetings were developed with the aim of bringing together Gaelic learners and local fluent Gaelic speakers for informal conversation entirely in Gaelic. The aim of the group was not just to help learners to become fluent but also to help strengthen Gaelic in a community where it is becoming seriously weakened and to strengthen links between native speakers and learners (Zall 1999). The Community Learning services of Glasgow City Council, Perth and Kinross Council and other local authorities have also successfully introduced *Abair Thusa* courses following the Skye example.[38]

The creation of a mentor scheme might also be suggested. The Welsh learners' group CYD, for example, operates a phone-pal and pen-pal scheme whereby fluent speakers act as mentors for learners. Such a scheme could be adapted for use in Scotland. CYD meetings also aim to bring learner and fluent speaker together rather than be confined to learners.[39] Also useful and cost-effective would be the systematic production of badges indicating that people can speak or are learning Gaelic.

While social groups are important, they are only one way in which Gaelic can be promoted informally. This has led to a movement to create Gaelic community centres, *Taighean Gàidhlig*, literally Gaelic houses. This began in Edinburgh in the mid-1990s with the *Taigh na Gàidhlig* project which aimed to create a centre to provide a venue for Gaelic classes, Gaelic groups and Gaelic-medium events and would also be home to a café/bar, a bookshop and a Gaelic playgroup. Such a drop-in centre would provide a focus for the Gaelic community in Edinburgh and would enable Gaelic learners and fluent speakers to come together in informal settings. While the Edinburgh *Taigh na Gàidhlig* plan has not yet come to fruition, and now seems unlikely to (NicDhòmhnaill forthcoming 2007), such Gaelic houses on a smaller scale have been set up at various times in the Isle of Arran, in Melness, Sutherland and in Dingwall, Ross-shire. That Gaelic centres such as these should be established was a very frequent suggestion made by respondents to the Gaelic Learners' Survey.

Plans are also afoot at present for a Glasgow Gaelic centre, *An Lòchran*. At the time of writing, it seemed relatively likely that this project would go ahead, possibly as part of the Gaelic school campus planned for Glasgow.[40] It should be noted, however, that there is a danger that large-scale projects such as this will not actually serve to promote the use of Gaelic unless serious consideration is given to the position of Gaelic within these centres and unless the Gaelic language is the focus of these projects. *An Lòchran*, for example, is billed as being a centre for the Highland and Irish community, for those with an interest in Celtic culture and for cultural events, in addition to being a Gaelic language centre (CnaG *et al.* 2000, *An Lòchran* Newsletter 2002).[41] In such circumstances, and given that English is normally the

---

[38] Eddy Cavin, Glasgow City Council Community Education Service, personal communication: telephone conversation, 25.05.99; various subsequent Glasgow City Council community education leaflets.
[39] CYD information taken from Welsh Language Board website www.bwrdd-yr-iaith.org.uk.
[40] See also www.anlochran.co.uk
[41] See www.anlochran.co.uk

language of 'Gaelic arts' events (Lang 2006), there is a serious danger that English would be the primary language of the centre and that the centre would aid rather than reverse language shift.

The importance of providing Gaelic-medium events not directly related to the language is undoubtedly of great importance if Gaelic is not to become merely the language which one learns in order to talk about Gaelic. The now-defunct Taigh na Gàidhlig project in Edinburgh has in the past provided Gaelic-medium classes in art-related subjects, for example. Advances have also been made by Glasgow City Council's Community Learning Department, which has been moving away from the traditional model of promoting of traditional evening classes alone to also supporting less formal groups and organising Gaelic-medium events and fun days with Gaelic classes and lectures on various subjects through Gaelic.[42] While such opportunities to use Gaelic remain very infrequent, these provide a model which can be emulated by others.

Two Gaelic night clubs have been formed in the mid-2000s: Bothan in Edinburgh and Ceòl is Crac in Glasgow. These clubs meet once a month and provide a range of entertainments for Gaelic speakers, such as music and quizzes in a fun environment. While not aimed specifically at learners, these clubs provide a Gaelic-speaking environment where learners can practice their oral skills.

Many of these events and initiatives mentioned are intended for both fluent speakers and learners. This reinforces the point that the needs of fluent speaker and learner are often identical given that both groups often have little opportunity to use the language. The lack of opportunity to use Gaelic, particularly in fun contexts, is undeniably one of the greatest challenges facing the language. Most other European minority languages face similar challenges. Without more opportunities to use the language, learners are unlikely to become fluent, fluent speakers are unlikely to meet Gaelic-speaking partners and/or to raise Gaelic-speaking children and Gaelic-medium pupils are unlikely to use Gaelic outside the school. As Johnstone has argued:

> The longer-term future of the language lies with its being used by a significant minority of Scotland's population as a chosen first language, enabling them to maintain or to find a Gaelic identity and way of life that at the very least matches their English speaking identity and way of life. [...] A major objective of the current developments therefore must be to provide contexts, opportunities and incentives to young speakers and learners of Gaelic that will encourage them to use it with sufficient regularity for it to remain or to become one of their first languages (1994: 77).

While some suggestions have been made here relating to informal opportunities for Gaelic learners to speak/hear Gaelic, the sheer scope of the problem of creating more domains for the use of Gaelic as mentioned above largely places it outwith the remit of the present study. As this is common to numerous other languages such as Welsh, Irish and Basque, however, it is an area on which there is always ongoing research and where well-formulated new research is always to be welcomed.

---

[42] Eddy Cavin, Glasgow City Council, personal communication: conversation, 19.02.99.

Reading and Writing as an Informal Learning Resource

In addition to opportunities to hear and speak the language, it is also crucial that learners should have opportunities to read and write the language. Reading Gaelic serves as an important informal learning opportunity, particularly given that reading is a more fertile source of vocabulary and idiom for learners than is spoken Gaelic. At present, there is relatively little printed Gaelic in newspapers and magazines, with the exception of a number of Gaelic columns in newspapers such as *The Scotsman*, *West Highland Free Press*, *Stornoway Gazette*, *Inverness Courier*, *Ross-Shire Journal* and *Oban Times*, the monthly newspaper *An Gaidheal Ùr,* the quarterly Gaelic learners' magazine *Cothrom* and, until recently, the quarterly publication *Gairm*, which has now been replaced by the quarterly *Gath*.

As well as being limited in quantity, the Gaelic published in the periodical press tends to be high-register and confined to serious topics. While such material is suitable for more advanced learners, it is less suitable for those at the earlier stages of learning and also leaves a gap in provision for fluent speakers. This suggests the need for a wider range of Gaelic periodicals (and indeed books), for Gaelic columns in more newspapers, and particularly for lighter and less intellectual columns in the tabloid newspapers, where there are currently none. An increased quantity of Gaelic in newspapers would also serve to bring the language to the attention of a larger number of people. For these reasons, it can be argued that achieving more Gaelic columns should be a lobbying priority for Gaelic organisations. Some of these could be geared specifically towards learners. The need for more Gaelic columns was one of the recommendations of the *Feumalachdan* report (1992: 50).

One possible suggestion for an expansion in printed Gaelic would be the creation of community Gaelic newspapers based on the Welsh *Papurau Bro*. The first Welsh-language neighbourhood newspaper was founded in Cardiff in 1973 and was followed by a large number of others, there being 52 in total by 1992 with a combined circulation of 75,000. These papers are mainly monthly and rely on voluntary, unpaid effort with a minimum of public subsidy (Davies 1993: 83). There are no similar papers in Scotland. Many Gaelic-speaking areas have community papers, but these are English-language papers, some of which have a limited Gaelic content. All-Gaelic community papers would provide a forum for Gaelic writing in a variety of registers and on a variety of subject matters and would help in the creation and maintenance of Gaelic communities and in the involvement of learners in Gaelic affairs.

Gaelic books can also be an important resource for learners. While books for adult fluent speakers are normally too difficult for all but the most advanced learners, and while Gaelic books for adults are limited in quantity and scope in any case, many Gaelic novels and short stories have been produced for secondary and upper primary pupils by groups and publishers such as An Stòrlann which are suitable resources for adult learners. Talking books have been produced to accompany the Ùr-Sgeul series of new Gaelic novels for adults and are another useful learning aid.[43] Existing books for fluent Gaelic-speaking children and adults could be graded for their suitability for learners, advertised to learners and accompanying talking books or study guides created.

Another suggestion for future development would be the production of novels and short stories in simplified Gaelic specifically for adult learners on the model of

---

[43] For more details of the series see: www.ur-sgeul.com

books published by Welsh-language publishers such as Y Lolfa. Bilingual books with English and Gaelic on facing pages would also be a useful resource for learners as would audio CDs to accompany these new books.

Broadcasting as a Learning Resource: Television

The *Feumalachdan* report emphasised the importance of broadcasting for learners, showing that both tutors and learners surveyed felt that insufficient provision was made for learners by the broadcasting media and recommending that all sections of the media should increase their commitment to Gaelic learners, both in terms of overall Gaelic output and in dedicated output for learners (CnaG/CLI 1992: 40, 52, 65, 67).

This recommendation has been implemented to a considerable extent, as the amount of Gaelic television broadcast increased greatly shortly after the *Feumalachdan* report as a result of the establishment of the Gaelic Television Fund. As part of this television expansion, the graded multimedia learners' course *Speaking Our Language* was commissioned.

In a study of Gaelic broadcasting five years after *Feumalachdan*, MacNeil and MacDonald identified television as a key learning resource for learners, concluding that television provides learners with "access to an authentic speech community" as it enables viewers to be exposed to various different registers and dialects of Gaelic and to see the language being used in various contexts (1997: 4). Their survey of Gaelic learners found that around 90% of respondents watched Gaelic television programmes for the purpose of enhancing their Gaelic (1997: 2, 15). Over half of the respondents also undertook follow-up learning activities related to their viewing such as the jotting-down of words or phrases or the recording of programmes for reuse (1997: 26). Many found subtitles useful to the learning process (1997: 24).

In addition to the direct learning benefits of television, programmes can also sustain learners' interest in Gaelic (1997: 27) and give learners more understanding of Gaelic-speaking communities through the programmes based on and intended for these communities.

Two Scottish Executive reports (Fraser 1998, Gaelic Broadcasting Taskforce [GBT] 2000) have recommended that a dedicated digital Gaelic television channel, available throughout the UK on all digital platforms, should be established. There can be no doubt that such a channel would benefit those learning Gaelic. A Gaelic channel would enable greater co-ordination of Gaelic broadcasts, screening of more Gaelic at peak times and weekends, and an overall increase in the amount and range of Gaelic programming (Fraser 1998, CCG 1997, GBT 2000). This would allow learners greater access to Gaelic television. Unlike conventional broadcasters, a dedicated Gaelic television station would have the potential to be part of a holistic language planning strategy in partnership with other Gaelic organisations and could make RLS a key aim of the organisation (CCG 1997: 2). It would also be able to give more weight to educational programming (Fraser 1998: 12; GBT 2000: 7). The Gaelic Broadcasting Taskforce has argued that Gaelic learners should be considered a key audience category at which the service should be aimed and that the proposed channel should provide support for Gaelic learning (2000: 12).

The Gaelic Broadcasting Committee [Comataidh Craolaidh Gàidhlig – CCG], Fraser, and the Gaelic Broadcasting Taskforce have all argued that a Gaelic television channel should make use of innovative new technology (Fraser 1998: 12; GBT 2000: 4, 13; CCG 1997: 5). This is particularly important given the increased convergence between radio, television, teletext, the internet and mobile telephony and the increased interactivity of broadcasting at the present time. Fraser suggests for example that Radio nan Gaidheal and Gaelic television schedules should be arranged so as to provide the Gaelic audience with integrated viewing and listening. Given that a full-time Gaelic television station would not be likely in the short term, Fraser further suggests a multimedia approach to the simultaneous transmission of Radio nan Gaidheal output on television at off-peak times with text, visuals and information (1998: 12). Internet and teletext services linked to the channel are also suggested (GBT 2000: 13). A Gaelic text service could contain material such as local and national news, news of new publications, details of Gaelic events and classes and clubs. Such measures would be of assistance to learners and would promote literacy in addition to spoken/oral proficiency in the language.

The growing interactivity of digital television also has potential for Gaelic learning. A 1998 report by the BBC pointed out that a return path on set-top boxes would in future allow viewers to play along with game shows, vote in TV polls and receive background information about programmes (BBC 1998: 6). Such features have now largely become a reality and are of obvious use to Gaelic learning programmes and other Gaelic broadcasts.

Digitalisation will also mean that teletext and subtitles will be available to all digital television viewers, but could also mean that viewers will also have the choice not to watch subtitles, both of these factors being of aid to Gaelic learners (MacNeil and MacDonald 1997: 24; Johnstone 1994: 65). There is also the possibility of the provision of a choice of subtitles in English or a variety of different levels of Gaelic.

In addition to such high-tech support materials for Gaelic learning, a Gaelic television channel could also lead to an enhancement in more traditional educational fields (CCG 1997: 6). The CCG have at times produced materials to accompany television series. Books and videos were produced for the *Mire Mara* children's series as were videos of a small number of other television series for younger viewers such as *An Taigh Tapaidh* and *Calum Clachair*. Tapes, videos and books have also been produced for the Speaking our Language learners' series. A dedicated Gaelic channel would have increased potential for the production of videos, books, CD-ROMs, talking books and additional backup materials likely to be of use to learners. New series specifically intended for learners could also be introduced.

MacNeil and MacDonald's 1997 report recommended that tutors and learners be given greater guidance as to how to make use of television as a resource for learners and that back-up materials based on Gaelic programmes should be made for learners and tutors (1997: 32). A dedicated Gaelic channel would have the potential to implement such recommendations together with other Gaelic promotional and educational bodies.

Progress towards a Gaelic television channel has been slow, with six years having passed since the publication of the Gaelic Broadcasting Taskforce report. A number of reforms were made to Gaelic broadcasting through the *Communications Act 2003* which reconstituted the Gaelic Broadcasting Committee as Seirbheis nam Meadhanan Gàidhlig / Gaelic Media Service (GMS) and gave the group the power to produce programmes and seemingly to develop into a Gaelic-medium broadcaster itself (Dunbar 2006: 10). Despite this, however, the act made no commitment to a Gaelic television channel (DTI/DCMS 2002, *West Highland Free Press* 2002, Dunbar 2006: 9). There has also been an ongoing disagreement between the Scottish Executive and the UK Government as to who should accept responsibility for funding the new channel (Dunbar 2006: 10).

At the time of writing, reports from the media and broadcasters strongly suggest that an announcement is imminent that a Gaelic television channel is to be established as a result of an agreement between the BBC and GMS to work together towards this goal and following the agreement of a funding package between the Scottish Executive and other stakeholders (M. MacLeòid 2006b, Sheppard 2006, GMS 2006). Due to limited funding, this channel would fall short of the recommendations of the taskforce, however, only broadcasting 1.5 hours of new material per day supplemented with repeats. More seriously, it is likely that the channel will only be available on digital satellite and not also via digital terrestrial Freeview with the result that fewer Gaelic learners will have access to the service (M. MacLeòid 2006b). Limited funding is also likely to restrict the amount of education work undertaken by the channel. While such a Gaelic broadcasting would mark an advance for learners in many respects, therefore, its potential to act as a learning resource would be far less than that envisaged by Fraser and the Gaelic Broadcasting Taskforce.

Broadcasting as a Learning Resource: Radio

Radio, like television, is an area where the *Feumalachdan* recommendations have largely been put into practice. The report called for a dedicated Gaelic programme for learners and for accessibility to Gaelic radio for those learners who could not then receive Gaelic radio (CnaG/CLI 1992: 45, 52).

Radio is also an important learning resource for learners. While fewer than 300 hours of Gaelic television are currently broadcast annually, the total amount of Gaelic radio aired yearly is over 2500 hours. The Gaelic radio station BBC Radio nan Gaidheal, founded in 1985, currently broadcasts for an average of around 63 hours per week, this total having risen from 53 in June 2002 and from 45 in 2001 (An Gàidheal Ùr 2002a).

Radio nan Gaidheal provides a useful resource for learners with its varied range of programmes. The news programmes provide learners with the use of formal, high-register Gaelic. The fact that most learners are in touch with current affairs through the English language media means they will normally have some idea of what is being discussed in Gaelic. This eases the learning of new words and phrases. Chat programmes give learners the opportunity to hear colloquial Gaelic from various different dialects used to discuss a variety of subjects. Gaelic Church services and children's programmes also provide the use of different registers. Radio also provides news about Gaelic and Gaelic events and can act as a link for the learner to the island Gaelic communities through its coverage of Gàidhealtachd issues. Evidence from the Gaelic Learners' Survey suggests that there is a high level of awareness of the availability of Radio nan Gaidheal amongst learners and a high level of Gaelic radio use amongst those able to receive it.

Since 1999, Radio nan Gaidheal has featured a programme for Gaelic learners: *Litir do Luchd-Ionnsachaidh* (the learners' letter). This programme, which is aimed at higher intermediate and advanced learners, takes the format of a five-minute letter broadcast each week in relatively simple Gaelic and delivered slowly and clearly. The text of each programme is published prior to the programme both in the *West Highland Free Press* newspaper and on the BBC Alba website, along with a glossary[44] of difficult terms and interesting idioms and grammar points arising from the text.

---

[44] www.bbc.co.uk/alba

A book and audio DVD of the series has been produced and the programmes are also available on demand on the website as sound files or as podcast (MacIlleathain 2005). This programme has now been joined by *An Litir Bheag* (the little letter), a similar weekly programme for less advanced learners for which the text and sound files are also available on the BBC Alba website.

In addition to the improvements in terms of dedicated provision for learners and in the expansion of the amount of radio broadcast since 1992, there have also been improvements for learners in terms of access to Gaelic radio. Prior to 1996, the full Radio nan Gaidheal output was only available on FM in the Highlands and Islands with a very limited amount being broadcast nationally through Radio Scotland on medium wave. Since April 1996, however, Radio nan Gaidheal has broadcast its full range of programming on the 103.5–105 FM frequency to the Central Belt as well as the Highlands and Islands. The full service was further extended to the Aberdeen city area in July 1996. Along with this expansion in service, however, came the cessation of the national MW transmission of Gaelic radio with the result that Radio nan Gaidheal was no longer available in the areas of Scotland not served by the dedicated Gaelic frequencies.

While this move left many areas without access to Gaelic radio, further expansion of Radio nan Gaidheal took place in 2002 with gaps in coverage in the Highlands being filled and with Gaelic radio provision being extended to transmitters serving Dundee and most of Perth and Kinross, Aberdeenshire, Angus and Fife. While gaps remain in Radio nan Gaidheal availability in south-east and south-west Scotland and in some other areas, this is nonetheless a considerable advance. The BBC's plan is to expand Radio nan Gaidheal to cover all of Scotland though it is not clear at present when this might happen. It is important for Gaelic learners that such expansion should take place.

Lack of exposure to the spoken language is a key problem faced by learners living outwith Scotland. In such places access to Gaelic classes or Gaelic speakers is typically more difficult and without sufficient opportunity to hear the language it is unlikely that a learner will ever reach any level of fluency. Many learners living in areas where Radio nan Gaidheal was not available, including many outwith Scotland, indicated in the Gaelic Learners' Survey that they wished to be able to access Gaelic radio. This is a very important issue, given that Galloway (1995b) has identified around 15,000 individuals outside Scotland undertaking some form of Gaelic learning activity. Such learners now have access to Radio nan Gaidheal via the BBC Alba website, established in 2000, which carries live streaming of all of Radio nan Gaidheal's output and which also carries their audio files for listening on demand. Text for news bulletins is also available on the website, complete with glossary. Since 2002, Radio nan Gaidheal has also been available via Sky satellite which can be accessed throughout the UK. Radio nan Gaidheal is also now available in many areas of Scotland through DAB digital radio.

Despite the considerable advances in the Gaelic radio service, however, some further practical improvements might be suggested for the benefit of the Gaelic learner. Firstly, an increase in output would be highly desirable. Despite increases in the amount of radio output, weekend output is still relatively meagre, broadcasting only until 1pm on Saturdays and for only 1.5 hours in total on Sundays. There are also several gaps in weekday provision, from midday to 2.00pm and from 7.00pm to 9.00pm. Extension of the hours of Gaelic broadcasting, and particularly of those in the evening and at the weekends would allow more learners access to the language.

Expanding BBC Radio nan Gaidheal would follow the example set by Ireland's Raidió na Gaeltachta which has been upgraded to a 24 hour, seven days a week service.

An increase in hours broadcast would also enable a widening of the range of programming carried. At present a large percentage of Gaelic radio is aimed at the island Gaelic communities, with a substantial percentage of output also being devoted to traditional music and folklore. An expansion in hours of radio broadcast would create room for more programmes likely to be of greater interest to Gaelic learners without entailing any reduction in the broadcasting aimed at the island Gaelic communities or at those with interest in traditional music or folklore. A wider range of music and more discussion of subjects relevant to urban life might be suggested. More comedy, drama and sports coverage would be of interest both to the traditional Gaelic communities and to learners. Some progress has been made in this front with the introduction of two programmes, namely *2–4* (since replaced by the similar *Siubhal gu Seachd*) playing Radio 2 style music and *Rapal*, playing contemporary rock and pop music and aiming at a teens and twenties audience. There can be no doubt, however, that far more progress could be made on this front to ensure that Gaelic radio reflects the interests of learners and of all sections of the Gaelic community.

Another way in which Gaelic radio could be used to help learners both within and outwith Scotland would be the production of learning materials to accompany Gaelic radio programmes. Talking books based on radio drama would be one possibility as would booklets to go along with certain series. Raidió na Gaeltachta, the Irish radio station, for example, have produced some Irish talking books. A useful learning resource has also been produced by BBC Radio Cymru in Wales: a series of mini dictionaries of Welsh news terms used on the radio station. Acen Ltd has also produced a learners' guide to the news in Welsh. Such materials would also be useful in Scotland. There is currently a short list of new terminology on the Radio nan Gaidheal website which could easily be expanded upon.

While discussion has so far centred on Radio nan Gaidheal, the importance of English-language radio must not be forgotten. There is at present no radio programme for Gaelic learners on BBC Radio Scotland. A bilingual Gaelic learners' series on Radio Scotland would not only be a useful resource for learners, but would also help encourage more people to learn Gaelic through bringing the language to a wider audience. Radio Wales, the national English-language radio station of Wales, broadcasts *Catchphrase*, a five-minute nightly slot for Welsh learners. Such a slot would interest non-Gaelic listeners and act as a teaching resource whilst being sufficiently short not to make other listeners switch channel. This arrangement could perhaps be complemented with a series of fuller related programmes on Radio nan Gaidheal or tied in with television or internet Gaelic courses.

The Internet

One learning medium which was barely in existence at the time of the *Feumalachdan* report was the internet. In the intervening period, the internet has become a significant formal and informal Gaelic learning resource. The internet helps learners worldwide to overcome isolation by allowing them to gather information about Gaelic learning opportunities, to access written and spoken Gaelic and to communicate with other Gaelic learners and speakers. By facilitating contact with other learners and speakers and providing news and views on Gaelic matters, the internet also enables learners to engage more closely with the Gaelic speech community.

The internet has expanded access to the written Gaelic in the newspapers as several Gaelic columns are now available online such as those in *The Scotsman*, *Scotland on Sunday*, *Press and Journal*, *West Highland Free Press*, *Inverness Courier* and *Ross-shire Journal*.

A range of Gaelic-related websites have now been developed, many of these by Gaelic groups such as Comunn na Gàidhlig, Bòrd na Gàidhlig and Stòrlann Nàiseanta na Gàidhlig. One particularly notable, and long-established, site is that of Sabhal Mòr Ostaig, the Gaelic college, which has been at the forefront of Gaelic internet development and which provides extensive links and information about Gaelic learning and Gaelic development in both Gaelic and English.[45]

The website of the Gaelic learners' organisation, Clì Gàidhlig, is also significant to learners as it provides information about Gaelic learning opportunities worldwide, as does the Learn-Gaelic website developed by Clì Gàidhlig and the Community Learning and Development Review Group for Gaelic.[46] Of all Gaelic websites, however, the site with the most resources for learners at present is that of BBC Alba.[47] As seen previously, BBC Alba offers live streaming of Gaelic radio and contains on demand audio files. It also features written news in Gaelic, Gaelic radio and TV listings, educational materials for schools and websites for many BBC Gaelic programmes. In addition to carrying the sound files and texts of the learners' series *Litir do Luchd-Ionnsachaidh,* the BBC Alba site also has an online introduction course for beginners *Beag air Bheag* (little by little) containing exercises, sound files and a bulletin board.

The internet provides the opportunity for learners to engage in informal learning by means of Gaelic internet mailing lists. The first Gaelic list, Gaelic-L, was established in 1989 for discussion in Gaelic, Irish and Manx. Due to the large volume of mail on Gaelic-L, additional Gaelic lists were established in 1996.[48] The Scottish Gaelic lists created were Gaidhlig-A and Gaidhlig-B, the former being discussion in Scottish Gaelic for fluent speakers and the latter for bilingual discussion for learners. A further Gaelic list, Gaidhlig4u, was established for beginners in the USA in 1997. In addition to these large lists, there are also a variety of smaller Gaelic lists through the Yahoo Groups.

The lists have many advantages for learners. They help to reduce the isolation of the individual learner, bringing together Gaelic learners world-wide. They also give learners the opportunity to use their Gaelic and to discuss their questions about Gaelic grammar and usage. Relative anonymity and the fact that learners do not face the pressure of conversation in the physical presence of fluent speakers is a further advantage (Lloyd 1995: 78). Lists act as a platform for the dissemination of Gaelic-related information and the discussion of Gaelic-related issues.

Despite their advantages, however, the lists at present exhibit many weaknesses. There is little posting to Gaidhlig-A list and little posting to Gaelic-L in Scottish Gaelic, with the effect that relatively little fluent Gaelic is available through the lists. The main disadvantage with the lists aimed at non-fluent learners is that there is relatively little involvement from fluent speakers and particularly from native speakers. This means that the correction of mistakes and answering of questions

---

[45] www.smo.uhi.ac.uk
[46] www.cli.org.uk; www.learn-gaelic.info
[47] www.bbc.co.uk/alba
[48] For more details of the Gaelic lists, see: http://www.smo.uhi.ac.uk/liosta/

relies disproportionately on the goodwill of a small number of people. It also means that mistakes may occasionally go uncorrected and that incorrect discussion of grammar may go without challenge. Weaknesses aside, however, the Gaelic lists are a very useful resource for learners.

There have also been a proliferation of Gaelic-related internet forums, enabling Gaelic learners to see and use written Gaelic since the late 1990s. The largest forum at time of writing was *Foram na Gàidhlig*.[49] A more recent innovation is that of the Gaelic Blog. These web-logs also allow learners to see and use written Gaelic. There are now a number of Gaelic bloggers, all of them now linked through the umbrella website *Tìr nam Blog* on which over 20 blogs were represented at the time of writing.[50] A Gaelic programme has also been established via podcast featuring news and current affairs in Gaelic by Gaelic speakers in the USA and this represents another way in which the internet can be used to aid Gaelic learning.[51]

Attracting Learners

One area which is not normally considered during the discussion of the Gaelic learning infrastructure is the means of attracting Gaelic learners. Though helping existing learners to reach fluency is crucial, it is equally important that new learners be attracted – particularly in the strategically important under-25 age group. Little attention has so far been given by Gaelic groups to attracting new learners.

To increase the number of learners, more publicity for Gaelic will be necessary given its currently low profile in most of Scotland and given the high level of public ignorance as to the history and present place of Gaelic in Scottish society (McLeod 2001a: 6, McLeod 2006b, A. Gillies 2000, Ó Maolalaigh 2000). There are two ways in which the language can be promoted, the first of these being the increased use of Gaelic in public life. The most important example of this has been the increase in the amount of Gaelic television, which has achieved high viewing figures and, as discussed below, may have had an effect in influencing people to learn.

Also making Gaelic more obvious since the 1990s has been the increasing use of Gaelic on signage in the Western Isles and the Highlands including road signs on many of the regions trunk roads, the expansion of Gaelic signage at stations on the Highland mainline railway and an increase in Gaelic signage in public buildings owned by Highland council.[52] Gaelic signage in the Lowlands too has been increasing, with bilingual signs in Glasgow Queen Street station, in Partick, on some signs in Airdrie town centre and other towns where the Mòd has been held and most notably, in the Scottish Parliament in Edinburgh and on its giftware. Like television, these signs seem to have raised the profile of the language without causing any significant adverse reaction from the public. Gaelic television has shown that there is a considerable amount of passive support for the language and that the level of hostility to Gaelic is less than is often assumed (Moffat 1995: 18; Cormack 1994: 128; MacKinnon 1991a: 135). As Grin and Vaillancourt have noted in their study of

---

[49] http://31.freebb.com/gaidhlig/gaidhlig.html
[50] http://www.tirnamblog.com
[51] http://www.gaelcast.com
[52] For details of bilingual signage on trunk roads, see the following Scottish Executive news releases: www.scotland.gov.uk/News/Releases/2003/01/2947. For details for expanded signage on the Highland mainline, see:
http://195.173.143.171/cx/pressreleases/archive2001/oct2001/signs.htm

bilingual road signs in Wales, "the symbolic and psychological impact of bilingual signs [...] must not be underestimated" (1999: 27).

The visibility of the language may also increase as a result of the limited official status granted to Gaelic by the *Gaelic Language (Scotland) Act 2005*. The drawing-up of language policies for public bodies and local authorities under the Act will be likely to lead to increased bilingualism in the public faces of these bodies in such areas as letterheads, websites and public signs. Any such public use of Gaelic would be likely to increase the esteem in which the language is held (McLeod 1996: 3, Bentahila and Davies 1993: 367, Grin and Vaillancourt 1999) and therefore might lead to an increase in the numbers of learners. It is therefore important that Bòrd na Gàidhlig actively encourage public visibility of the language through the policies drawn up by public bodies in accordance with the *Gaelic Language Act*.

It should be noted, however, that no research has yet been conducted in Scotland into the effect of such initiatives as signage in RLS terms. As McLeod has argued, there has been a tendency to assume that raising the profile of Gaelic via initiatives such as television and signage is directly and automatically linked to Gaelic learning and use (McLeod 2002a: 289). While the position of Gaelic in Scottish life has certainly been strengthened by such initiatives through increased awareness and interest in the language, however, there has been little or no research on the subject of how far and how directly such initiatives aid acquisition, use and transmission of the language (McLeod 2002a: 289). Similarly, there have been few public opinion surveys on Gaelic with the exception of the BBC opinion poll of 2003 and MacKinnon's survey of 1981. Such research has an important role to play in informing policy for attracting Gaelic learners.

The second way in which the language can be promoted is through active marketing of the language by means of publicity campaigns. Such a tactic has been widely used to promote minority languages as diverse as Maori and Catalan (e.g. Nicholson 1997; Fishman 1991: 307). Research by various groups has shown that there is a great deal of public support for Gaelic but that this is not always matched by accurate knowledge about the language or about how to find out more about it (e.g. MacKinnon 1981, CCG 1996, BBC 2003). A 1996 survey conducted by System 3 Scotland for Gàidhlig '96 found that 86% of a representative sample of people agreed that the Gaelic language and way of life should be maintained. It also found, however, that 62% of the same groups felt that it was either difficult for people in Scotland to access information regarding Gaelic or that they had never been aware of the existence of such information (Gàidhlig '96 1997).

More directly related to the learning of Gaelic was a 1996 study by BBC Scotland which found that 5% of a representative sample of Scots were very interested in learning Gaelic and a further 18% were quite interested (CnaG 1999b: 12).[53] An opinion poll conducted for the BBC in 2003 found that 16% of a representative sample of the Scottish public, when asked whether they would consider learning Gaelic in the future, answered 'yes' with a further 16% answering 'maybe'. It also discovered, however, that only 31% of the sample agreed 'if I wanted to learn Gaelic it would be easy to find the course'. While these figures can in no way be taken as indicative of the number of people who actually will learn Gaelic, it suggests that there is much interest in learning Gaelic were there adequate facilities for learning and adequate publicity of learning opportunities.

---

[53] Margaret Mary Murray, BBC Scotland, personal communication: email, 1998.

The task of a publicity campaign would be to combine the high level of passive public support with a greater level of knowledge about the language in order to increase the number of people actively involved in Gaelic. The importance of marketing for Gaelic has been recognised by Comunn na Gàidhlig, who have published a brochure about the Gaelic revival for tourists (*Fàilte*), a pack to encourage Gaelic speakers to teach the language (*Thig a Theagasg*), a booklet advertising Gaelic career opportunities (*Bith Beò ann an Gàidhlig*) and promotional posters and booklets to explain and encourage Gaelic-medium education (*Fios is Freagairt*) (CnaG 2004, 2000, 1997d). None of these efforts have centred on adult learners to date, however.

A broader PR campaign for Gaelic was established in the mid-1990s: Gàidhlig '96/'97. This project aimed "to raise the profile of Gaelic nationally in a positive manner" and drew up detailed plans as to who should be targeted and how. In practice, this campaign came to little with most events being centred on Gaelic Matters, a week of events in 1997 including some Gaelic events, photo opportunities for the press, the distribution of leaflets at five shopping centres around Scotland and an increase in Gaelic television for the week. In practice Gaelic Matters received very little national media coverage and had very little presence on the ground. The Gàidhlig '96/'97 project failed to fulfil its aims to any noticeable extent. This was mainly due to a lack of funding (Gàidhlig '97: 4). Despite recommendations from Gàidhlig '97's final report that a publicity campaign on its model should be continued, this did not happen.[54]

As part of an overall RLS strategy for Gaelic, more publicity for Gaelic in a systematic fashion will be necessary in order to make people aware of the existence of the availability and advantages of Gaelic-medium education, Gaelic adult learning opportunities and so on. This could perhaps be organised by a permanent marketing/publicity campaign under the auspices of Bòrd na Gàidhlig. The need for such a publicity campaign is noted in the Ministerial Advisory Group on Gaelic report, which suggests that "a comprehensive awareness-raising campaign is needed to bring about attitudinal change, and culture shift to give the wider Scottish population ownership of Gaelic" (2002: 31).

A central publicity aim from the point of view of Gaelic learners should be to attract learners who are younger and from a wider range of social classes. It is important for this reason that Gaelic is presented at all times as a modern language relevant to people throughout Scotland, that the diversity of the modern Gaelic-speaking community be reflected and stereotypes avoided.

As part of a publicity campaign, the production of a book or booklet about how to learn Gaelic would be useful. Such books of varying sizes have been produced in Wales for those wishing to begin learning to give them ideas as to what means of learning are available and as to the length of time it would take to learn the language under these different methods (e.g. Finch 1978). Such a book or booklet would also be useful in Scotland, giving details of all the different types and providers of Gaelic courses in one booklet.

---

[54] A one year campaign to encourage the learning of Gaelic is being planned as part of the Highland 2007 initiative but few details were available at the time of writing. See: www.highland2007.com/air-splaoid.html

Gaelic in the Primary School

Making a decision to learn a language in adulthood requires some level of information regarding that language. Traditionally the school system in Scotland has not imparted information to its pupils regarding Gaelic, its history and present situation (MacInnes 1992: 101; McLeod 2001c: 96; McLeod 2001a: 6; McLeod 2004: 6; A. Gillies 2000; Ó Maolalaigh 2000; Robasdan 2006: 107). As McLeod has argued: "the Scottish educational system gives most Scots almost no instruction either in or about the Gaelic language" (2001: 7). This has been part of a broader lack of teaching of Scottish history and Scottish culture in Scotland's schools. The Scottish Consultative Council on the Curriculum's Scottish History Review Group, for example, referred to a "Scottish history deficit" in Scotland's schools (SCCC 1997: 13). A Scottish cultural deficit might also be identified in the school system.

If pupils are not given some level of accurate information about Gaelic during their school career they are unlikely to be aware of the part which Gaelic plays and has played in Scottish society and are unlikely to see through popular fallacies and stereotypes surrounding the language and are therefore unlikely to learn Gaelic in adulthood (McLeod 2001a: 7, 26; McLeod 2001c: 96; McLeod 2004: 44; Robasdan 2006: 107). For example, "most Scots do not realise that Gaelic was once spoken far more widely in Scotland than it is today" (McLeod 2001a: 7).

For these reasons, recommendations have been made by Comunn na Gàidhlig and by Gaelic educationalist Boyd Robertson to ensure that all children learn something about Gaelic language and culture. Robertson has suggested that the history and heritage of the Celts and the Gaels should be included in the primary school curriculum in all Scottish schools (CnaG 1998: 4; Robertson 1999: 255; Robasdan 2006: 88, 105, 107). This could also form the basis of a short course in secondary school (Robasdan 2006: 107). He has further suggested that a Gaelic pack based around the study of place-names might be a useful way to introduce Gaelic studies to the classroom.[55] Comunn na Gàidhlig have suggested that:

> All primary schools throughout Scotland should ensure, as recommended in the 5–14 development programme, that pupils have some knowledge and understanding of Gaelic culture. This should be done through environmental studies and the expressive arts and should contribute also to the 5–14 knowledge of language strand. (CnaG 1997c: 7).

Such recommendations would, if implemented, do much to increase knowledge about Gaelic and would encourage the learning of the language by adults. They should therefore be seen as a priority of any strategy to increase numbers of Gaelic learners and, through increasing awareness and tolerance for Gaelic, for RLS in general. They also have the advantage of being very low-cost, not adding significantly to an already crowded school curriculum, through avoiding the potentially contentious issue of 'compulsory Gaelic' and through not requiring the use of scarce Gaelic teachers.

One factor likely to facilitate increased Gaelic awareness teaching in the primary school would be the production of a high-quality Gaelic awareness teaching pack

---

[55] Boyd Robertson, personal communication: interview, 02.10.98.

(Robasdan 2006: 107). The cost of producing such support materials would be relatively low and would be cost-effective in terms of the impact which they would have in RLS efforts through helping to raise awareness of the language's existence and through helping to dispel common misconceptions regarding the language.

Given that even the availability of resources might not be sufficient to encourage all schools to include Gaelic-related studies on the curriculum, Comunn na Gàidhlig suggested as part of their proposal for a Gaelic Language Act that:

> There should be a statutory requirement that the contribution of Gaelic Scotland to Scotland's history and culture be included as an essential and compulsory part of the national curriculum at both the primary and secondary school levels (CnaG 1997b: 28).

Such a legal requirement would be of great benefit to RLS through enforcing the teaching of some Gaelic-related studies throughout Scotland. While this suggestion was not included in the *Gaelic Language (Scotland) Act* enacted in 2005, it is an area which should be pursued by Bòrd na Gàidhlig via Gaelic language plans and educational guidance for local authorities. Lo Bianco has made a similar suggestion in his recommendations for a language policy for Scotland, suggesting that there should be a compulsory language awareness course covering Gaelic, Scots, BSL and ethnic minority languages (Lo Bianco 2001: 65).

While discussion has so far centred on Gaelic awareness teaching, it should be noted that Gaelic is taught as a subject in English-medium education in some schools, a factor which is likely to encourage uptake of Gaelic in the secondary school and to encourage some pupils to learn Gaelic as adults in later life. Comunn na Gàidhlig has recommended that Gaelic be taught as a second language in primary schools in areas where Gaelic is available as a subject in secondary schools:

> All schools associated with secondary schools in which Gaelic is taught should be expected to teach some basic Gaelic (e.g. to a level equivalent to Gaelic 5–14 Learners' Elementary). Support for this should be provided on the model of the primary modern languages initiative (CnaG 1997c: 7).

The Modern Language for Primary Schools (MLPS) initiative referred to is a national scheme whereby teachers are granted day release for a specified number of weeks in order to learn a modern language to teach to upper primary pupils. All primary schools in Scotland take part in this scheme. As recommended by Comunn na Gàidhlig, a Gaelic Language for Primary Schools (GLPS) pilot programme similar to MLPS was established by Argyll and Bute Council and Highland Council in 1999–2000 to teach Gaelic to pupils in English-medium education (Gaelic Medium Teachers' Action Group 2005). Following the success of the pilot, Highland Council has continued to provide training and Argyll and Bute has formed a consortium with Stirling, East Ayrshire, Perth and Kinross and North Lanarkshire Councils to provide GLPS training in the Central Belt.

This group has since expanded and the authorities joining the consortium or requesting GLPS training have included Edinburgh, East Dunbartonshire, the City of Glasgow, North Ayrshire, Inverclyde and West Dumbartonshire.[56] In addition to

---

[56] Linda Roberts, Scottish Executive Gaelic Unit, personal communication: email, 06.04.06.

the GLPS training programme, Gaelic teaching to English-medium primary pupils is also delivered in all Comhairle nan Eilean Siar primaries by fluent Gaelic speaking teachers and in Perth and Kinross Council a peripatetic teacher teaches Gaelic in selected Highland Perthshire schools.

GLPS provision is delivered mainly in schools where GME is delivered (Gaelic Medium Teachers' Action Group 2005: 17). In the 2005–6 session, roughly 6,500 pupils were participating in GLPS: 3,900 in Argyll and Bute and its central belt consortium partners through 77 schools, 1,639 pupils in the Comhairle nan Eilean Siar area in 38 schools, and approximately 1,000 pupils in 40 schools in the Highland Council area.[57]

If a GLPS scheme were implemented in all primary schools feeding into secondaries where Gaelic is taught, as recommended by CnaG, it would ensure that all children entering these secondaries had some familiarity with Gaelic. This would be likely to increase the uptake of Gaelic as a subject at secondary school. Robasdan has similarly recommended an expansion of GLPS and has suggested as a target that the scheme should roll out to every local authority where Gaelic-medium education is available within a decade (Robasdan 2006: 108).

One initiative which might lead to an expansion in the GLPS scheme is a course which Aberdeen University is currently developing for primary teachers who have already completed the GLPS programme. This aims to develop further their knowledge of Gaelic language and skills in delivering the 5–14 Gaelic learners curriculum to pupils in upper primary and lower secondary. The target groups are primary and secondary teachers who have the equivalent of GLPS and who wish to teach Gaelic to learners in primary and S1/S2. This course would enable teachers to deliver and assess the entire 5–14 curriculum and to deliver at Standard Grade level (Gaelic Medium Teachers' Action Group 2005: 18). It could, therefore, enable an expansion in Gaelic for learners in secondary school as well as primary school. The Scottish Executive appointed Gaelic Medium Teachers' Action Group has stated its "strong support for the continuation and expansion of GLPS courses" and calls upon the Scottish Executive to support Aberdeen University's new course (Gaelic Medium Teachers' Action Group 2005: 19).

It is far from certain at present, however, whether there will be any significant expansion of Gaelic subject teaching at the primary level. *Citizens of a Multilingual World*, a report on the future of school language teaching on behalf of the Scottish Executive, recommended a diversification in languages taught in primary schools (Ministerial Action Group on Languages 2000). It was very vague and ambiguous, however, as to the position which Gaelic subject teaching should have in future provision. The Scottish Executive response to the report failed to clarify the position of Gaelic within school language teaching and also failed to release significant new resources for school language teaching as recommended by the report (Scottish Executive 2001). The framework established by the report further devolves most control over choice of languages taught to local authorities. These factors are likely to hinder future development of Gaelic subject teaching in the primary school.

The area of Gaelic subject teaching within English-medium primary education has so far received relatively little discussion or research by Gaelic educationalists, agencies or activists. It is, however, a most important area and more research and discussion about the contribution of this area to RLS and about ways in which

---

[57] Linda Roberts, Scottish Executive Gaelic Unit, personal communication: email, 06/04/06.

provision in this area might be expanded would be useful. Bòrd na Gàidhlig should further this objective via Gaelic language plans and educational guidance for local authorities.

Broadcasting as a Means of Attracting Gaelic Learners: Television

Television is important to the learning of Gaelic, not only as a learning resource, but also as a mechanism for attracting new learners. This section will investigate television as a factor in encouraging people to learn Gaelic.

Gaelic television changed almost beyond recognition in 1993 when the quantity of Gaelic broadcasting increased from under 100 hours per annum to almost 300. This revolution followed the 1990 Broadcasting Act which established the £9.5M Gaelic Television Fund and the Gaelic Television Committee (CTG), later to become the Gaelic Broadcasting Committee (CCG), and now known as Seirbheis nam Meadhanan Gàidhlig (GMS), which was to distribute this fund for the production of Gaelic television with effect from 1993.

This trebling of Gaelic output brought the language to the attention of Lowland Scotland to a greater extent than ever before and can be considered to have been a key factor in leading to the common perception that a Gaelic revival is currently underway (McLeod 2001a: 3). Important in this was the fact that Gaelic television programmes were being produced more professionally than previously and were spread across the main television channels, often being shown in prime time slots.

While these facts in themselves might have been expected to increase interest in Gaelic amongst non-Gaelic speakers, many programme makers were keen to go further and actively target this group as potential supporters and learners of the language. Programmes changed not only in terms of quantity and quality, but also often in terms of their content. As Rhoda MacDonald and Alistair Moffat, then both involved in Gaelic television within Scottish Television, have pointed out, the company actively pursued a strategy in the early-mid 1990s of trying to re-symbolise Gaelic through associating it with the 'good things in life' and in attempting to place it at the centre of modern Scottish life (MacDonald 1993, Moffat 1995). MacDonald has talked of using television to make Gaelic 'trendy' and 'sexy' (MacDonald 1993: 16). Such tactics have been by no means limited to Scottish Television.

Prior to the establishment of the CTG (Comataidh Telebhisein Gàidhlig – The Gaelic Television Committee), Gaelic television tended to deal mainly with religion, traditional music and the traditional Hebridean way of life, often doing so in a highly stereotyped fashion (Cormack 1994). Such images were unlikely to be of interest to younger Gaels or to non-Gaelic speakers.

By avoiding such images, Scottish Television (STV) and other broadcasters aimed to gain more viewers for Gaelic television and to improve the image of Gaelic amongst speaker and non-speaker alike. STV, for example, produced a number of series of subtitled Gaelic programmes covering modern subjects which were not being served by Scottish-made English language programmes at the time; subjects such as cookery, cars, DIY and fashion. The intention was to attract viewers to Gaelic television and thus to Gaelic itself through attracting them to the subject matter of the programmes (MacDonald 1993: 15). Such series have also sought to show Gaelic as a modern, living language suitable for the rigours of modern and urban life, and as a language which is relevant to today's youth. The Gaelic soap opera *Machair* was also notable in this respect through its warts-and-all portrayal of a modern-day Gaelic community (CTG 1993: 7).

Other innovations in the 1990s following the expansion of Gaelic television were *Eòrpa*, a BBC-produced European current affairs programme specialising in issues not covered elsewhere and *Telefios*, a Grampian Television-produced Gaelic news bulletin. Such programmes served to apply the use of Gaelic to new broadcasting domains.

The portrayal of Gaelic in an all-Scotland sense has been a very noticeable strand in the strategy of Gaelic broadcasters. This, as Cormack has argued, is based on a desire by broadcasters to place Gaelic in the centre of Scottish affairs once more, and is derived from the principle that Gaelic can only survive if it is perceived as a national language (Cormack 1994, MacDonald 1993, S. Macdonald 1997: 256, Moffat 1995). The learners' series *Speaking Our Language* is a particularly notable example of this desire to re-symbolise Gaelic. Rather than showing Gaelic speakers mainly in a Western Isles setting, *Speaking Our Language* (SOL) was largely filmed in cities such as Glasgow and Edinburgh and showed Gaelic being used in fashionable shops, bars and restaurants at least as much as on the croft or the fishing boat. The SOL mini-dramas were both set in Glasgow and the series visited a large number of Lowland towns stressing their connections with the language.

There is much evidence to suggest that Gaelic broadcasters met with a significant degree of success both in their attempts to raise the profile and awareness of Gaelic and also in their more ambitious attempts to encourage people to learn the language. The increase in Gaelic television from 1993 gained a great deal of publicity and the scatter of programmes between three channels, often in peak slots, meant that more people than ever before came into contact with the language. The backlash which many pro-Gaelic campaigners had feared might occur against the expanded Gaelic television service failed to materialise (Moffat 1995: 18; Cormack 1994: 128; MacKinnon 1991a: 135).

Audience research surveys in the 1990s evidenced a large degree of support for Gaelic broadcasting and for Gaelic in general on the part of the Scottish population as a whole. All-Scotland System 3 polls for the CTG and CCG found that a great majority of viewers strongly or slightly agreed that "it is important that the Gaelic language is kept alive in Scotland through Gaelic programmes on TV". In 1993 40% agreed strongly and 35% slightly with the proposition and in 1996 43% strongly agreed with 36% slightly agreeing (CTG 1994: 24, CCG 1996: 21).

Viewing figures for subtitled Gaelic programmes have often been impressive. NOP polls for Grampian Television in 1993 and 1996 found that over 50% of the audience in the Grampian transmission area watched Gaelic programmes even though only 6% were Gaelic speakers (Grampian Television 1994, CCG 1996: 21). Research carried out throughout Scotland in 1994 and 1996 demonstrated that around 40% of those sampled in each of the years had watched a Gaelic programme in the previous week (CTG 1994, 1996: 7).

Machair gained viewing figures of over 500,000 at its peak and continued to receive viewing figures far in excess of the number of Gaelic speakers for its entire run. It is estimated that 1.85 million people out of the population of 3.35 million living in the Scottish Television transmission area tuned into a programme of the first series of the learners' series *Speaking Our Language* for at least three minutes (MacCaluim 1995: 10). The importance of Gaelic television in public opinion terms has been demonstrated by Sproull and Chalmers who have identified television as a crucial factor in influencing the emergence of positive attitudes to the language (Sproull and Chalmers 1998).

The learners' series *Speaking our Language* was not only successful in terms of its ratings, but also, in terms of encouraging the learning of Gaelic. By 1994, over 10,000 viewers had purchased programme support materials with 30,000 learners contacting the broadcasters for information (CTG 1994: 8; Johnstone 1994: 54). That Gaelic television in general might be a factor in encouraging the learning of Gaelic is also suggested by the Gaelic Learners' Survey as 28.8% of 392 respondents in Scotland stated that Gaelic television was very important in their decision to learn and a further 45.4% that it was quite important.

It should be noted, however, that while Gaelic television has certainly served to raise awareness of the language, to create more sympathetic attitudes and to encourage the learning of Gaelic, there has been little or no research to ascertain how far and how directly television encourages the acquisition, use and transmission of the language (McLeod 2002a: 289; Cormack 2006: 218, 219). Such research is essential for future RLS efforts (Cormack 2006: 219).

While Gaelic television has been an important factor in increasing general awareness and encouraging the learning of the language up to this point, there are currently several factors which are serving to limit the potential of television to be able to fulfil such a role in future. One such factor is the failure of Border Television to screen Gaelic programming. The Carlisle-based station, which serves Cumbria and Mann in addition to the Southern Uplands of Scotland, was exempted from any responsibility to show Gaelic television under the 1990 Broadcasting Act and has refused to show any Gaelic television up to this point.

The amount of Gaelic television shown has tends to vary by season and by day of the week, with less Gaelic being shown in the summer or at the weekends than at other times. The BBC has also confined virtually all of its adult Gaelic viewing and much of its children's viewing to Thursday evenings on BBC2. Such developments ensure that Gaelic television is less likely to be seen by non-Gaelic viewers. The CTG/CCG/GMS has been unable to intervene in scheduling decisions as it has no powers in this area.

The visibility of Gaelic on the screen has decreased drastically since the later 1990s with, it is presumed, a knock-on effect on levels of public awareness and a diminution of the power of television to act as a means of attracting Gaelic learners. Cuts to the Gaelic Television Fund from £9.5M to £8.5M in the late 1990s and a failure of the government to link its level to inflation have led to a decrease in the fund in real terms. By 1998 this financial situation had resulted in a decrease of 40 hours per annum in Gaelic television output (Fraser 1998: 6; GBT 2000: 24).

The late 1990s and early 2000s have also saw the completion of the *Speaking our Language* series and the cancellation of *Machair* and *Telefios*, these being highly popular programmes which in many ways can be said to be have been the flagships of the 1993 Gaelic television expansion. Cuts in funding mean that they have not in the main been replaced by similarly high budget and high profile series and have limited the development of such areas as Gaelic drama.

Increased competition between the BBC and the ITV companies and increased commercial pressure on the ITV companies has led to a greater tendency for the screening of television programmes at anti-social hours and for the dropping of peak-time Gaelic slots (GBT 2000: 2, 8). In late 2005, an agreement between Ofcom and the Scottish and Grampian Television companies reduced the hours of peak-time Gaelic television on ITV from 26 to only 6 hours per annum (C. MacLeod 2005, Ofcom 2005).

While some Gaelic television is now available digitally, the initial presence of Gaelic on digital terrestrial television is not unlike the limited and somewhat piecemeal provision currently seen on analogue. S4C Digital Networks, the licensee for Multiplex A, is required to broadcast at least 30 minutes of Gaelic programming during peak evening viewing time: 6.00–10.30 pm (GBT 2000: 20).[58] This service, TeleG, is available via Freeview between 6 and 7pm each day. As a digital channel, and one broadcasting for only a few hours per week at that, its potential in attracting new Gaelic learners is very limited.

Such deficiencies in current Gaelic television provision have lead to increased discussion of the future for Gaelic television by Gaelic broadcasters and by the government itself. 1998 saw the publication of the Scottish Office-funded Fraser report; a consultation paper on Gaelic broadcasting (Fraser 1998). In his report, Fraser identified a lack of co-ordination of Gaelic broadcasting and of accountability on the part of broadcasters, referring to many of the factors mentioned above and concluding with regard to analogue television that:

> The tendency will be towards more and more mainstream competitive programming at the expense of public service minority interest elements such as Gaelic. In this scenario an overall strategic plan and a comprehensive, consistent and coherent Gaelic broadcasting service is impossible to create and sustain (Fraser 1998: 9).

Due to the constraints of the present analogue television set-up and the huge expansion which is now taking place in digital television, the discussion of the future of Gaelic television has increasingly shifted towards the possibility of a dedicated digital Gaelic television channel in order to bring about an expanded television service where peak time slots can be guaranteed and which would be more answerable to the Gaelic community (Fraser 1998, GBT 2000).

Fraser concluded that such a channel is the only way forward for Gaelic television. A study by the CCG in 1997 also backed the concept of a digital Gaelic channel (CCG 1997). A Gaelic Broadcasting Taskforce was appointed following the Fraser report in order to "examine from the standpoint of technical feasibility, finance and programming the practicability of establishing a dedicated Gaelic television channel" (2000: 2). This taskforce endorsed the arguments made by Fraser and concluded that such a channel would be both practicable and desirable. Following these reports, the Scottish Executive, UK Government, SMG and broadcasters have been in negotiation with the view to establish a Gaelic television channel and an announcement is expected soon (M. MacLeòid 2006b, Sheppard 2006, GMS 2006).

While the debate on Gaelic broadcasting in recent years has been a debate on how best to achieve a Gaelic channel, however, many Gaelic speakers had previously argued against the establishment of such a channel. The main argument against a Gaelic channel has been that this would serve to ghettoise Gaelic, and would lose the value of Gaelic television as a means of attracting learners and raising awareness in general.[59] Until the later 1990s, opposition to a Gaelic channel would seem to have been the majority position amongst Gaelic agencies and viewers. The CCG chairman stated in 1995, for example, that the CCG had not yet been convinced as to the case for a separate Gaelic television channel given that this might entail the loss of many

---

[58] For more details, see www.teleg.co.uk

[59] For the opposing view that Gaelic television should be for traditional Gaelic-speaking communities rather than for attracting outside interest, see Wilson 1995, D.MacLeod 1995.

non-Gaelic viewers (*Stornoway Gazette* 24.08.95). In the mid 1990s, several broadcasters and academics also expressed scepticism as to the value of such a channel in view of its reduced awareness-raising potential and opinion polls indicated that a Gaelic television channel was not supported either by a majority of Gaelic speakers or non-Gaelic speakers (MacDonald 1993; Moffat 1993; Grampian Television 1994; *Cothrom*: winter 95–96: 22; Johnstone 1994: 67).

From the later 1990s, however, support for a separate Gaelic television channel has come to be the mainstream view (Allardyce 1996) with both the CCG and the Scottish Office/Executive moving closer to the idea of a Gaelic channel and with audience research for the CCG in 1998 finding widespread support for the concept, with 60% of all respondents and 71% of Gaelic respondents supporting a channel dedicated exclusively to Gaelic programmes (*West Highland Free Press* 08.03.96; Fraser 1998: 11, CCG 1997).

This movement in opinion reflects the weaknesses in current provision identified above. It also reflects the fact that the large number of digital television channels potentially available means that the traditional strategy of attracting non-Gaelic speakers to Gaelic television through the screening of Gaelic programmes on English-language channels will become less and less effective as a means of attracting learners and raising awareness in general.

While there are many strong arguments for a Gaelic television channel, from the point of view of television as a learning resource, the counter-argument that such a channel would be a 'ghetto' was until recently a very widely held belief and has only lost support in the face of changing technological and commercial circumstances which have rendered the status quo untenable (McLeod 2001c: 104). Despite the centrality of this debate to discussion of Gaelic broadcasting, however, nothing is said in the Fraser report or in the Gaelic Broadcasting Taskforce report regarding the whole issue of awareness-raising and attracting potential Gaelic learners and no recommendations are made to this end. This issue has also been ignored in the ongoing debate on the establishment of a Gaelic television channel in the years since the publication of the taskforce report. This is a highly worrying omission given the important role previously played by television in this respect.

It is clear that a digital Gaelic television channel would not be able to act as an awareness-raiser for Gaelic or to attract new learners to the same extent or in the same ways as the previous system. It is important that this fact be acknowledged in the debates on the establishment of a Gaelic television channel and general Gaelic development in order to ensure that the new broadcasting structures act as a tool for encouraging Gaelic learning as far as possible. Given that the potential of a Gaelic television channel to attract new learners will be limited, however, it is crucial that action is taken to identify ways of replacing the awareness-raising function once filled by Gaelic television.

From the point of view of interesting more people in Gaelic, continued provision of Gaelic programmes on English-language channels would be of great benefit. A reasonable suggestion would be the continuation of a limited amount of subtitled, high-quality Gaelic programmes such as news bulletins or learners' programmes on analogue and digital public service channels at strategic peak times following the establishment of a Gaelic television channel and a legal requirement for these channels to publicise the Gaelic television channel.

A new high-quality and high-profile programme for Gaelic learners to be

---

[60] For more details of *Turas Teanga*, see: www.rte.ie/tv/turasteanga

screened on English-language channels would also be useful. A good model for such a course is RTÉ's *Turas Teanga* Irish-language course which was recently aired on RTÉ 1 despite the existence of the Irish language channel TG4.[60] Programmes in English about issues relating to Gaelic and linked to publicity for learning opportunities would also help to encourage and facilitate learning. The BBC's recently screened *Colin and Cumberland* series is a good example of how English-language television can be used to promote Gaelic learning. This comedy cartoon is an introduction to the language aimed at adults with a backup interactive website which aims to teach a few basic phrases in the language and encourage viewers to take language learning further.[61]

While there are more channels available on digital than on analogue television, there are still relatively few on digital terrestrial – currently just over 30 channels, some of which are pay-to-view. This fact, combined with the continuation of familiar channels such as BBC 1 and BBC 2, ITV, Channel 4 and Channel 5 on digital and the arguably poor quality of many of the new channels means that the viewing behaviour of the public is not likely to change greatly in the short term. This is also likely to be the case to a lesser extent for digital satellite television despite the far larger number of channels available. This adds weight to the argument for the continuation of some Gaelic broadcasting outwith the Gaelic channel, should one be established.

Broadcasting as a Means if Attracting Gaelic Learners: Radio

English-language radio could also play a role in attracting Gaelic learners. This could happen, for example, through a Gaelic programme for learners on Radio Scotland as recommended above. Attention could also be drawn to the existence of Gaelic radio and to Gaelic in general through advertising of BBC Radio nan Gaidheal through BBC Radio Scotland. The BBC promotes its output both on radio and television and has produced a number of high-budget promotional campaigns on television, but such advertising has not normally included any mention of Radio nan Gaidheal. Mentioning Radio nan Gaidheal in television and radio advertisements promoting BBC Scotland's output would not add to the cost of production of the advertisements and would serve to draw attention to the service and to the language.

Gaelic Learners' Organisations

There are presently three organisations with a remit specifically relating to Gaelic learners. These are Clì Gàidhlig, Lìon – the national network for Gaelic learners' services and the Community Learning and Development Review Group for Gaelic (CLDRG).[62]

Clì Gàidhlig, which was formed in 1983 as Comann an Luchd-Ionnsachaidh (CLI) with financial assistance from the Highlands and Islands Development Board, was constituted as a membership organisation with the following aims: to design and produce relevant new courses, to co-operate with groups and classes to bring learning facilities to all, to maintain teacher training, to give the public an information service and to represent learners to the education and broadcasting authorities (*Cuairt Litir Ionnsachaidh* 1). Two publications were also produced three times a year: *Cainnt*, an all-Gaelic magazine, and *Cuairt Litir Ionnsachaidh*, a bilingual information

---

[61] www.bbc.co.uk/colinandcumberland/
[62] Formerly known as the Community Education Review Group for Gaelic: CERG.

newsletter. CLI was very much involved in teaching Gaelic in the 1980s, organising a large number of summer schools, weekend courses, and intensive four week 'crash courses' at reasonable prices. It also provided training days for tutors.

When the initial grant from the HIDB came to an end in 1986, CLI was unable to find financial support to enable it to continue at the same level and lost its director. Between 1986 and 1989, CLI continued to operate with no paid staff, concentrating mainly on a joint project to produce the *Siuthad* learners' course (*CLI Newsletter*, December 1987).

The slow recovery of CLI began in 1989 when an administrator was employed, first on a part-time basis and later full-time. CLI were further assisted from 1992 by CnaG's creation of a post of Adult Learners' Development Officer. The duties of this officer included liaising with CLI, administering Lìon and encouraging the establishment of Gaelic clubs. There were several further advances during this period: the CLI newsletter was expanded and upgraded, mechanisms for providing of information to learners about classes and courses were improved, a yearly glossy magazine was introduced and a series of cassettes for learners was developed.

The present incarnation of CLI dates from 1995 when the position of full-time director for CLI was created with financial assistance from CnaG, replacing CnaG's Adult Learners' Development Officer post, and when CLI moved into its own premises for the first time. The aims of the new CLI were: to act as the voice of Gaelic learners, to disseminate information of Gaelic affairs to learners, to promote improved Gaelic learners' facilities and to promote the participation of learners in Gaelic affairs (*Cothrom* 4, 1995: 11).

CLI membership grew fairly steadily from around 200 in 1989 to over 1000 in the late 1990s. In 2006, membership stood at just over 890. The percentage of members living in Scotland has varied from around 60% to around 70%, with members in England constituting the second single largest group.[63]

The main activities of Clì Gàidhlig, as the organisation has been known since 2003, are the production of the quarterly high-quality bilingual magazine *Cothrom* and the provision of information about Gaelic classes and courses, including the maintenance of a website detailing learning opportunities (www.learn-gaelic.info). In addition to the director and administrator, Clì Gàidhlig have since 1999 operated a Community Course project, employing a part-time and later a full-time officer to provide Gaelic short courses nationally with funding initially from the National Lottery, later from the Scottish Executive and currently from Bòrd na Gàidhlig. In 2006, it is expected that more than 15 courses will be planned, ranging from one to five days depending on the demand of learners in the respective regions.

Despite the expansion of CLI in the mid-1990s, however, it can be argued that the group never fulfilled its full potential until well into the new millennium. Due to financial and staff shortages, the group's director and administrator largely had to concentrate on the production of the magazine, website and database. This has meant that the group was unable to become involved to any great degree in encouraging more people to learn Gaelic, to plan strategically for the learning of Gaelic or to become more involved in areas directly relating to education, such as the production of materials or the teaching of tutors. CLI also had to abandon a range of potential development projects due to lack of funding.

---

[63] Sarah NicEachainn, Clì, personal communication: email, 11.06.2002; Siùsaidh Hardy, Clì, personal communication: telephone interview, 09.05.2006.
[64] Siùsaidh Hardy, Clì Gàidhlig, personal communication: telephone interview, 09.05.2006.

In the early-mid 2000s, however, there have been many positive developments at Clì Gàidhlig under directors Peadar Morgan and later Siùsaidh Hardy who replaced him in January 2005. The appointment a part-time editor for *Cothrom* in 2004 with financial assistance from Bòrd na Gàidhlig has enabled the director to spend more time on strategic issues.

Under its new director, Clì has increasingly focussed on direct provision of learning opportunities in addition to strategy for learners.[64] Not only has the programme of Clì Gaelic weekend courses expanded but the group has also published the *Leabhar nan Litrichean* book and DVD set (MacIlleathain 2005) and has revised the content of Cothrom magazine to make it more useful as a learning resource.[65] The group has further developed a three day high-level grammar course for fluent speakers, has piloted workplace based Gaelic taster courses for Highland Council, SNH and HIE and is currently working on a Gaelic awareness training course. Clì Gàidhlig is also currently in discussion with publishers about the possibility of producing reading books aimed specifically at adult learners and is seeking funding for a proposed learners' gathering in 2007. Perhaps the most significant of the group's projects at present is a proposal from Deiseal Ltd that Clì Gàidhlig pilot the Ulpan method of immersion teaching for Gaelic. A funding application has been submitted to Bòrd na Gàidhlig for this project.[66]

While Clì Gàidhlig plays a very important role for adult learners, both in terms of strategy and direct provision for Gaelic learners, it has, however, only a narrow budget. Its potential strategically to influence the Gaelic for adults sector is limited by the ad hoc and uncoordinated nature of current provision and the large number of providers currently involved. The current director of Clì Gàidhlig has therefore suggested that a national strategy and a national co-ordinator for Gaelic learners is necessary to increase strategic co-ordination and improve provision.[67]

The Community Learning and Development Review Group for Gaelic (CLDRG) referred to above is another organisation concerned with the adult learner.[68] It is an inter-authority standing group with the remit of promoting Gaelic within the field of community learning and development, including adult learners. CLDRG itself is funded through the Scottish Executive Specific Grants for Gaelic Education scheme and membership consists of those local authorities in receipt of specific grants for Gaelic, along with a number of Gaelic organisations who attend as observers. CLDRG produces three-year plans, holds regular meetings and a public annual conference and has in the past organised study trips. The group acts to share information and good practice between local authorities and has supported the piloting of new Gaelic community projects on a national scale which could then be followed up by individual authorities. Recent projects have included the holding of some training courses for adult tutors, Gaelic family learning weeks and the funding of a low-key national Gaelic learners award. More recently the group has commissioned a handbook for Gaelic tutors (MacIlleathain 2006).

---

[65] Siùsaidh Hardy, Clì Gàidhlig, personal communication: telephone interview, 09.05.06. *Leabhar nan Litrichean* is discussed in more detail in the section above on broadcasting (radio) as a learning resource.

[66] Siùsaidh Hardy, Clì Gàidhlig, personal communication: telephone interview, 09.05.06.

[67] Siùsaidh Hardy, Clì Gàidhlig, personal communication: telephone interview, 09.05.06.

[68] I would like to thank Peadar Morgan, formerly of CLI; Siùsaidh Hardy, current director of Clì Gàidhlig and Eddy Cavin, Glasgow City Council for discussing CERG/CDLRG with me on a number of occasions.

CLDRG has been successful in providing a forum for discussion of Gaelic affairs and in undertaking the initiatives outlined above. One problem faced by the group, however, has been the fact that not all councils entitled to participate in the group have been doing so. Another has been that Gaelic has often only been a very small part of the job description of some of the community learning and development officials involved in the group. This has meant that the authorities and individual officers who are most committed to Gaelic have had to shoulder a disproportionate amount of work. These factors have served to reduce the effectiveness of the group, as has the group's small budget, this typically being around £12,000–£15,000 each year.

The final main group with regard to Gaelic learners is Lìon, the Gaelic learners' network, which was established following the *Feumalachdan* report to help co-ordinate the efforts of all the groups involved with Gaelic learners in an attempt to inject more co-ordination into the Gaelic for adults sector. When established, Lìon had over 20 member groups, including Gaelic development bodies, broadcasters and colleges.

In the early 1990s, Lìon provided a forum for discussion and information-sharing. Lìon held a triennial Gaelic learners' conference between 1992 and 1998. Lìon was also involved in lobbying, playing an important role in bringing about advances such as the screening of *Speaking our Language* throughout the UK on BBC2's late-night educational series *The Learning Zone* and in achieving the broadcasting of Gaelic radio in the Central Belt. Lìon was also involved in the development of immersion courses. Despite these achievements, however, the network had no budget or staff of its own, its administrative expenses being covered by CnaG and CLI. As Boyd Robertson, the chair of Lìon, has pointed out, this to some extent limited the activities of the group.[69] In addition to these structural weaknesses, the group has also been dormant since the late 1990s with the series of Gaelic learner's conferences having come to an end and with the group not having met or undertaken any activity for over five years.[70]

Some improvements to the current organisations can be suggested to increase their effectiveness. For example, increased funding for Clì Gàidhlig, as recommended by both by the 1995 and 1998 Gaelic Learners' Conferences held by Lìon, would enable them to become more involved in long-term planning for learners, to intensify its lobbying on behalf of Gaelic learners, to co-operate with other groups in the production of teaching materials and to liaise more closely with local and national Gaelic groups.

Some obvious tasks for an expanded Clì Gàidhlig would be the development of a network for those teaching Gaelic to adults and the creation of a newsletter for Gaelic tutors to provide information about teaching methods and training opportunities, these having been recommended in *Feumalachdan* (CnaG/CLI 1992: 36). An expanded Clì Gàidhlig could also employ a member of staff to administer and co-ordinate a revitalised Lìon or an equivalent group.

An expansion of the Clì Courses project might enable the course organiser, augmented by one or more assistants, to arrange more community courses and to liaise with learners in areas where courses had previously been held in order to help ensure continuity of Gaelic provision through advice on the organisation of classes or social/self-help groups. In addition to learners' courses, an expanded Community Courses project could also organise tutor training weekend courses, perhaps in tandem with learners' courses.

---

[69] Boyd Robertson, personal communication: interview, 17.05.99.
[70] Boyd Robertson, personal communication: email, 17.03.06.

Another idea which would be worth investigating as part of an expanded Clì Gàidhlig or as part of alternative structures for Gaelic learning would be the possibility of establishing local adult learners' officers in different parts of Scotland to help co-ordinate informal Gaelic groups, distribute information and involve fluent speakers. CYD, the Welsh learners' association, employs eight part-time officers to cover all parts of Wales and also operates a volunteers scheme.[71]

An expansion of Clì Gàidhlig and revitalised Lìon as recommended above would enable an improvement in services provided to Gaelic learners and an expansion in lobbying, information-sharing and strategic thinking on issues relating to adult Gaelic learning. Even should this happen, however, there would still be an overall lack of co-ordination in the provision for Gaelic learners due to a lack of authority on the part of Clì Gàidhlig and Lìon over basic fields such as college and local authority evening classes and immersion courses, for example. Structural weaknesses such as these and ways in which they might be tackled will now be discussed.

Structural Weaknesses in the Learning Infrastructure

It has been seen that there are many structural weaknesses in the Gaelic learning infrastructure. The most significant of these will now be summarised and recommendations made for possible improvements. Tutor training will be investigated first, followed by funding and then by strategic co-ordination and planning.

Tutor Training and Support

A key weakness identified in the Gaelic learning infrastructure by the *Feumalachdan Luchd-Ionnsachaidh* report was a serious shortage of Gaelic tutors and a lack of training and support for such tutors. At the time of the report, there was no training provision for Gaelic tutors. *Feumalachdan* found that around half of the tutors surveyed had no training or experience in teaching. The study also found that the provision of Gaelic classes was heavily dependent on the availability of Gaelic-speaking school teachers, who constituted almost one-half of tutors surveyed (CnaG/CLI 1992).

To remedy this situation, the report suggested a number of measures including day, weekend or week-long induction courses for Gaelic tutors, regular in-service training, the production of a tutors' handbook, the creation of a national support network, resource centre and newsletter for tutors (CnaG/CLI 1992). It was further recommended that fluent speakers not trained in teaching should increasingly play a part in Gaelic classes or informal Gaelic groups through acting as language assistants rather than as conventional tutors (CnaG/CLI 1992: 8).

Of the recommendations made by the *Feumalachdan* report for improvement in tutor training and support, progress has been limited and slow. There is still no national resource centre, national support network or newsletter for tutors. There has been progress in terms of training courses but this has been less than envisaged by the report. CLDRG and its member authorities have run a variety of one-off, one-day or short residential training seminars for evening class tutors over the past decade. In the early-mid 2000s these courses have become increasingly frequent and professional, including an annual tutor training weekend at Sabhal Mòr Ostaig and occasional training days in

---

[71] www.cyd.org.uk
[72] Eddy Cavin, CLDRG, personal communication: telephone conversation, 12.05.06.

different local authorities, particularly in Glasgow City and Highland. These courses have been aimed mainly at existing evening class tutors teaching in local authority classes. The CLDRG has also recently commissioned a tutor training manual by writer and broadcaster Ruairidh MacIlleathain to be used in future courses (MacIlleathain 2006).[72]

While this has been significant progress, however, these short courses are necessarily limited in scope, being short in duration and intended for local authority evening class tutors, and there is still no organised support or systematic training structure for Gaelic tutors in general. Longer, more frequent and more detailed courses, including ab initio courses, are still necessary to increase the number of and expand the skills of tutors through enabling them to deal with different types of classes and course.

Despite the CLDRG training enabling some new tutors to enter the market, Gaelic tutors are still in short supply 14 years after the *Feumalachdan* report.[73] There is also the added complication that a large proportion of tutors are retired or nearing retirement age.[74] The lack of tutor training available has implications for the quality as well as the quantity of tutors. One area which was frequently raised in the Gaelic Learners' Survey is the variable quality of Gaelic tuition resulting from the widespread use of fluent speakers with little or no teaching experience. Without quality tuition, it is unlikely that a learner will proceed to fluency.

Any strategy for growth in the number of Gaelic learners will require more trained tutors. It will also require a wider and more flexible range of Gaelic classes including parents' classes, work-based classes, immersion courses, distance learning and weekend courses. These courses, particularly immersion courses, will require some tutors to have more specialised training than that required for conventional evening classes. This suggests that there is the potential or, indeed, the necessity, for the emergence of a sector of professional Gaelic-for-adults tutors who will teach Gaelic to adults for a living, whether working full-time in one course or through varying day, evening, weekend and other classes throughout the year. Very few tutors indeed make a living from teaching Gaelic to adults at present.

For the purposes of RLS, it is clear that action is needed to ensure adequate training for tutors. One suggestion could be a certificate scheme for Gaelic tutors based on the development of Scottish Qualifications Authority modules in teaching Gaelic to adults. Such modules would form a flexible basis for a range of different tutor-courses such as open/distance learning, certificated summer schools or intensive weekend courses leading to a certificate over a period of months. Such a scheme might also take account of those fluent speakers wishing to lead Gaelic self-help or social groups as language assistants rather than as tutors of formal classes.

To provide for the creation of professional Gaelic tutors as described above, a more ambitious longer-term aim would be the establishment of a Postgraduate Certificate of Education course in teaching Gaelic to adults. A professional study into possible ways of establishing, funding and assessing demand for certificated tutors would be a good way of taking such proposals forward.

---

[73] Siùsaidh Hardy, Clì Gàidhlig, personal communication: telephone interview, 09.05.06.
[74] Peadar Morgan, Clì, personal communication: interview, 22.04.98.
[75] Siùsaidh Hardy, Clì Gàidhlig, personal communication: telephone interview, 09.05.06.
[76] For more details of the Ulpan course in Wales, see Pritchard Newcombe and Newcombe 2001.

Another means of improving the availability and quality of tuition alongside the schemes suggested above would be the adoption of the Ulpan system of intensive language teaching for Gaelic, a possibility which Clì Gàidhlig are currently investigating.[75] This system originated in Israel where it is used to teach immigrants Hebrew and has since been adopted in Wales to teach Welsh to adult learners.[76] Based around language drills augmented with role-play and games, Ulpan is based around the spoken language but is structured so as to develop an understanding of grammar and also introduces reading and writing. The course as used in Wales is based around a written course manual featuring progressive units. Ulpan has the advantage of reducing the level of training required by tutors as they can rely mainly on the course materials, having only to learn the basic teaching skills rather than having also to master the teaching of grammar and to identify or produce resources. This would help increase the number of and improve consistency of tutors.

In addition to its advantage for tutors, the course is also structured in units which can be used for courses of varying intensity and duration such as evening classes, weekend courses and residential courses. The introduction of Ulpan to Scotland would, therefore, be able to inject more consistency and interchangeability to Gaelic courses.

Funding

Funding for Gaelic learners' provision is another area of significant weakness in the present Gaelic learning infrastructure. As seen above, the strategically important immersion courses sector and the further education sector in general have particular funding difficulties. At present, no specific Gaelic-related funding is available for the tertiary or higher education sectors, while Gaelic immersion courses also attract a low funding weighting factor. Further and Higher Education funding arrangements also make it difficult for graduates or would-be graduates to undertake immersion courses (Robertson 2001a: 10). Given these difficulties, both the Scottish Executive Taskforce on Public Funding of Gaelic and the Ministerial Advisory Group for Gaelic recommended that funding for Gaelic in the tertiary sector be addressed, with the latter recommending an initial annual budget of £100,000 (Taskforce on Public Funding of Gaelic 2000: 17, MAGOG 2002: 51). Similarly, Robertson has concluded that "special funding arrangements are required for Gaelic immersion courses if they are to play their full part in the regeneration of the language", suggesting that these arrangements take account of factors such as the intensive nature of the courses, the likelihood of smaller-than-average sizes and the need to remove financial impediments from prospective students (Robertson 2001a: 12).

Possible future funding arrangements to enable a growth in the immersion course sector might include an increase in the funding weighting given to intensive Gaelic courses, the establishment of a specific grant scheme for Gaelic tertiary and higher education and a reform in student funding arrangements for those wishing to undertake intensive Gaelic courses.

In addition to reform of current funding structures, the Gaelic adult learners sector would also benefit greatly from a general increase in the level of funding allocated by the Scottish Executive / Bòrd na Gàidhlig within present structures. The Gaelic for adults sector currently receives only a small portion of government funding for the language. At present, the national Gaelic resource centre Stòrlann Nàiseanta na Gàidhlig has no resources for the production of materials for adult learners.

Similarly, while Gaelic local authority community education projects may apply for funding under the Specific Grants for Gaelic Education scheme, the scheme's budget is relatively small, being £4,114,000 per annum in 2006–7, with the large majority of funding under the scheme currently going to primary and secondary education.

The lack of funding and, arguably, of priority allocated to Gaelic for learners by the Executive can also be seen from the level of direct government funding to the Gaelic learners' association CLI, which received just £22,000 in 2000–01. In the same year far larger amounts were given to two associations far less closely linked to the intergenerational transmission of Gaelic: £100,000 was allocated to An Comunn Gaidhealach, organisers of the Mòd, and £128,000 to the Columba Initiative, which aims to foster cultural and linguistic ties between Gaelic-speaking Scotland and Ireland (Taskforce on the Public Funding of Gaelic 2000: 32).

Bòrd na Gàidhlig has now taken over responsibility for distribution of grant funding to most areas of Gaelic development, with the exception of the Gaelic Broadcasting Fund and Specific Grants for Gaelic Education scheme. Funding for Gaelic development has also increased overall. The Bòrd has increased the financial support for Clì Gàidhlig to over £60,000. Even so, the Gaelic for adults sector still receives only a relatively small proportion of Gaelic development funding, as can be seen from Bòrd na Gàidhlig's annual reports (Bòrd na Gàidhlig 2004, Bòrd na Gàidhlig 2005). It should be remembered, however, that Bòrd na Gàidhlig has only been in existence for around two years and that it has not yet published its national plan for Gaelic, which will determine future Gaelic development priorities. It could be, therefore, that the Gaelic for adults sector will be afforded higher priority and funding in future. It is certainly to be hoped that this will be the case.

An expansion in specific grant funding available, an increase in the direct funding to Gaelic learners' organisations, and the allocation of funding to the national Gaelic resource centre for the production of Gaelic learners resources would all help enable the creation of a more effective Gaelic learning infrastructure.

Strategic Co-ordination and Planning

A lack of co-ordination of a language planning based approach and of an overall development policy for Gaelic has been identified as the key characteristic and weakness of RLS efforts in Scotland (McLeod 1999; Lo Bianco 2001: 7; Taskforce on Public Funding of Gaelic 2000). This has led two government-appointed taskforces on Gaelic to recommend a language planning approach for future Gaelic development efforts (Taskforce on Public Funding of Gaelic 2000, Ministerial Advisory Group on Gaelic 2002).

With regard to education, CnaG have argued that there is currently a lack of strategic co-ordination at all levels, including the adult learners' sector and in response have recommended a national policy for Gaelic education (CnaG 1997c). As seen during the course of this chapter, a lack of co-ordination is particularly notable within the adult learners sector. In 1992, *Feumalachdan* concluded that "provision for adult Gaelic learners is fragmented, lacks co-ordination and needs a more structured approach" and called for "immediate steps be taken by Comunn na Gàidhlig, CLI and other Gaelic development agencies together with local authorities to work out a co-ordinated strategy aimed at securing effective provision for Gaelic learners at all levels" (CnaG/CLI 1992: 65, 67).

In 2006, the situation has changed little. No co-ordinated Gaelic learners' strategy has been drawn up. Gaelic classes and courses are still provided by a range of different providers such as colleges, local authorities, individuals and Gaelic organisations, a situation which makes the teaching of Gaelic to adults difficult to co-ordinate or to plan for strategically either on the local or on the national scale. This lack of co-ordination, in combination with the funding difficulties identified above, means that there are serious gaps in provision such as a shortage of classes at advanced levels, a lack of diversity and flexibility in available learning opportunities and a high level of regional variation.

As discussed above, the national Gaelic learners' organisations Clì Gàidhlig, CLDRG and Lìon are currently in no position to co-ordinate or strategically plan for the improvement of the Gaelic learning infrastructure to any significant extent due to a shortage of funding and staff and a lack of power over areas such as fund allocation. This situation has left something of vacuum on the national scale, with no group able to co-ordinate and strategically direct the Gaelic learning infrastructure or to tackle issues such as tutor training or learning resource production which require a national rather than a local solution.

The creation of Bòrd na Gàidhlig to develop Gaelic by means of a language planning approach and the charging of the Bòrd under the *Gaelic Language (Scotland) Act 2005* with drawing up a national plan for Gaelic could enable the injection of more co-ordination and strategic direction to the Gaelic learners sector. It remains to be seen, however, whether the national plan and Bòrd will give priority to the Gaelic for adults sector.

Possible Solutions

For a truly co-ordinated strategy and infrastructure, it would be necessary for Gaelic groups to have more control over the Gaelic development infrastructure, something which would be most effectively done through having some say over the distribution of government funding for higher, further and community education Gaelic provision for adults.

One possible framework would be to establish a national consortium for adult Gaelic learners based on the model of the eight Welsh for Adults consortia in Wales.[77] Each Welsh for Adults consortium brings together all providers of Welsh classes for adults in a particular area in order to determine the function of each provider and develop a joint approach to organising and marketing the courses. Each consortium draws up a strategic plan every three years in addition to an annual plan of action. This approach is intended to avoid duplication of effort and gaps in provision and to ensure maximum co-ordination, with the expansion of the numbers of fluent Welsh speakers as a clear overall goal.[78]

The membership of a national Gaelic adult learners consortium could include colleges, community education departments and other providers of Gaelic courses and Gaelic development organisations. Such a consortium could be charged with drawing up plans for the provision of those classes which receive government funding. The plans would aim to ensure that there was no duplication of effort or

---

[77] Due to the smaller number of learners and providers of services in Scotland one consortium might suffice initially.

[78] For more details of the Welsh for Adults Consortia, see the Welsh Language Board website: www.bwrdd-yr-iaith.org.uk.

gaps in provision (geographically or in terms of types of courses offered) and that all efforts have the goal of RLS in mind.

To ensure participation of class providers and to ensure the maximum co-ordination of different Gaelic classes, the learners' consortium would have to have some power over the financing of Gaelic courses. It might therefore be suggested that any applications for government funding for adult learners classes would have to be approved by the consortium before being allowed to proceed to the government for consideration, whether this be for Specific Grant funding or for further education funding. Any proposals which were not compatible with the consortium's strategy would not receive approval.

An increased weighting in the funding for further education Gaelic courses and an increase in the Specific Grant budget as recommended above would enable the expansion in provision for adult learners. If this should happen, the learners' consortium/consortia would be able to invite colleges and community education departments in areas lacking provision for learners' courses to make bids for funding and to advise them on such matters.

This consortium could be based upon the model of Lìon, serviced by a full-time Lìon officer employed by Clì Gàidhlig. Alternatively, such a Gaelic learning consortium might come directly within the remit of Bòrd na Gàidhlig.

In 1999 Lìon recommended that a study be commissioned into the Gaelic learners' infrastructure in order to inform the "formulation of a coherent strategy and the creation of a dedicated and responsive infrastructure" for adult learners (1999). The consultancy remit developed recommends "a review of the overall strategy for Gaelic language acquisition and to make recommendations for a national development strategy to be presented to the Scottish Parliament and Executive". This review would consider the role and effectiveness of providers of courses at all levels, the relationship between, and functions of CLI, CnaG and Lìon and the support structures required to meet learners' needs and aspirations, including the possible establishment of a Gaelic language acquisition agency to develop and implement a national policy at all levels. Other areas to be considered in the proposed review are current funding mechanisms and future funding strategy, the integration of the Gaelic learners' sector into the overall Gaelic infrastructure, the effecting of closer engagement with the Gaelic communities within the adult learning sphere, and the scope of provision of courses and resources for Gaelic learners. Although this research proposal did not receive funding and did not go ahead, there can be no doubt that a study of this type would be invaluable in informing the learning infrastructure of the future and it is to be strongly recommended that funding be made available to carry out such important research.[79]

It may well be that such a review would come up with different organisational recommendations from those tentatively made above. Whatever decision might be made on the form of infrastructure required, however, it is very clear that an expansion in the number of people employed in promoting the learning of Gaelic for adults and in the amount of money available for adult learners will be necessary if more adults are to learn and to become fluent in Gaelic. It is also clear that structures will be necessary to improve the co-ordination of provision.

It is important too that any strategy for Gaelic learners be closely linked to an overall strategy for Gaelic education and for Gaelic development in general to ensure

---

[79] A detailed study of this type was carried out on the Welsh for Adults sector in 2003 (Powell and Smith 2003).

that Gaelic learners provision is viewed and treated as an integral part of Gaelic development as a whole rather than as a discrete and perhaps peripheral area. This ties in with the view of Comunn na Gàidhlig (1997c) and the Ministerial Advisory Group for Gaelic (2002) that a Gaelic education strategy and an overall plan for the language are needed. It is to be hoped that this will be the case in the national plan for Gaelic which Bòrd na Gàidhlig have been charged with drawing up.

Conclusion

The 14 years since 1992 have seen both great change and great continuity in the infrastructure for Gaelic learners. Gaelic broadcasting has been significantly upgraded, published Gaelic courses have improved in their range and Clì Gàidhlig has considerably expanded. The most significant advances have been the development of immersion courses (bearing in mind, however, these are still few in number and that many of them have now folded) and the Sabhal Mòr Ostaig Gaelic access course. For the first time, these courses have offered some learners the opportunity to become fluent in a short time. Advances aside, however, such expansion of provision as has been achieved has taken place within the existing uncoordinated framework.

Feumalachdan Luchd-Ionnsachaidh concluded that "provision for adult Gaelic learners is fragmented, lacks co-ordination and needs a more structured approach" (CnaG/CLI 1992: 65). This conclusion is just as valid in 2006 as it was in 1992. The key recommendation of the 1992 study was that "immediate steps be taken by Comunn na Gàidhlig, CLI and other Gaelic development agencies together with local authorities to work out a co-ordinated strategy aimed at securing effective provision for Gaelic learners at all levels" (CnaG/CLI 1992: 67). While there was for a time increasing co-operation between groups through Lìon, this was short-lived and there is still nothing resembling a co-ordinated strategy for Gaelic learners at all levels. Provision is still largely ad hoc and uncoordinated, with no overall steering mechanism but a bewildering range of groups and institutions having a range of distinct but overlapping responsibilities.

While *Feumalachdan Luchd-Ionnsachaidh* led to the establishment of a Gaelic learners' development officer and later to the appointment of a CLI director, and while media provision for learners has increased, other priority reforms recommended by the report have failed to be implemented. Tutor training, where an expansion was envisaged, is still very limited and piecemeal and there is still no resource centre for learners. The proposed setting-up of Gaelic social groups has also failed to progress to any significant extent.

The effect of the gaps and inadequacies of the Gaelic learning infrastructure identified is quite simply that few Gaelic learners are able to reach fluency in the language. The failure of all but very few learners to reach fluency is an characteristic feature of the Gaelic learning scene and has been documented in a number of studies, including chapter 5 in the present study (MacNeil and MacDonald 1997, Wells 1997, Robertson 2001a). While immersion courses and Gaelic-medium courses have enabled larger numbers of Gaelic learners than ever before to reach fluency in the language, the numbers of learners reaching fluency are still very small both in absolute numbers, numbering dozens rather than hundreds each year, and as a percentage of all Gaelic learners. Development of such intensive courses has also been very slow and uneven. From the point of view of RLS, learners are simply not reaching fluency in sufficient numbers to make up for the numbers of Gaelic learners lost each year. Census data indicates that over 700 new Gaelic speakers would have to be created each year to maintain numbers of Gaelic speakers at their current level. While no research has yet been carried out into the number of adult learners reaching fluency, there can be no doubt that there are fewer than 700 per year. In fact, it is likely that fewer than 700 adult learners have learned the language to fluency in total.

Rather than being central to Gaelic RLS, the infrastructure for Gaelic learning is, in fact, peripheral in many respects. At present this sector is uncoordinated and ineffective in bringing more than a small number of learners to fluency each year. The Gaelic learning infrastructure is also peripheral in terms of its level of funding, both in absolute terms and in comparison with other sectors of Gaelic development such as Gaelic-medium education. Another mark of the peripherality of the Gaelic learners sector has been the lack of development in this sector within the last decade.

These facts point to the continued need for an overall strategy and institutional framework for Gaelic learning as part of a broader strategy for the language. The aim of any learners' strategy should be to increase the number of Gaelic learners and to increase the proportion of learners becoming fluent. It is important that any strategy for learners be closely linked to an overall RLS strategy to ensure that the importance of learners to other fields of Gaelic development, such as parenting Gaelic-speaking children, filling Gaelic-related jobs and consuming Gaelic products and services, is recognised.

A strategy for learners would have to cover a variety of areas. In the first place, increased co-ordination would be required between all the various different groups and institutions providing classes, courses and other services to learners, as will an appropriate infrastructure and funding structure to ensure such co-ordination. This will require a great expansion of the organisational infrastructure for Gaelic learning. This is a matter which will require further research and it is to be hoped that a study of this area of the type proposed by Lìon over six years ago will go ahead.

To increase numbers of fluent learners, a strategy would require greater flexibility in Gaelic courses, with courses of various types and degrees of intensity being available, offering clear routes of progression and funding structures and enabling access to the maximum number of people. Closely linked with this is the need for a national tutor training scheme. A strategy for the identification and filling of gaps in the production of learning and teaching materials for learners will also have to be determined.

A strategy should be concerned with Gaelic learning for adults in the very broadest sense, looking at all relevant factors from primary school education to satellite broadcasting. It should not only be concerned with existing learners, but also with the attraction of new learners to the language.

In summary, it might be argued that while progress has been made in the infrastructure for Gaelic learners, an outer limit has been reached in the amount achievable within the present framework. If fluent Gaelic learners are to emerge in significantly increased numbers and to be tied in with broader RLS goals, a new framework will be necessary.

4: The Social Identity of Gaelic Learners

> It is difficult for you who are born Welsh-speakers to understand how much the language can mean to us who are born without it.
> (Welsh learner, quoted in Thomas 1971: 116).

Introduction

While the learning of a language is a fundamentally social phenomenon, very little has so far been written on the social experience of learning Gaelic as an adult, whether from a sociological, sociolinguistic or anthropological viewpoint. Only one paper directly addressing the social identity of the adult Gaelic learner has been published to date (Morgan 2000) with other authors such as Chapman, Dorian, S. Macdonald, Fraser and Rogerson and Gloyer having touched upon the subject during the course of broader works (Chapman 1978, Chapman 1992, Dorian 1970, 1979, Fraser 1989, Glaser 2004, 2006; S. Macdonald 1997, Oliver 2005, 2006; Rogerson and Gloyer 1995, Wmffre 2004). More has been written about the learners of other minority languages such as Welsh (e.g. Trossett 1986, Bowie 1993, Pritchard Newcombe 2002, Wmffre 2004) and Irish (e.g. Leyland 1996, McCoy 1997, Maguire 1991) from a social scientific viewpoint. This chapter will investigate the social identity of Gaelic learners, seeking to develop what has already been written on the subject in Scotland and making use of the existing literature on other minority languages. Material from the Gaelic Learners' Survey will be also be used and in parts I will supplement the material with my own knowledge of the Gaelic learning world.

This chapter will begin by investigating the relationship between learner and native speaker and will then look at the relationship between Gaelic learners and non-Gaelic speakers and, finally, at the broader question of what part learners come to occupy in the Gaelic community (however this might be defined) by virtue of learning Gaelic. The implication of the issues in question for RLS will also be considered.

The meaning of the terms 'learner' and 'native speaker'

As one of the central topics of this chapter is the relationship between Gaelic learners and native speakers, it is very important that these terms should be investigated at the outset. As noted in the Introduction, both the terms 'learner' and 'native speaker' and, indeed, even the term 'Gaelic-speaker' carry significant ambiguities in the early twenty-first century.

The term 'Gaelic learner' is normally used to describe a spectrum of people ranging from those in the very first stages of language learning to those who have learnt Gaelic to a very high level of fluency.[80] Due to this ambiguity, care will be taken in this chapter to distinguish between fluent or near-fluent learners on one hand and those with a lesser command of the language on the other where this distinction is of importance.

The expression 'native speaker' too conceals a variety of different abilities and backgrounds in the language.[81] Indeed, while it is very frequently used in common

---

[80] Wmffre 2004 makes a similar point regarding Welsh learners (2004: 150).
[81] Wmffre 2004 makes a similar point regarding Welsh native speakers (2004: 153).

parlance, the very concept of 'native speaker' is ambiguous and difficult to define (Davies 2003). Usually the term is used to refer to people who have been brought up speaking Gaelic as a sole or a joint first language, normally in a Gaelic-speaking community. As Gillies points out with relation to his university students, however:

> Where a century ago you were either a native speaker of Gaelic in the fullest sense, or you were not, nowadays we find increasing numbers of what one might call 'half-Gaelic speakers' – brought up with Gaelic speaking parents in the city, or with one Gaelic speaking parent in the Highlands, for instance (W. Gillies 1989: 19).

Almost 20 years later, even many children raised by two Gaelic-speaking parents in a Gaelic-speaking area might be added to Gillies' list of 'half-Gaelic speakers' (see also Hunter 1995: 13; Black 1999: xxiii; L. MacDonald 1999: 27). Ability in Gaelic varies greatly between different people brought up speaking Gaelic. While some speakers may be highly proficient in Gaelic over a wide range of registers, others, particularly those in younger age groups, can have a very imperfect knowledge of the language and its different registers and are often less fluent in Gaelic in all or most areas than they are in English. Contrary to previous practice, very few children in Gaelic-speaking households are now being raised as Gaelic-speaking monoglots in their pre-school years. Some children with two Gaelic speaking parents and living in houses where Gaelic is commonly spoken are not being raised as Gaelic speakers at all, with their parents relying on Gaelic-medium education to pass on a knowledge of Gaelic to their offspring.

It can be expected that these trends will continue in future, leading to further diversity in the linguistic ability of those described as native speakers. The situation will be complicated additionally as increasing numbers of young adults emerge from Gaelic-medium education having learnt their Gaelic at school and as fluent Gaelic learners raise children as Gaelic speakers.[82] It is likely, therefore, that the term 'native speaker' itself will in future become more ambiguous and that there will be growing debate over its definition as natives, learners and GME pupils draw ever closer together in terms of accent and linguistic ability. Though learners are an atypical minority at present, the formerly almost black-and-white native speaker/learner distinction will increasingly break down into a spectrum as highly fluent native speakers who have learned the language at home become less and less numerous. In a real sense, therefore, it is likely that most Gaelic speakers will be able to be described as learners in some sense by the end of the second or third decade of the 21st century.

As such, it can be argued that the term 'native speaker', like the term 'learner', encompasses a spectrum of people with varying backgrounds and abilities in the language. A failure to appreciate this diversity is common amongst learners (at least in the initial stages of learning Gaelic) and is often a factor affecting learner/native speaker relations.

Even the term 'Gaelic speaker' might cause misunderstanding. Virtually all English speakers in Scotland are fully fluent in English and are able to read and write the language as well as to speak it. It goes without saying that almost without exception, people who are able to speak English in Scotland do so regularly. Many who do not come from Gaelic-speaking communities, including Gaelic learners, can

---

[82] The latter group could perhaps be labeled 'neo-native speakers'.

fail to recognise that being a Gaelic speaker is not identical to being an English speaker in this respect. As has already been seen, ability in Gaelic is not uniform. Literacy rates in Gaelic are also low and many people who are able to speak Gaelic do so rarely, for particular purposes only, with certain people only, or not at all. As will be discussed below, failure to recognise these distinctions can also be an important factor affecting the nature of the relationship between Gaelic learners and those with some native ability in the language.

The various distinctions drawn above should be borne in mind in the following sections. Care will be taken, however, to define what is being meant by both 'native speaker' and 'learner' at any one time as far as possible so as to avoid confusion.

Gaelic Learners and Native Gaelic Speakers

In looking at the social identity of the Gaelic learner, the most significant relationship to be investigated is that between the native speaker and learner of Gaelic. This relationship can sometimes be an uneasy one.

A frequent complaint made by Gaelic learners is that native speakers can be unhelpful to learners, anti-learner and even anti-Gaelic (M. MacLeòid 1999, 2006a). An article in the Gaelic learners' magazine *Cothrom* entitled 'Despairing of Native Speakers' for example, accused native speakers of resenting learners, of being unhelpful to learners and of elitism (MacPhàdruig 1998). Such views are expressed not uncommonly in the magazine by its readers. Montgomery's study of Gaelic learners in Glasgow found that many learners shared such a view, finding native speakers "in general critical and negative" and accusing native speakers of having such qualities as a "keep off attitude to learners and some condescension" (Montgomery 1989: 79). CnaG and CLI's 1992 questionnaire survey of Gaelic learners also found that many learners felt this way, with native speakers being "variously described as being 'unhelpful', 'prone to mickey-taking' and 'unwilling to spend time with us'" (1992: 7, 12, 42). These findings comport with Moffat's assessment (1995: 21) and Fraser's 1989 study of parents involved in Gaelic-medium education, as well as the Gaelic Learners' Survey.[83]

While many learners would strongly disagree with any notion that native speakers are a hindrance to learners or to the wellbeing of Gaelic, the fact that so many learners are critical of native speakers makes the issue worthy of investigation. In the first place, however, it must be noted that this opinion is by no means universal (Morgan 2000: 129). It must also be noted that there is a geographical element to be considered. Gaelic speakers living in the Lowlands and in the cities are much more likely to have met with and to be experienced in speaking to and encouraging Gaelic learners than are those living in traditional Gaelic-speaking communities, where an encounter with a Gaelic learners is "a rarity and a novelty" (Morgan 2000: 129,132). Similarly, as learners in the Lowlands will normally meet native speakers through Gaelic-related activities, those whom they meet will mainly be enthusiastic about the language (see Fraser 1989: 374).

Complaints by learners regarding native speakers can be subdivided into two basic types. These are firstly that native speakers can be unhelpful towards Gaelic learners, and secondly that many native speakers do not want people to learn Gaelic and can be anti-Gaelic. Many examples of such views can be seen in Appendix 2.

---

[83] Examples of the views of Gaelic learners regarding native speakers can be seen in Chapter 5 and Appendix 2.

While these allegations are often made together in practice, it is important to separate them in theory as it does not follow, for example, that a native speaker who is unhelpful towards learners will necessary be anti-learner or anti-Gaelic.[84]

The sometimes uneasy relationship between learner and native speaker can be analysed at on two different levels. The first of these is on the level of relatively superficial communication problems and the second consists of the deeper sociological differences which exist between the two groups in terms of matters such as identity and views regarding Gaelic. The frequently heard claim that many native speakers are unhelpful to learners comes mainly under the heading of communication problems. Occasionally, of course, learners may meet with native speakers who are unhelpful due to a hostility to Gaelic learners or to an opposition to the promotion of Gaelic, but this will be examined later.

Non-fluent learners often argue that native speakers are unwilling to speak Gaelic to them or that their efforts to speak Gaelic are answered by replies in English. This leads many to ask "how can I become fluent in Gaelic when native speakers won't talk to me in Gaelic?" There can be no doubt that learners often do find it difficult to get native speakers to use Gaelic with them (Dorian 1979: 258, 1981: 98; Chapman 1992: 144; Montgomery 1989: 40; 84, Fraser 1989: 324; Ó Maolalaigh 2000; Cormack 2000). That this is not a new problem can be seen from the experiences of J. S. Blackie and Edward Dwelly, who reported similar difficulties in the late nineteenth and early twentieth centuries (Blackie 1882: 35; Dwelly 1994: IV). This phenomenon is not limited to Gaelic and has been documented for other minority languages (e.g. Trossett 1986: 169; Lloyd Humphreys 1992: 251; Kabel 2000: 135). While many learners do not understand the reasons for this, however, or even consider the failure to use Gaelic with learners to be a failing on the part of fluent speakers, the reasons for this situation are often uncomplicated.

Where the learner has friends or relatives who can speak Gaelic, language bonding will already have long since occurred, meaning that the Gaelic speaker is already used to speaking English with the relative/friend in question. To use basic or broken Gaelic when both people are used to speaking English to each other can seem very artificial to both participants in the conversation and can often lead to the use of English (S. Macdonald 1997: 138).[85] It is also unlikely that the native speaker will be accustomed to speaking with those who are learning Gaelic or best know how to best encourage the learner's skills.

Where non-fluent learners attempt to try their limited Gaelic on people with whom they are not well acquainted, similar problems frequently ensue. As previously stated, native speakers will not normally be used to speaking with those who are learning Gaelic and will often turn to English through not understanding what the learner has to say or through a desire to communicate more effectively. To hold a prolonged conversation in very basic Gaelic with a non-advanced learner is likely to prove embarrassing to a native speaker. As Trossett has argued:

> language learners are essentially like small children in their linguistic ability: they need to be spoken to fairly simply, to have a chance to repeat what is said to them, and to be corrected when they make mistakes. Because most Welsh learners are mature adults, it is

---

[84] This point is also made with regard to native Breton speakers by Lloyd Humphreys (1992: 251).
[85] For similar points regarding Welsh and Irish, see Trossett 1986: 173; Maguire 1991: 112.

embarrassing for everyone concerned for them to be treated like infants. Therefore both the learners and the native speakers are likely to opt for the English language in which they can interact according to their appropriate social level of maturity (1986: 171).

Speaking Gaelic to a non-advanced learner in such circumstances means that the medium of the conversation takes priority over the content. This is not a choice which is likely to be favoured by most fluent speakers, with the result that English is often used with learners (Trossett 1986: 171, Kabel 2000: 135).

In addition to not being accustomed to using Gaelic with adult learners, many native speakers will not be used to using the language with anybody other than members of their immediate family and local community. In particular, many native speakers will be unaccustomed to using Gaelic with strangers. These factors also can often lead to the use of English.

Another factor which may lead native speakers to use English with non-advanced Gaelic learners is the fact that very few learners become fluent in Gaelic. Experience of people who have attended Gaelic classes and subsequently dropped out or who have remained perpetual beginners may have given some Gaelic speakers the impression that learners all speak very basic Gaelic, simply do not achieve fluency and, therefore, that there is little point in speaking to them in Gaelic. For this reason, even advanced or fluent learners might find their ability in the language underestimated by native speakers who may turn to English when this is unnecessary (Trossett 1986: 169, 175; Ó Maolalaigh 2000). Conversely, but for the same reasons, native speakers might often exaggerate the achievements of non-fluent learners with whom they are acquainted given that they may have low expectations of what learners can achieve and given that Gaelic is often perceived to be difficult due to the lack of learners becoming fluent (Trossett 1986: 175).

An additional difficulty is that non-fluent learners in the initial stages of learning are unlikely to understand the varying shades of the term 'native speaker' as discussed above. Learners might not appreciate that individuals who can speak Gaelic might actually prefer and/or be more proficient in English. They might also fail to appreciate that some people whom they believe to be Gaelic speakers might be passive bilinguals or semi-speakers rather than fluent Gaelic speakers or that many younger Gaelic speakers do not consider it to be 'cool' to be seen speaking Gaelic. Low literacy levels also mean that many fluent speakers are unable to answer the classic learners' question of 'how do you spell that?' Like most monolingual English speakers, most Gaelic speakers will also be unable to explain the grammar of their language to others.

Trossett has argued that Welsh learners are often seen by others primarily in their capacity as Welsh learners: "learners are perceived mainly in terms of what they have done: as 'the learning of Welsh' rather than as 'people who are learning Welsh'" (1986: 174). A similar case could be made that Gaelic learners tend to see native speakers primarily in their role as Gaelic speakers; as a language resource, rather than as individuals. It could be argued that those at early stages of learning Gaelic often expect too much of native speakers. MacPhàdruig for example has argued that "many learners regard native speakers as role models and even as objects of near-worship" (1998: 14).[86] With such high expectations, reality often disappoints when learners are

---

[86] See also Montgomery 1989: 78.

unable to find any native speakers with whom to converse or when they find that many native speakers will not hold sustained conversations with them in Gaelic. Meeting native speakers who are unwilling to speak Gaelic or, more rarely, who mock the efforts of learners can severely dent the self-confidence of a learner and his/her determination to continue learning.[87]

It is likely that the situation described above will gradually change both due to the shifting demography of the Gaelic community and the implementation of measures to improve the native-speaker/learner relationship. At present there are relatively few Gaelic learners of any kind and very few fluent Gaelic learners, the latter of these groups probably only numbering a few hundred and the former only a few thousand. These groups are both vastly outnumbered by native Gaelic speakers (Galloway 1995b; W. Gillies 1987: 27; McLeod 1998c, 2000b; MacAulay 1994: 43). The development of Gaelic immersion courses and other intensive courses will produce fluent Gaelic learners in increasing numbers and will provide native Gaelic speakers with examples of people who have learnt Gaelic to a sufficient level to converse easily. This will make native speakers more accustomed to learners. Learners having studied Gaelic through immersion courses will also be better able to make use of native speakers by easily being able to strike up and continue conversations in Gaelic without causing alienation.

A key advantage of the immersion courses is that they bring learners to a meaningful level of fluency within the college environment and in a short period of time. This means that learners are more easily able to converse with native speakers on completion of the course and that native speakers are less likely to be exposed to near-beginners. Intensive Gaelic courses such as immersion courses reduce the dependency of learners on native speakers and encourage a more fruitful relationship between the two groups. Social factors such as these would be worthy of consideration in the drawing-up of any future national strategy for Gaelic learning.[88]

Increased teaching of Gaelic in the Western Isles in summer schools and the like would also make more native speakers used to dealing with Gaelic learners. This has happened in the Irish Gaeltacht, for example, where summer Irish courses for children and adults have made native speakers used to meeting learners and have acted as a source of income (Maguire 1991: 155; Ó Maolalaigh 2000). As Hindley has pointed out, however, such courses can, if carried out on a large scale, be a double-edged sword, both through increasing the amount of English spoken in the Gaeltacht and through reinforcing the perception that learners do not become fluent, given that the majority of students are beginner or intermediate level students (Hindley 1990).

Recommendations are made elsewhere in this study for a training scheme for the tutors of adult learners and for the production of a 'how to learn Gaelic' book or booklet. Any such training scheme could encourage tutors to teach some basic background information about native Gaelic speakers and their relationship with the language as described above. Tutors could teach their students, for example, that not all Gaelic speakers can read/write Gaelic or actually use their Gaelic, or are helpful to learners or strongly supportive of the language. Such information should also be included in any 'how to learn Gaelic' book/booklet.

Having looked at some of the more superficial differences affecting the relationship between Gaelic learners and native speakers it is now necessary to look at the situation in more depth. As has already been seen, many learners feel that native

---

[87] A similar point regarding Irish is made by Maguire (1990: 155).
[88] For discussion of the prospect of a Gaelic learners' strategy, see Chapter 3, "The Gaelic Learning Infrastructure".

speakers do not want others to learn Gaelic and that they can be 'anti-Gaelic'. This section will investigate both the negative and the more positive aspects of the learner/native speaker relationship and will touch upon the relevance of this to RLS efforts. While discussion so far has centred on non-fluent learners, this section will look more closely at fluent or near-fluent learners.

It has already been seen that native speakers are mainly unaccustomed to meeting Gaelic learners due to the relatively small number of those learning Gaelic. A related factor is that native speakers are also typically unaccustomed to meeting Gaelic speakers who come from a different background to their own (Morgan 2000: 132). As McLeod has pointed out:

> A high proportion of Gaelic speakers, relative to the UK's other autochthonous languages communities, are native speakers born and brought up in Gaelic-speaking communities in the Hebrides and west Highlands. It would be safe to say that at least 90% of Gaelic speakers come from such backgrounds whereas the Welsh language community contains significant proportions of learners and non-traditional speakers. In the case of Gaelic, then, there is a very significant link between the ability to speak the language and a distinct culture and way of life, and the language is the badge of a community that has long been outside the societal mainstream (1998c).[89]

Not only are all remaining Gaelic-speaking areas rather homogeneous, but they also differ from the rest of Scotland in many respects:

> Although the principal factor differentiating the Gaels from other Scots is the use of the Gaelic language itself, it can well be argued that the language is actually the medium of a distinct and separate culture, manifested in a variety of ways including deep-rooted traditions of poetry, song and music, and unique forms of religious worship. To some extent at least, this distinctiveness extends to material existence as well, the present-day crofting communities remaining substantially different in their way of life from the highly urbanised Scottish mainstream (1998c).

As Trossett has indicated, "no one speaks a language in isolation from other people; to learn a language is to enter a community of people who speak it" (1986: 6). As the vast majority of Gaelic learners hail from the Lowlands or from anglicised areas of the Highlands, most learners are seeking to enter a community from which they significantly differ. Morgan has graphically illustrated this through his description of:

> Neo-Gaels who don't cut peat, don't have a love-hate relationship with CalMac ferries, don't think that the world revolves around on a Glasgow-Stornoway axis, don't think that West is best. Few can aspire to be island crofters and most would probably not want to (2000: 131).

---

[89] Wmffre by contrast has estimated that native speakers and learners of Gaelic (in which he includes both adult learners and those learning Gaelic through GME) are roughly equal in number (2004: 157). However, this estimate is fundamentally flawed as it is based on the mistaken assumption that the 45% of Gaelic speakers based in the Lowlands are mainly non-native speakers.

By learning Gaelic, learners are displaying what represents a badge of community to Gaelic speakers without actually being members of that community or exhibiting its attributes. They do not demonstrate the normal link between the ability to speak the language and the possession of a distinct culture and way of life as referred to above. In her study of Highland by-names, Dorian, herself a fluent learner of Gaelic, pointed out some of the consequences of an outsider learning Gaelic:

> By learning the local dialect I became the only exception to an otherwise hard-and-fast rule that use of the local Gaelic is synonymous with blood membership in the group. That is to say that I became a bizarre phenomenon, a speaker competent in a linguistic system but incompetent in the social system underlying it. (1970: 306)

While Dorian is here referring to the moribund East Sutherland dialect, her comments could also be applied to Gaelic in general. Dorian has further noted that many Gaelic speakers in East Sutherland found it very difficult to comprehend that total outsiders with no blood connections to the community should learn the language (1979: 258).

Trossett has identified a similar phenomenon with respect to Welsh learners and has explained this situation in terms of a conceptual duality in the minds of Welsh speakers between the 'Welsh' and the 'English', whereby the 'Welsh' are native Welsh speakers and the 'English' are monoglot English speakers, including Welsh people who do not speak Welsh (1986: 172).

Welsh learners do not readily fit into either of these categories: "Welsh learners [...] are a group for which there is no category. Learners are 'English' people who speak Welsh, and that without being either fluent or native Welsh speakers, thereby defying all the basic tenets of the classification" (1986: 172). While Trossett has argued that the fluent learner can "come closer to acquiring some sort of Welsh identity", even becoming fluent is no guarantor that the learner will become reclassified as 'Welsh', and ambiguity is likely to remain (Bowie 1993). Trossett has also blamed the lack of a concept of an 'English' person able to speak Welsh in part for the common failure of Welsh speakers to speak the language to learners.

Learners upset the traditional perception that people either speak Welsh natively or do not speak Welsh at all. Learners may speak Welsh despite coming from a different background from most native speakers and can participate in Welsh language only events despite having learnt the language. For these reasons, Bowie has argued that "there is a sense in which the Welsh learner remains the 'joker in the pack', fitting neatly neither into the English nor the Welsh category" (1993: 171).

The situation in Scotland could be said to be similar to that of Wales, with a conceptual duality existing in the minds of native Gaelic speakers between Gaelic speakers and English speakers. The former are Gaelic speakers who come from a homogeneous background and are native speakers of the language.[90] The latter are monolingual English speakers who do not speak any Gaelic. Such a conceptual system does not properly address Gaelic learners, who fit into neither category. This is particularly the case for fluent learners. For these reasons, it seems highly unusual to many native Gaelic speakers that there should be Gaelic speakers who have learned the language, who have come from very different backgrounds and who might be

---

[90] Passive bilinguals and semi-speakers of Gaelic from the same background would also fit into this category.

unfamiliar with aspects of Gaelic culture such as Gaelic church services or Gaelic song or who might speak the language with a non-Highland accent.

Trossett argued in 1986 that it was possible that Welsh speakers would develop a mental category for Welsh learners in the future should the numbers of learners increase and that some had already developed such a concept (Trossett 1986: 173). The numbers of Welsh learners have indeed increased greatly since Trossett's article was written with recent figures showing that only 54% of speakers have learned the language at home (Welsh Language Board 2006: 23). While a majority of those learning Welsh outside the home have learned at school, there are nonetheless substantial numbers of adult learners of the language, though as in Scotland, there is a high drop-out rate (Wmffre 2004: 158).

In Scotland too, there can be no doubt that some native speakers have developed a mental category for learners. While this is probably only the case for a minority at present, it is likely that many more Gaelic speakers will develop such a category in future as more learners become fluent and as larger numbers of people take up learning.

In addition to helping explain why native speakers often do not speak Gaelic to learners and can find it difficult to relate to learners, the difference in background between native Gaelic speakers and most Gaelic learners also helps to explain many of the differences between the two groups in terms of their perception and use of the language. Gaelic, like other languages, can be invested with various different meanings by different people who speak the language (Chapman 1978, Chapman 1992, Bowie 1993, Malcolm 1997, McCoy 1997, McDonald 1989, S. Macdonald 1997). Macdonald has demonstrated that there is no uniform native speaker perception of Gaelic and it could similarly be argued that there is no single learner perception (S. Macdonald 1997, Morgan 2000).[91] Even so, noticeable differences between learners and native speakers can be identified when these groups are taken as a whole.

As native speakers generally come from communities in which Gaelic is spoken it is natural that many should mainly associate the language with the area from which they come, the lifestyle of that area and the way in which the language is used there. Macdonald has demonstrated this in relation to the Gaelic-speaking community on the Isle of Skye which she studied in the 1980s (S. Macdonald 1997). For many native speakers in Gaelic-speaking areas, using Gaelic is an everyday, normal, unselfconscious activity which merits little consideration and is taken for granted. As identities, including local or national identities, draw on a variety of different factors, native speakers do not always see Gaelic as a key component of their identity, though many do (S. Macdonald 1997).

For Gaelic learners, the situation is very different. Learning Gaelic is a conscious decision and becoming fluent in Gaelic requires a great deal of commitment and motivation. It is unsurprising, therefore, that many have given a great deal of consideration to Gaelic issues and feel very strongly about the language, often exhibiting the zeal of the convert (Morgan 2000: 128; Wells 1996a: 1; Moffat 1995: 21). It is also the case that most learners tend to visualise the significance of the language in national or Highland terms rather in terms of any particular community. As the results of the Gaelic Learners' Survey demonstrate, not only do most learners strongly support the language, but most are motivated partially or wholly by identity-related reasons such as national identity or a desire to become closer to their roots. Very few

---

[91] See also the discussion of learners' attitudes to the language in Chapter 5.

learn Gaelic for mainly instrumental reasons. People who purposefully learn Gaelic may see it as being central to their identity in a way that native speakers might not. As learners tend not to come from Gaelic communities where the language is in palpable decline, many can also see the decline of the language as being less natural or inevitable than might native speakers.

Given that these qualities are commonly exhibited by learners of minority languages, Trossett has suggested that such learners can act as language consciousness raisers. She has argued that:

> Unlike Welsh speakers learning English, Welsh learners are *not* motivated by practical necessity; instead, their voluntary acquisition of the minority language is an expression of their respect for the Welsh-speaking community and is significant of a desire to prevent the impending death of the Welsh language. [...] Learning Welsh constitutes an affirmation of Welsh-Wales to continue to exist, and the existence of Welsh learners is indicative of the possibility of its doing so (1986: 174).

By learning Welsh, according to Trossett, learners are demonstrating to others that they are concerned about the future wellbeing of the language. By doing so, learners may lead native speakers to think about the state of the language and about their own relationship to it (1986: 175).

It could easily be argued that Gaelic learners in Scotland can play a similar role given the numerous learners involved in Gaelic promotion and in Gaelic events, societies, campaigns and the like on a national or a local scale and given the high levels of motivation and commitment which they bring to the language.[92] By learning Gaelic, learners may bring new perspectives to the language, encourage native speakers to see the language in a new light and give them more hope for its future survival. Some of the enthusiasm for the language might also rub off on native speakers with whom learners come into contact. This is clearly a positive contribution of Gaelic learners to language maintenance efforts. The sort of positive impact which learners can have through consciousness-raising is hinted at from the following comment by Kenna Campbell, herself a native speaker, in which she discusses recent language developments:

> many of these innovative ideas originate from the increasingly numerous body of the non-Gaelic learners of the language, who do not have the built in "blessed is he who expecteth little" attitude to matters Gaelic that many of the native population tend to have. Consequently, more attention has been focused on the importance of Gaelic not only to the Gaels as their birthright and identity, but to Scotland as a whole as a key to its past and present, and also possibly to its future (1993: 13).

In making native speakers think about their language, however, and in symbolising respect for and the possible survival of that language, the consciousness-raising function of learners can also lead to less positive results where they encounter native speakers with less favourable views towards the language or who view the language in a very different light from themselves.

---

[92] For a similar point regarding Irish language learners, see Leyland 1996: 153.

Being outsiders to Gaelic-speaking communities means that learners often do not understand that not all native speakers see the language in the same terms as they do. As Morgan points out, "The learner [...] may not appreciate that the native speaker might have mixed or no feelings about the language" (Morgan 2000: 128). Speaking Gaelic natively, after all, is no guarantee that any given individual will be supportive of Gaelic in general or of any particular measures to support the language. Many native speakers will simply use Gaelic as an unselfconscious means of communication, not having given very much thought to issues such as the status or future of the language (Chapman 1978: 216, 227). Gaelic speakers may also have fatalistic or ambivalent attitudes regarding the language or even be opposed to its promotion (S. Macdonald 1997). Such ambivalent feelings have been described by Gillies as a "passionate war of attrition between a passionate devotion to the language of one's forefathers, homeland and childhood, and an equally strong motivation to escape from it as a bar to success and fulfilment" (W. Gillies 1987: 29). Fraser has similarly argued that:

> Within the last century the attitudes of the Gaelic speaking community seem dominated by a perception of Gaelic culture as a personal or local aberration with strong sentimental connections but less and less practical relevance within the ever-widening parameters of modern society. This attitude has by no means been completely dispelled amongst today's young people (1989: 349).

Such feelings are still very common among Gaelic communities and are related to factors such as the traditional lack of economic value in the language, the former discouragement of Gaelic in education, the memory of the stigma and disadvantages of monolingualism in Gaelic, the shrinkage of the domains in which Gaelic might be used and to unfavourable attitudes towards Gaelic outwith Gaelic-speaking areas (MacKinnon 1972: 127; MacKinnon 1984: 499; M. MacLeòid 1999; CnaG 1997b: 15; MacAulay 1994: 37; Chapman 1978: 12; Fraser 1989: 349).[93]

As most learners come from outside Gaelic-speaking communities, few will exhibit the love-hate relationship with the language or the fatalism as to the language's future which characterises many native speakers. Meeting native speakers who are hostile or indifferent to Gaelic is often a great disappointment to Gaelic learners who, as mentioned above, tend to view native speakers as being authentic representatives of the language and to value their views accordingly.

Differing conceptions of a language and its importance can, therefore, be a cause of division and misunderstanding between learners and natives. This has been demonstrated in Brittany, for example, where McDonald has shown how native speakers of Breton tended to associate the language with family and community identities whereas many language activists, often learners, conceived the language in term of a broader nationalist and left-wing cause (M. McDonald 1989). Passionately committed learners might, therefore, find that native speakers of the language might not agree with them on linguistic matters. In Scotland, Sharon Macdonald has suggested that there is a division between those whom she terms 'Gaelic revivalists', who visualise Gaelic mainly as a national language and the native Gaelic speakers living in traditional Gaelic communities who often see the language more in terms of

---

[93] For a similar discussion of Breton speakers' often ambiguous attitudes to their language and its causes, see Press 1994.

the local community. While Macdonald does not properly define these 'Gaelic revivalists', it is clear that she feels that second-language speakers of Gaelic constitute a significant part of this group, and it can be seen from the results of the Gaelic Learners' Survey that most learners do indeed hold views which Macdonald terms 'revivalist', such as support for Gaelic-medium schooling, official status for Gaelic and Gaelic road-signs (S. Macdonald 1997, 1999).[94]

Many such policies, though widely supported by learners, often met with a less than supportive response in 'Carnan', the Gaelic-speaking area which she studied in the 1980s. Promotion of Gaelic could cause division in a community where many were unable to speak Gaelic and where many rated community unity as being more important than the language (see also MacKinnon 1984: 499; Rothach 2006: 236). Even those supportive of the 'Carnan' Gaelic playgroup and concerned with language maintenance tended to visualise Gaelic in the context of the local community, seemingly wishing to retain for Gaelic the role which it then held as the language of the home and of a few limited public uses rather than trying to bring the language into new domains such as signposts, education and official forms. While Macdonald's work goes on to point out that the people of 'Carnan' subsequently became more supportive of Gaelic promotion measures, her work has nonetheless helped to show that divisions can exist between the perceptions of Gaelic learners and native speakers.

Macdonald quotes one Gaelic-speaking 'Carnan' resident as being highly worried by Gaelic becoming 'middle class and posh' in the Lowlands:

> I like the Gaelic. But if it's going to become something artificial, then, well, I won't feel like speaking it at all. I don't want Gaelic to be kept alive by making it artificial ... For myself I'd prefer if it died (1997: 218).

Such a view, which according to Macdonald was not uncommon in 'Carnan', raises the important issue of the ownership of the language. By learning the language, Gaelic learners can appear to native speakers to be claiming joint ownership of the language, regardless of whether this is actually their intention (Morgan 2000: 128; Moffat 1995: 21; Chapman 1978: 148). This can cause resentment, with some native speakers feeling that learners have no right to the language. By seeking to use Gaelic in contexts where it would not normally be used in Gaelic communities, or by trying to promote Gaelic outwith traditional Gaelic communities, Gaelic learners might be seen by some native speakers as doing something which is 'artificial' or 'unnatural' or which is irrelevant to the 'real' Gaelic communities (M. MacLeòid 2006a).[95] In other words, Gaelic learners may be seen by native speakers as appropriating their language and using it in illegitimate contexts (Martin 1996: 7; MacCaluim forthcoming 2007; M. MacLeòid 2006a). This has led Wmffre to talk of a "struggle for power" between learners and native speakers for ownership of the Celtic languages (Wmffre 2004: 170).

---

[94] For a critical discussion of Macdonald's use of the term 'revivalist' see MacCaluim 1998b. This does not, however, affect the broader point that learners are generally supportive of measures which could be described as 'revivalist' and mostly see Gaelic as having national importance.

[95] For examples of such a view, see D. MacLeod 1998, 1999, 2002.

The fact that Gaelic learners might be seen by native speakers to be claiming joint ownership of the language does not necessarily mean that they are in fact attempting to do so, however. While many learners do feel that Gaelic belongs to them, many others feel that the language belongs to native speakers and can never really belong to even the fluent Gaelic learner.[96]

Whether consciously or not and whether intentionally or not, however, Gaelic learners are acting to redefine Gaelic. As Morgan has pointed out:

> There is a common unity to the existing communities on which religious and dialect differences have little impact. A unity in which pressures of relative isolation, harsh elements and poor land quality are shared, as is dependence on supplementary small-holding agriculture and dominance by large estates. Most even vote in the same constituency and are served by the same local authority, the Western Isles Council [...]. What threatens to dilute the strength of this modern-day ethnic identity is the increase in language users with a different experience (2000: 131).

Gaelic learners, as Morgan further points out, "have their own local cultures and traditions, their own economic and social patterns and, though each language carries an intrinsic heritage, their own perceptions of Gaelic's past and future" (2000: 131). By seeking to live these different experiences and ways of life through Gaelic, Gaelic learners necessarily introduce new perceptions of and uses of Gaelic which might not always be to the taste of native speakers (Oliver 2005). This can come about unconsciously due to the fact that learners come from different backgrounds from native speakers. It can also come about consciously, however, due to learners having a very different view of Gaelic or even through a more deliberate wish on their part to re-symbolise Gaelic.

It has already been argued that most fluent Gaelic learners speak the language without possessing many aspects of the culture or material lifestyle which normally accompanies fluency in Gaelic. Many learners have a deep interest in and respect for the culture and lifestyle of the Gaelic-speaking communities and may aspire to that culture and/or lifestyle, some learning Gaelic primarily for this reason. At the same time, many Gaelic learners are uninterested in many of the aspects of the Hebridean lifestyle and culture and can even be highly critical of them and actively favour a redefinition of what constitutes 'Gaelic culture', the meaning of the 'Gaelic community' and the significance of the Gaelic language itself. Some learners, for example, feel that traditional Gaelic music and song are irrelevant to modern Gaelic speakers. Much more commonly, Gaelic learners will see no place for Highland-style Presbyterianism in their vision of Gaelic, despite the fact that many islanders consider this to be central to their identity and closely linked to Gaelic. Also very common among learners is the perception of Gaelic as a national language rather than a local or Highland language. As one of Montgomery's sample of Gaelic learners argued: "Some native speakers think of Gaelic as *their* language. It is NOT – it belongs to the Scottish and Irish people" (1989: 79).

---

[96] It might be hypothesised that this fact has an effect on the participation of learners in RLS with some learners feeling that it is inappropriate for them to take actions such as publicly speaking out in favour of the language or becoming involved in certain RLS activities due to a feeling the language does not belong to them.

Some native speakers can be resistant to such a re-symbolisation of Gaelic. This can be due to the ambivalent or sceptical attitudes felt towards the language in general, but, as already noted, can also result from native speakers feeling that the use of their language by non-native speakers from very different backgrounds to their own to be cultural imperialism or artificial (D. MacLeod 2002, M. MacLeòid 2006a).

In addition to challenging native speakers' perceptions of the value and significance of the language, learners can also challenge the conventional views of where, when and with whom it is appropriate to use Gaelic and where it is appropriate to use English. This once again ties in with Trossett's concept of the learner as a consciousness-raiser. In Gaelic-speaking areas, Gaelic has long been used in a diglossic context, with English being used in some domains and Gaelic in others. Gaelic native speakers are used to this situation and understand the social conventions as to where each of the languages should be used. As Thomson has pointed out:

> It would probably be fair to say that only a very small minority [of Gaelic speakers] is familiar with, or can confidently handle, a wide range of Gaelic usage [...] the majority of Gaelic speakers use the language for everyday chat and gossip, household purposes, telling jokes and stories, perhaps talking of crops and sheep and fishing, and would think of it as a natural language for fank-day (a communal gathering for shearing and dipping sheep), for a visit to the pub, for church in some areas, basically for rather local and parochial purposes, and they would easily turn to a more mixed discourse, with a high degree of code-switching, if the conversation turned to politics, or consumer topics, or dress and fashion, etc. [...] Only a small minority would tend to insist on using Gaelic for a wide range of speaking and writing, and they would be regarded, often, as somewhat élitist or eccentric: their Gaelic might be referred to as 'deep' or 'difficult', or occasionally as 'artificial' (1994: 232).

A similar view is taken by Chapman:

> Gaelic has become associated with the familial, domestic, expressive and essentially 'non-serious' aspects of life, [...] English is by comparison associated with business, economics, education and the hard and rational outside world (1978: 217).[97]

Learners' views on where and how Gaelic should be used are normally very different as they have not been socialised into the unwritten rules of Gaelic communities as to where Gaelic should and should not be used. For monolinguals used to using one language for everything, or to bilinguals speaking two major languages, the fact that Gaelic should be used for some purposes and not for others can often seem absurd and unnecessary, particularly when this involves Gaelic speakers using English with one another. As a matter of principle, many learners also object to the fact that English rather than Gaelic is normally associated with and used for the more 'important' things in life (Cox 1998: 74). As Fraser has argued (1989: 360), and as is also suggested by the works of Chapman (1978), S. Macdonald (1997, 1999) and MacKinnon (1981),

---

[97] See also Black 1992:147.

Gaelic learners are more likely to view the matter of language and language policy as a political matter and a matter of human rights than are native speakers.

For these reasons, fluent Gaelic learners are typically just as likely to use Gaelic for more formal and more important matters as they are for the more everyday purposes referred to by Thomson (1994: 231).[98] Learners can also be more resistant to calques and English loanwords than native speakers. Learners also typically attach much more importance to the writing and reading of Gaelic than do native speakers with fluent learners of Gaelic being almost universally literate in the language as opposed to just over half of native speakers. Learners are also often to the forefront of campaigns to increase the usage and profile of Gaelic in public life, including dealings with public authorities, areas which are not always considered to be of the first order of importance by Gaelic campaigners who are native speakers and who are used to the exclusion of Gaelic from these areas.[99] An argument can be made, however, that while the views of learners and native speakers are often different, they may prove complementary in practice, with the different groups giving priority to different pro-RLS measures and often in different parts of the country in a way which benefits the language generally (Fraser 1989: 361; Montgomery 1989: 80).

While some disagreement can be caused between learners and native speakers over matters such as where it is appropriate to use Gaelic, this is clearly an area where Gaelic learners are acting as consciousness-raisers and sources of strength to RLS efforts. Linked closely to Trossett's concept of learners as consciousness-raisers is the argument touched upon by Fraser that Gaelic learners, as outsiders to Gaelic-speaking communities, can often be more objective about the language than native speakers who are used to the present situation of Gaelic (Fraser 1989: 60). In the linguistic matters and matters of language policy just discussed, learners often find it absurd that Gaelic speakers should use English with one another for certain matters, and that Gaelic has in the past been excluded from such areas as schooling, signage and government administration. More importantly, learners by their very nature as outsiders can sometimes perceive the linkage between the patterns of usage of Gaelic in communities and the language shift taking place in favour of English in a way that people raised in these communities cannot.

Discussing a Harris Gaelic community in the 1970s, MacKinnon argued that: "Bilinguals, within a situation of societal bilingualism see both of their languages as having their proper place and do not necessarily see language-contact in terms of power, domination or conflict" (1977: 170). The fact that many Gaelic learners, unlike the native bilinguals referred to above, see the relationship between Gaelic and English in *exactly these terms* is a strength which learners lend to RLS efforts.

---

[98] It might be hypothesised that Gaelic learners are, if anything, more likely to be more comfortable in using Gaelic for formal matters than for some varied everyday matters such as deep emotions, spiritual matters and sex due to the difficulty in learning the relevant vocabulary for these areas or in gaining opportunity to use Gaelic in some of these fields.

[99] Gaelic campaigning groups of the past such as Comann na Cànain Albannaich in the 1970s and Ceartas and Strì in the 1980s and Fàs in the early 2000s which laid great weight on such matters were mainly composed of learners as is Clì Gàidhlig, the association for Gaelic learners which has been very involved in campaigns for increased usage of Gaelic in public life. It is important not to exaggerate this tendency, however, for even if a far larger proportion of fluent Gaelic learners than native speakers are involved in Gaelic development and language activism, native speakers nonetheless form a clear majority of those involved in Gaelic promotion in areas such as education, broadcasting and language development in general.

Through doing so, learners can help to denaturalise social conventions concerning the use of Gaelic which are encouraging language shift.

This section has discussed areas of tension between native speakers and learners but has also attempted to show the more positive aspects of the relationship. Any such discussion will inevitably tend to accentuate the aspects of that relationship which are most worthy of comment rather than those which are most typical. It is useful, therefore, to stop at this point to evaluate the relative importance of the different tendencies. This is particularly important given that many influential commentators on Scottish Gaelic have tended to emphasise the differences and antagonisms between native and learner at the expense of similarities and solidarity and have tended to polarise the debate between revivalist learners on one hand and non-revivalist native speakers the other (Chapman 1978, 1992; Rogerson and Gloyer 1995). Such a distinction is an oversimplification.

As will be investigated further in the course of the discussion of Gaelic learners and their relationship to the 'Gaelic community' and the identity of 'Gael', it is important to reiterate that there is no one view of Gaelic among either native speakers or learners. While learners *tend* towards some views of the type which are described (somewhat ambiguously) as revivalist by Macdonald and native speakers *tend* towards more community-based views of the language, this is by no means universally true, as some learners have a community-based view of Gaelic and many native speakers a revivalist one. Many learners, for example, value Gaelic as the language of a particular community or of the Highlands, for example, and may not see the value in many proposals being made by Gaelic groups such as the right to use Gaelic in courts.[100] Conversely, many native speakers view Gaelic as a national language and support strong legislative measures for its promotion (see, for example, R. MacDonald 1993, A. P. Campbell 1999). There is also some evidence to suggest that the boundaries between these different views of Gaelic are tending to blur in practice.

As mentioned above, many native Gaelic speakers are very helpful to learners and supportive of attempts to promote Gaelic, encouraging and being encouraged by learners.[101] It is also the case that there is a geographical element to the relationship, with learners being more likely to meet highly enthusiastic Gaelic speakers and with native speakers being used to dealing with learners in the Lowlands, cities and large Highland towns. While native speakers in the Hebrides might be less used to meeting learners, this cannot be equated with a dislike of learners. Rather, the learner is very likely to find a great deal of encouragement even if less positive attitudes are sometimes encountered.

Any Gaelic learner who reaches fluency will meet both helpful and unhelpful Gaelic speakers and will encounter a variety of attitudes towards the language. Learning about the native speakers of Gaelic and their relationship with the language is itself a part of the process of learning Gaelic. This experience is best described by the following quotations from Gaelic learners.

Describing his fieldwork with the Linguistic Survey of Scotland in the 1950s in

---

[100] For an example of a community-based view of Gaelic from a fluent Gaelic learner, see Gordon Wells, letter to the editor, *Cothrom* 17, 1998.

[101] Trossett 1986: 168 "Welsh speakers are usually delighted when an outsider takes the trouble to try to learn Welsh. Learners receive a warm welcome in Welsh Wales, having by their effort demonstrated their respect and concern for the language and its survival." The same point is equally applicable to Scottish Gaelic speakers.

Highland Perthshire, Anthony Dilworth observed:

> In all these places I met people who loved their language and culture and welcomed you if you showed an interest in Gaelic and were pleased to help you; people who despised their language and despised others who were interested in it and wanted to learn it: people who had been belted at school for speaking Gaelic but had refused to give it up and people who regretted that their parents had kept it to themselves and so deprived them of their heritage. All in all it was a complex situation with a lot of complex attitudes. Isn't it high time some of the complex and self-destructive attitudes were sorted out? (Anthony Dilworth, letters, *West Highland Free Press*, 06.09.96).

A younger Gaelic learner, Niall Gòrdain, gave a similar account of his experiences:

> A thaobh nan Gaidheal fhèin, is cinnteach gun tig an neach-ionnsachaidh an cois a h-uile seòrsa: bidh feadhainn ann a tha cuideachail, is feadhainn nach eil. Chan e rud ùr annasach a tha seo! Am measg na chualas leamsa air feadh nam bliadhnaichean a dh' fhalbh, tha " 's e luchd na Beurla a bhruidhneas a' Ghàidhlig"; neo thuirt cailleach rium uaireigin, "why do you learners all pretend that you never spoke a word of English in your lives?" Bidh seo a' tachairt gus an tiormaich na cuantan – na gabhaibh dragh air, a luchd-ionnsachaidh chòir (Niall Gòrdain, letters, *Cothrom* 18, 1998).[102]

Gaelic Learners and Non-Gaelic Speakers

As previously discussed, Trossett has argued that learners can act as linguistic consciousness-raisers, promoting the use of the language amongst native speakers. She has further asserted that Welsh learners also serve as language consciousness-raisers amongst non-Welsh speakers (1986: 174).

By learning Welsh, learners draw the attention of others to the language and indicate their respect for the language and their desire for its survival. Fluent learners also show that the language can be learned. By learning, however, "learners have made their social identity ambiguous, with the result that English as well as Welsh speakers are drawn into negotiations of their own identities, both with respect to the learners and to the Welsh language" (Trossett 1986: 175). As previously seen, learners do not fit into the normal dichotomous classification system by which people either come from a certain background and speak Welsh natively or do not speak Welsh at all (Bowie 1993: 171, Trossett 1986: 172). By challenging these conventional categories, in other words, learners may cause people to think about the Welsh language in new ways.

---

[102] "As regards the Gaels themselves, it is certain that the learner will meet every type: some will be helpful, others won't. This isn't a strange new thing! Amongst what I've heard through the years are "it's English speakers who speak Gaelic"; or an old woman who said to me once, "why do you learners all pretend that you never spoke a work of English in your lives?" This will happen until the seas dry up – don't worry dear learners!" All translations are by the present author unless otherwise stated.

Such an argument can also be made with regard to Gaelic learners. Gaelic learners could certainly be said to act as consciousness-raisers for the language amongst non-Gaelic speakers given the widespread involvement of learners (fluent or otherwise) in activities to publicise and promote the language. Less formally, learners will frequently talk to friends and others about the language and thereby help to raise awareness.

Trossett's contention that Welsh learners challenge people's existing perceptions regarding Welsh speakers and non-Welsh speakers can also be easily applied to the Scottish situation. Like most native speakers of Gaelic, most non-Gaelic speakers in Scotland tend to assume that all Gaelic speakers come from a traditional Gaelic-speaking community, and that they are native speakers.[103] It could be argued, therefore, that non-Gaelic speakers, like native Gaelic speakers, generally have no real concept to cover a Gaelic speaker who has learnt Gaelic but who does not hail from a traditional Gaelic-speaking community.

Media discussion of questions such as the provision of services for Gaelic speakers normally centres on the discussion of 'native speakers' and Gaelic as a 'mother tongue', due to a lack of recognition that those wishing to use Gaelic might be learners. One example of the tendency to equate speaking Gaelic with being a native speaker comes from a House of Commons debate on the role of Gaelic in the Scottish Parliament, where discussion centred exclusively on Gaelic as a 'first language' or 'native language' (*Hansard* [H.C] January 29 1998).

Where Gaelic learners do come to people's attention, they serve to draw the attention of others to the language and show that the language can be learnt. More symbolically, learners could be taken to represent the possibility of the continued survival of Gaelic Scotland (Trossett 1986: 174). By learning Gaelic, an individual makes people with whom s/he is in contact think about the state of the language and about their relationship with it. This can have different effects on different groups of people.

Trossett and Bowie have shown that reaction to Welsh learners can be both positive and negative. By symbolising that Welsh can be learned, learners encourage those who are sympathetic to the language to learn or to take other action to support the language. Many of these people have felt a sense of regret or guilt that they could not speak Welsh, some feeling incompletely Welsh through not having a command of the language. For others with less positive views towards the language, however, the Welsh learner can provoke feelings of hostility by showing that the language can be learned and by showing that it is possible for the language to survive. Those hostile to the language include many people who do not see the Welsh language as central to Welsh national identity, who feel the language is a redundant relic from the past or who feel a mainly British sense of nationality (Bowie 1993: 189). As Bowie has argued, this is "a complex issue with feelings of guilt, resentment and nostalgia associated with the disappearance and, to some extent, reappearance, of the Welsh language" (1993: 186).

There can be no doubt whatsoever that the learning of Gaelic also causes non-speakers of Gaelic to face similar complex feelings, although there is a different relationship between language and Scottish national identity. Although many people do see Gaelic as a national language, Gaelic is nowhere near as widely perceived as an

---

[103] In the case of native Gaelic speakers, this assumption is likely to be borne of experience whereas in the case of non-Gaelic speakers it is more likely to be borne of assumptions and/or stereotypes.

important element of national identity in Scotland as Welsh is in Wales (McLeod 2001: 7). In addition to national identity, the matter of Highland identity also comes into consideration.

As in Wales, Gaelic learners, both by their actions and by their very existence, encourage those who have sympathetic feelings towards the language to learn, symbolising that the language can be learned and showing that it is not the exclusive preserve of the native speaker. By drawing people's attention to the language, however, and by showing that the language may be learned, learners can also provoke the ire of the minority who are less supportive of the language. Non-Gaelic speakers who do not perceive Gaelic as part of their national identity, for example, might see the promotion of Gaelic as a threat to their sense of Scottish national identity as might those living in the Highlands who do not see Gaelic as an important part or, indeed, as any part of modern Highland identity (MacInnes 1992: 128).

The concept of artificiality, already mentioned during the discussion of the relationship between native speakers and learners, is also important here. Many people who hold anti-Gaelic views take greater exception to the promotion of Gaelic by learners than by native speakers, feeling that the use or promotion of the language by learners is 'artificial' and is 'artificially' prolonging the life of the language. One letter-writer to *The Scotsman*, for example, argued that:

> Gaelic should be allowed to live out its life with dignity, as spoken in the rich vein of the people of Stornoway and Lewis [sic]. It should not suffer the indignity of the political activist, the urban nouveaux Gael, the life-support machine and the Edinburgh Parliament (Imlach Shearer, Letters, *The Scotsman* 12.02.98).

The journalist Tim Williams has also levelled the charge of artificiality against Gaelic learners, saying that:

> It will, after all, not be your average Gaelic-speaking law breaker who will take advantage of his new right to speak his 'mither tongue' in court; it will be the SNP supporter, almost certainly a blow-in, possibly even English and thus guilt-ridden, who is learning the language of other people's forebears, badly as a political statement (Williams 1999).[104]

Similarly, a correspondent in the *Strathspey and Badenoch Herald* attempted to play down the importance of a Gaelic campaign by pointing out that a leading protagonist was from Surrey (Alan Cameron, Letters, *Strathspey and Badenoch Herald,* 04.01.96). By learning Gaelic, learners are seen by many opponents of the language to be helping to artificially promote a dying language which does not belong to them in the first place, a language which is foreign to them. Another common complaint made by those holding anti-Gaelic views is that is that Gaelic is becoming a hobby for the

---

[104] John MacKay, then MP for Argyll, made a very similar argument during the debate on the ill fated 1981 Gaelic (Miscellaneous Provisions) Bill where he spoke of a Liverpudlian, Scottish nationalist Gaelic learner living in Argyll who, should he have had to appear in court might "insist on the hearing being in Gaelic, for political and disruptive reasons". The clear implication of this comment was that it is not legitimate for Gaelic services to be provided to non-native speakers of Gaelic, and particularly to those who view Gaelic in a political light (*Hansard* [H.C] 1147 Feb 13, 1981).

middle class (e.g. J. MacLeod 1996; Williams 1999a, 1999b).

Gaelic learners, like Welsh learners, are in many ways the 'joker in the pack' referred to by Bowie, fitting neither into the category of native speaker or non-Gaelic speaker. One consequence of this position is that learners are more likely than native speakers to be subject to criticism from those opposed to Gaelic. Many people are unwilling to express anti-Gaelic views to native speakers. To do so might be considered rude or unfair given that being a native Gaelic speaker is an aspect of a person's life which s/he has not chosen and has no control over. For learners who have chosen to learn the language, however, this consideration does not apply.

While discussion has so far centred on non-Gaelic speakers in general, it is worth noting at this point that reaction to Gaelic learners is not necessarily the same throughout Scotland. In the Lowlands, where Gaelic generally impinges very little upon the lives of the vast majority of people, Gaelic meets with relatively little hostility and can rely on the passive goodwill of most people. Its connection with Scottish identity is also perceived as rather weak. In the Highlands, however, the situation can be different given that Gaelic has a higher profile, was widely spoken throughout the area in the recent past and is still spoken in many places. Many people living in the Highlands who do not speak Gaelic will have (had) Gaelic-speaking parents or grandparents. The perceived connection between Gaelic and Highland identity is also much stronger than that between the language and national identity. In the Highlands, and particularly in areas where Gaelic is still widely spoken, many of the ambivalent attitudes regarding Gaelic which have been discussed with reference to native speakers can live on.

As Comunn na Gàidhlig have pointed out:

> For those who retain close links to the language but have lost the ability to to speak it, there is frequently a sense of loss, of social separation and fragmentation, and of confusion as to social and linguistic loyalties (CnaG 1997b: 15).

For those who have close family links to the language or who live in Gaelic-speaking (or recently Gaelic-speaking) areas without speaking the language, these feelings can result either in pro-Gaelic sentiment or in an opposition to the promotion of Gaelic. Trossett has made a similar argument regarding non-Welsh speakers in Wales:

> Many Anglo-Welsh people are somewhat uncomfortable with the ambiguity of their own cultural identity, and therefore it is not surprising that they often feel very ambivalent toward Welsh learners, who are admired for having done what many of them wish they could do, but who have usurped their own Welshness [...] Uncertain of their own Welshness, many Anglo-Welsh people are unwillling to allow true outsiders by origin to find a place within the community they themselves are unable to enter.

---

[105] Such negative attitudes towards Gaelic are not confined to the learning of Gaelic by adults. Stockdale *et al.*, for example, demonstrated apparent antipathy towards Gaelic-medium education amongst first generation non-Gaelic speakers in the strongly Gaelic-speaking communities which they studied, contrasting with significant support amongst fluent Gaelic speakers and recent non-Gaelic speaking incomers from outwith Scotland (Stockdale *et al.* 2003: 41).

By learning Gaelic, learners are learning a language which not everybody in Gaelic-speaking communities is able to speak. Those who live in Gaelic communities and have Gaelic-speaking parents or grandparents but do not speak Gaelic themselves are often hostile to the learning of Gaelic (Galloway 1995: 184; MacAulay 1994: 46; Neill 1997b: 51).[105] This is particularly the case when learners are outsiders to the community, hailing from large Highland towns such as Inverness or Fort William, from the cities or from outwith Scotland. By drawing attention to the language question, learners can encounter hostility from non-Gaelic speakers who feel that their identity as a Highlander, a Gael or an Islander is being drawn into question. This is particularly the case given that many living in Gaelic communities feel that the language belongs to them and to their community even if they do not speak the language themselves. In such situations, Gaelic learners from outwith the community can be seen as appropriating a language which does not belong to them in the first place and therefore as doing something which is 'artificial' and non-authentic. Such views, which are likely to be experienced by any Gaelic learner spending any time in a Gaelic-speaking community, are expressed clearly by one young non-Gaelic speaking Skyeman in the following letter:

> Gaelic is on the decline among the indigenous population and [...] the resurgence is a purely cosmetic one bolstered by incomers and holiday Gaelic-speakers, and perpetuated by the Gaelic Mafia. Personally, I believe that the machinations of the nouveau Gaels and the Gaelic Mafia do nothing but alienate many indigenous non-Gaelic speakers. I also believe that Gaelic is a very important part of the culture of the Highlands and Islands and I take no pleasure in seeing its decline, but I do recognise that there is more to being Highland and Scottish than just the language (D.J MacLennan, Letters, *West Highland Free Press*, 30.08.96).

Such common sentiments may be explained partly in terms of jealousy on the part of those living in bilingual communities who have been raised monolingually and who resent others learning the language which they have been denied. They are also related to the perception of Gaelic as a backward and rural language which can 'hold people back' which still continues to exist to some extent in Gaelic communities.[106] The decline of Gaelic in traditional Gaelic communities and the lack of opportunities to use the language for modern pursuits has also led to the language being seen by many young people as the language of old people or of more isolated areas. Given that learners of Gaelic typically view Gaelic in a very different light, it is unsurprising that they may encounter hostility from non-Gaelic speakers living in Gaelic communities.

In summary, it can be concluded that there is no one view of Gaelic learners among non-speakers of Gaelic any more than there is one view amongst native Gaelic speakers. Awareness of the existence of learners of Gaelic is also very low. Despite this, however, and despite occasional hostility, reaction to learners amongst non-Gaelic speakers is generally positive insofar as there is awareness of their existence.

---

[106] See Fraser 1989: 28.

Gaelic Learning as a Process

In investigating the social identity of learners, it is important to remember that learning a language is not an event but a process. Learning Gaelic does not take place overnight but, rather, takes much time. Learning Gaelic is also a process in social terms. As learners make progress with Gaelic, their relationships to and understandings of native speakers are likely to change, as are their own identities. In other words, the social identity of the Gaelic learner is not static but evolves alongside the learner's level of proficiency in Gaelic (Leyland 1996). As Trossett has argued with regard to Welsh learners: "to be a Welsh learner is to occupy not a social category, but a transitional state" (1986: 188).

Recognising Gaelic learning as a social as well as a linguistic progress raises several important questions. The first must be the question of exactly how transitional Gaelic learning is. While there can be no doubt that all Gaelic learning involves transition from one level of proficiency in Gaelic to another with any attendant social consequences, the transition from being a complete beginner in Gaelic to a fluent speaker is a rare one. As Chapman has argued, "the illusion that Gaelic-learners are on a straight and unproblematic, if lengthy, route towards being Gaelic-speakers [...] is simply not true" (1978: 215). For reasons investigated elsewhere, the vast majority of Gaelic learners do not reach fluency.

Chapman and McEwan-Fujita have not only suggested that most learners fail to become fluent, but also that most do not aim at fluency (Chapman 1978, McEwan Fujita 1998: 20). In Chapman's words:

> the learning of the language is a gesture whose validity is not entirely dependent upon how much is learnt. [...] Learning Gaelic is essentially a 'holiday pursuit', with all that entails. It would not be unjust to argue that the essential message of a Gaelic course is contained in the attendance and the intention, and achievement comes as an added but not entirely necessary bonus (1978: 214).

Chapman's assertion does not ring true for the majority of learners. The Gaelic Learners' Survey has shown, for example, that the vast majority of learners sampled aim at fluency and literacy in the language. While a distinction might be drawn between the aspiration to fluency and the actual expectation of reaching fluency in practice, the fact remains that most learners have been shown by a variety of surveys to be motivated mostly or wholly by integrative motives such as a family tradition of speaking Gaelic, or national or Highland identity. Research has tended to suggest that, like many of the parents involved in Gaelic-medium education surveyed by Fraser, "many [...] feel a sense of dislocation (varying in the degree and manner of its conscious articulation) from their own cultural heritage" (Fraser 1989: 1). For most people desiring to learn Gaelic for such reasons, failure to learn Gaelic fluently can be due more to the inadequacies in the Gaelic learning infrastructure and to lack of opportunity rather than to the lack of a real desire to learn. Failure to progress can be a real cause of regret to many learners. While the point must be conceded that some learners do not aim at fluency, such learners are a small minority.

If not all learners reach the goal of fluency and some do not even aim to reach this goal, it is also the case that Gaelic learners do not all start from the same base point. Some learners are semi-speakers, passive bilinguals, lapsed native speakers, have a

Hebridean accent or come from a Gaelic-speaking community/family. As will be investigated later, these factors can often be of great importance in determining the social experience of learning.

Having recognised that the process of learning Gaelic does not always start from the same point and does not necessarily result in fluency, we must now investigate the question of what exactly a Gaelic learner becomes when s/he reaches fluency. With regard to the Welsh language, Trossett has argued that "to be a Welsh learner is to occupy not a social category but a transitional state. It is only by moving beyond this state and adopting the full status, linguistic and cultural, of a Welsh speaker, that it is possible for a nonnative speaker to achieve a legitimate social identity within Welsh-Wales" (1986: 189). While a learner can "come closer to acquiring some sort of Welsh identity", however, Trossett has argued that the only true way to *finish* being a learner is to pose as a native speaker. Bowie too has argued that some ambiguity is likely to remain regarding the identity of Welsh learners even after they have achieved fluency (Bowie 1993).

The question of what exactly a learner becomes on reaching fluency is pondered with regard to Gaelic by Morgan:

> The term 'learner' is (in Scotland at least I would argue) both ambiguous and loaded: how fluent does a new user need to be before he or she ceases to be a learner? Is it the height of their linguistic ambition to earn the yes-but-label of 'fluent learner' – it can be fairly insulting to the person who has been able to make Gaelic the first language of his or her daily routine, with the ability and desire to use it in each and every possible circumstance encountered, to be lumped in with those stuttering through their first few sentences (2000: 126).

As Morgan has suggested, the process of learning Gaelic never ends in the sense that a fluent learner (in all but the most exceptional cases) will always be recognisable to native speakers as a learner and will always be liable to be considered as a 'learner' (Morgan 2000: 128, MacKay 1974: 5, L. MacDonald 1999: 28). Gaelic is spoken as a community language over a far smaller range of the country than is Welsh in Wales and Gaelic dialectal variations are far less significant that those of Welsh. For all these reasons, Trosset's argument that some fluent learners can 'finish' being a learner by posing as and being accepted as a native speaker are far less applicable to Scotland than they are to Wales. This tactic could only be expected to work in a tiny number of cases in Scotland.

As the fluent learner cannot ever become a native speaker and is very unlikely to be able to pass as one, the question remains as to what exactly someone who reaches fluency in Gaelic becomes. One possibility which has received some discussion is that of whether or not fluent Gaelic learners are Gaels.

The issue of the meaning of the word 'Gael' is a very complex one. As MacAulay has argued, "the answer to 'who is a Gael?' depends on when you ask it and of whom you ask it – and indeed, what language you ask it in" (1994: 42). As a subjective identity, the idea of what constitutes being a Gael is not a static one but one which is open to reinterpretation in line with changing circumstances (Glaser 2006: 169). When the Highlands were strongly Gaelic-speaking, the term Gael was an unambiguous one meaning both a Highlander and a Gaelic speaker. However, the meaning of 'Gael', and perhaps the importance attached to the identity of Gael, have changed greatly in the last hundred and fifty years with the decline of Gaelic in the Highlands, the migration of Highlanders to the Lowlands and the emigration of Highlanders. This has allowed varying interpretations of the term Gael which range from the Highlander (Gaelic-speaking or otherwise) to those able to speak Gaelic (Highlander or otherwise) to those of Highland descent or, more traditionally, to the native Gaelic-speaking Highlander (Glaser 2006: 169; Oliver 2005).

The full ambiguity of the term is captured by MacAulay in the following paragraph:

> If you ask it [who is a Gael?] of a non-Gaelic-speaking Scot, the most likely answer you get is 'a Hielander' – they have problems with the difference between 'What is a Gael?' and 'Who is a Gael?': a Gael is, generally, someone who lives vaguely north by west. If you ask a Gaelic-speaking Scot who has learned Gaelic as a non-native language (and perhaps some politically correct attitudes at the same time) they are likely to say 'Some one from Gaeldom' (excluding themselves, even if they are Gaelic speakers). If you ask a native community Gaelic-speaker, in English (they are all bilingual), they are likely to say 'Someone from the Gàidhealtachd', and get into trouble with narrower definitions – in terms of language, for example; and broader definitions – in terms of parental origins, for example. If you ask a traditional Gaelic-speaker in Gaelic, there does not appear to be such indecisiveness: *'Duine aig a bheil Gàidhlig bho dhùthchas'*, 'A native speaker of Gaelic' (or words to that effect) will be your most likely answer. Language will be the primary criterion. Traditionally the term *Gaidheal* contrasted with *Gall, Gaidheal* denoting a member of the Gaelic community and *Gall* denoting someone who was not. [...] At the present time, of course, an added complexity has arisen which separates out the ethnic and linguistic components. Many people have learned the Gaelic language who do not belong to the Gaelic community. They pass the linguistic test, however. On the other hand many young members of the Gaelic community fail to learn the Gaelic language, and so they do not fulfil the linguistic criterion. And, meantime, we have traditional speakers. We need to develop terms which will, neutrally, differentiate among them. As we said Gaelic identity is a complex question (1994: 43).

The Gaelic learner and poet William Neill has raised the question of the meaning of the term Gael in a variety of articles in Gaelic and English (Neill 1997a, 1997b, 1997c, 1997d. 1998). He has argued that equating Gael with 'Highlander' is problematic as Gaelic has been spoken as a community language outwith Highland bounds until fairly recently, pointing out that "much of the Lowland area of Scotland is that of a people who, until fairly late historical times, shared a common culture with Gaeldom" (Neil 1997d). He has argued, therefore, that "the term 'Gael' is not racial, but linguistic. A Gael is a person who speaks Gaelic as a first language. One may be a Highlander, a Scot, an Irishman, a Manxman or a Nova Scotian, but without Gaelic, no Gael" (Neill 1997d).

Morgan has similarly argued that Gael is a linguistic term: "no Gaelic and you're not a Gael" (Morgan 1997: 9). He seems to go further than Neill, however, by implying that Gaelic learners can become Gaels: "If it is accepted that language is the defining characteristic of a Gael, then the Gaelic world must remember that it includes a variety of traditions and backgrounds. And this is true of the Gàidhealach Gaels of the Islands as much as it holds for Gaelic learners." He further talks of the possibility of monolingual youngsters becoming Gaels (1997: 9). As Morgan himself notes elsewhere, however, a primarily linguistic definition of 'Gael' is not universally accepted: "it is a term sometimes applied to, and claimed by, non-speakers who were brought up in a Gaelic community or exhibit some perceived qualifying characteristics." In Gaelic communities "locals without Gaelic do not want to be alienated; local Gaelic speakers identify as one of themselves someone with the same sense of humour, musical tastes, geographical and occupational experiences regardless of which of their two languages is used" (Morgan 2000: 127).[107]

That there is no one generally agreed definition of Gael is not only true for the public in general, but also for Gaelic learners. The Gaelic Learners' Survey has shown that there are greatly divergent views amongst learners as to what exactly constitutes a Gael, with some emphasising linguistic factors and others factors of background and ethnicity. Given such differing understandings, the extent to which any Gaelic learner can become a Gael depends on the definition of the word Gael adopted.

In general, however, it would be fair to conclude that it would normally be inappropriate to consider fluent Gaelic learners to be Gaels. In the first place, the idea that any Gaelic speaker, regardless of his/her background constitutes a Gael is not one which is widely subscribed to. Definitions of Gaels as Highlanders, as native Gaelic speakers or as native Gaelic-speaking Highlanders are far more common. More importantly, as suggested by MacAulay above, very few fluent Gaelic learners consider themselves to be Gaels. This is supported by the results of the Gaelic Learners' Survey, where few fluent learners indicated that they strongly felt themselves to be Gaels, as well as the BBC radio series *Na Gaidheil Ùra*, which indicated a general consensus among the fluent Gaelic learners interviewed that becoming a Gaelic speaker could not be equated with becoming a Gael (Dick 1999).

If a Gael is defined as a Gaelic speaker from a Gaelic-speaking community, it is clear that most fluent learners cannot become Gaels (L. MacDonald 1999: 29). Under such a definition, to become a Gael through learning Gaelic is no more possible than to become French through learning the French language. It is possible, however, for some learners to be accepted as Gaels if they already fulfil most of the other social categories implied by the term Gael. A lapsed native speaker, a semi-speaker or a passive bilingual becoming fully fluent in Gaelic is likely to become fully accepted as a Gael, as is someone native to a Gaelic community who learns the language fluently from scratch. For most learners, however, being accepted as a Gael in this way is not possible.[108]

Not only is it clear that most learners cannot hope to become Gaels according to such a definition, but most Gaelic learners would not aspire to many aspects of the material and cultural lifestyle typical of native Gaelic speakers in Gaelic-speaking communities which are seen by members of that community as being central to being a Gael. In this respect a distinction might be drawn between Gaelic learners who wish merely to become Gaelic speakers at one end of a spectrum and those wishing to become as much like a Gael as possible at the other.

---

[107] See also Glaser 2006: 172.
[108] For a similar discussion regarding the Welsh language, see Bowie (1993: 177).

While fluent Gaelic learners cannot normally become Gaels, however, they are sometimes described as 'new Gaels', 'nouveau Gaels', 'Gàidheil Ùra' or 'Nua-Ghàidheil'. Terms such as these are normally used to describe those who have learned Gaelic but come from outwith the Gaelic-speaking communities. They thus have rather different connotations from the term 'Gael'. Until recently, such terms were not common, however, and were used more as descriptive tags than an identity which a Gaelic learner would be likely to associate him/herself with.

The term 'new Gael' or 'nouveau Gael' has been used in two distinct ways. Opponents of RLS sometimes use 'new Gael', or more likely 'nouveau Gael', as a pejorative term to stress the discontinuity between the native speaker and learner and to suggest the illegitimacy and inauthenticity of learning Gaelic.[109] The term 'new Gael', however, can also be used by those wishing to stress the continuity between traditional Gaels and Gaelic learners and the legitimacy of learning Gaelic. The term 'new Gael' has increasingly come to be used in this latter sense following the re-branding in 2001 of the national Gaelic learners' association, Comann an Luchd Ionnsachaidh[110] (CLI), as Clì –na Gàidheil Ùra[111] and the expansion of the group's scope to include Gaelic speakers who have gone through Gaelic-medium education.[112]

This re-branding of CLI was motivated by several factors, according to the group's then director.[113] As seen above, the term 'new Gael' can be used to stress continuity and linkage between native Gaelic speakers and Gaelic learners and to assert that Gaelic learners are a part of the Gaelic community. The change in nomenclature also partly reflects a reaction by the group against the use of the term 'nouveau Gael' in a pejorative sense. Use of the term 'new Gael' was also thought to address the question of what a learner becomes on successfully learning Gaelic through enabling the fluent learner to escape the term 'learner'.

The use of the term 'new Gael' received a mixed reception, being accepted enthusiastically by some but being criticised by others.[114] Criticism came from those who feel that the use of the term 'new Gael' is divisive, creating a distinction rather than a continuity between 'new' and 'traditional' Gaels or who feel that the term 'new Gael' insinuates that learners are replacing the 'traditional' Gaels within the Gaelic community rather than merely joining them within it on equal terms. The expression has also been unpopular amongst those for whom 'Gael' is defined in other than linguistic terms.

The name change was also criticised from a very different perspective by some of those who feel Gaelic to be a national language, who argued that linking Gaelic learners to the identity of 'Gael' or 'new Gael' reinforces the perception that Gaelic is a language relevant primarily or solely to the Gàidhealtachd rather than to Scotland

---

[109] See the letters from Imlach Shearer and D.J MacLennan quoted above, for example, see also "Study dashes hopes of a Gaelic revival", *Sunday Times,* 11/8/96, p. 7; J. MacLeod 1996; P.H Hainsworth: letter to the *West Highland Free Press*, 20.09.96.
[110] Literally "the Learners' Society".
[111] "The New Gaels".
[112] For further information about the reason's for the group's name change, see Morgan 2001 and the Naidheachdan ChLÌ sections of *Cothrom* 28 (2001: 40), *Cothrom* 30 (2001: 44).
[113] Peadar Morgan, personal communication: email, 23.04.02..
[114] ibid.
[115] For some of the reactions to the term "New Gaels", see *Cothrom* 30 (2001:43), 31(2001: 38).
[116] Peadar Morgan, personal communication: email, 23.04.02.

as a whole.[115] Such was the reaction to the expression 'new Gael' that the group dropped the term and officially adopted the name 'Clì Gàidhlig' instead in 2003.

While the term 'new Gael' has gained some degree of acceptance, it is still too early to say whether or not the term will pass into everyday usage or whether the identity of 'new Gael' will be accepted either by those who are learning the language or by native speakers of the language. For these reasons, it is also too early to tell whether or not this identity will allow learners to escape the label 'learner' on reaching fluency and thus to finish the process of Gaelic learning in this sense. It can be said, however, that the adoption of the term 'new Gael' by CLI encouraged a healthy debate on the meaning of such concepts as 'Gael', 'learner' and 'native speaker'.[116]

These debates notwithstanding, how much do definitions of the term 'Gael' really matter to Gaelic learners? Research by MacKinnon has suggested that the identity of 'Gael' might not actually be felt particularly strongly by native Gaelic speakers: "the perceptions of Gaelic speakers in ethnic terms such as 'Gael', 'Highlander' did not appear to be so strong as national identity as 'Scottish' or more specifically local terms as 'Leòdhasach' etc., or Islander" (MacKinnon 1998: 7). It would similarly be reasonable to argue that the issue of the meaning of the word Gael and of whether or not they, as Gaelic learners, constitute Gaels, is one to which most Gaelic learners attach little or no importance.

While the discussion of the meaning of the term Gael might be seen as a purely academic exercise with no practical implications, this question is part of the broader question of exactly what position the Gaelic learner occupies in Gaeldom or in the national Gaelic community. It is, indeed, part of the question of how these very entities are to be defined. As will be investigated below, such questions have a huge practical impact on language policy.

To explore these questions further, it is now time to return to the more basic question of what exactly learners become on reaching fluency in Gaelic. As has already been seen, a fluent Gaelic learner will always be considered to be a learner regardless of fluency in the tongue. The learner, however, will also have become a Gaelic speaker and will normally be considered to be such both by native Gaelic speakers and by non-Gaelic speakers, regardless of whether or not s/he is considered to be a Gael or a member of the Gaelic community.

The identity of 'Gaelic speaker' or 'fluent Gaelic speaker' is one which has so far received little discussion in academic works. This is perhaps because authors such as Chapman and Rogerson and Gloyer have tended to stress divisions between Gaelic learners and native speakers and to posit a dichotomy between activist, revivalist learners and non-activist, non-revivalist native speakers (Chapman 1992, Rogerson and Gloyer 1995).[117] Such a model would be challenged by the 'Gaelic speaker' identity, which might, in some cases, bridge these suggested divisions. In practice, many native speakers subscribe to views of Gaelic which might be described as revivalist.[118] Works focusing on native speaker/learner divisions have failed to acknowledge that many native Gaelic speakers perceive the situation more in terms of Gaelic speaker / non-Gaelic speaker rather than in terms of Gael/non-Gael or whether or not learners belong to the Gaelic community. For many native Gaelic speakers, the fact that a Gaelic learner speaks fluent Gaelic is far more important than where s/he hails from. This view is not, however, universal.

---

[117] Unfortunately, no real definition is given of terms such as 'activist' or 'revivalist' in these works.
[118] For a similar discussion in the Irish context, see Kabel 2000: 133.

While fluent learners are more or less universally accepted as speakers of Gaelic by native speakers, however, the perceived importance of being a Gaelic speaker can vary depending on the native speaker's view of the language. This might be investigated in terms of the extent to which fluent Gaelic learners are perceived as belonging to the Gaelic community. Like nations, communities such as 'the Gaelic community' or 'Gaeldom' are imagined communities (Anderson 1983, Glaser 2006: 170). This is to say that they are not physical communities where everyone knows each other, but rather socially created ideas which nonetheless have a reality of their own because people think in terms of these ideas. As imagined communities such as nations are ultimately ideas, they are subject to different interpretations by different people within the community even though there is normally a great deal of overlap between these interpretations.

Whether or not, or to what extent, fluent Gaelic learners are seen to constitute part of the Gaelic community depends, therefore, on how the Gaelic community is defined by different individuals. Where ability to speak Gaelic is understood as the defining point of the Gaelic community, the Gaelic learner will easily be seen as a member. Where speaking Gaelic is seen as only one, perhaps peripheral, characteristic of membership in the Gaelic community, fluent Gaelic learners will be perceived as peripheral to or outwith the Gaelic community. As McLeod has pointed out:

> For those who have acquired the language, however, it is by no means clear that this accomplishment is sufficient to admit them fully into the Gaelic community. Various degrees of resentment against so-called 'new Gaels' are very familiar, where the value of *Dùthchas* (inherited tradition) remains paramount (1998c).

MacAulay has also stressed that importance of *dùthchas* and *dualchas* (people/kin), to Gaelic-speaking communities, arguing that these are: "the traditional basis of identity and are very much recognised as such in the remnants of traditional society to this day" (MacAulay 1994: 41). Where such factors are considered to be of prime importance in the definition of the Gaelic community, Gaelic learners can never hope to be considered to be 'one of us' by those who adopt such a view.

Even where *dùthchas*- and *dualchas*-based definitions dictate that learners cannot be fully accepted as members of the Gaelic community, however, learners can still be accepted as belonging to the community to some extent.[119] How much this is the case depends on factors such as the extent to which learners wish to enter that community. As already argued, many learners not only wish to become Gaelic learners, but wish to become like Gaels. Morgan, for example, has spoken of learners who "attempt to go native in outlook as much as in language" (2000: 128). Other learners may mainly wish to become Gaelic speakers without necessarily harbouring any desire to become like the Gaels or be accepted as such. How much learners are accepted as, or desire to be accepted as, belonging to the Gaelic community depends partly on such factors as how much interest they take in the material and cultural lifestyle of Gaelic-speaking communities.

Given that fluent Gaelic learners will never be fully accepted as full members of the Gaelic community by a large section of native speakers, and perhaps even by

---

[119] Bowie has similarly argued with relation to Welsh that: "Speaking Welsh does not necessarily enable the learner to 'become Welsh' but [...] it can, in some circumstances at least, invest the individual with an 'honorary Welsh' status" (1993: 180).

learners, Gaelic learners are both within and outwith the Gaelic community. In Chapman's words:

> Those learning Gaelic are drawn into a somewhat ambiguous fraternity in which they become a party to secrets that are not shared with the common tourist. They do not, however, by this become in any simple sense a part of Gaelic society. Indeed, Gaelic-learners are often subject to another kind of dismissive derision from those for whom Gaelic is as ordinary as white bread, and for whom the part-time pieties of the would-be Gael are somewhat grotesque. Gaelic is, in many different ways, representative of the intimate interiority of the society of the Highlands and Islands. It is not surprising that outsiders learning or knowing Gaelic would present to that society a rather more complex problem than does the tourist, who can be discreetly and politely excluded (usually without his knowing it) from more intimate affairs (Chapman 1978: 228).

While Chapman stresses the negative aspects of the ambiguous position of a Gaelic learner, Bowie's discussion of Welsh learners shows that there are also many positive aspects:

> There is a sense in which the Welsh learner remains the 'joker in the pack', fitting neatly into neither but can also, on occasions, mean that the learner can play both cards. Observing the shifts that take place as they are categorised as English or Welsh, and the meanings given to these categories, reveals the ways in which identities are negotiated and in which the symbolic boundaries of the community are maintained (1993: 171).

Trossett has similarly said of the relationship between Welsh learners, native Welsh speakers and non-Welsh speakers that "learners do not necessarily act as mediators between these two groups, but they are in a good position to do so, since, unlike native speakers, they know how the Welsh-speaking community appears from the outside" (1986: 176). The position of a fluent Gaelic learner is, therefore, one which also carries many advantages and one which few if any learners would regret achieving.

As noted above, the social identity of the Gaelic learner is not a static but a developing one. This developing process might start and finish at different points for different learners. While the Gaelic learner will always be seen as a 'learner' as opposed to a native speaker or a Gael, s/he will come to be seen as a Gaelic speaker upon reaching fluency and may be accepted as belonging to the Gaelic community to a greater or lesser extent. How much this is the case depends on factors such as the background of the learner, how native speakers visualise the Gaelic community, how the learner visualises Gaelic and how much s/he wants to become part of this community.

As reaching fluency in Gaelic almost always involves interacting with native speakers, becoming fluent in Gaelic will normally also be accompanied by a deeper understanding of the relationship between native speakers and their language. While learners may, at present at least, occupy a somewhat ambiguous and semi-detached position in the Gaelic world, their position is one which is by no means without advantage. Fluent learners, as already seen, are able to act as consciousness-raisers. They are also both partly within and partly without the Gaelic community and come from different backgrounds from native Gaelic speakers and are, therefore, able to act in some senses as a bridge between native Gaelic speakers and non-Gaelic speakers.

The Practical Implications of the Social Identity of Gaelic Learners for RLS

A final point to be made about the social identity of the Gaelic learner is that the position Gaelic learners occupy in the Gaelic community has significant implications for RLS. It has already been seen that Gaelic learners can play a role in encouraging RLS on the individual level through acting as language consciousness raisers, through having high levels of support for Gaelic and through bringing new perceptions and experiences to the language.

Regardless of the qualities which learners may bring to RLS efforts as individuals, however, how much of a role Gaelic learners as a group will actually be able to play in RLS on the national scale depends to a great extent upon the nature of Gaelic policies drawn up by government and by Gaelic organisations. The nature of these policies depends in turn upon social identity issues such as how the Gaelic community is defined by policy makers and how much Gaelic learners are seen to belong to or be relevant to this community.

How concepts such as the Gaelic community are defined by policy makers have significant implications for language policy. Where discourse focuses on Gaelic as a 'mother tongue' or 'native language' and on Gaelic speakers from and within traditional geographical Gaelic communities, for example, the needs and aspirations of Gaelic learners and their possible contribution to RLS are unlikely to be taken into account or to be given any priority. If however, policy is underpinned by a discourse whereby learners are seen as an integral part of the Gaelic speech community, the outcome is likely to be very different.

To date there has been relatively little discussion or debate within Government, Gaelic development agencies or the Gaelic community in general on the question of what constitutes the modern Gaelic community. This means that little consideration has been given to issues such as what place adult learners of Gaelic and the areas of Scotland in which they tend to live should have within Gaelic development policy.[120]

This lack of attention to issues relating to the position of Gaelic learners in the Gaelic community or within RLS efforts, reflects the broader lack of a strategic language planning based approach to Gaelic development efforts in Scotland. These have instead tended to date to be "uncoordinated and haphazard, driven without the guidance of theory or the control of planning" (McLeod 2002a: 279). A notable feature of this lack of strategy has been the absence of debate on certain fundamental issues facing the future of the language, including the position of the Gaelic learner within the Gaelic community and within RLS efforts.[121] As W. Gillies has pointed out:

> The Gaelic speaking community as a whole faces big questions which to my mind are quite unresolved regarding (for instance) Gaelic language priorities *versus* educational priorities, Gaelic as a community

---

[120] See Chapter 5 for a discussion of the geographical distribution of Gaelic learners. For discussion of the significance of Lowland and urban Scotland and of Gaelic learners in these areas to reversing language shift, see MacCaluim and McLeod 2001, MacCaluim forthcoming 2007.

[121] For the importance of such debate in RLS, see Fishman 1991:10, 394.

[122] It could be argued, however, that the lack of clarification of the position of Gaelic learners in the Gaelic community may be one factor in explaining why the priority and funding afforded to the Gaelic for adults sector within the limited current Gaelic development efforts has been so much less that that afforded to Gaelic-medium education and broadcasting.

language *versus* Gaelic as a 'national language', Gaelic language priorities *versu*s economic priorities and similar. We lack serious debate on these crucial matters of principle, not to mention discussion of strategies to attain the objectives decided on. [...] Gaelic desperately needs its philosophical debates. (W. Gillies 1989b: 28).

As Gaelic development efforts in Scotland have been rather limited to date, the lack of clarification of the position of Gaelic learners within the Gaelic community has not been a matter of great practical consequence.[122] This situation is likely to change in the near future, however, as a result of expansion of Gaelic development efforts pursuant to the Gaelic Language (Scotland) Act 2005, the establishment of the Gaelic development agency Bòrd na Gàidhlig, charged with developing Gaelic through a language planning approach, and the likely development of a Gaelic television channel in the near future.

Any such stepping-up of Gaelic development efforts will necessarily involve the taking of a number of policy decisions based on a definition, whether conscious or unconscious, as to what constitutes the Gaelic community. The position which learners are seen to have within this community will affect a wide range of policies on areas of importance to learners. These include matters as diverse as what emphasis should be placed upon creating fluent learners of Gaelic, to what extent broadcasting should reflect the interests and experiences of learners, and as to which geographical areas should be targeted in Gaelic development policy.

How the Gaelic community is defined by future policy makers is, therefore, a matter of fundamental importance to Gaelic learners and to the future development of Gaelic. The part which Gaelic learners are seen by politicians and policy makers to occupy within the Gaelic community will determine to a large extent whether learners will be in the centre or the periphery of the future Gaelic community and RLS efforts. At present it is unclear how Gaelic policy makers will define the position of Gaelic learners within the Gaelic community. There can be no doubt, however, that this definition will have a crucial effect on the future development of the language.

Conclusion

This chapter has dealt with several social aspects of Gaelic learning, seeking to build upon previous studies and looking at issues not previously covered by others. The relationships between Gaelic learners and native speakers and between Gaelic learners and non-Gaelic speakers have been investigated, as has the question of the position Gaelic learners come to occupy in the Gaelic community on achieving fluency. The relevance of these issues to reversing language shift has also been discussed. At all times, efforts have been made to understand the situation of the Gaelic learner from the perspective of the Gaelic learner and not only, as has characterised the analysis of many previous commentators such as Chapman and Hindley, from the perspective of the native speaker (Chapman 1978, 1986; Hindley 1993). Care has also been taken to stress the equal validity of the views of learners and native speakers.

It has been seen that the Gaelic learner occupies a somewhat anomalous position between the native speaker and the non-speaker of Gaelic and challenges conventional perceptions, whereby the language is believed either to be spoken natively or not at all. The position of the Gaelic learner contains some disadvantages, such as the charge of 'artificiality' and the ambiguous semi-detached relationship which learners may feel they have with the Gaelic community. This same position, however, carries many advantages such as the opportunity to gain an understanding both of the views of the Gaelic and non-Gaelic communities as regards each other and as regards the language. The learner can also bring new experiences and perceptions to the language and act, for native speakers and learners alike, as a consciousness-raiser.

The relationship between Gaelic learners and native speakers described in this chapter can sometimes, though by no means always, be an uneasy one due to the different backgrounds and perceptions of these two groups. Some suggestions have been made for the improvement of this relationship, such as the expansion of immersion courses and the discussion of the relationship between native speakers and their language as an integral part of the formal Gaelic learning process.

While there is some division between native speaker and learner at times as to the value, role and future direction of Gaelic, it is also the case that the relationship between Gaelic learners and native speakers is a changing one. For the first time, small but significant numbers of Gaelic learners are now reaching high levels of fluency in the language and significant numbers of children from non-Gaelic-speaking homes are becoming Gaelic speakers through Gaelic-medium education. Numbers of native Gaelic speakers also continue to decline and Gaelic continues to weaken as a community language in the Western Isles.

As these trends progress and as increasing numbers of adult and GME learners play prominent roles in Gaelic circles life, it is to be expected that native speakers will be increasingly likely to recognise the existence of learners as they come into contact with them and come to understand their perspectives and recognise them as part of the Gaelic community. This has already become the case to a large extent in the cities, where both Gaelic learners and native speakers play an integral role in Gaelic-related organisations and activities.

The changes currently occurring in the demography of the language are likely with time to lead to a redefinition of what is meant by terms such as 'the Gaelic community' and 'Gaeldom' and to a clarification of the position of learners within this community (A. Gillies 2000: 103). Indeed, recent works by Glaser and Oliver suggest that this process is now underway (Oliver 2005; Glaser 2004: 185, 195). At present, however, the question of whether or not learners are members of the Gaelic community (however this might be defined) has still not been fully answered. This uncertainty has significant implications for language policy and for reversing language shift.

5: The Gaelic Learners' Survey

> Ag ionnsachadh na Gàidhlig – cha tug dad sam bith an uiread toileachais dhomh, 's an uiread bròin cuideachd.[123]
> (Gaelic learner, from questionnaire)

Introduction

In order to gather further data about Gaelic learners, a questionnaire was distributed between Summer 1998 and Spring 1999 (see Appendix 1). The aim of this questionnaire was to investigate four main research issues namely:

- What is the social background of Gaelic learners?
- What is their motivation for learning?
- What is the impact of learners on Gaelic affairs and on regenerating the language?
- How do learners view the language?

Through the survey, it was intended to provide a broad overview of a representative sample of learners and to investigate a wide range of issues with relevance to RLS and the position of Gaelic learners within the Gaelic speech community.

The questionnaire was in English and was divided into sections roughly corresponding to the headings above, with the addition of a blank section at the end in which opinions were invited from the respondents.

Methodology

An initial draft of the questionnaire was produced and piloted on a small national sample of 40 Gaelic learners. Minor amendments were then made. The final draft of the questionnaire was distributed in the first instance to the membership of the Gaelic learners association Comann an Luchd Ionnsachaidh (CLI).[124] This was done through the summer 1998 issue of CLI's magazine *Cothrom*.[125] The questionnaire was accompanied by a freepost envelope. The survey was carried out with the full co-operation of CLI.

A short article by the author explaining the questionnaire and the Gaelic Learners' Survey was printed in the magazine to encourage response.[126] A bilingual reminder letter from the author was also printed in the next issue to encourage members to complete and return the survey. Attention was further drawn to this letter through the magazine's editorial.[127]

CLI's personal membership stood at 1107 at the time of the questionnaire's distribution, 647 of whom lived in Scotland.[128] The response rate for questionnaires sent out to CLI members was as follows:

---

[123] "Learning Gaelic – nothing else has ever given me so much pleasure and so much sadness too."
[124] Now known as Clì Gàidhlig.
[125] *Cothrom* 16
[126] *Cothrom* 16, p. 10
[127] *Cothrom* 17, p. 9, 34
[128] CLI did not have current addresses for ten members in Scotland and one in England. This has been taken into account in the response rate.

Total response:	458	Response rate:	42%
Response of Scottish sample:	266	Response rate:	42%
Response of remainder of UK:[129]	128	Response rate:	45%
Response outwith UK:	61	Response rate:[130]	29%
Country not stated	3		

The response rate within the UK is reasonably good for a postal questionnaire and the respondents can, therefore, be taken as being representative of the more committed Gaelic learners within CLI. The length of the questionnaire and the time needed to complete it (around 30–45 minutes for most respondents) was undoubtedly a factor in discouraging more learners from returning questionnaires.

The nature of CLI's membership should be borne in mind when assessing the response rate. While primarily a body for learners, CLI also attempts to encourage members who are involved in teaching/promoting Gaelic or who support Gaelic whilst not necessarily learning it. The subtext on *Cothrom* magazine, for example, is "For Learners, Supporters and Speakers of Scots Gaelic" and its content is likely to be attractive to anybody with an interest in Gaelic. Given that the questionnaire was aimed at learners of Gaelic, no native speakers or members who had never made an attempt at learning Gaelic answered. These factors mean that the rate of response from CLI learners who are actually learning or have learned Gaelic can be taken to be slightly higher than the overall figure quoted above.[131] The word 'slightly' should be stressed, however as Peadar Morgan, director of CLI at the time of the survey, felt that only a small proportion of CLI members were either native speakers or non-Gaelic speakers who have no real desire to learn.[132]

While the membership of CLI was chosen as a sample likely to be broadly representative of Gaelic learners as a whole, there were a few potential biases in the sample. As a membership organisation, there was a possibility that people in CLI were more likely to be what might be termed 'joiners', i.e. people with an above-average propensity to join clubs and societies. As CLI membership costs money, and as much information about Gaelic and Gaelic learning is not easily available except through CLI, there might also be a tendency for learners joining CLI to be amongst the more dedicated Gaelic learners.

Another hypothesis was that some classes of Gaelic learners were likely to be under-represented amongst the organisation's membership. People on full-time Gaelic courses with more regular contact with Gaelic and less in need of information of the sort provided by CLI might be expected to be less likely to join, for example.

For these reasons, the main sample was supplemented by questionnaires distributed at summer and weekend courses for learners and to full-time Gaelic courses and Gaelic immersion courses at colleges and universities. Questionnaires

---

[129] Of these questionnaires, 117 were from England, 9 from Wales, 1 from Cornwall and 1 from Northern Ireland.

[130] The low level of response outwith the UK is most likely accounted for by postage costs. As the UK Freepost service is not available outwith the UK, respondents living outside the UK had to pay the full postal costs in order to return the questionnaire.

[131] The author was able to identify 15 people in Scotland from the CLI membership list whom he knew to be native speakers. The number of Gaelic supporters within CLI's ranks who are not learning Gaelic is impossible to assess, but is likely to be larger.

[132] Peadar Morgan, personal communication: interview, 22.04.98.

were given out at Sabhal Mòr Ostaig, (August, September 1998), An Ceathramh, the Gaelic learning centre in Sutherland (August, September 1998), a Gaelic weekend at Wansfell College, Essex (November 1998) and Gaelic evening classes held in London with a strong connection to this Gaelic weekend (Autumn 1998). This was done with the help and approval of the Short Course Organiser at Sabhal Mòr Ostaig, the director of An Ceathramh and the teachers of the Wansfell College course. These courses were chosen due to being the largest and most widely known Gaelic summer courses. With support from course organisers, questionnaires were also given out at a weekend Gaelic course at Taigh na Gàidhlig, Edinburgh and at CLI weekend community courses held in Dumfries, Fort William, Melrose, Plockton and Benbecula in 1998 and 1999.

Questionnaires were sent out to all immersion courses in operation during the 1998–99 session and were distributed at all courses with the exception of those in Falkirk and Perth. Questionnaires were also distributed to students studying Gaelic within the Celtic Departments of Aberdeen, Edinburgh and Glasgow Universities.

It did not prove possible to calculate response rates for those respondents who received questionnaires at the Summer courses / community courses or full-time courses. Despite the distribution of a returnable information form to tutors / course organisers, figures were not received back from all courses as to the number of students or the number of students who had already received a questionnaire through another source. As some Gaelic learners will have attended more than one of the courses or classes in question and as many of the students of these courses are CLI members, duplication in questionnaire distribution is likely to have been considerable. Evidence from the courses from which detailed information was received,[133] however, indicates that the response rate (taking into account duplication of questionnaire distribution) was similar to that received from CLI members through the *Cothrom* mailing detailed above.

Altogether, the following number of questionnaires were received back from sources other than the mailing of CLI members through *Cothrom*:[134]

Full-time courses   75 (15 living outside Scotland)[135]
Weekend courses / evening classes   61 (22 living outside Scotland)
Summer courses   74 (41 living outside Scotland)

Given the high level of duplication of questionnaire distribution, the fact that many participants on the above courses were CLI members and the relatively small number of questionnaires received from these sources, the results of these questionnaires have been analysed alongside those of the larger CLI sample rather than separately. Through supplementing the main CLI sample in this way, it was hoped to ensure that the learners sampled were as representative as possible of Gaelic learners in general.

---

[133] This being around half of the courses.

[134] Some respondents from these courses were CLI members. The CLI members are therefore included both within the overall total for CLI members responding as well as in the figures given here for respondents from full-time/summer/weekend courses. They are, however, only included once within the overall total for all questionnaires received.

[135] Here "living outside Scotland" refers to those whose main place of residence is outside Scotland. This is taken to include university and college students whose home address is outside Scotland

Altogether, 643 questionnaires were returned.

For the purposes of analysis, three main divisions have been made in the overall sample for use in different tables. These are:

All Scottish respondents	392 respondents
Respondents in the rest of the UK	159 respondents
Respondents in the rest of the world	89 respondents

Relevance of Questionnaire Results to the Present Day

As the Gaelic Learners' Survey dates from 1998–1999, it is important to consider to what extent the questionnaire results are relevant to Gaelic learning in 2006 before these findings are described and discussed in detail.

In general, it would be safe to conclude that the survey results still broadly reflect Gaelic learning in 2006. As seen in chapter 3, there have been few significant developments in the Gaelic learning infrastructure since the late 1990s, with the result that, to this day, few Gaelic learners are successful in reaching fluency in the language.

The only major development significantly affecting the daily experience of Gaelic learning has been the expansion of internet access and the resulting worldwide availability of Gaelic broadcasting, mailing lists and reading materials. The Gaelic Learners' Survey showed that the learners participating in the survey made little use of the internet. This situation has now changed, with the internet now being very widely used as a resource for Gaelic learning.

While it is more difficult to assess how accurately the survey figures reflect the social profile of today's Gaelic learners, there is nothing to suggest that there have been any major changes in this respect since the late 1990s. Indeed, the picture painted in this chapter of the social background of Gaelic learners in terms of matters such as social class and political affiliation will be very familiar with today's Gaelic tutor. While there has been a lack of research into the social background of Gaelic learners since the Gaelic Learners' Survey, available evidence with regard to matters such as the current age and gender profile of Gaelic learners suggests that there has been little change in their makeup, as shown later in this chapter.

Questionnaire Results

Section 1: Social Background of Learners

Sex of Respondents

The issue of the sex of Gaelic learners is an important area of study as any significant imbalance in the gender balance of speakers of the language would likely have a detrimental effect on language development efforts. To date, the results of studies which have touched upon this issue make it difficult to draw an overall conclusion. Comunn na Gàidhlig and CLI's 1992 study, for example, found that 58% of respondents were female and 42% male (CnaG/CLI 1992). A gender balance in favour of women was also found in Pringle's earlier study of Gaelic weekend courses (Pringle 1985). More girls than boys choose Gaelic as a school examination subject (NicCoinnich 1998). A 1997 study of CLI members by the Lèirsinn research centre on the subject of Gaelic broadcasting as a learning resource, however, found the gender balance of their respondents to be 58.1% male and 41.8% female (MacNeil and MacDonald 1997). As will be seen below, the findings of the present Gaelic Learners' Survey confirmed the difficulty of drawing an overall conclusion as to the gender balance of Gaelic learners nationally.

Learners were asked in the Gaelic Learners' Survey whether they were male or female. The results can be seen in Table 3.

Table 3: Sex of all respondents

Sex	% Scotland 2001 Census	Scotland[136] N	%[137]	UK N	%	World N	%
M	48.05	211	53.8	99	62.3	45	50.6
F	51.95	175	44.6	60	37.7	41	46.1
Not Stated	-	6	1.5	-	-	3	3.4
Total	**100**	**392**	**100**	**159**	**100**	**89**	**100**

It can be seen that men were over-represented amongst respondents. This was the case not only with respondents in Scotland, but also with respondents in the remainder of the UK and, to a lesser extent, in the rest of the world. The fact that survey respondents were predominantly male cannot, however, be taken to mean that such a pattern of male prevalence is representative of Gaelic learners as a whole, as significant variations existed between the gender balances of questionnaires which had been distributed through different sources.

---

[136] Throughout this chapter, the use of (Sc) or Scotland in tables signifies responses from Scotland, UK signifies the responses coming from parts of the UK *other than Scotland* and World responses from outside the UK.

[137] Throughout this chapter, percentages in tables have been rounded up to one decimal place. Totals do not, therefore, always add up to 100%

The large percentage of males in the sample reflects the fact that questionnaires were mainly distributed through CLI, an organisation with a predominantly male membership (see Table 4). In addition, within the CLI membership, there was a higher questionnaire response rate amongst males than females, meaning that the gender balance of the CLI members in Scotland who filled in a questionnaire was: 61.3% male, 36.5% female and 2.3% unknown.

Table 4: Sex of entire CLI membership:[138]

	% (all members)[139]	% (Sc)	% (UK)	% (world)
M	58.1	54.5	65.6	60.2
F	41.8	45.5	34.4	39.8
Total number	1053	604	262	186

This pattern of male predominance was not replicated in the remainder of the questionnaires. Questionnaires returned from summer, weekend, college and university courses showed a majority of women on each of these types of course. In Scotland, the gender balance of those who returned questionnaires received from these sources combined was: 40.4% male, 59.6% female, with the total number of questionnaires being 136. This reflects the research of Comunn na Gàidhlig and of Pringle whose studies of Gaelic evening and weekend courses found that a disproportionate number of women attended such classes (CnaG 1992, Pringle 1985).

A range of providers of Gaelic learning opportunities were contacted for details of the gender balance of their courses in the late 1990s and early 2000s. Between 1998 and the end of 2000, CLI's weekend 'Community Courses' were attended by 639 people, 60% of whom were female.[140] The main Gaelic summer course provider, Sabhal Mòr Ostaig, also reported a majority of female participants on its courses, with 62% of the 355 course participants in the year 2000 being female and 38% being male, this being a typical yearly gender balance for the courses.[141] Universities also reported a female dominance amongst the learners on their courses.[142] This is also typical of the full-time intensive Gaelic courses (Robertson 2001: 3). At Inverness College, for example, roughly two-thirds of students on the immersion course were female and in Sabhal Mòr Ostaig the intake over the years 1998–2000 for intensive Gaelic courses has consisted of 94 students, 60% female and 40% male.[143] The largest provider of

---

[138] The sex of CLI members was worked out through analysis of the CLI membership list.

[139] The sex of 25 CLI members could not be ascertained from their entries on CLI's membership list. These members have been excluded from the table, as have corporate members.

[140] Màiri Rhind, Community Course Manager, CLI, personal communication: telephone conversation, 12.03.01.

[141] Gavin Parsons, Short Courses Manager, Sabhal Mòr Ostaig, personal communication: email, 11.01.01.

[142] Ronald Black, Senior Lecturer in Celtic, Edinburgh University, personal communication: email, 10.01.01; Carol Smith, Secretary, Department of Celtic, Glasgow University, personal communication: email: 12.03.01.

[143] Iain MacIlleChiar, tutor, Inverness College Gaelic Immersion Course, personal communication: email: 13.01.01; Wilson McLeod, then Lecturer, Sabhal Mòr Ostaig, personal communication: email, 12.03.01.

Gaelic distance learning courses, Edinburgh's Telford College, further reports a long-standing majority of female learners of around the same order.[144]

In order to update the figures for the mid-late 2000s, a sample of course providers were contacted in 2006: Clì Gàidhlig, Edinburgh's Telford College, Inverness College and the Celtic departments of Glasgow, Edinburgh and Aberdeen Universities. All reported a significant majority of female students.[145] Figures supplied by the Scottish Executive's Gaelic unit for students studying Gaelic at any level through further education colleges showed that there were 1,015 students in the 2004–5 session of whom 60.6% were female and 39.6% male.[146]

It has already been seen that two tendencies can be observed amongst the questionnaire responses: a male bias amongst CLI respondents and a female bias amongst questionnaires returned from summer, weekend and college/university courses. Evidence such as the CLI membership list, the earlier studies referred to above and the gender balance figures from the various types of course mentioned suggest that the patterns of gender balance seen in the questionnaire are representative of the Gaelic learners scene as a whole, with females forming a majority in most types of Gaelic courses nationally but with men forming a majority of CLI members. If the roughly 6:4 female: male ratio quoted for many of the courses mentioned is anywhere near representative of the Gaelic learners scene as a whole, this female majority would be less than that which might be expected for the learning of other modern languages in Scotland.

The female majority on courses such as summer, university and weekend courses reflects the well-documented tendency for women to be more likely than men to learn languages and for languages to be perceived by many to be 'women's subjects' (Nuffield Languages Enquiry 2000: 46). The male bias of the CLI membership, on the other hand, could be said to reflect the tendency of men to be more likely than women to join organisations (Skogen 1996: 457).

One factor which has been argued to attract male learners to learning certain languages is politics. Pritchard has shown evidence of a greater interest in learning the Irish language in West Belfast on the part of males than females, both in school and in post-school education, which she attributes to the political significance of the language (Pritchard 1990: 31).

This may also be a factor affecting the gender balance of the Scottish sample of learners, given the strong level of support for political nationalism shown amongst respondents, and may well be a factor in ensuring that the seeming female majority amongst Gaelic learners is not as large as it often is for the learners of other languages.

---

[144] Katie Murray, Gaelic flexible learning tutor, Telford College, Edinburgh, personal communication: email, 15.03.01.

[145] Carol Smith, Secretary, Department of Celtic, Glasgow University, personal communication: email: 28.02.06; Wilson McLeod, Senior Lecturer in Celtic, Edinburgh University, personal communication: e-mail: 26.02.06; Rob Dunbar, Reader in Law and Celtic, University of Aberdeen, personal communication: e-mail, 01.03.06; Katie Murray, Gaelic flexible learning tutor, Telford College, Edinburgh, personal communication: email: 26.02.06, Iain MacIlleChiar, tutor, Inverness College Gaelic Immersion Course, personal communication: e-mail: 27.02.06; Siùsaidh Hardy, Director, Clì Gàidhlig, personal communication: telephone conversation: 09.05.06.

[146] Douglas Ansdell, Scottish Executive Gaelic Unit, personal communication: e-mail: 13.3.06.

While the discussion here has suggested tentatively that the difference in proportion of males and females learning Gaelic is probably not so large as to be a matter for concern, there can be no doubt that the gender balance of Gaelic learners (both those learning and those who have become fluent) is an area which requires further research.

Age of Respondents

The age of respondents is set out in Table 5. Respondents in Scotland tended to be slightly older than the Scottish population as a whole, while learners in the remainder of the UK tended to be noticeably older than the general population. In Scotland, for example, 16.9% of respondents were between 15 and 29 as opposed to 22.9% of the population aged 15 or over in Scotland as a whole. While the age range of respondents in Scotland is not very greatly older than the population as a whole, the demographic picture of Gaelic learners emerging from this study is nonetheless not hopeful for RLS. Similar findings with regard to the age of learners have been observed in a number of previous national studies (CnaG 1992, MacCaluim 1995, MacNeil and MacDonald 1997).

Table 5: Age of all respondents

Age[147]	% Scotland[148]	Scotland N	Scotland %	UK N	UK %	World N	World %
15-19	7.64	29	7.4	3	1.9	6	6.5
20-24	7.57	21	5.4	5	3.1	14	15.2
25-29	7.64	16	4.1	8	5	11	12
30-34	9.20	31	7.9	4	2.5	9	9.8
35-39	9.70	37	9.4	16	10.1	7	7.6
40-49	17.22	93	23.8	50	31.45	15	16.3
50-59	15.38	63	16.1	39	24.5	15	16.3
60-69	12.05	51	13	22	13.8	6	6.5
70-79	8.96	24	6.1	7	4.4	4	4.34
80+	4.65	10	2.6	-	-	-	-
Not Stated	-	15	3.8	5	3.1	5	5.4
Total	100	390	100	159	100	92	100

To maximise the impact of learners on RLS, learners would have to tend to be significantly younger than the population as a whole. If few people are attracted to learning Gaelic in the 15–25 age group then it is unlikely that many learners will meet

---

[147] There were also two respondents aged younger than 15. These respondents have been excluded from the table.
[148] % Scotland = percentage of people in Scotland over the age of 15 who fall within each age group. Data is drawn from the 2001 Census.

Gaelic-speaking partners or learn the language prior to becoming parents. If learners are to play a part in intergenerational transmission of the language, more young learners must be attracted to and become fluent in the language. Even for intergenerational donation of the language by means of Gaelic-medium education, the questionnaire response is not promising, as over 60% of learners are 40 or older.

In many ways it could be said to be easier for younger people to learn Gaelic than for older people, as there are opportunities to undertake Gaelic as a college or university course on leaving school, and as people in their teens and early twenties typically have fewer family and job responsibilities than people in older age groups and may, therefore, have more time and energy to devote to language learning. If people learn Gaelic relatively early in life, it also probably more likely that they will enter Gaelic-related employment than they would when in an established career or with a family to support. This is an important factor given the significance of Gaelic-related employment such as teaching and broadcasting to RLS and the difficulty often encountered in filling Gaelic-related jobs (Galloway 1994: 144).

Table 6: Age of respondents in Scotland excluding university students

Age[149]	% Scotland	N (Sc)	% (Sc)
15-19	7.64	10	2.9
20-24	7.57	11	3.1
25-29	7.64	13	3.7
30-34	9.20	31	8.9
35-39	9.70	32	9.1
40-49	17.22	93	26.6
50-59	15.38	62	17.7
60-69	12.05	51	14.5
70-79	8.96	24	6.9
80+	4.65	10	2.9
Not Stated	-	13	3.7
Total	100	350	100

It should be noted that the overall age pattern amongst respondents hides some variations, as can be seen from Table 6. The learners aged under 20 recorded in the figure for respondents as a whole largely consisted of learners who were studying Gaelic as a university course at one of the three university Celtic departments, with there being very few learners in this age group in the remainder of the questionnaires. Learners in the 15–34 age group tended to be under-represented throughout all sectors of Gaelic learning sampled with the exception of these university courses.

Geographical Location of Respondents

Respondents were classified according to their normal country of residence in Tables 7 and 8.

---

[149] The two respondents aged under 15 have been omitted once again.

Table 7: Distribution of Gaelic learners by country of residence

Country / Area	N	%
Scotland	392	61
Rest of UK	159	24.7
Rest of Europe[150]	41	6.4
U.S and Commonwealth[151]	47	7.3
Other[152]	1	0.2
Not stated	3	0.5
Total	**643**	**100**

Table 8: Location of all respondents living in UK by country of residence

Country / Area	N	%
Cornwall	1	0.2
England	148	26.9
Northern Ireland	1	0.2
Scotland	392	71.1
Wales	9	1.6
Total	**551**	**100**

As might be expected, most respondents were resident in Scotland. The single largest concentration of learners outwith Scotland was to be found in the remainder of the UK, overwhelmingly in England. Smaller but significant numbers of learners also resided elsewhere in Europe and in the US and Commonwealth. Very few respondents resided elsewhere.

Place of Upbringing of Respondents

Respondents were charted by place of upbringing in Tables 9–11. Learners living outside Scotland are covered in Tables 9 and 10; learners living in Scotland in Table 11.

Table 9: Place of upbringing: respondents in the UK but outwith Scotland

Country	N	%
Scotland[153]	50	31.45
Rest of UK	101	63.5
Rest of Europe	1	0.6
USA	3	1.9
Commonwealth	1	0.6
More than one country	2	1.3
Not Stated	1	0.8
Total	**159**	**100**

---

[150] Austria 1, Brittany 2, Catalonia 1, Denmark 1, France 2, Galicia 1, Germany 13, Irish Republic 5, Isle of Man 4, Italy 1, Netherlands 3, Poland 1, Russia 1, Spain 1, Sweden 3, Switzerland 1.
[151] Australia 9, Canada 7, New Zealand 4, USA 26, Zimbabwe 1.
[152] Argentina 1.
[153] Including 6 respondents who were partially brought up in Scotland.

Table 10: Place of upbringing: respondents outwith the UK

Country	N	%
Scotland	5	5.6
Rest of UK	4	4.5
Rest of Europe	34	38.2
USA	26	29.2
Commonwealth	18	20.2
Other	1	1.1
More than one country	1	1.1
Not Stated	-	-
Total	89	100

It can be seen from Table 9 that almost one-third of learners living in the remainder of the UK were brought up wholly or partially in Scotland. This suggests that a Scottish upbringing may be a factor in leading many respondents to learn Gaelic. This factor, along with the factor of Scottish descent, will be investigated further below.

Of the respondents living furth of the UK, few were born in Scotland, with most respondents having been born in the country in which they were resident.

Table 11: Place of upbringing: respondents resident in Scotland

Country	N	%
Scotland[154]	303	77.3
Rest of UK	58	14.8
Rest of Europe	10	2.55
USA	5	1.3
Commonwealth	4	1
More than one country (not including Scotland)	3	0.8
Unknown	9	2.3
Total	392	100

Of the learners living in Scotland, just over three-quarters had been raised in Scotland. A significant number also hailed from the remainder of the UK. This compares with the figures of 87.15% of Scottish residents born in Scotland and 9.07% born in the remainder of the UK as seen in the 2001 Census.

Place of Residence within Scotland

One question which this study aimed to investigate was the geographical location of Gaelic learners. As questionnaires were distributed partly at community courses and other courses attended largely by people living in a particular area, it was felt that results from the questionnaire might not accurately reflect the geographical balance of Gaelic learners within Scotland. For this reason, the geographical location of Gaelic learners in Scotland will be investigated through the place of residence of CLI members at it stood on 01.09.98, shortly after the questionnaire was distributed, as the geographical distribution of the CLI membership is likely to be representative of Scottish based Gaelic learners in general.

---

[154] Includes three respondents brought up partially in Scotland.

The distribution of CLI members in Scotland by local authority area can be seen in Tables 12 and 13. Due to the large number of local authorities in Scotland, CLI members have also been tabulated by pre-1996 regions in order to simplify matters. In each table, the percentage of the entire Scottish population living in each area according to Census data is shown in the column entitled "% Scottish Population (2001 Census)".

Table 12: Place of residence: CLI members in Scotland by local authority area

Local Authority	N	%	% Scottish Population (2001 Census)
Aberdeen City	19	2.8	4.19
Aberdeenshire	19	2.8	4.48
Angus	15	2.2	2.14
Argyll and Bute	31	4.5	1.80
Clackmannanshire	5	0.7	0.95
Comhairle nan Eilean Siar	23	3.4	0.52
Dumfries and Galloway	18	2.6	2.92
Dundee	12	1.8	2.88
E. Ayrshire	5	0.7	2.38
E. Dunbartonshire	13	1.9	2.14
E. Lothian	6	0.9	1.78
E. Renfrewshire	6	0.9	1.76
Edinburgh	95	13.9	8.86
Falkirk	8	1.2	2.87
Fife	23	3.4	6.90
Glasgow	67	9.8	11.42
Highland	168	24.6	4.13
Inverclyde	4	0.6	1.66
Midlothian	9	1.3	1.60
Moray	9	1.3	1.72
N. Ayrshire	15	2.2	2.68
N. Lanarkshire	9	1.3	6.34
Orkney	0	0	0.38
Perth and Kinross	25	3.7	2.67
Renfrewshire	10	1.5	3.41
S. Ayrshire	14	2	2.21
S. Lanarkshire	18	2.6	5.97
Scottish Borders	15	2.2	2.11
Shetland	1	0.1	0.43
Stirling	9	1.3	1.70
W. Dunbartonshire	5	0.7	1.84
W. Lothian	7	1	3.14
Total	683	100	100

Table 13: Place of residence: CLI members in Scotland by pre-1996 region

Region / Island area	N	% CLI members	% Sc. Pop (2001 Census)
Borders	15	2.2	2.11
Central	22	3.2	5.52
Comhairle nan Eilean	23	3.4	0.52
Dumfries and Galloway	18	2.6	2.92
Fife	23	3.4	6.90
Grampian	47	6.6	10.39
Highland	168	24.6	4.13
Lothian	117	17.1	15.38
Strathclyde	197	28.8	43.61
Tayside	52	7.7	7.69
Orkney Isles	0	0	0.38
Shetland Isles	1	0.1	0.43
Total	**683**	**100**	**100**

It can be seen from the tables that Gaelic learners were spread throughout the country. As might be expected, there tended to be more learners in areas where Gaelic is or has recently been spoken as a community language and also in Scotland's main urban centres, Glasgow and Edinburgh, where there are large populations, many people with family links to the language and a range of Gaelic groups and happenings. Even in regions of Scotland where there were fewer Gaelic learners than would have been the case if learners were distributed in proportion to the Scottish population as a whole, there were nonetheless respectable numbers of learners in all former regions, with the exception of the Orkney and Shetland Isles areas, where Gaelic has never been spoken as an autochthonous language. These figures look hopeful with regard to RLS, showing that a level of interest exists in the language nationally and that there are concentrations in areas of strategic importance to the language: the Highlands and the cities.

Proportion of the sample living in or raised in the Highlands and Lowlands

One issue which the questionnaire aimed to investigate was the extent to which Gaelic learners had connections with the Highlands through, for example, living in or coming from the Highlands. This was part of the broader investigation of the extent to which Gaelic learners had personal or family connections to the language or areas in which the language is or has recently been spoken. Whether interest in Gaelic is largely restricted to groups of people with such connections to the language or whether the appeal of the language is broader is a significant question for RLS.

In order to investigate the proportion of respondents in Scotland living in or hailing from the Highlands, a series of tables was drawn up. This presented some difficulty in that the geographical boundaries of the terms 'Highlands' and 'Lowlands' are very difficult to define.[155] After what are now known as the Lowlands had mainly ceased to be Gaelic-speaking by the end of the fifteenth century, the term

---

[155] See MacInnes 1989, Newton 2000, Withers 1984, 1988, 1992 for detailed discussion of the term 'Highlands'.

'Highlands' came to be used to describe the area of northern and western Scotland where Gaelic was consolidated and remained as the vernacular. Several factors have served to blur this long-standing definition of the Highlands in recent times. Most importantly, Gaelic has ceased to be spoken in much of the Highland area from late 18th century onwards. Factors such as population change, administrative boundaries, trading and transport links have also served to render the southern and eastern boundaries of the Highlands ambiguous (Withers 1984, 1988, 1992).

For these reasons, in attempting to categorise respondent's place of upbringing and place of residence, the decision was taken to draw up two different definitions of the Highlands. The 'Core Highlands' has been defined as the areas of Argyll and Bute Council, the Highland Council and Comhairle nan Eilean Siar. This was to ensure as far as possible that the areas in question were considered to be Highland by the people living in or hailing from these areas. A further definition of the 'Greater Highlands' has also been drawn up to represent as far as possible the full extent of the traditional Highlands, including also traditionally Highland areas of the Aberdeenshire, Angus, Moray, North Ayrshire, Stirling, Perth and Kinross and West Dunbartonshire council areas, areas in which Gaelic was spoken until fairly recently.[156] It cannot be assumed, however, that all of those coming from or living in these areas are necessarily aware of the Gaelic-speaking history of these areas or consider the areas to be part of the Highlands. In practice, very few respondents lived in these latter areas.

Respondents in Scotland were categorised according to Highlands or Lowlands residence in Table 14 and according to upbringing in Table 15. In Table 16, they were tabulated according to whether they were resident in or raised in the Highlands.

Table 14: Residence in the Highlands or Lowlands: respondents in Scotland

Place of Residence	N	%
The Greater Highlands	135	34.4
The Core Highlands	129	32.9
The Lowlands	247	63
The Highlands and Lowlands	4	1
Not Stated	6	1.5
Total	392	100.0

Table 15: Upbringing in the Highlands or Lowlands: respondents in Scotland

Place of Upbringing	N	%
The Greater Highlands	72	18.4
The Core Highlands	69	17.6
The Lowlands	216	55.1
Highlands and Lowlands	11	2.8
Outwith Scotland	81	20.7
Not stated	12	3.1
Total	392	100.0

---

[156] The exact outer boundaries of this Greater Highland area would be difficult to define in theory. In practice, however, no respondents lived in boundary areas where definition as Highland or Lowland would be difficult.

Table 16: Upbringing or residence in the Highlands: respondents in Scotland

Place of Upbringing / Residence	N	%
Raised or resident in the Greater Highlands[157]	174	44.27
Neither raised nor resident in the Greater Highlands	212	53.9
Raised or resident in the Core Highlands	165	42
Neither raised nor resident in the Core Highlands	221	56.4
Not stated	6	1.8
Total	**392**	**100**

It can be seen that while a significant minority of respondents were raised in the Highlands, a majority of respondents were raised elsewhere in Scotland. A majority were also resident outwith the Highlands. Even when these two factors were taken together, a majority were neither resident nor raised in the Highlands regardless of the definition of 'Highlands' employed. This finding bodes well for the regeneration of Gaelic, showing as it does that the learning of Gaelic is not mainly confined to people living in or coming from areas where the language is or was spoken as a community language in the recent past.

Education

Respondents were tabulated by level of educational qualification gained in Tables 17–19. Respondents living in Scotland are charted by level of qualification and in Tables 18 and 19 are compared with the Scottish population as a whole.

Table 17: Level of qualification: respondents in Scotland

Qualification	N	%
No Formal Qualifications	25	6.4
Basic Vocational / Scotvec	6	1.5
O' Grades / Standard Grades / O' Levels or Equivalent	21	5.4
Higher / A' Levels or Equivalent	66	15.3
ONC / OND	6	1.5
HNC / HND / Dip HE or Equivalent	28	7.1
Teachers' Certificate / Nursing Qualification	30	7.65
First Degree	63	16.1
Postgraduate Certificate / Professional Diploma	81	20.7
Higher Degree	60	15.3
Other	-	-
Not Stated	6	1.5
Total	**392**	**100**

---

[157] All figures for those raised or resident in the Highlands in this table include those who were raised partially in the Highlands or who live both in the Highlands and in the Lowlands. One respondent is counted both within the totals for the Greater Highlands and Core Highlands due to living in one and having been raised in the other.

Table 18: Level of qualification: respondents in Scotland vs. 1991 Census[158]

Level of Qualification	N (Sc)	% (Sc)	% Scotland 1991 Census
Level a	60	15.3	0.8
Level b	144	36.7	6
Level c	64	16.3	7.2
Any of above	268	68.4	14

It can be seen from Tables 17 and 18 that the respondents as a whole have a far higher level of education than the Scottish population as a whole. A similar pattern is also shown for Gaelic learners furth of Scotland in Tables 19 and 20. The significance of these high levels of educational qualification are further investigated below in connection with the social class makeup of the respondents.

Table 19: Level of qualification: respondents in UK outwith Scotland

Qualification	N	%
No Formal Qualifications	13	8.2
Basic Vocational / Scotvec	5	3.1
O' Grades / Standard Grades / O' Levels or Equivalent	9	5.7
Higher / A' Levels or Equivalent	9	5.7
ONC / OND	1	0.6
HNC / HND / Dip HE or Equivalent	6	3.8
Teachers' Certificate / Nursing Qualification	12	7.55
First Degree	36	22.6
Postgraduate Certificate / Professional Diploma	33	20.75
Higher Degree	33	20.75
Other	2	1.3
Not Stated	-	-
Total	159	100

[158] Census figures in this table ('% Scotland') are based on 10% figures from Table 2 of the 1991 Census Qualified Manpower Great Britain report. Qualifications are defined as: level a: higher degrees of UK standard, level b: first degrees and all other qualifications of UK first degree standard and level c: qualifications that are (i) generally obtained at 18 and over, (ii) above GCE 'A' Level standard; and (iii) below UK first degree standards. In the 2001 Census, the categories used for measuring level of qualification were: No qualifications; Group 1 ('O' Grade, Standard Grade, Intermediate 1, Intermediuate 2, City and Guilds Craft, SCQ Level 1 or 2 or equivalent); Group 2 (Higher Grade, CSYS ONC, OND, City and Guilds Advanced Craft, RSA Advanced Diploma, SVQ Level 3 or equivalent); Group 3 (HNC, RSA Higher Diploma, SVQ Level 4 or 5 or Equivalent); Group 4 (First Degree, Higher Degree, Professional Qualifications). The figures for each group in the 2001 Census were: No qualifications 33%, Group 1: 25%, Group 2: 16%, Group 3: 7%; Group 4: 19%. Figures are based on Table 24 of the Registrar General's 2001 Census Report to the Scottish Parliament. It was not possible to re-anbalyse the questionnaire figures in terms of these categories as the questionnaire database no longer exists; nevertheless, it can still be clearly seen that the respondents tended to be qualified to a higher level than the Scottish population as a whole.

Table 20: Level of qualification: respondents outwith the UK

Qualification	N	%
No formal qualifications	14	15.7
Basic vocational / Scotvec O' Grades / Standard Grades / O' Levels or equivalent	4	4.5
Higher / A' Levels or equivalent	9	10.1
ONC / OND	-	-
HNC / HND / Dip HE or equivalent	1	1.1
Teachers' certificate / nursing cualification	4	4.5
First degree	19	21.35
Postgraduate certificate / professional diploma	13	14.6
Higher degree	14	15.7
Other	7	7.9
Not stated	4	4.5
Total	89	100

The socio-economic status of respondents was also recorded (Tables 21 and 22) and these figures were then compared with Census data (Table 23).

Table 21: Socio-economic status: respondents in Scotland

Status	N	%
Employed full-time	130	33.2
Employed part-time	39	10
Unemployed	15	3.8
Armed Forces	1	0.3
Permanently sick or disabled	3	0.8
In full-time Education	76	19.4
On a government training or employment scheme	2	0.5
Looking after house full-time	14	3.6
Retired	90	23
Other[159]	19	4.8
Not Stated	3	0.8
Total	392	100

---

[159] Including 14 self-employed respondents. As a question on being self-employed was not included on this table in the questionnaire, it is likely that some self-employed respondents may have entered themselves as being in part-time or full-time employment.

Table 22: Socio-economic status: respondents in UK outwith Scotland

Status	N	%
Employed full-time	85	53.5
Employed part-time	15	9.4
Unemployed	8	5
Armed Forces	-	-
Permanently sick or disabled	2	1.3
In full-time education	6	3.8
On a government training / or employment scheme	-	-
Looking after house full-time	4	2.5
Retired	29	18.2
Other[160]	9	5.7
Not Stated	1	0.6
Total	**159**	**100**

Table 23: Economic position: Scottish and UK respondents vs. Scottish Census data

	% Scotland[161] (1991 Census)	% Scotland[162] (2001 Census)	% (Sc)	% (UK)
Economically active:	60.4	64.97	51.2	72.3
In employment	54.1	54.1	47.4	67.3
Full-time	38.4	40.25	33.3	53.5
Part-time	9.3	11.12	10	9.4
Self-employed	5.3	6.6	3.6	4.4
On a government scheme	1	-	0.5	-
Unemployed	6.2	3.97	3.8	5
Economically inactive	39.6	35.01	46.8	25.8
Students	3.6	4.28	19.4	3.8
Permanently sick	5.6	7.44	0.8	1.3
Retired	18.1	13.89	23	18.2
Other inactive	12.2	9.40	3.6	2.5

It can be seen that the economic position of the respondents in Scotland was relatively similar to that of the Scottish population as a whole with the exception that there was a larger percentage of students in the sample than in the population as a whole, reflecting the students learning Gaelic at university within the sample. The *permanently sick* and *other inactive* categories were also noticeably under-represented amongst respondents. For the respondents outwith the UK, larger percentages were economically active and particularly in full-time employment than in the general population. As in Scotland, the 'permanently sick' and 'other inactive' categories were under-represented.

---

[160] Including 7 self employed respondents.
[161] Census figures in this table ('% Scotland 1991 Census') are based on 100% figures from Table 1 of the 1991 Census Economic Activity Scotland report.
[162] Census figures in this table ('% Scotland') are based on 100% figures from Table 13 of the Registrar General's 2001Census Report to the Scotland Parliament. Please note that there were some changes to the categories for the 2001 Census. The category of *On a Government training scheme* was removed and *Economically active full-time studentrs* were counted as a separate category from economically inactive students. The questionnaire data cited in the table was analysed in terms of the categories as were used in the 1991 Census data and it was not possible to re-analyse the questionnaire figures as the questionnaire database no longer exists

Social Class

Respondents were placed into social class in Tables 25–28. The scheme of social class used was Social Class Based on Occupation [Registrar General's Social Class] as used in the UK Census.

Table 24: Social Class based on occupation: [Registrar General's Social Class]

	Class
I	Professional etc. occupations
II	Managerial and technical occupations
III (N)	Skilled occupations: non-manual
III (M)	Skilled occupations: manual
IV	Partly skilled occupations
V	Unskilled occupations

Scottish respondents currently in employment were charted by social class and compared with the social class makeup of Scotland as a whole in Table 25. In Table 26, all Scottish respondents were charted regardless of whether in employment or not. The social class position of learners living in the rest of the UK and in the rest of the world are recorded in Tables 27–28.

Table 25: Social Class based on occupation: Scottish respondents currently in employment

Class	N (Sc)	% (Sc)	% Scotland 1991 Census[163]
I	45	21	4.8
II	119	55.6	26.8
III (N)	20	9.35	22.6
III (M)	11	5.1	21.5
IV	7	3.3	15.4
V	2	0.9	7.2
Armed Forces	2	0.9	0.8
Occupation inadequately described or not stated	8	3.7	0.9
Total	214	100	100

Table 26: Social Class based on occupation: all Scottish respondents[164]

Class	N (Sc)	% (Sc)
I	76	24.1
II	169	53.65
III (N)	32	10.2
III (M)	16	5.1
IV	9	2.9
V	2	0.6
Armed Forces	2	0.6
Occupation inadequately described or not stated	9	2.9
Total	315	100

Questionnaire Results

Table 27: Social Class based on occupation: respondents in UK outwith Scotland

Class	N (Sc)	% (Sc)
I	31	27.4
II	56	49.6
III (N)	9	8
III (M)	7	6.2
IV	3	2.65
V	1	0.9
Armed Forces	1	0.9
Occupation inadequately described or not stated	5	4.4
Total	**113**	**100**

Table 28: Social Class based on occupation: respondents outwith UK in employment

Class	N (Sc)	% (Sc)
I	18	29.5
II	30	49.2
III (N)	4	6.6
III (M)	3	4.9
IV	1	1.6
V	3	4.9
Armed Forces	-	-
Occupation inadequately described or not stated	2	3.3
Total	**61**	**100**

It can be seen from Tables 25–28 that respondents in Scotland, the rest of the UK and the rest of the world were largely drawn from the highest social classes with very few coming from the manual working classes. As can be seen from Table 25, respondents in Scotland were disproportionately drawn from classes I and II with all other classes

---

[163] Census figures in this table ('Scotland') are based on 10% figures from Table 14 of the 1991 Census Economic Activity Scotland report for Scotland for the working population aged 16+. As of the 2001 Census, a new socio-economic classification has been used in place of Social Class based on Occupation. This is the NS-SeC (National Statistiucs – Socio-Economic Classification). It has not been possible to re-analyse the questionnaire data in terms of these new categories as the questionnaire database no longer exists. For purposes of comparison with the 1991 Census data, the figures in the 2001 Census (Table 16) for the Scottish population aged 16–74 in employment according to the NS-SeC were: Large employers and higher managerial and professional occupations: 4%; Higher professional occupations: 7%; Lower managerial and professional occupations: 25%; Intermediate occupations: 13%; Small employers and own account workers: 8%; Lower supervisory and technical occupations: 10%; semi-routine occupations: 16%; Routine occupations: 12%; Full-time students in employment: 4%; Occupation not stated or inadequately described: 0% (General Register for Scotland: 2003).

[164] In this table, all respondents in Scotland, whether economically active or inactive, are placed into social class based on occupation wherever possible. The retired and unemployed are classified according to previous occupations, those looking after the house or permanently ill are categorised according to partner's occupation. Students are excluded as are unemployed or retired people who did not state their previous occupation.

being under-represented in comparison with the population as a whole. A similar pattern emerged outside Scotland.

This pattern of class participation is not unique to Gaelic learning but rather is common to many cultural, educational and voluntary organisations and social movements, as is the tendency for participants to be highly educated. Forster's study of the Esperanto movement, for example, shows a pattern of class participation similar to that shown above (1968: 306). This trend is also mentioned by Bottomore, who points out that such a pattern is particularly notable in cultural and educational organisations and movements (1954: 363). Many other sociologists have also noted the predominantly middle-class makeup of such 'new social movements': social movements engaged mainly in the politics of lifestyle, culture and identity as opposed to the politics of class.[165]

Many reasons can be suggested for the predominance of classes I and II in such groupings. Bottomore has suggested that "participation […] is strongly influenced by the individual's level of education, which is closely correlated with his occupational status" (1954: 363). This factor is also pointed out by Forster, who argues with reference to the Esperanto movement that learning and gaining the fullest use of a language "implies a need for verbal facility and an inclination for reading which in turn strengthens the middle-class social composition of the movement" (Forster 1968: 308). It has already been seen that respondents tended to be educated to a high level. Another possible factor in the class makeup of the sample is that of finance. This, too, is mentioned by Bottomore who says that: "it is reasonable to suppose that those from the lowest occupational groups are in practice excluded from some of these organisations by the high subscriptions, and not merely self-excluded by not having developed the appropriate cultural interests" (1954: 364).

While perhaps not as important as the reasons above in leading to the largely middle-class make-up of respondents, money must certainly be one factor influencing the composition of the Gaelic learners' movement, as learning involves many costs for services and materials such as evening classes, books and summer schools which would tend to exclude those with lower incomes.

In addition to the general middle class predominance among respondents, certain sectors of this class such as teachers, lecturers, the clergy and those involved in the medical profession were particularly well represented. A tendency for those involved with social movements to be drawn disproportionately from the educational and caring professions as opposed to sectors such as finance and industry has been noted to be common to many new social movements (e.g. Cosgrove and Duff 1980: 340, Forster 1968: 310).

Some commentators such as Cosgrove and Duff have suggested that this predominance of what they call the 'non-productive service sector' in social movements reflects the class interests of this particular class fraction. Such groups are said to be on the fringes of capitalist society due to their work being 'non-productive' in terms of industrial capitalism. Involvement in such social movements as the Green movement can, therefore, be explained in terms of a "concern to win greater participation and influence and thus to strengthen the political role of their members"

---

[165] For some examples of high levels of middle-class participation in a range of different new social movements, see Cotgrove and Duff 1980 (green movement), McAllister Groves 1992 (animal rights), Parkin 1968 (anti-nuclear movement) and Beardsmore and Kial 1992 (vegetarianism).

(1980: 340) and a desire to reduce their peripherality. Interestingly, McEwan-Fujita comes close to making a similar argument with regard to Gaelic through arguing that the use by Gaelic activists (many of whom are learners) of the discourse of Gaelic as a component of group identity is "an attempt on the part of cultural elites to achieve cultural legitimisation, garner a larger share of economic resources, and consolidate their social position in the wider arena of Europe as well as in the context of the UK" (1998: 6). The cultural elites referred to are, as might be expected, middle class (McEwan-Fujita 1997, 1998).

Class-based explanations of the type given by Cosgrove and Duff have, however, been criticised for gross economic/class reductionism (Bagguley 1992, 1997: 149), as have those of the type made by McEwan-Fujita (Fishman 1985: 508). An alternative explanation for the fact that middle class people involved in social movements such as Gaelic have a tendency to work in fields such as education, medicine and the clergy could be that those choosing this type of profession may be more likely to have done so through an interest in education and learning or a desire to change or improve society than are those who have chosen a career in sectors such as finance or industry. As Bagguley has pointed out, a further explanation of the disproportionate involvement of this fraction of the middle class in social movements is that they tend, more than other sections of the middle class, to have skills as producers and organisers of knowledge (1992: 48).

Politics

Respondents were asked which political party they felt closest to. The results for respondents in Scotland are charted in Table 29. In order to compare the questionnaire respondents with the population as a whole, the political preferences were placed in opinion poll format whereby *don't knows*, *wouldn't votes* and those who did not answer the question were excluded, so that only those intending to vote and expressing party preference are included. This figure was then compared with two newspaper opinion polls for Westminster voting intentions which were conducted at the time when the questionnaires were being received (Table 30).

Table 29: Political affiliation: respondents in Scotland

Party	N	%
Conservative	18	4.6
Labour	51	13
Liberal Democrat	45	11.5
Scottish Green Party	13	3.3
Scottish National Party	197	50.3
Other Party[166]	7	1.8
Wouldn't Vote	6	1.5
Don't Know	37	9.4
Not Stated	18	4.6
Total	392	100

---

[166] Other parties: Communist Party of Scotland: 1, "Independent": 1, Mebyon Kernow (Cornish nationalists): 1, Pro-Life Party: 1, National Front: 1, Socialist Party of Great Britain: 1, US Republican:1.

Table 30: Political preference: respondents in Scotland vs. opinion polls (UK General Election)

Party	Respondents	Herald System 3 Poll[167]	Scotsman ICM Poll
Conservative	5.4%	14%	18%
Labour	15.4%	43%	41%
Liberal Democrat	13.6%	9%	10%
Scottish Green Party	3.9%	included in 'other' below	included in 'other' below
Scottish National Party	59.5%	33%	30%
Other Party	2.1%	1%	1%
Total number	**331**	**-**	**-**

As opinion polls had begun for Scottish parliamentary voting intentions by the time the questionnaire was conducted, the political preference of respondents in Scotland has also been compared with a Scottish parliamentary poll based upon the proportional representation system used in Scottish elections (Table 31). It should be noted that the questions used in the opinion polls asked about voting intention and were thus slightly different from that used in the questionnaire which asked which party respondents felt closest to.

Table 31: Political preference: respondents in Scotland vs. opinion poll (Scottish Parliament Election)

| Party | Respondents | Scotsman ICM Poll[168] | |
		Constituency	Region
Conservative	5.4%	9%	11%
Labour	15.4%	36%	36%
Liberal Democrat	13.6%	14%	15%
Scottish Green Party	3.9%	included in 'other' below	included in 'other' below
Scottish National Party	59.5%	39%	36%
Other Party	2.1%	2%	2%
Total number	**331**	**-**	**-**

Many significant trends can be seen. Firstly, there is a very low level of support for the Conservative party. Secondly, the pattern of support for the Labour party and SNP amongst the respondents are very different from that of national opinion polls, with very high levels of support for the Nationalists and far lower levels of support for the Labour party. In fact, just over half of all respondents in Scotland said that they felt closest to the SNP (almost 60% in opinion poll format) whereas only 13% of all respondents said that they felt closer to Labour.

---

[167] Data is from the *Scotsman* ICM poll, July 31 1998 and from the *Herald* System 3 poll, July 1998 as quoted on the Scottish Politics Pages: http://www.alba.org.uk/polls/index.html
[168] Data from *Scotsman* ICM poll, 31.07.98.

Table 32: Political affiliation: respondents in UK outwith Scotland

Party	N	%
Conservative	20	12.6
Labour	46	28.9
Liberal Democrat	35	22
Plaid Cymru	5	3.1
Scottish Green Party	5	3.1
Scottish National Party	24	15.9
Other Party[169]	3	1.9
Wouldn't Vote	5	3.1
Don't Know	10	6.3
Not Stated	6	3.8
Total	**159**	**100**

In Table 33, the response is tabled in opinion poll format and compared with a contemporary opinion poll. Major opinion polls are normally conducted on a GB basis (excluding Northern Ireland due to the different political parties in the area) and do not normally distinguish between voting preferences of the individual nations and regions of the UK. For this reason, UK respondents living outwith Scotland have of necessity been compared with a GB poll. This is not likely to have a significant effect on the comparability of the results, however.

Table 33: Voting intentions : respondents in the UK outwith Scotland

Party	Respondents	Mori Poll[170]
Conservative	14.5%	27%
Labour	33.3%	56%
Liberal Democrat	25.4%	13%
Plaid Cymru	3.6%	Scottish / Welsh Nationalist 3%
Scottish National Party	17.4%	Scottish / Welsh Nationalist 3%
Green Party	3.6%	1%
Other Party	2.2%	1%
Total number	**138**	-

As with the respondents in Scotland, respondents in the rest of the UK showed a far lower level of support for the Conservatives than the population as a whole. Interestingly, 17% of respondents said that they felt closest to the SNP despite living outwith Scotland. This reveals a high level of political interest in the Scottish constitution and identity even amongst those living outside Scotland.

As in Scotland, the level of support for the Labour party was lower amongst respondents than in the public in general. It may be hypothesised in this context, however, that much of the discrepancy between the level of Labour support amongst 'rest of UK' respondents and opinion poll data may have been due less to hostility

---

[169] Other parties: Communist: 2, Referendum Party: 1.

[170] Data from the Times Mori poll, 02.07.98. Question = "how would you vote if there was a General Election tomorrow? If undecided or refused: which party are you most likely to support?"

towards the Labour party than to Labour voters stating a preference for the SNP. This is suggested by the fact that several respondents in England stated that while they voted Labour, they would vote SNP were they able to. It was also hinted by the fact that a large majority of SNP supporters placed themselves on the left or in the centre on the left-right scale elsewhere in the questionnaire.

The level of support for the Liberal Democrats was also higher amongst respondents than might have been expected from national opinion poll data. This further lends to the impression that the respondents tend towards the parties of the political left and centre rather than towards the political right.

Table 34: Political affiliation of respondents outwith the UK

Party	N
Centre Left[171]	17
Centre[172]	5
Centre Right[173]	3
Green	7
Nationalist[174]	16
Socialist	1
Other	1
Wouldn't Vote	3
Don't Know	22
Not Stated	14
Total	89

The political preferences of respondents outwith the UK were recorded in Table 34. While the small number of respondents in this category mean that these figures cannot be analysed in any detail, they do suggest that Gaelic learners outside the UK share similar political affiliations to those seen in Scotland and the remainder of the UK.

Respondents were also asked in the questionnaire to place themselves on a left-right political spectrum where 0 represented the hard left, 5 the absolute centre and 10 the far right. The results are shown both graphed and tabulated below for all respondents.

Table 35: Self-identification on a left-right spectrum: respondents in Scotland

Position	0	1	2	3	4	5	6	7	8	9	10
N	10	19	52	81	70	70	32	13	8	3	0
%	2.8	5.3	14.5	22.6	19.55	19.55	8.9	3.6	2.2	0.8	0

Total = 358 – question not answered by 34 people.

---

[171] Labour, NDP (Canadian Labour), US Democrat.
[172] Liberal Democrat, Canadian Liberal, Fianna Fáil.
[173] Conservative, Dutch Christian Democrat, US Republican.
[174] SNP 14, Mec Vannin 1, ERC (Catalunya) 1. Despite the distinction made between "nationalist" and "left" in this table, it should be noted that all three nationalist parties represented here are left of centre.

Figure 1: Self-identification on a left-right spectrum: Scottish respondents

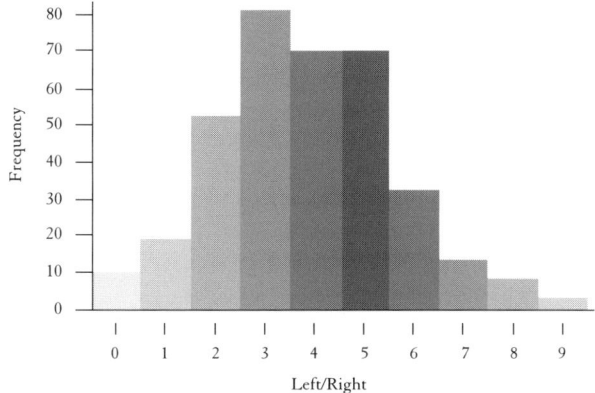

Table 36: Self-identification on a left-right spectrum: respondents in rest of UK

Position	0	1	2	3	4	5	6	7	8	9	10
N	4	4	15	36	30	31	16	5	6	2	0
%	2.7	2.7	10.1	24.1	20.1	20.8	10.7	3.4	4	1.3	0

Total = 149 – question not answered by 10 people.

Figure 2: Self-identification on a left-right spectrum: respondents in rest of UK

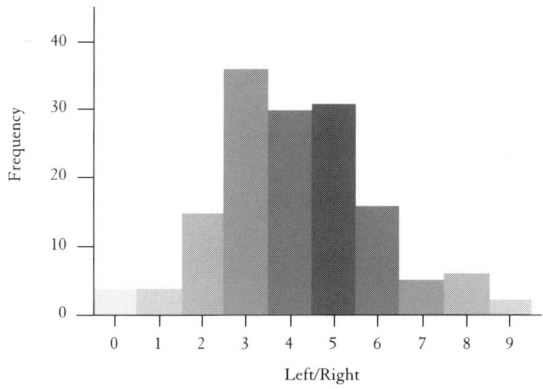

Table 37: Self-identification on a left-right spectrum of respondents outwith the UK

Position	0	1	2	3	4	5	6	7	8	9	10
N	2	3	8	17	11	13	7	6	2	-	3
%	2.8	4.2	11.1	23.6	15.3	18.1	9.7	8.3	2.8	-	4.2

Total = 72 – question not answered by 17 people.

Figure 3: Self-identification on a left-right spectrum: respondents outwith the UK

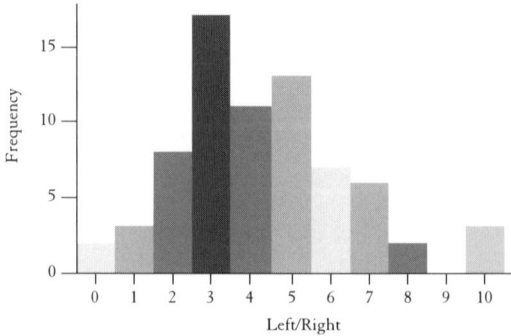

In all three groups studied, there was a clear tendency for the majority of respondents to define themselves as being left of centre, with significant numbers also defining themselves as being in the political centre. In Scotland, for example, 64.75% of respondents described themselves as being left of centre, 19.55% as being on the dead centre and 15.5% as being on the right of centre. These results serve to confirm the impression from the question on political affiliation that the sample tend towards the centre, and particularly the left, of politics.

National Identity

Respondents living in Scotland were asked to state which national identity category best described them from a range of options. The results were recorded in Table 38 and compared with the results of an opinion poll on the same issue.

Table 38: National identity of respondents in Scotland

Description	N	%	Opinion poll[175] %
Scottish not British	165	42.1	25
More Scottish than British	119	30.4	32
Equally Scottish and British	49	12.5	26
More British than Scottish	4	1	3
British not Scottish	7	1.8	11
Other[176]	29	7.4	1
Not Stated	19	4.85	2
Total	392	100	-

A large majority of the respondents displayed a predominantly Scottish sense of national identity: 72.5% felt either Scottish not British or more Scottish than British,

---

[175] ICM Scotland poll, *The Scotsman*, 2 April 1999, http://www.icmresearch.co.uk
[176] Other: American 4, Anglo-Welsh Scot 1, British and N. Irish 1, British not English 1, "Celt (Irish Citizen)" 1, Cornish 1, English 7, Equally Scottish, English and Irish 1, Equally Scottish and Irish 1, Equally Scottish and English 1 Equally Scottish and European 1, German-Cantonese 1, Icelandic 1, Irish 2, "I identify with all Celtic nations" 1, More Irish than Scots 1, New Scot 1, Naturalised Scottish not British 1, European 1, Welsh 2, world 1, "don't think of myself in these terms" 1.
[176] Of those stating that they considered themselves to be "British not Scottish" or "more British than Scottish", all but one were born in England.

while only 12.5% felt equally Scottish and British and only 2.8% either more British than Scottish or British not Scottish.[176] The level of identification with Scottish as opposed to British national identity was far higher within the sample than in the opinion poll with which it is compared. This, along with the high level of SNP support seen earlier, confirms the strong feeling of Scottish national identity within the sample.

The question of nationality / national identity was also investigated for respondents furth of Scotland, as shown in Tables 39, 40. The two nationalities given most frequently were British and English, with significant numbers also describing themselves as Scottish or Scottish/British.

Outside the UK, learners came from a large number of countries and had many different nationalities. Few of those outwith the UK stated themselves to be Scottish. Of those who did state themselves to be Scottish or partly Scottish, all but one were in the USA and Commonwealth. Learners in the USA and Commonwealth mainly stated that they had Scottish ancestors whereas those in Europe mainly did not report such connections with Scotland.

Table 39: National identity of respondents in rest of UK

Nationality	N	%
British	54	34
English	33	20.8
Irish	2	1.3
Scottish	24	15.1
Welsh	6	3.8
Scottish / British	13	8.2
Other[178]	12	7.5
Not Stated	15	9.4
Total	159	100

Table 40: National identity of respondents outwith UK

Nationality	N	%	Nationality	N	%
American / USA	22	24.7	Manx	3	3.4
Argentine	1	1.1	New Zealand	2	2.2
Australian	5	5.6	Polish	1	1.1
Austrian	1	1.1	Russian	1	1.1
Breton	1	1.1	Scottish	6	6.7
British	3	3.4	Spanish	2	2.2
Canadian	5	5.6	Swedish	2	2.2
Danish	1	1.1	Zimbabwean	1	1.1
Dutch	2	2.2	Dual nationality (not including Scottish)	5	5.6
Galician	1	1.1	Dual nationality (including Scottish)[179]	6	6.7
German	12	13.4	Not stated	1	1.1
Irish	4	4.5			
Italian	1	1.1	Total	89	100

---

[178] Other: English/British 2, English/British/European 1, Irish/British 1, Welsh/British 1, German 1, New Zealand 1, UK Citizen 2, Yorkshire 1, Northumbrian 1, Scottish-Canadian 1.

[179] Dual nationalities containing Scottish: Australian (born in Scotland) 1, Aussie/Scot 1, Canadian/Scottish 1, Irish and Welsh heritage 1, New Zealand Gael 1, Scottish and Franconian 1, Scottish-American 1.

Other Identities

Respondents were also asked to assess their identification with a variety of other identities alongside their national identities. This question was based on one used in the 1994–5 Euromosaic survey (MacKinnon 1998b) with additional options added for the purposes of this survey. The results for Scotland are given in Table 41, followed by the results for other respondents.

Replies to this question also revealed a far stronger identification with the Scottish than with the British identity. Over 70% identified themselves as *very much Scottish* as opposed to only 8.7% identifying themselves as *very much British*. In fact, more respondents stated that they did not feel British than that they did. As for the European identity, a majority stated that they felt European, but most of these felt themselves to be European *on the whole* rather than *very much so*, and a significant minority of respondents did not feel themselves to be European.

Table 41: Identities of Scottish respondents

N = 392	Yes, Very Much So		Yes, On The Whole		No / Not Really		Not stated	
Identity	N	%	N	%	N	%	N	%
Gael	59	15.01	68	17.35	222	56.6	43	10.9
Gaelic Speaker	46	11.7	114	29.1	187	47.7	45	11.5
Highlander	73	18.6	50	12.8	224	57.1	45	11.5
Islander	27	6.7	29	7.4	285	72.7	50	12.8
Local Identity[180] (Please specify)	59	15	50	12.8	113	28.8	170	43.3
Scottish	283	72.2	50	12.8	29	7.4	29	7.4
British	34	8.7	134	34.2	182	46.4	42	10.7
European	68	17.35	160	40.8	125	31.9	39	9.95
Celt	107	27.3	107	27.3	132	33.7	46	11.7
Other[181]	19	4.8	17	4.3	20	5.1	336	85.7

---

[180] Local identities: Aberdeen 3, Abrach / Lochaber 7, Argyll 5, Arran, Ayrshire 2, Badenoch and Strathspey, Borderer 4, Buchan, Cathcart, Caithness, Caithness and Sutherland roots, Central Scotland 2, Cowal, Argyll, Doric speaker, Dubliner, Dundonian 2, East Coast Gael, East of Scotland south of Moray Firth to Lothians, Easter Ross, Edinburgh 5, Fear à Raineach, Fife 4, Fort William, Gallovidian 2, Glaswegian 6, Greenockian, Gall-Ghaidheal and 'Lowland', Hawick, Invernesian 2, incomer, Kelso, Kirkintilloch, Lanarkshire, Lanarkshire and Strathspey, Lewisman 2, Londoner, Lowlander 8, Lowlander with Highland ancestry, Lowlander whose heart is in Highlands and Islands, Moravian, Native of East Dunbartonshire, NE Scotland, North Uist, Northern England, North west coast, Oirthir an Iar, Partick, Glasgow, Paisley, Rogart, Rosach, SE Scotland 2, Skye / Sgitheanach 3, SE Scotland, SW Scotland 2, Tobermory, West Coast, West Fifer, Uist, Not stated 3.

[181] Other: An incomer with strong Celtic leanings, adopted Scottish as a homeland, Anglo-Irish, Asian (white) because practising Buddhist, Cornish 2, country (not town), "cultural stateless person", Doric 2, dual British and Irish, English 2, English Scot, English ancestrally Scottish culturally, Esperantist, German-Cantonese, Gaelic learner 2, Icelandic, Irish 3, immigrant, Lowlander, New Yorker, Pictish, Scandinavian, Scot with Gaelic identity from Irish ancestry, Welsh, Welsh / English / Highland, white, world.

Respondents' level of identification with the terms *Gael* and *Gaelic speaker* were also recorded. While 15.01% of the sample identified strongly with the identity *Gael* and 17.35% felt themselves on the whole to be Gaels, a majority did not feel themselves to be Gaels. This compared with the 62% of MacKinnon's 1994 quota sample of fluent Gaelic speakers who identified 'very much' with the term and the 11.5% who identified with the term 'as a whole' (MacKinnon 1998b: 2). As discussed above, the term Gael has an ambiguous and contested meaning, with different emphasis being put on the linguistic and ethnic elements of the identity by different people.[182] The meaning of the term Gael could now be said to form a spectrum, with the centre being the traditional definition as 'a Gaelic-speaking Highlander' and with the poles being definitions as 'any Highlander regardless of ability to speak Gaelic' on one side and 'any Gaelic speaker regardless of place of origin' on the other.

For this reason, self-identification with the term *Gael* has been tabulated according to fluency in spoken Gaelic (Table 42) and to Highland or Lowland upbringing and residence (Table 43).

Table 42: Identification with *Gael* identity by level of fluency in spoken Gaelic: respondents in Scotland

Gael	Yes, Very Much So	Yes, On The Whole	No / Not Really	Not stated	Total
	%	%	%	%	N
All respondents	15	17.4	56.6	10.9	392
Fluent learner	29.3	26.8	39	4.8	41
Advanced learner	29.6	25	36.4	9	44
Intermediate learner	10.5	18.8	61.6	9	133
Basic learner	12.2	11.6	64.6	11.6	164

As can be seen, there is a correlation between level of identification with the term *Gael* and level of ability in Gaelic, with fluent and advanced learners being more likely to consider themselves to be *Gaels* than intermediate or basic learners. A majority of those in the former groups felt themselves to be *Gaels* as compared with a minority in the latter groups. Among the groups where a majority felt themselves to be *Gaels*, there was a relatively even numerical split between those who strongly identified themselves as *Gaels* and those who considered themselves to be *Gaels on the whole*.

Table 43: Identification with *Gael* identity by place of upbringing: respondents in Scotland

Place of Upbringing	Yes, Very Much So		Yes, On The Whole		No / Not Really		Not stated		Total
	N	%	N	%	N	%	N	%	N
All respondents	59	15	68	17.4	222	56.6	43	10.9	392
Greater Highlands	22	27.2	22	27.2	27	33.3	10	12.4	81
Core Highlands	19	24.4	22	28.2	27	34.6	10	12.8	78
Lowlands	24	11	36	16.5	139	63.8	19	8.7	218
Outwith Scotland	9	11.1	10	12.4	51	63	11	13.6	81

---

[182] See Chapter 5.

Analysis of the figures for those hailing from the Highlands found that there was a correlation between coming from the Highlands and self-identification as a *Gael*. As might be expected, the group of respondents coming from the Highlands identified themselves more strongly with the identity of *Gael* than those coming from the Lowlands or from outwith Scotland. It can also be seen, however, that the *Gael* identity was by no means confined to Highlanders, as around a quarter of respondents raised in the Lowlands or outwith Scotland also claimed this identity. While those raised within the Highlands were the more likely to call themselves *Gaels*, this identity was not represented particularly strongly even within the sample of Highland respondents, as only around one-half of this group identified with the term *Gael*, with more respondents saying that that they did not feel themselves to be *Gaels* than said that they *very much* identified with the label.

Table 44: Identification with *Gaelic* identity by place of residence: respondents in Scotland

Place of Residence	Yes, Very Much So		Yes, On The Whole		No / Not Really		Not stated		Total
	N	%	N	%	N	%	N	%	N
All respondents	59	15	68	17.4	222	56.6	43	10.9	392
Greater Highlands	27	19.6	21	15.2	72	52.2	18	13	138
Core Highlands	27	20.4	21	15.9	66	50	18	13.6	132
Lowlands	30	12	47	19	147	59.3	24	9.7	248

For respondents living in the Highlands (regardless of place of upbringing), levels of identification with the term *Gael* were lower than those seen for respondents brought up in the Highlands (regardless of place of residence in Scotland). The fact that many Highland residents were raised elsewhere is likely to explain this in part.

Table 45: Identification with *Gaelic speaker* identity by level of fluency in spoken Gaelic: respondents in Scotland

Gaelic speaker	Yes, Very Much So	Yes, On The Whole	No / Not Really	Not stated	Total
	%	%	%	%	%
All respondents	11.7	29.1	47.7	11.5	392
Fluent learner	61	29.3	2.4	7.3	41
Advanced learner	31.8	50	11.4	6.8	44
Intermediate learner	3	42.1	43.6	11.3	133
Basic learner	1.8	12.8	72.6	12.8	164

In addition to the complicated and contested identity of Gael, the more linguistically based identity of *Gaelic speaker* was also tabulated. 11.7% strongly identified with the *Gaelic speaker* identity and 29.1% identified with this identity *on the whole*, with 47.7% not feeling themselves to be *Gaelic speakers*. As might be expected, however, there were large variations within the sample on this point, with those able to speak more Gaelic being more likely to consider themselves as *Gaelic speaker*. While only 1.8% of learners with a basic level of Gaelic considered themselves *very much* to be *Gaelic speakers*, for example, 61% of fluent learners did so. It should also be noted that *fluent/advanced Gaelic learners* tended to identify themselves more strongly as *Gaelic speakers* than as *Gaels*.

Respondents were also asked to say how much they identified with the identities of *Highlander* and *Islander*. The responses to these questions have been tabulated in Tables 46 and 47.

Table 46: Identification with *Highland* identity: respondents in Scotland

Place of Upbringing	Yes, Very Much So		Yes, On The Whole		No / Not Really		Not stated		Total
	N	%	N	%	N	%	N	%	N
All respondents	73	18.6	50	12.8	224	57.1	45	11.5	392
Greater Highlands	49	60.5	17	21	7	8.6	8	9.9	81
Lowlands	15	6.9	22	10.1	155	71.1	26	11.9	218
Outwith Scotland	6	7.4	9	11.1	58	71.6	8	9.9	81
Place of residence									
Greater Highlands	42	30.4	25	18.1	56	40.6	15	10.9	138
Lowlands	29	11.7	23	9.3	167	67.3	29	11.7	248

It can be seen that those brought up in the Highlands mainly did feel themselves to be *Highlanders*, 60.5% *very much so* and a further 21% *on the whole*. Of those respondents not brought up in the Highlands, a small minority nonetheless considered themselves to be *Highlanders*. For respondents living in the Highlands (regardless of place of upbringing), levels of identification with the term *Highland*, like the term *Gael*, were far lower than those for respondents brought up in the Highlands (regardless of place of residence in Scotland). Again, this is likely to be due to the large percentage of Highland residents who were brought up elsewhere. As can be seen below, a similar pattern emerged for the identity of *Islander*.

Table 47: Identification with *Island* identity: respondents in Scotland

Place of Upbringing	Yes, Very Much So		Yes, On The Whole		No / Not Really		Not stated		Total
	N	%	N	%	N	%	N	%	N
All respondents	27	6.7	29	7.4	285	72.7	50	12.8	392
Island	11	64.7	3	17.6	-	-	3	17.6	17
Elsewhere	14	3.8	27	7.4	279	76.9	43	11.8	363
Place of residence									
Island	6	16.2	14	37.8	14	37.8	3	8.1	37
Elsewhere	20	5.7	16	4.6	268	76.8	45	12.9	349

Other identities covered in the questionnaire were local identities and *other* identities. While a significant minority of the sample identified themselves by a local identity, only 15% of the sample *very much* felt themselves to belong to such an identity. Even fewer stated that they identified with an *other* identity. The local and other identities named can be seen in the footnotes to Table 41.

It has already been argued that the meaning of the term *Gael* is both difficult to define and contested. This is even more the case with the term *Celt*, which can be defined in terms of language, ethnic factors, place of residence or other factors.[182] As the terms *Celt* and *Celtic* have been the subject of much academic and media discussion in recent years, the term was included within the questionnaire to see whether or not respondents identified with it. The level of identification with the term *Celt* amongst respondents in Scotland turned out to be fairly high, with 27.3% identifying *very much* and a further 27.3% *on the whole*.

Identities: Respondents outside Scotland

Table 48: Identities of UK respondents outwith Scotland

N = 159	Yes, Very Much So		Yes, On The Whole		No / Not Really		Not stated	
Identity	N	%	N	%	N	%	N	%
Gael	13	8.2	21	13.2	111	69.8	14	8.8
Gaelic Speaker	9	5.7	36	22.6	98	61.6	16	10.1
Highlander	17	10.7	16	10.1	110	69.2	16	10.1
Islander	5	3.1	6	3.8	127	79.9	21	13.2
Local Identity (Please specify) [184]	16	10.1	15	9.4	57	35.85	71	44.6
Scottish	48	30.2	25	15.7	63	39.6	23	14.7
British	47	29.6	73	45.9	26	16.35	13	8.2
European	32	20.1	42	26.4	63	39.6	22	13.8
Celt	40	25.2	35	22	61	38.4	23	14.5
Other[185]	19	11.9	10	6.3	8	5	122	76.7

The identities asserted by those living in the remainder of the UK can be seen in Table 48. For the identities of *Gael, Gaelic speaker, Highlander* and *Islander*, a similar pattern emerges to the one already seen for Scotland. While minorities identified with each of the identities mentioned, these were significant minorities in most cases; it is also fair to assume that there was a far higher level of identification with these identities among the respondents than would be found amongst the population as a whole. As might be expected, however, fewer people identified themselves as *Gaels, Gaelic speakers, Highlanders* or *Islanders* in the remainder of the UK than did so in Scotland, reflecting the lower levels of people hailing from the Highlands and Islands and in line with the lower numbers of respondents who were advanced or fluent in Gaelic outwith Scotland.

Also noteworthy in relation to the *rest of UK* respondents is the high level of identification with the *Scottish* identity. Just over 30% (30.2%) of respondents

[183] For some examples of very different views on the term 'Celt', see Berresford Ellis 1993, Chapman 1993.

[184] Local identities (English): Anglo-Saxon Southerner, Birmingham, Cumbria 2, Lake District, Lancastrian 3, Londoner 3, Midlander, North West, Northumbrian, South East, Southern English, Warwickshire, Yorkshire 4. Local identities (Scottish): Arbroathian, Argyll, Barra 2, Fifer, Glaswegian, Isle of Skye, Lowlander, Small Isles: Isle of Muck. Local identities (other): Derry, Ulsterwoman. Not stated 1.

[185] Other identities: Canadian, Citizen of the World 3, English 8, Irish, Yorkshire, Welsh 6, 'Lloegryn' an Englishman who speaks Welsh, Scottish related identities: Married to a Scot, feel Scottish by marriage, North Briton, "Scottish ancestry, but otherwise no identity – a bit rootless", Gaidheal à Sasainn or Anglo-Scot, 'second hand Scot', second generation Scot, striving to be a Celtic Gaelic speaker, South Uist/Barra.

identified *very much* with this identity, slightly more than identified *very much* with the *British* identity. Altogether, 45.9% of the *rest of UK* identified themselves as Scottish to some extent. While much of this can be explained by the large percentage of *rest of UK* respondents raised in Scotland (31%), this is insufficient to explain the full extent of this identification. This suggests that many of the sample, while not born in Scotland, have other connections with Scotland such as family ties or feel Scottish for other reasons. Some of these reasons can be seen from the *other identities* section of the Table.

It is also noteworthy that a large percentage of the *rest of UK* sample identified themselves as *Celts* – 25.2% very much so and 22% on the whole and that self-identification as *British* was not particularly strong. Identification with the *British* identity was far weaker within this section of the respondents than was identification with the Scottish identity within the sample living within Scotland.

Table 49: Identities of respondents outwith UK

N = 89	Yes, Very Much So		Yes, On The Whole		No / Not Really		Not stated	
Identity	N	%	N	%	N	%	N	%
Gael	22	24.7	14	15.7	47	52.8	6	6.7
Gaelic Speaker	12	13.5	24	27	47	52.8	6	6.7
Highlander	8	9	11	12.4	62	69.7	8	9
Islander	8	9	8	9	67	75.3	6	6.7
Local Identity (Please specify)[186]	17	19.1	5	5.6	32	36	35	39.3
Scottish	16	18	13	14.6	50	56.2	10	11.2
British	2	2.2	9	10.1	68	76.4	10	11.2
European	12	13.5	19	21.35	50	56.2	8	9
Celt	27	30.3	21	23.6	33	37.1	8	9
Other[187]	24	27	12	13.5	6	6.7	47	52.8

The identities of respondents living outwith the UK are charted in Table 49. Once again, it can be seen that noticeable minorities define themselves as *Gaelic speakers*, *Gaels*, *Highlanders* and *Islanders*. As was the case with UK respondents, identification with identities such as *Highlander*, *Islander* and *Gael* can partly be explained by people coming from the Highlands and Islands or through having ability in the language. Once again, however, this does not account for everything as fewer than 6% of respondents resident outwith the UK had been brought up in Scotland and only 8% defined themselves as *fluent or advanced in spoken Gaelic*.

---

[186] Local identity: Baden, Californian of Gaelic descent, Cape Breton, Castilian from Madrid, Cracovian, French, Galician, Inverness/Nairn area, Irish 3, Isle of Mull and Barra, Lochaber/Moidart, Manks, Ostgote, Perthshire – Bruar Falls, San Franciscan, Southern USA, Torontonian, Vogtland (German region).

[187] Other: American 6, Australian – but I'd love to be Scottish, Australian of highland/island descent, Australian of Scottish Highland Origins, Berliner, Breton 2, Canadian 2, Catalan, Citizen of the World, Conamarach Gearmánach, Dutch, Franconian, German 3, Immigrant to US, Irish, Italian, Manx, Nordic, Nova Scotian, Pictish, Polish, Scandinavian, Scotch-Canadian, Scots descendent, Scottish Australian, person of Scottish, Irish, Welsh, French and German descent, Southerner of mainly Celtic extraction. US, descendant of Highland Scots immigrants to US.

The local and *other* identities given once again show some evidence of Scottish connections on the part of the learners. In local identities, many learners in the USA and Commonwealth reveal that they are descended from Scottish or Highland families or that they come from areas of Canada with strong Gaelic connections. Further weight is given to this impression by the question on reasons for learning Gaelic below, in which a large number of learners outwith Scotland say that they are learning Gaelic to 'get closer to my roots' and also in the comments section of the questionnaire in which many respondents revealed Scottish ancestry.

In the case of the identity *Gael*, it should also be pointed out that several Irish and Manx respondents were present in the sample who also identified with the identity, an identity which is also common in Ireland and the Isle of Man. It should also be noted once again that there was a rather high level of identification with the term *Celt* with a majority of respondents defining themselves as such. This may also be due to a large extent to Scottish descent or through connections by birth or family to other Celtic countries such as Ireland and Wales.

While many respondents did have direct or indirect connections with Scotland, not all respondents did so, particularly those who did not live in the New World. Most respondents living in Europe did not come from Scotland and, as will be seen later during the discussion of reasons for learning, were not of Scottish descent. Interestingly, some respondents indicated in the *other* identity section that they come from areas where other minority languages are spoken such as Ireland, the Isle of Man, Wales, Catalonia and Galicia. For many other respondents, however, they did not come from any such area and were not involved with any other minority languages.

Knowledge of Languages

A specific question was asked concerning knowledge of languages other than Gaelic and English and respondents were asked to give some indication of their fluency. The responses to this question have been tabulated in Tables 50–54. 60.7% of respondents in Scotland and over 70% of other respondents had knowledge of a language other than Gaelic and English. This high percentage of speakers/learners of other languages suggests a heightened level of interest in and awareness of languages amongst Gaelic learners, as does the fact that over half of the respondents who stated that they knew or were learning a language other than English had ability in more than one other language.

Knowledge of languages appears to be significantly higher amongst the respondents in this survey than in society as a whole. While no authoritative official figures exists in this regard, a study of a representative sample of 4000 adults in Great Britain provides useful comparable data on knowledge of languages (Tuckett and Cara 1999). When asked "are there any other languages [than your mother tongue] that that you use or can understand, speak or communicate, or have learned at any time in the past", 42% of GB respondents answered that there were (29% cited one language other than their mother tongue and 13% more than one). In Scotland, the study found that only 31% of their sample of 360 people were able to speak a language other than their mother tongue. Similar findings were also revealed in the *Europeans and Language* report, which found that 66% of a representative sample of the UK population had absolutely no knowledge of any language other than English (Osborn 2001).

Table 50: Ability to speak languages other than Gaelic and English: all respondents

	Scotland		UK		World	
	N	%	N	%	N	%
Yes	238	60.7	116	73	72	80.9
No	151	38.5	43	27	17	19.1
Not stated	3	0.8	-	-	-	-
Total	392	100	159	100	89	100

Table 51: Number of languages spoken: respondents with languages other than Gaelic and English

	Scotland		UK		World	
	N	%	N	%	N	%
1	102	42.9	39	33.6	22	30.6
2	57	24	28	24.1	17	23.6
3	45	18.9	22	19	14	19.4
4	22	9.2	7	6	8	11.1
5	4	1.7	9	7.8	8	11.1
6	5	2.1	7	6	2	2.8
7	1	0.4	1	0.9	-	-
8	1	0.4	2	1.7	1	1.4
9	1	0.4	-	-	-	-
10+	-	-	1	0.9	-	-
Total	238	100	116	100	72	100

Table 52: Languages of which respondents in Scotland have knowledge

Language	N	Language	N
Cornish	4	Latin	27
Dutch	9	Russian	21
French	188	Portuguese	7
German	90	Spanish	39
Greek[188]	11	Scots	11
Hebrew	4	Urdu	4
Irish	16	Welsh	12
Italian	27	Other minority languages[189]	9
Japanese	5	Other languages[190]	30

A large number of different languages were represented amongst respondents. As might be expected, major European languages such as French, German and Spanish were known by the largest number of respondents. The fact that these languages are widely taught at school partly explains this. This is also the case for Latin, which was widely taught in the past. It should be pointed out, however, that figures for languages known represent much more than a residual school knowledge: many of

---

[188] "Greek" and "Hebrew" in this, and the following tables, represent both the modern and ancient varieties of these languages as it was not possible to ascertain which form was meant in every case.

[189] Breton: 2, Catalan, Basque, Manx, Maori, Navajo, Sorbian, Yiddish.

[190] Arabic: 2, Chinese: 2, Danish: 2, Esperanto: 3, Old English, Farsi, Hindi: 2, Icelandic, Old Irish, Mongolian, Norwegian: 3, Polish: 3, Slovak, Swahili: 2, Swedish: 3, Thai, Turkish.

Table 53: Languages of which respondents in the rest of the UK have knowledge

Language	N	Language	N
Breton	3	Japanese	3
Cornish	3	Latin	15
Dutch	5	Portuguese	5
French	88	Russian	15
German	61	Spanish	31
Greek	13	Swedish	4
Hebrew	3	Welsh	19
Irish	8	Other languages[191]	23
Italian	19		

Table 54: Languages of which respondents outwith the UK have knowledge

Language	N	Language	N
Breton	3	Latin	6
Dutch	6	Manx	4
French	37	Russian	9
German	31	Spanish	24
Greek	3	Swedish	5
Irish	16	Welsh	10
Italian	7	Other languages[192]	22
Japanese	5		

those with a knowledge of French or German were fluent in the languages, for example. The fact that most of the languages cited by respondents are taught rarely, or not at all, in Scottish schools further emphasises this.

In addition to the major European languages, many minority languages were represented. It is significant that knowledge of all Celtic languages is present within the sample, including Cornish and Manx, which only have a few hundred speakers each, as well as Irish and Welsh which have hundreds of thousands. Several other minority languages are also present, ranging from European languages to a few Amerindian and Australasian examples. This suggests that those interested in Gaelic are often interested in other minority languages. It is also interesting that three respondents in Scotland and two elsewhere had a knowledge of the international auxiliary language Esperanto.

Membership of interest/pressure groups

In order to gain further information about the interests, recreational activities and political persuasion of Gaelic learners, respondents were asked to state whether they were members of any interest or pressure groups other than Gaelic groups.

---

[191] Arabic, Chinese: 2, Old/Middle English, Esperanto, Finnish, Flemish, Gujerati, Hungarian, Icelandic, Indonesian, Malay: 2, Manx, Nepali, Old Norse, Norwegian, Polish: 2, Punjabi, Sanscrit, Serbo-Croat: 2, Turkish, Urdu.

[192] Afrikaans, Arabic, Basque, Catalan: 2, Chinese, Czech, Danish, Esperanto, Galician: 2, Hindi, Hebrew, Maori, Ndebele, Norwegian, Polish, Portuguese: 2, Sanskrit, Silesian, Turkish.

Table 55: Membership of non-Gaelic interest / pressure groups

	Scotland		UK		World	
	N	%	N	%	N	%
None	188	48	71	44.6	71	79.8
1	82	20.9	20	12.6	5	5.62
2	38	9.7	19	12	7	7.8
3	29	7.4	13	8.2	2	2.2
4	20	5.1	10	6.3	1	1.1
5	14	3.6	7	4.4	1	1.1
6	6	1.5	3	1.9	-	-
7	2	0.5	4	2.5	1	1.1
8	6	1.5	4	2.5	-	-
9	2	0.5	3	1.9	-	-
10+	3	0.8	5	3.1	-	-
Not answered	2	0.5	-	-	1	1.1
Total	392	100	159	100	89	100

In Scotland and the rest of the UK, a majority of respondents were members of at least one pressure or interest group, as compared with only around 20% of respondents outwith the UK. The majority of those who were group members had membership in between one and three groups, though many respondents had membership in far more.

As a very large number of different organisations were mentioned, the groups of which respondents were or had been members were classified into several broad categories. Before looking at these categories, it should be noted that the groups mentioned most often in Scotland were: RSPB: 48, CND: 34, National Trust for Scotland: 33, Amnesty International: 23, Greenpeace: 21, Scottish Wildlife Trust: 21, Friends of the Earth Scotland: 19, SNP: 15.

Table 56: Nature of membership groups: respondents in Scotland[193]

Category of Groups	Number of mentions
Community organisations	30
Conservation Groups	147
Cultural / literary Groups	30
Environmental / anti-nuclear groups	79
Health / welfare charities	15
Historical / archaeological groups	23
Trade Unions / Professional Associations	18
Political parties	30
Political pressure groups	119
Recreational groups	43
Religious groups	6
Miscellaneous / unclassifiable groups	14

The interest represented most strongly amongst the sample was conservation, with a large number of respondents belonging to groups ranging from wildlife and nature

---

[193] The group membership of respondents outside Scotland was very similar to those within Scotland and has not, therefore, been analysed in detail.

conservation to the preservation of historic buildings, but with the wildlife and nature element being by far the most strongly represented. Many of these were Scottish conservation groups such as the Scottish Wildlife Trust, the National Trust for Scotland, the Cairngorms Campaign and the John Muir Trust. A large number of political pressure organisations were also mentioned. The largest single group of these were environmental/anti-nuclear groups, which have been given their own category due to the large number of respondents (79) who belonged to them.

A very large range of groups were covered within the 119 mentions given to other political pressure groups. Numbers of mentions are recorded in brackets. The main areas covered were: human rights and civil liberties (including gay rights and youth rights) [28], animal rights [5], rights of way campaigns [4], devolutionary and nationalist campaigns for Scotland and other countries (e.g. the Campaign for a Scottish Parliament, the Celtic League) [13], other UK constitutional reforms (Charter 88) [4], local and national public transport campaigns (e.g. Sustrans, Spokes, Railway Development Society) [10], international development campaigns [14], campaigns for other international issues such as Cuba, Tibet, Palestine, Native Americans and tribal people of the world [9], language campaigning groups for languages other than Gaelic (Cymdeithas Yr Iaith Gymraeg, Scots Language Society, Manx, Breton, Cornish and Esperanto groups) [15], the campaign against Skye Bridge tolls [3] and the anti-poll tax campaign [3]. Several other groups were mentioned only once. It is noticeable from this list that most of the groups represented here are what might be termed radical or left-wing groups.

Recreational groups were mentioned 43 times and covered a very wide range of interests ranging from railway and boating groups to horse breed societies and chess clubs. The most commonly mentioned recreational pursuit was rambling, which was mentioned ten times.

Community groups such as community councils, parent-teacher associations, school boards and neighbourhood watch groups were mentioned thirty times as were cultural/literary groups. Of this latter category, the overwhelming majority of organisations related to Scottish music and culture such as traditional/folk music and dance and Scottish literature.

Thirty mentions were also given to political parties. The most strongly represented of these was the SNP, which was mentioned fifteen times. There were also two members each of the Scottish Communist and Liberal Democrat parties and one member each of the Conservative and Green parties. Interestingly, there were also four members in Scotland both of Welsh nationalists Plaid Cymru and of Cornish nationalists Mebyon Kernow and one member of the Breton nationalist party Emgann.

Historical and archaeological interests were also relatively well represented amongst respondents. Again, most of the groups in question related to Scottish matters including local historical societies / Comainn Eachdraidh, local museum support groups, family history societies, archaeology groups and the Scottish Place-name Society.

Relatively few respondents registered membership of trade unions or professional organisations. This was surprising given the large number of respondents from professions with a high level of union/professional organisation membership. The wording of the question may have been partly responsible for the low figure obtained given that this sector of organisations was not mentioned as an example of interest or pressure groups in the question.

The group membership of the respondents tend to confirm several trends seen elsewhere; namely that many respondents are interested in Scottish history and culture or in walking in and conserving the Scottish countryside, and that a significant proportion are involved in progressive politics.

Religion

Respondents were asked a range of questions relating to their religious beliefs. The results are summarised in Tables 57–60. Due to the rapid decline in church adherence and attendance figures in the past 20 years and the lack of adequate comparable data regarding church attendance/adherence in Scotland, these figures are printed here without commentary. It is hoped, however, that these figures may be useful to other researchers.

Table 57: Religious affiliation: all respondents
Question: *Are you a member of a religious group or affiliation?*

	Scotland		UK		World	
	N	%	N	%	N	%
Yes	198	50.5	87	54.7	50	56.2
No	191	48.7	72	45.3	39	43.8
No answer	3	0.8	-	-	-	-
Total	392	100	159	100	89	100

Table 58: Association with religious groups / denominations: all respondents
Question: *If yes, which denomination or religious group are you connected with?*

	Scotland		UK		World	
	N	%	N	%	N	%
Buddhist	3	1.5	-	-	-	-
Jewish	-	-	-	-	2	4
Church of Scotland	106	53.5	10	11.5	5	10
Church of England	-	-	27	31	3	6
Episcopalian	13	6.6	-	-	4	8
Free Church	7	3.5	2	2.3	1	2
Roman Catholic	37	18.7	21	24.1	15	30
Christian (no denomination stated)	15	7.6	6	6.9	5	10
Christian (other)	12[194]	6.1	18[195]	20.6	14[196]	28
Other	-	-	1[197]	1.1	1[198]	1.1
Not stated	5	2.5	2	2.3	-	-
Total	198	100	87	100	50	100

---

[194] Baptist: 1, Christian Brethren: 1, Ecumenical Christian: 1, Jehovah's Witness: 1, Lutheran Evangelical: 2, Methodist: 2, Quaker: 2, more than one church: 2.
[195] Baptist: 1, "Church in Wales": 1, Congregational: 2, Ecumenical Christian: 1, Judeo/Christian: 1, Methodist: 2, Presbyterian Church of Wales: 1, Quaker: 6, Spiritualist: 1, URC: 1, more than one church:1.
[196] Baptist: 2, Church of Christ: 1, Dutch Reformed: 1, "Fundamental Protestant": 1, Lutheran: 2, "Presbyterian": 4, Unitarian: 1, Uniting Church of Australia: 1.
[197] "messianic Judaism (although I am a gentile)"
[198] "Jewish, Presbyterian"

Table 59: Involvement with religious groups / denominations: all respondents
Question: *Are you a full member?*

	Scotland		UK		World	
	N	%	N	%	N	%
Yes	140	70.7	56	64.4	31	62
No	58	29.3	31	35.6	19	38
Total	198	100	67	100	50	100

Table 60: Frequency of religious group involvement: all respondents
Question: *Apart from special occasions, how often do you attend religious services or meetings?*[199]

	Scotland		UK		World	
	N	%	N	%	N	%
Once a week or more	81	40.9	31	35.6	16	32
Several times a month	28	14.1	14	16.1	5	10
At least once a month	15	7.6	8	9.2	8	16
Several times a year	35	17.7	11	12.6	10	20
At least once a year	7	3.5	6	6.9	4	8
Less often than once a year	26	13.1	15	17.2	5	10
Not stated	6	3	2	2.3	2	4
Total	198	100	87	100	50	100

Table 61: Ability of parents to speak Gaelic: all respondents
Question: *Did either of your parents speak Gaelic?*

	Scotland		UK		World	
	N	%	N	%	N	%
Yes[200]	91	23.2	19	11.95	6	6.7
No	276	70.4	127	79.9	78	87.6
Don't know	5	1.3	4	2.5	1	1.2
No answer	20	5.1	9	5.7	4	4.5
Total	392	100	159	100	89	100

---

[199] This table is based on those who regard themselves as belonging to a particular religion.
[200] 4 of those answering "yes" in Scotland, 3 in the remainder of the UK and 1 in the remainder of the UK were referring to Irish Gaelic.

Table 62: Ability of grandparents to speak Gaelic: all respondents
Question: *Did either of your grandparents speak Gaelic?*

	Scotland		UK		World	
	N	%	N	%	N	%
Yes[201]	132	33.7	37	23.3	16	18
No[202]	211	53.8	105	66	68	76.4
Don't know	30	7.65	8	5	1	11
No answer	19	4.85	9	5.7	4	4.5
Total	392	100	159	100	89	100

Respondents were asked to specify if any of their parents or grandparents had been Gaelic speakers. It can be seen from Table 61 that a significant minority did have at least one Gaelic-speaking parent but that a majority did not. In Scotland, 23.2% of respondents had Gaelic-speaking parents but 70.4% did not. In the remainder of the UK too, a noticeable minority of 11.95% of respondents had Gaelic-speaking parents. Outwith the UK, figures were lower at 6.7% of respondents.

As would be expected, an even larger number of respondents stated that they had or had had at least one Gaelic-speaking grandparents. In Scotland, just over a third answered affirmatively, as did just under a quarter of respondents in the rest of the UK and one fifth in the remainder of the world. Once again, however, a majority of respondents did not have any Gaelic-speaking grandparents. There was some geographical variation in the response within Scotland, with a majority of 54% of those raised in the Greater Highlands having had a Gaelic-speaking parent or grandparent as compared to 30% of those raised in the Lowlands.

The results for this question show that most learners do not come from a family in which Gaelic was spoken in the recent past. This is encouraging for RLS efforts as it suggests that learning Gaelic is not mainly confined to those with Gaelic-speaking parents or grandparents, a group of people who will decline in number in line with the decrease in number of native Gaelic speakers.

The results also show, however, that a higher percentage of respondents have Gaelic-speaking parents or grandparents than would be expected in the population as a whole. This suggests that having Gaelic-speaking (grand)parents is a factor influencing many learners' decision to learn the language. This will be investigated later during discussion of motivation for learning Gaelic.

---

[201] Eight of those answering "yes" in Scotland and five in England were referring to Irish Gaelic. One in England was referring to Manx Gaelic. One respondent outwith the UK was referring to Irish and another to Manx.

[202] Three respondents in Scotland noted that they had not had Gaelic-speaking grandparents but that their fathers had learned Gaelic. Another respondent noted that while having no Gaelic-speaking grandparents that his mother had learned Gaelic and another that his mother was a Gaelic speaker but that he was unsure whether or not he had any Gaelic-speaking grandparents.

Section 2: Learning Gaelic

The second section of the questionnaire entitled 'learning Gaelic' looked firstly at respondents' progress in learning Gaelic and then at their motivation for learning.

Level of competency in Gaelic

A series of questions were asked regarding respondents' level of ability in Gaelic. Respondents were asked firstly whether or not they were currently learning Gaelic. They were then asked what level of ability they had in speaking, reading, writing and understanding Gaelic and were further asked what level of fluency they aimed to achieve and for how long they had been learning Gaelic.

Table 63: Learners of Gaelic: CLI respondents
Question: *Are you currently learning Gaelic?*[203]

	Scotland		UK		World	
	N	%	N	%	N	%
Yes	174	65.4	94	73.4	50	82
No	92	34.6	34	26.6	11	18

Table 64: Status of learners of Gaelic: CLI respondents in Scotland
Question: *If not, please indicate which of the following best describes you.*

	N (Sc)	% (Sc)
I made an attempt or attempts at learning Gaelic but am no longer doing so	6	6.5
I have been learning Gaelic on and off but am not learning at the moment	31	33.7
I have learnt Gaelic to fluency	34	37
Other[204]	1	1.1
No answer	20	21.7
Total	92	100

From Table 63, it can be see that of the CLI members, around one-third of respondents in Scotland and around one-quarter and one-fifth respectively in the rest of the UK and the rest of the world were not learning Gaelic at the time of filling in the questionnaire. As Table 64 shows, of those CLI members not learning Gaelic, a small number indicated that they had given up learning Gaelic. Most learners not currently learning Gaelic, however, indicated either that they had learned the language to fluency or that they had been learning the language on and off and were not learning the language at that time. Some comments were: "Have been learning for 3 years on and off", "49 years with lengthy interruptions", "have been learning Gaelic on and off with no definite plan" and "have been learning for at least 10 years with gaps since about 1960".

---

[203] The results for this question have been tabulated for CLI members only as all questionnaires going out to non-CLI members were distributed at Gaelic learning classes/courses and therefore reached almost exclusively those who were actively learning Gaelic.
[204] Other: "no classes in my area".

For the question regarding levels of fluency, the figures for both CLI respondents in Scotland and the Scottish respondents as a whole are shown due to the fact that the CLI sample contained many fluent speakers whereas the Gaelic learning classes and courses sampled consisted almost entirely of those who were not fluent. It can be seen from Tables 65 and 66 that apart from the larger proportion of fluent speakers within the CLI respondents the proportions of learners at each of the other levels of competence in the language throughout the Scottish respondents are roughly similar.

Table 65: Ability in Gaelic: CLI respondents Scotland
Question: *What level of ability in Gaelic would you say you have at present in terms of speaking, understanding, reading and writing?*

N = 266	Fluent		Advanced		Intermediate		Basic		No answer	
	N	%	N	%	N	%	N	%	N	%
Speaking	37	13.9	32	12	90	33.8	101	37.9	6	2.3
Understanding	40	15	38	14.3	100	37.6	81	30.4	7	2.6
Reading	43	16.2	55	20.7	93	35	68	25.6	7	2.6
Writing	33	12.4	43	16.2	83	31.2	95	35.7	12	4.5

Table 66: Ability in Gaelic: respondents in Scotland

N = 392	Fluent		Advanced		Intermediate		Basic		No answer	
	N	%	N	%	N	%	N	%	N	%
Speaking	41	10.5	44	11.2	133	33.9	164	41.8	10	2.5
Understanding	45	11.5	53	13.5	149	38	134	34.2	11	2.8
Reading	46	11.7	76	19.4	130	33.2	126	32.1	14	3.6
Writing	36	9.2	52	13.3	123	31.4	160	40.8	21	5.4

In Scotland, significant majorities of learners considered themselves to have either a basic or intermediate ability in speaking, reading, writing and understanding Gaelic, with notable minorities considering themselves to be advanced or fluent. For speaking, understanding and writing, over 70% of respondents fell into the basic or intermediate categories with 65.3% falling into these categories for reading. This reflects the situation commented on elsewhere that there tend to be more people at the less advanced end of the Gaelic learning scale due to a high drop-out rate amongst learners and the inadequacies of the Gaelic learning infrastructure, which mean that many learners become 'perpetual beginners' or reach a plateau in their knowledge of Gaelic which they are unable to overcome.

Levels of ability in Gaelic outwith Scotland differed significantly from those recorded for respondents in Scotland, with far fewer learners either being fluent or advanced in Gaelic than in Scotland and with far more being intermediate and, especially, basic learners. The low level of fluency outwith Scotland reflects the isolation experienced by learners outside Scotland where there is little in the way of a Gaelic learning infrastructure.

---

[205] One further respondent stated that s/he had no ability in speaking the language at all.
[206] See also Chapter 4, "The Social Identity of Gaelic Learners".
[207] Other: fluent in speaking and reading Gaelic 1, fluent in speaking and understanding Gaelic 1, "to have it as my mother tongue" 1, fluency to Higher level 1, Simple sentences/conversations and hobby/interest 1, wish to fully comprehend Gaelic even if not able to speak fluently 1.

Table 67: Ability in Gaelic: respondents in the rest of UK

N = 159	Fluent		Advanced		Intermediate		Basic		No answer	
	N	%	N	%	N	%	N	%	N	%
Speaking[205]	5	3.1	7	4.4	45	28.3	98	61.6	3	1.9
Understanding	5	3.1	15	9.4	49	30.8	84	52.8	6	3.8
Reading	8	5	21	13.2	51	32.1	75	47.2	4	2.5
Writing	5	3.1	10	6.3	52	32.7	87	54.7	5	3.1

Table 68: Ability in Gaelic: respondents in the rest of the world

N = 89	Fluent		Advanced		Intermediate		Basic		No answer	
	N	%	N	%	N	%	N	%	N	%
Speaking	3	3.4	7	7.9	19	21.4	57	64	3	3.4
Understanding	4	4.5	8	8.9	22	24.7	50	56.2	4	4.5
Reading	3	3.4	12	13.5	34	38.2	35	39.3	1	1.1
Writing	3	3.4	4	4.5	32	36	44	49.4	5	5.62

Level of Fluency aimed for

Respondents were also asked what level of fluency they aimed to achieve. A large majority of respondents aimed at fluency in speaking, reading and writing Gaelic. This becomes an overwhelming majority when supplemented by those aiming for fluency in at least one of these fields. In Scotland, 71.4% aimed for full fluency and literacy in Gaelic, with a further 14.5% desiring to become fluent in speaking Gaelic only and 5.6% in reading and writing Gaelic only. Only small numbers of learners in Scotland wished to learn a limited amount of Gaelic or to learn sufficient Gaelic to help with a hobby or interest. The picture was broadly similar furth of Scotland, with a large majority seeking fluency. There were, however, larger proportions of learners seeking to learn limited or specialised Gaelic than was the case in Scotland. These findings challenge the view of Chapman and McEwan-Fujita that a large proportion of Gaelic learners do not aim for fluency in the language but rather take part in Gaelic learning activities as a gesture (Chapman 1978: 214, McEwan-Fujita 1998: 20).[206]

Table 69: Level of target fluency: respondents in Scotland
Question: *What level of fluency do you aim for?*

	N	%
I would like enough Gaelic to understand simple sentences / conversations	16	4.1
I would like to learn enough Gaelic to help me with a hobby or interest	9	2.3
I would like to become fluent in reading and writing Gaelic	18	5.6
I would like to become fluent in speaking Gaelic	57	14.5
I would like to become fluent in speaking, reading and writing Gaelic	280	71.4
Other[207]	6	1.5
Not Stated	6	1.5
Total	392	100

Questionnaire Results

Table 70: Level of target fluency: respondents outwith Scotland
Question: *What level of fluency do you aim for?*

	UK		World	
	N	%	N	%
I would like enough Gaelic to understand simple sentences / conversations	13	8.2	7	7.9
I would like to learn enough Gaelic to help me with a hobby or interest	10	6.3	7	7.9
I would like to become fluent in reading and writing Gaelic	10	6.3	2	2.25
I would like to become fluent in speaking Gaelic	10	6.3	2	2.25
I would like to become fluent in speaking, reading and writing Gaelic	111	69.8	65	73
Other[208]	1	0.6	5	5.6
Not Stated	4	2.5	1	1.1
Total	159	100	89	100

Respondents were then asked to state whether or not they expected to reach the level of fluency which they aimed for.

Table 71: Expectancy of reaching target fluency: all respondents
Question: *Do you expect to reach the level of fluency that you have indicated above?*

	Scotland		UK		World	
	N	%	N	%	N	%
Yes	166	42.4	73	45.9	56	62.9
No	100	25.5	39	24.5	13	14.6
Have done	29	7.4	6	3.8	2	2.2
Maybe	19	4.8	9	5.7	2	2.2
Hopefully	34	8.7	18	11.3	8	9
Other[209]	16	4.1	6	3.8	4	4.5
Don't know	5	1.3	3	1.9	1	1.1
Not Stated	23	5.9	5	3.1	3	3.4
Total	392	100	159	100	89	100

---

[208] Other: Simple sentences/conversations, reading and writing fluent 2, speaking and reading fluent 1, "I want to be skilled enough to communicate with Irish/Scot Gaelic speakers using mainly Manx but able to phrase things to make my self understood" 1, "enough Gaelic to understand/read/write (with dictionary/grammar) most texts" 1.

[209] Other (Scotland): if I can get onto an immersion course 5, "when I retire and have more time" 1, Probably not 3, only if I can make enough time for it 3, "yes, when I retire" 2, "determined to work towards fluency", "I only expect to become fluent in reading and perhaps speaking" , "not unless I can pursue it in US" , "not within University institution". Other (rest of UK): "probably not in speaking, but definitely in reading and writing", "Only if can spend enough time on it", "I wish I could be fluent – not good with linguistics", "I think I will become partially fluent". Other (rest of world): "not for speaking", "probably only fluent in reading", "I think in Gaelic all the time", "not in Holland but yes if I go to Scotland", ""if circumstances allow me to spend more time in Gaelic speaking areas", " If I have time, I will come to Alba to learn, but now it's impossible for me".

It can be seen that under half of all respondents in Scotland, 42.4%, expected to reach the level of fluency which they had stated. 25.5% did not expect to reach this level and many were uncertain as to whether or not they would. A further 7.4% said that they had already reached the level of fluency for which they aimed. The figures for the remainder of the UK were broadly similar in most respects.

It seems that UK respondents tend to be somewhat pessimistic about the likelihood of reaching their desired level of fluency. In practice, however, it could be said that there may be a tendency towards over-optimism on the part of the 42.4% in Scotland and 45.9% in the remainder of the UK saying that they do expect to reach their desired level of fluency given the very low percentage of Gaelic learners attaining fluency in the language.

Qualifications in Gaelic

Table 72: Formal qualifications in Gaelic: all respondents
Question: *Do you have any formal qualifications in Gaelic?*

	Scotland		UK		World	
	N	%	N	%	N	%
Yes	160	40.8	21	13.2	12	13.5
No	232	59.2	138	86.8	77	86.5
Total	392	100	159	100	89	100

Respondents were asked if they had any formal qualifications in Gaelic. 40.8% of learners in Scotland and around 13.2% of learners outwith Scotland stated that they did have qualifications in Gaelic. The qualifications most frequently noted were Scotvec/SQA modules and Highers, although many others such as HNC courses and university courses were also noted.

Length of Time spent Learning Gaelic

Learners were asked for how long roughly they had been learning Gaelic. The level of fluency in Gaelic was then compared with length of time which they had spent learning. The results can be seen in Figures 4–6 and in Tables 73 and 74.

Figure 4: Time spent learning Gaelic: respondents in Scotland:
Question: *For how long have you been learning Gaelic?*

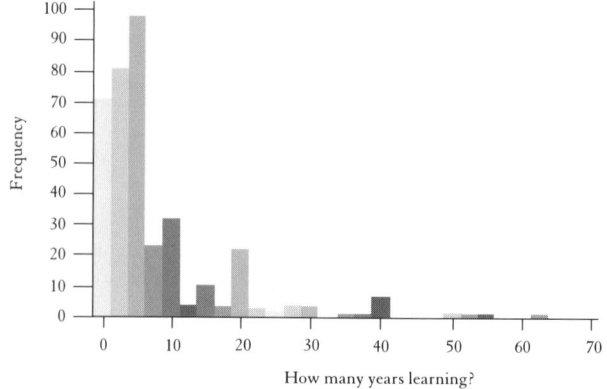

Figure 5: Time spent learning Gaelic: respondents in UK outwith Scotland
Question: *For how long have you been learning Gaelic?*

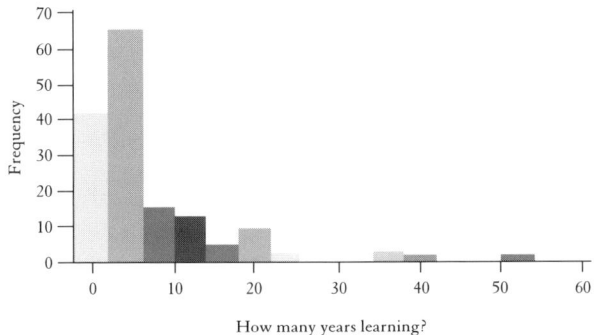

Figure 6: Time spent learning Gaelic: respondents outwith UK
Question: *For how long have you been learning Gaelic?*

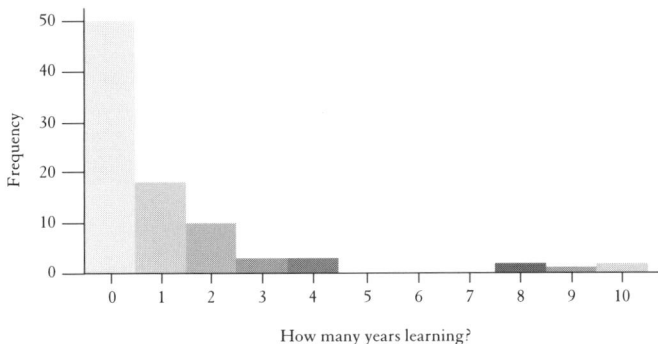

Table 73: Length of time learning Gaelic: all respondents

	Scotland		UK		World	
Time spent learning	N	%	N	%	N	%
Three years and under	151	38.5	79	49.7	61	68.5
Four to ten years	155	39.5	54	34	15	16.8
Over ten years	70	17.8	23	14.5	13	14.6
Not stated	16	4.1	3	1.9	0	0
Total	392	100	159	100	89	100

While a significant percentage of learners in Scotland (38.5%) had been learning for under three years, respondents had on average spent a long time learning, with 57.3% having been doing so for at least four years. As seen above, this learning often had an 'on and off' character or tended to stall at the beginner or intermediate stage rather than progressing steadily towards fluency. From the following table, it can be seen that despite the large percentage who had been learning for many years, the pace and extent of progress in learning Gaelic amongst respondents tended to be slow and limited. This can be seen clearly from the fact that after learning for four to ten years, only 10.5% of respondents had reached fluency and that even after ten years only 30.9% had become fluent and 13.2% advanced in Gaelic. Amongst those who had been learning for fewer than three years, very few respondents had progressed beyond intermediate level. These figures are a cause for concern as far as RLS efforts are concerned as they suggest that the current infrastructure for Gaelic learning is not resulting in a large percentage of learners reaching fluency and is not enabling learners to make fast progress in the language.

Table 74: Pace and level of ability : respondents in Scotland and rest of UK (based on speaking ability) [210]

Time spent learning	% Respondents				
	Fluent %	Advanced %	Intermediate %	Basic %	N[211]
Scotland:					
Three years and under	0.7	6.1	29.7	62.8	(147)
Four to ten years	10.5	15.7	40.5	33.3	(153)
Over ten years	30.9	13.2	36.8	19.1	(68)
Rest of UK:					
Three years and under	-	2.6	24.4	73.1	(78)
Four to ten years	5.8	3.8	36.5	53.8	(52)
Over ten years	4.4	13	30.4	52.2	(23)

Learners living outside Scotland tended to have been learning for shorter periods of time than those in Scotland. As there is no evidence to suggest that there was a surge in the level of interest in learning Gaelic outside Scotland in the three years up to the composition of the questionnaire, the figures seem to reflect a high drop-out rate caused by the difficulty in making progress in or sustaining an interest in Gaelic outside Scotland where facilities for learning the language are limited. The difficulty in making progress with learning Gaelic outside Scotland can also be seen from the fact that learners outside Scotland tended to make less progress in learning the language over a given period of time than learners living in Scotland. In Scotland, 10.5% of those who had been learning for between four and ten years, for example, had reached fluency in the language and a further 15.7% an advanced level as compared with only 5.8% and 4.4% in the remainder of the UK. These figures are also a matter of concern for RLS.

---

[210] Those living outside the UK have been excluded from this table due to the small numbers involved.
[211] Those who failed to state their level of fluency or the number of years spent learning Gaelic are excluded.

Questionnaire Results

Motivation for learning

Table 75: Motivation for learning: respondents in Scotland
Question: *Please rate the importance of each of the following to your decision to learn Gaelic by ticking the appropriate boxes. Which of the reasons (A–R) mentioned was the most important to your decision to learn Gaelic? Please write down only one reason.*

Reason	Very Important	Quite Important	Not Important at all / Not applicable	No Answer	Main Reason for learning[212]
N = 392	%	%	%	%	%
(a) I would be able to enjoy Gaelic music better	24.2	48.2	23	4.5	3.95
(b) I would be able to understand Gaelic TV	28.8	45.4	21.9	3.8	0.5
(c) I would be able to understand Gaelic literature	42.35	43.9	9.7	4.1	5.3
(d) I would be helping to keep Gaelic alive	67.9	25	4.3	2.8	25.8
(e) I live in a Gaelic speaking area	10.2	10.2	72.45	7.1	1.6
(f) Adult members of my family can /could speak Gaelic	16.1	11.5	68.9	3.6	4.5
(g) Gaelic would be useful for my hobbies or interests (e.g. place-names, tracing ancestry)	21.9	37	36.2	4.85	4.7
(h) Gaelic would be useful in present /future employment	17.9	26.8	49	6.4	3.95
(i) As a Scot/someone living in Scotland, I feel that I should speak Gaelic	42.9	37.8	15.6	3.8	9.5
(j) As a Highlander / Islander /someone living in the Highlands and Islands I feel I should speak Gaelic	26.8	14.8	53.6	4.85	5.3
(k) Gaelic would help me get closer to my roots	27.8	28.8	39.3	4.1	6.8
(l) I did not feel like a complete Scot without a knowledge of Gaelic	26.5	24	44.4	5.1	6
(m) My children are in Gaelic-medium education	7.65	3.6	82.65	6.1	2.9
(n) I have Gaelic speaking friends	23	33.9	38.8	4.3	3.4
(o) I am interested in languages	24.2	38.8	31.6	5.4	3.7
(p) I want to live in the Highlands /in Scotland	14.8	18.6	60.7	5.87	1.05
(q) I like to visit the Highlands/Islands	25.3	29.3	37.8	7.65	0.8
(r) Other Reasons	12.8	3.1	8.2	76	10.3

Learners were asked to rate the importance of seventeen common reasons for learning Gaelic to their decision to learn the language and were also given the opportunity to add any reasons not suggested in the questionnaire. Respondents were further asked to state which of the reasons was the most important to their decision. The responses to this section of the questionnaire were recorded for Scotland in Table 75 and for elsewhere in Tables 80 and 81.

Before noting the patterns emerging from the tables, it is interesting that several learners mentioned in this section that their motivation for learning had changed over the years and that they had continued learning for reasons different from those which had motivated them to start. Altogether, thirteen comments of this type were made, such as "Many of the above reasons are important now, but they were not when I started learning nearly 30 years ago in Canada", "my reasons have changed as my knowledge has increased". Most learners also had several reasons for doing so, with most respondents citing a number of reasons on the table as having been important to their decision to learn.

Respondents in Scotland

While the figures from the table are mostly self-explanatory, some of the main patterns may be commented on. First of all, it can be seen that a wide range of main reasons for learning were cited by respondents, with the largest single motivation only consisting of around one-quarter of the respondents (25.8%).

The reason for learning most commonly quoted as being very important was *I would be helping to keep Gaelic alive*, which was said to be very important by 67.9% of Scottish respondents and as quite important by another 25%. Only 4.3% of those who answered the question said that this factor was not important/applicable. This was also the most frequently chosen main reason for learning, picked by 25.8% of respondents in Scotland. This shows a high level of concern with the well-being of Gaelic and suggests that most respondents do not see their learning of Gaelic as a purely personal pastime, but rather see it as part of the effort to reverse language shift in Scotland.

The reason for learning which was mentioned second most often both as being very important and as a main reason for learning was *As a Scot / someone living in Scotland, I feel that I should speak Gaelic*. 42.9% said that this was very important and a further 37.8% quite important, with 9.5% of respondents stating that this was their main reason for learning.

Cited third most often as being a very important reason for learning was *I would be able to understand Gaelic literature*, which was deemed very important by 42.4% of respondents, quite important by 43.9% and as a main reason for learning by 5.3% of the respondents. Other reasons cited by a majority of respondents as very or quite important to their decision to learn Gaelic were reasons (a) Gaelic music (72.4%), (b) Gaelic television (74.2%), (g) hobbies or interests (58.9%), (k) getting closer to ones roots (56.6%), (l) not feeling like a complete Scot without Gaelic (50.5%), (n) having Gaelic-speaking friends (57.2%), (o) an interest in languages (63%) and (q) liking to visit the Highlands and Islands (54.6%).

The hobbies and interests mentioned by learners as being important to their decision to learn Gaelic were recorded in Table 76.

---

[212] This excludes 12 respondents who did not answer this question.

Table 76: Hobbies / interests influencing respondents to learn Gaelic [213]

Hobby	N
Music / singing / choirs[214]	117
Place-names	82
Hill walking / mountaineering	72
Scottish / Highland / Celtic History[215]	82
Other[216]	33
Genealogy	26
Visiting Highlands / Islands / travelling	28
Gaelic culture / literature folklore	75
Interest in languages	15

Interestingly, only 44.7% of respondents cited reason (h) *Gaelic would be useful in present/future employment* as a reason for learning Gaelic (17.9% very important, 26.8% quite important), with only 3.85% citing this as being their main reason for learning. A similar lack of enthusiasm about learning Gaelic for employment-related reasons was reported in Comunn na Gàidhlig and CLI's *Feumalachdan Luchd-Ionnsachaidh* report (1992: 6) and by MacNeil and MacDonald (1997: 11). This finding is perhaps significant given that much of the promotional effort undertaken by Gaelic agencies for the language puts particular stress on the job opportunities and economic benefits which can come through Gaelic. The findings of this section of the questionnaire, however, suggest that idealistic motivation (also called integrative or expressive motivation) to learn the language is more important to most respondents than instrumental motivation (also called practical motivation).[217] In other words, factors such as personal, local or national identity, political reasons such as nationalism, community-related or cultural reasons tend to be more important in influencing learners to learn Gaelic than the prospect of gaining employment or material gain through the language. The fact that under 4% of respondents cited job opportunities as their main reasons for learning Gaelic, taken together with the fact a significant minority said that such reasons were important (mainly *quite* rather than *very important*), suggests that while job opportunities are often one factor influencing learners, this is rarely the main reason.

Of the other reasons cited as being important only by a minority of respondents, most were reasons in which a large percentages of those responding answered *not applicable*. For possible motivations such as having children in Gaelic-medium education, for example, many learners answered *not applicable* as they did not have children in Gaelic-medium education. While Table 75 gives an idea of the relative importance of different reasons for learning within the sample of respondents as a whole, some further analysis is required of the possible reasons for learning which

---

[213] As hobbies/interests both in Scotland and elsewhere were similar, hobbies for all respondents are recorded here. It should be noted that many learners had more than one hobby or interest.

[214] Of those interested in music, four specifically mentioned Runrig and eleven indicated that they are or were Gaelic choir members.

[215] Types of history mentioned included local history, Celtic history, ecclesiastical history, clan history and Highland military history amongst others.

[216] Other: anthropology 2, archaeology 3, Celtic art 4, crafts 1, dancing 3, education 2, general interest in Scotland 3, meeting people 2, reading tombstones 1, Scottish politics/current affairs 6, spinning 2, sailing 1, video production 1, watching/listening to Gaelic broadcasts 2.

[217] For a discussion of instrumental and integrative motivations, see Wright 2000, 234-5.

were only applicable to certain sections of the respondents such as Highland dwellers or people with Gaelic-speaking family members. For this reason, a selection of the possible reasons for learning have been tabled, with the *not applicable* responses removed. It can be seen that majorities of those living in Gaelic-speaking areas, of those who have or had Gaelic-speaking members of their family and of those with children in Gaelic-medium education stated that these factors were important in their decision to learn the language and that a very large majority of those living in or from the Highlands/Islands felt that *As a Highlander / Islander / someone living in the Highlands and Islands I feel I should speak Gaelic*. The percentage of those stating *I did not feel like a complete Scot without a knowledge of Gaelic* also increased when those not considering themselves to be Scots were excluded.

Table 77: Main reasons for learning Gaelic

Reason	Very Important	Quite Important	Not Important	No Answer	Total
	%	%	%	%	N
(e) I live in a Gaelic speaking area	26.8	26.8	27.5	18.8	149
(f) Adult members of my family can/could speak Gaelic	38.5	30.4	21	10.1	148
(g) As a Highlander / Islander /someone living in the Highlands and Islands I feel I should speak Gaelic	52.5	29	9	10	200
(l) I did not feel like a complete Scot without a knowledge of Gaelic	33.4	30.2	29.9	6.4	311
(m) My children are in Gaelic-medium education	38.5	18	12.8	30.8	78

Learners who chose option (r) on the questionnaire and stated that an *other* reason for learning was important were asked to specify the reason. As many comments were received from respondents regarding *other* reasons for learning, responses have been categorised under a number of headings. No distinction is made between responses from those living in Scotland and those living outside Scotland, as these were similar in composition.

Some respondents stated that Gaelic was a recreational activity. (e.g. "looking towards retirement", "at my age it is important to be mentally active", "Gaelic is a sociable and inexpensive hobby", "the Gaelic community in the Borders is very friendly and the language is a way of making friends"). Similarly, some stated that they were learning the language for fun (e.g. "for the craic", "just because I like it"). Altogether, fifteen comments were received of this type.

Not everybody was sure as to why they were learning. Eight learners stated that they were unsure as to why they wanted to learn the language (e.g. "have always wanted to speak Gaelic – unsure why", "I feel a totally irrational emotional connection with the language", "just to know it for its own sake"). Another eight stated that they were learning the language as they felt it to be beautiful (e.g. "it's a beautiful language", "inherent appeal of the language", "love the sound of the spoken word").

Various instrumental and practical reasons were cited by eleven learners. These included reasons such as a desire to communicate with Gaelic-speaking clients, working in a school where Gaelic was used, the need to learn Gaelic to conduct certain research and the fact that Gaelic was a part of a university degree course chosen by the respondent. One learner also stated, "Gaelic is becoming more used and I don't want to be left behind when it becomes more important (in Parliament etc) in the future".

The desire to achieve a Gaelic mindset or view of the world through the language was mentioned by four learners. One learner stated: "It is a very ancient language and, although it must have developed and changed, the way of expressing thoughts is very different from present languages. So it illustrates a different 'mindset' that might be useful to understand when reading ancient history", while another expressed the view that "languages open their own consciousness in a person, to the extent I have learned Gaelic, it is like getting an additional soul", "every language mirrors the things that are valuable to the community. Gaelic will help me understand the Highlands".

Eleven learners stated that their decision to learn Gaelic was influenced by their interest in Scottish or Canadian culture as a whole. (e.g. "I feel that all of Scotland's culture is important and probably the Gaelic language most of all", "the whole package of literature, culture and history", "I believe Gaelic to be an integral part of Scottish culture", "Gaelic is Scottish heritage and culture"). The connection between Scottish and Irish culture as a reason for learning was also mentioned three times.

The desire to revitalise Gaelic was cited by three learners who stated that the statement *I would helping to keep Gaelic alive* offered in the questionnaire did not go far enough. ("It is not simply a matter of 'keeping Gaelic alive' it should be restored to the people of Scotland", "I would like to see Gaelic return to those parts of Scotland where it was once spoken. (i.e. most of it)", "to revenge myself in a small way against the people who tried and largely succeeded in extirpating the language in many parts of the Highlands"). Two people mentioned Gaelic radio as an important motivation for learning.

In addition to the reasons for learning which were mentioned by several learners, several reasons were mentioned only once. These are charted in Table 78.

Table 78: Other reasons for learning Gaelic

To become the greatest Gaelic prose author and modernise the language.

For the greater glory of God.

I would like to be a part of the Celtic church in the Highlands and Islands, helping to spread the word of God through the influences of our Celtic forebears.

I feel strongly about the attitude of some visitors towards the Welsh language, and felt that I had to try and learn Gaelic if I was to spend time in the Highlands.

I had it as a kiddie and don't want to lose it altogether.

I am very interested in Celtic spirituality and would like to be able to read in the original language which I am increasingly able to do so.

I feel Celtic in my heart and soul.

Political gesture and antidote to melancholy induced by commemorations of 1745 and Culloden in 1995 and 1996 (though had always intended to try to learn).

Poetry is subtle and doesn't survive translation. I want to enjoy it as a Gael would. I also have family. journals from the 18th and 19th centuries that I would like to be able to understand.

Galicia, my land is a country with Celtic Roots. Music (pipes), tradition and folklore are similar to Scotland, Eire, Brittany, and I think that it is very important to keep Gaelic alive.

I was made aware of the existence of Gaelic by way of Sword and Sorcery novels I read as a child / teenager and have always felt a strong affinity for Celtic things; plus it sure beats French! (Or Latin – UG!)

Of all the *other* reasons for learning Gaelic commented on by learners, by far the most frequently mentioned was the desire to learn Gaelic so as to reclaim something which respondents felt should belong to them but had been denied them. This included people who wished to reclaim their family, local or national linguistic heritage or identity and those who felt that their personal identity was incomplete due to an inability to speak Gaelic. Many learners expressed disappointment with the education system, which they felt had denied them the language to which they felt entitled. Several expressed anger, a feeling of incompleteness and/or a feeling of having been cheated. Sixteen learners put comments of this type down on the questionnaire as important *other* reasons for learning. Altogether, however, over 44 comments of this type were made throughout Section 2 of the questionnaire. A selection of representative comments can be seen in Table 79.

Table 79: The desire to reclaim Gaelic as a reason for learning

My father comes from Barra. I visit the island regularly and am embarrassed that I can't speak my own language.

I feel that being a Gael is part of who I am but have always felt cut off from my family and the Gaelic community by not being able to understand and speak the language. This has had a massive psychological impact which by learning Gaelic can to some extent be resolved for the future.

If you have no Gaelic then you are completely cut off from your heritage. (That applies to folk born and brought up here. If they haven't Gaelic they may be islanders and Highlanders, but they aren't Gaels).

Learning Gaelic has been for me a way of compensating for an education that at best ignored Gaelic culture and at worst condemned it as backward.

My ancestors were cleared from their land. After they went to Canada they changed their surname to an English one and gradually abandoned their language and culture. Learning Gaelic is my way of recovering something very important which was lost.

My own father refused to speak any Gaelic with me which made me very angry when I was older. I feel that I'm struggling to recover something that I should have been brought up with.

I felt cheated at not having the chance to learn Gaelic at school.

Gaelic should have been my inheritance.

It is personal but also political. We were stripped of our language – and consequently our culture. Scotland's diaspora feel the loss keenly. Learning is a gift to my ancestors and to my descendants.

Jealousy has played its part in my decision to learn. I felt there was something here which might have been mine and was denied me – and I wanted it!

Nuair a tha mi ag èisteachd ri luchd-turais a' bruidhinn nan cànan fhèin 's urrainn dhomh a ràdh "tha mo chànan fhèin agamsa cuideachd. (When I listen to tourists speaking in their own languages, I can say "I can speak my own language too").

I feel that I have missed out on a key dimension in my upbringing given that both parents spoke Gaelic.

Gaelic was denied to my generation. I was unaware of the fact it is the true language of the Scots until my 40s. I am angry I was taught to believe my language was English.

I am trying to make up for the failure of the Scottish education system to give me the opportunity of learning one of the indigenous language of my own country.

Gaelic should belong to me but has been denied to me – I wish to reclaim it.

Bha e a' cur orm nach b' urrainn dhomh mo chànan fhèin a bhuidhinn mar bu chòir. (It bothered me that I couldn't speak my own language as I should).

Having had two grandparents who spoke Gaelic but who did not see it advantageous to teach it to their children I felt a responsibility to reverse the decline in my family.

I can't describe it – Gaelic is a part of me.

Would understand myself better.

I feel that I have lost part of my culture and it's important to me to try to replace that loss. I feel a strong personal need which I can't properly describe. I am impelled towards it – my life would incomplete without Gaelic – it represents a fulfilment.

I was not provided with Gaelic at school (Mallaig High [!!!!]) and have always wanted to learn it.

I personally feel cheated that Gaelic was not available to me at primary or secondary school.

Table 80: Motivation for learning: respondents in rest of UK
Question: *Please rate the importance of each of the following to your decision to learn Gaelic by ticking the appropriate boxes. Which of the reasons (A–R) mentioned was the most important to your decision to learn Gaelic? Please write down only one reason.*

Reason	Very Important	Quite Important	Not Important at all / Not applicable	No Answer	Main Reason for learning[218]
N = 159	%	%	%	%	%
(a) I would be able to enjoy Gaelic music better	35.2	45.3	15.7	3.8	10.1
(b) I would be able to understand Gaelic TV	10.7	31.45	53.5	4.4	-
(c) I would be able to understand Gaelic literature	47.2	40.25	8.8	3.8	4.7
(d) I would be helping to keep Gaelic alive	66.7	22	8.8	2.5	25.5
(e) I live in a Gaelic speaking area	3.1	1.3	89.3	6.3	0.7
(f) Adult members of my family can /could speak Gaelic	7.55	8.2	77.4	6.9	3.4
(g) Gaelic would be useful for my hobbies or interests (e.g. place-names, tracing ancestry)	20.75	37.74	37.1	4.4	6.7
(h) Gaelic would be useful in present /future employment	5.7	13.2	74.2	5.7	-
(i) As a Scot/someone living in Scotland, I feel that I should speak Gaelic	8.2	10.7	8.2	6.3	2.7
(j) As a Highlander / Islander /someone living in the Highlands and Islands I feel I should speak Gaelic	8.8	2.5	82.4	6.3	3.4
(k) Gaelic would help me get closer to my roots	23.3	26.4	46.5	3.8	10.7
(l) I did not feel like a complete Scot without a knowledge of Gaelic	10.1	18.2	66.7	5	1.3
(m) My children are in Gaelic-medium education	0.6	-	92.45	6.9	-
(n) I have Gaelic speaking friends	17.6	23.9	52.2	6.3	0.7
(o) I am interested in languages	32.1	37.1	28.9	1.3	9.4
(p) I want to live in the Highlands /in Scotland	24.5	27.7	39.6	8.2	4.7
(q) I like to visit the Highlands/Islands	49.7	32.7	12.6	5	8.05
(r) Other Reasons	17.4	1.3	5.8	75.5	8.05

[218] This excludes 10 respondents who did not answer this question.

The results for learners in the remainder of the UK were similar in many ways to those in Scotland. As in Scotland, *I would be helping to keep Gaelic alive* was both the reason most commonly cited as being very important (66.7%) and the reason most often named as being the main reason for learning (25.5%).

Other reasons being cited by a majority of respondents as having been very or quite important to their decision to learn Gaelic in both Scotland and the remainder of the UK were (a) Gaelic music (80.5%), (c) Gaelic literature (87.45%), (g) hobbies or interests (58.5%), (k) getting closer to one's roots (49.7%), (o) an interest in languages (69.2%) and (q) liking to visit the Highlands and Islands (82.4%).

There were some differences between the Scottish and 'rest of UK' results, however. For example, wanting to live in the Highlands and Islands was mentioned by a majority of 'rest of UK' respondents but by a minority in Scotland. As might be expected, fewer respondents than in Scotland cited reasons such as Gaelic television, children in Gaelic-medium education, residence in Gaelic-speaking areas, having Gaelic-speaking friends, not feeling a complete Scot without Gaelic or other reasons relating to Scottish/Highland background or residence. Such differences can be explained largely in terms of factors relating to the non-residence of respondents in Scotland such as the non-availability of such services as Gaelic education and television outside Scotland, due to the fact that fewer of the Gaelic learners outside Scotland have been born in Scotland and due to the fact that Gaelic speakers are fewer on the ground outside Scotland. As can be seen from Table 81, this is also the case for learners living outside the UK.

Motivation amongst the 'rest of world' sample was similar in many respects to that in the 'rest of the UK' sample. Again, a desire to keep Gaelic alive was the factor most often mentioned both as being very important and as being the main reason for learning. Other reasons mentioned by a majority of respondents as important reasons for learning were Gaelic literature (91%), Gaelic music (83.2%), interest in languages (79.75%), hobbies (58.5%) and visiting the Highlands/Scotland (72%).

Table 81: Motivation for learning: respondents in rest of the world
Question: *Please rate the importance of each of the following to your decision to learn Gaelic by ticking the appropriate boxes. Which of the reasons (A–R) mentioned was the most important to your decision to learn Gaelic? Please write down only one reason.*

Reason	Very Important	Quite Important	Not Important at all / Not applicable	No Answer	Main Reason for learning[219]
N = 89	%	%	%	%	%
(a) I would be able to enjoy Gaelic music better	37.1	46.1	15.7	1.1	7
(b) I would be able to understand Gaelic T.V	14.6	24.7	56.2	4.5	-
(c) I would be able to understand Gaelic literature	49.4	41.6	6.7	2.2	9.3
(d) I would be helping to keep Gaelic alive	69.7	18	11.2	1.1	23.3
(e) I live in a Gaelic speaking area	2.25	1.1	94.4	2.25	-
(f) Adult members of my family can /could speak Gaelic	6.7	4.5	86.5	2.25	-
(g) Gaelic would be useful for my hobbies or interests (e.g. place-names, tracing ancestry)	22.5	36	38.2	3.4	2.3
(h) Gaelic would be useful in present /future employment	6.7	21.35	68.5	3.4	2.3
(i) As a Scot/someone living in Scotland, I feel that I should speak Gaelic	7.9	6.7	80.9	4.5	4.65
(j) As a Highlander / Islander /someone living in the Highlands and Islands I feel I should speak Gaelic	6.7	5.6	83.15	4.5	1.1
(k) Gaelic would help me get closer to my roots	25.8	21.35	50.6	2.25	9.3
(l) I did not feel like a complete Scot without a knowledge of Gaelic	12.4	11.2	75.3	1.1	3.5
(m) My children are in Gaelic-medium education	1.1	1.1	95.5	2.25	1.1
(n) I have Gaelic speaking friends	10.1	29.2	58.4	2.25	1.1
(o) I am interested in languages	39.3	40.45	19.1	1.1	13.95
(p) I want to live in the Highlands /in Scotland	14.6	22.5	57.3	5.6	3.5
(q) I like to visit the Highlands/Islands	36	36	23.6	4.5	2.3
(r) Other Reasons	21.35	5.6	5.6	67.4	15.1

[219] This excludes 3 respondents who did not answer this question.

A further question regarding motivation for learning was asked in the questionnaire, giving learners the opportunity to grade each of seven possible reasons for learning on a scale of 0–10 where 0 signified not important at all and 10 signified very important indeed. Results are tabled for Scotland in Table 82 and for the rest of the UK and rest of the world in Tables 83 and 84.

Table 82: Importance of learning motivation: respondents in Scotland
Question: *How important on a scale of 0–10 would you say that the following were to your decision to learn Gaelic?* (0 = not important at all, 10 = very important indeed)

N = 392	0	1	2	3	4	5	6	7	8	9	10	NA
	%	%	%	%	%	%	%	%	%	%	%	%
(a) Patriotic, nationalistic or national identity reasons	14	2.3	5.6	3.8	3.1	10.5	6.4	8.2	8.9	6.9	27.6	2.8
(b) Highlands and Islands identity reasons	34.2	2.8	3.3	5.6	3.6	5.6	4.6	6.6	9.95	2.8	17.6	3.3
(c) Cultural reasons (e.g. music, literature)	5.4	1.5	2	2.8	3.3	11	8.9	11	14	9.2	27.8	3.1
(d) Career or economic reasons	44.1	4.3	6.1	5.1	1.3	11	4.85	4.85	4.85	2.3	6.9	4.3
(e) Immediate family reasons	58.4	3.3	4.6	2.55	1.5	4.6	1	2.55	2.3	2.55	13.5	3.1
(f) Community reasons	44.1	4.6	6.1	4.3	4.6	12	3.8	3.6	5.6	2.3	5.4	3.6
(g) Family background /roots reasons	34.4	2.8	5.6	5.6	2.3	8.7	2.3	5.4	5.1	5.6	19.6	2.55

The results of this question for Scotland confirm the patterns seen in the previous tables to a large extent. Again, most learners cited a range of factors as having been important to some extent to their decision to learn Gaelic. Of these reasons, those related to culture and national identity were mentioned most often. Just over 80% of respondents placed cultural reasons at 5 or above on the scale with almost 30% placing them at number 10. Patriotic, nationalistic or national identity reasons were placed at 5 or above on the scale by 68.5% of respondents, with almost 30% rating them as being very important indeed (level 10 on the scale).

Many respondents also cited Highlands and Islands identity reasons, with 47.2% placing these at 5 or above on the scale and around 18% placing them at 10, as opposed to the 34.2% who said that these reasons were not important at all. Very similar figures were obtained for family background/roots reasons. Community reasons were not cited as being of great importance by as many people, with 34.7% of respondents rating them at 5 or above as compared with 44.1% who said that these reasons were not important at all and only 5.4% rating them at 10 on the scale. As for immediate family reasons, a majority of almost 60% of respondents said that such reasons were not important at all, but with 13.5% placing them at 10 on the scale. For community and immediate family reasons, the pattern suggests, as in the previous question, that these factors were considered important by the minority of respondents who had close family or community links with the language but that they were not considered to be important by those who did not have such connections.

Once again, instrumental reasons for learning Gaelic did not seem to be a primary reason for learning for most learners. Only 34.75% rated career or economic reasons at 5 or above on the scale as compared with 44.1% who said that such factors were not important at all.

Table 83: Importance of learning motivation: respondents in rest of UK
Question: *How important on a scale of 0–10 would you say that the following were to your decision to learn Gaelic?* (0 = not important at all, 10 = very important indeed)

N = 159	0	1	2	3	4	5	6	7	8	9	10	NA
	%	%	%	%	%	%	%	%	%	%	%	%
(a) Patriotic, nationalistic or national identity reasons	33.3	3.1	3.8	4.4	0.6	10.1	8.2	4.4	10.1	3.1	16.4	2.5
(b) Highlands and Islands identity reasons	48.4	3.8	4.4	2.5	3.8	3.1	6.3	5	5	1.9	11.3	4.4
(c) Cultural reasons (e.g. music, literature)	5.7	0.6	1.3	4.4	3.1	5.7	12	9.4	11.3	6.9	37.1	2.5
(d) Career or economic reasons	62.9	5	7.55	5	1.9	5.7	1.9	3.1	0.6	1.3	1.9	3.1
(e) Immediate family reasons	72.3	1.3	8.2	1.9	0.6	1.9	2.5	0.6	1.3	-	6.3	3.1
(f) Community reasons	59.1	4.4	5	2.5	3.8	5.7	3.8	1.3	2.5	1.3	6.3	4.4
(g) Family background /roots reasons	35.2	2.5	6.3	2.5	1.9	6.9	5.6	5	6.3	1.9	22	3.8

Table 84: Importance of learning motivation: respondents outwith the UK
Question: *How important on a scale of 0–10 would you say that the following were to your decision to learn Gaelic?* (0 = not important at all, 10 = very important indeed)

N = 89	0 %	1 %	2 %	3 %	4 %	5 %	6 %	7 %	8 %	9 %	10 %	NA %
(a) Patriotic, nationalistic or national identity reasons	38.2	5.6	4.5	4.5	2.25	10.1	2.25	1.1	6.7	4.5	15.7	4.5
(b) Highlands and Islands identity reasons	50.6	3.4	1.1	-	2.25	9	4.5	6.7	5.6	2.25	9	5.6
(c) Cultural reasons (e.g. music, literature)	6.7	2.25	-	3.4	1.1	4.5	6.7	4.5	14.6	4.5	48.3	3.4
(d) Career or economic reasons	56.2	3.4	5.6	2.25	3.4	12.4	1.1	4.5	2.25	-	4.5	4.5
(e) Immediate family reasons	67.4	6.7	2.25	3.4	1.1	4.5	-	2.25	2.25	-	4.5	5.6
(f) Community reasons	75.3	4.5	-	-	1.2	4.5	1.1	1.1	2.25	-	4.5	5.6
(g) Family background /roots reasons	39.3	1.1	2.25	1.1	3.4	10.1	3.4	3.4	3.4	2.25	25.8	4.5

Outside Scotland, as within it, cultural reasons were the factors rated most highly by the most respondents as being important to their decision to learn Gaelic. In the remainder of the UK and the rest of the world, over 80% of learners rated cultural reasons between 5 and 10 on the scale, with 37.1% and 48.3% respectively placing them at 10. The factors rated second most highly by learners as having been important to their decision to learn Gaelic were family background/roots reasons. In the rest of the UK, 22% of learners stated that these reasons were very important indeed to their decision to learn the language (level 10 on the scale) and 47.7% placed these reasons above 5 on the scale. Outside the UK, the comparative figures were 25.8% and 48.35%. There were also significant minorities citing Highlands and Islands identity as being factors in their decision to learn Gaelic both in the rest of the UK and the rest of the world.

Patriotic, nationalistic or national identity reasons were also said to have been important by many learners outside Scotland. Among the 'rest of UK' respondents, 52.3% of learners rated these reasons at between 5 and 10 on the scale, with 16.4% placing them at 10. Outside the UK, the figures were 40.35% and 15.7% respectively. Other reasons for learning – immediate family reasons, community reasons and career or economic reasons – were cited by relatively few respondents outside Scotland as having been important to their decision to learn, with large majorities of respondents stating that these reasons were not important at all in each case.

Ways of Learning Gaelic

Learners were invited to state their main ways of learning Gaelic in a specific box in the questionnaire and were given some possible examples of ways of learning Gaelic as illustrations (evening classes, summer courses, distance learning, using a published Gaelic course at home, going to live in a Gaelic community, full-time college/university courses).

As would be expected, a large range of learning methods were revealed. In Scotland, by far the most commonly used method was the conventional Gaelic evening or day class, which was mentioned by 222 respondents. Also commonly mentioned were the use of published Gaelic courses at home (118 mentions), university- and college-certificated Gaelic courses (91 mentions), summer and weekend classes (89 mentions) and flexible/distance learning (44 mentions). Other methods mentioned less frequently included the use of radio and television, books and newspapers, informal Gaelic self-help groups, internet mailing lists, talking to other Gaelic speakers and visiting Gaelic-speaking areas. Given the importance of practising spoken Gaelic to becoming fluent in the language, it is perhaps a matter of concern that few learners (32) noted that they used talking to fluent Gaelic speakers as a means of learning.

Outside Scotland, the use of evening classes was less widespread than in Scotland, reflecting the limited availability of such classes outside Scotland. Use of Gaelic broadcasting was also limited due to the then non-availability of Gaelic television and radio outwith Scotland. As in Scotland, however, published Gaelic courses were widely used for learning, as were flexible/distance learning and Gaelic summer and weekend courses. Altogether, 54 learners in the rest of the UK and 24 learners outside the UK had attended summer or weekend Gaelic courses, most of which were held in Scotland. 36 learners in the remainder of the UK and 10 learners in the rest of the world used distance learning. Use of the internet as a means for learning Gaelic was not common amongst the sample, reflecting the much lower level of internet use in 1998.

In order to look at the relationship between means of learning and progress in the language, levels of fluency and learning methods were cross-checked. Due to the nature of the question on learning methods, it was not possible to analyse the results of this section statistically and so a discussion of the trends which are obvious to the eye must suffice.

There was a greater incidence of the use of college and university courses amongst those who classified themselves as fluent or advanced than among the rest of the sample (15 out of the 41 fluent learners and 14 out of the 44 advanced learners in Scotland had attended such courses). Within the fluent and advanced groups, there were also higher incidences of using conversation with Gaelic speakers or of having spent time in Gaelic-speaking areas as means of learning than amongst respondents as a whole. Of the 32 learners who mentioned that they practised their Gaelic with fluent speakers, 23 were in the fluent and advanced categories. People in these groups also tended to have used more different ways of learning Gaelic than those in the less fluent categories. While many of the beginners and intermediate learners had been learning solely through evening classes or books, for example, almost all fluent and advanced learners stated that they had used a variety of different methods such as evening classes, home study, summer courses, radio and reading. These patterns aside, however, fluent and advanced learners had become fluent by a variety of different means.

Section 3: Using Gaelic

In Section 3, a number of questions relating to the use of Gaelic by respondents were asked in order to investigate the ways in which, and to what extent, the learners used Gaelic and to gain some idea as to what impact learners were having on Gaelic affairs and in RLS efforts.

Use of Gaelic Broadcasting and Media

Learners were asked firstly about Gaelic broadcasting. Table 85 shows that while most respondents in Scotland were able to receive the Gaelic radio station Radio nan Gaidheal, a significant minority of 17.6% were resident in areas where Radio nan Gaidheal could not then be received.[220] Of those able to receive Radio nan Gaidheal, most were regular listeners: almost 80% (77.2%) indicated that they listened to Radio nan Gaidheal on the average day. This suggests that Radio nan Gaidheal is being widely being used as a learning resource.

Table 85: Ability to receive Radio nan Gaidheal: respondents in Scotland
Question: *Can you receive Radio nan Gaidheal where you live?*

	N	%
Yes	253	65.3
No	69	17.6
Don't know	31	7.9
Not stated	36	9.2
Total	392	100

Table 86: Time spent listening to Gaelic radio: respondents in Scotland
Question: *If yes, how many hours of Gaelic radio do you listen to on the average day, if any?*

Amount	N	%	Amount	N	%
None	53	21	2-4	27	10.7
up to 1	106	41.9	4-6	7	2.8
1-2	51	20.2	6+	4	1.6
No answer	5	2	**Total**	253	100

A similar question was asked with regard to television. Over 90% of respondents stated that they were able to receive Gaelic television, with only 5% being unable to do so. This reflects the fact that, Gaelic television unlike Gaelic radio, is available in virtually all of Scotland with the exception of areas of the south west.[221] Many respondents in the Border TV area of southern Scotland noted, however, that they were only able to receive Gaelic television on the BBC as Border TV do not carry Gaelic broadcasts. Of those able to watch Gaelic television, most watched some Gaelic television each week, with 36.1% watching a few programmes and with 31% watching half or more of the programmes. Of those who stated that they viewed little

---

[220] As noted in chapter 3, availability of Gaelic radio has since greatly expanded.
[221] Some areas of south-western Scotland receive English rather than Scottish BBC 2 services meaning that BBC Scotland's Gaelic output cannot be seen. These areas are also within the Border TV broadcasting area, where no ITV Gaelic programmes are broadcast.

or no Gaelic television, over half noted that they either did not have a television or viewed very little television at all.

Table 87: Reception of Gaelic television: respondents in Scotland
Question: *Can you receive Gaelic television where you live?*

	N	%
Yes	355[222]	90.6
No	21	5.4
Not stated	16	4.1
Total	**392**	**100**

Table 88: Time spent watching Gaelic television: respondents in Scotland
Question: *If yes, how many of the Gaelic television programmes do you usually watch in an average week, if any?*

	N	%
All of them	6	1.7
Most of them	64	18
About half	40	11.3
A few	128	36.1
I watch Gaelic TV very occasionally	65	18.3
I don't usually watch any Gaelic programmes[223]	31	8.7
Not stated	21	5.9
Total	**355**	**100**

Several comments regarding broadcasting were made on the questionnaires. Ten respondents unable to receive Radio nan Gaidheal stated their unhappiness with this situation, as did eight living in the Border Television area who wished that Border would show Gaelic programmes.

Outwith Scotland, neither Radio nan Gaidheal nor Gaelic television were available at the time when the questionnaire was distributed, a situation upon which 36 respondents living furth of Scotland commented.[224] 28 respondents in the remainder of the UK stated that they wanted Gaelic radio and/or television to be available throughout the UK. Of these, 5 had listened to Radio nan Gaidheal when it had been available on medium wave. A further 3 said that they had people tape radio programmes for them. Three respondents outside the UK said that they wanted access to Gaelic broadcasting.

---

[222] Two noted that they could only receive Gaelic television on the BBC.
[223] Ten of these respondents noted that they had no television set.
[224] Radio nan Gaidheal's output has since become available via the internet.

Table 89: Gaelic publications read: UK respondents
Question: *Do you regularly read any of the following?*

	Scotland		UK		World	
Publication	Yes	No	Yes	No	Yes	No
	%	%	%	%	%	%
Gairm	16.8	83.2	20.8	79.2	22.5	77.5
Cothrom	69.1	30.9	79.9	20.1	69.7	30.3
An Gaidheal Ùr	32.9	67.1	20.1	79.9	16.8	83.2
The Scotsman Friday Gaelic column	33.2	66.8	8.2	91.8	5.6	94.4
The Scotsman Wednesday Gaelic column	35.2	64.8	8.8	91.2	5.6	94.4
Press and Journal (Highland Edition) Gaelic column	11.5	88.5	4.4	95.6	1.1	98.9
Gaelic columns or pages in local or community newspapers	30.4	69.6	17.6	82.4	14.6	85.4
Gaelic column or supplement in other newspaper or magazine	11.7	88.3	5.7	94.3	20.2	79.8
	Total = 392		Total = 159		Total = 89	

Table 90: Number of publications: all respondents

	0	1	2	3	4	5	6+
	%	%	%	%	%	%	%
Scotland	15.3	20.7	17.6	18.4	15.3	6.4	3.1
Rest of UK	12	45.6	18.4	17.1	4.4	1.9	0.6
Rest of World	22.5	30.4	25.8	12.4	7.9	1.1	-

Figure 7: Number of publications read: respondents in Scotland

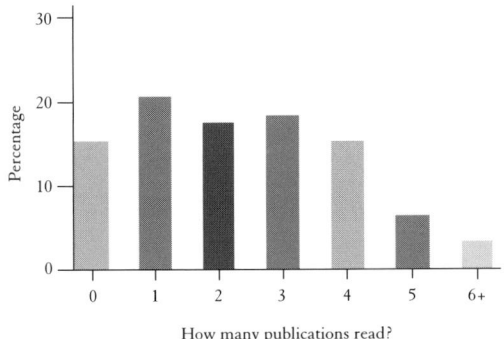

Respondents were asked which, if any, Gaelic publications they regularly read. As can be seen from Table 90, 85% of the sample in Scotland regularly read at least one Gaelic publication, with 64% reading at least one other than the Gaelic learners'

magazine *Cothrom*. A wide variety of publications were read by respondents, ranging from *Cothrom* to the literary magazine *Gairm*. Respondents read between them a large selection of columns and supplements which contained most or all of those available.[225] The most widely read magazine was *Cothrom*, reflecting the fact that the magazine is free to CLI members, a group which formed the lion's share of the questionnaire sample. Between 30 and 35% of respondents in Scotland read each of the following: *An Gaidheal Ùr*, *The Scotsman* Gaelic columns and Gaelic columns/pages in local newspapers.

Figures for the numbers of publications read and for the percentage of respondents reading individual publications tended to be lower outside Scotland, reflecting the generally lower level of fluency of this section of the sample and the increased expense and difficulty of obtaining Gaelic publications outside Scotland. The expansion of the amount of published Gaelic via the internet since the late 1990s, however, is likely to have increased use of published Gaelic by this group.

Table 91: Publications read by level of ability in reading Gaelic

	Gairm		*An Gaidheal Ur*		*Scotsman Wednesday*	
	N	%[226]	N	%	N	%
Fluent	33	71.7	35	76.1	32	69.6
Advanced	17	22.4	36	47.4	37	48.7
Intermediate	10	7.7	41	31.5	46	35.4
Basic	6	4.7	16	12.7	23	18.2

Readership of a selection of Gaelic publications were cross-tabulated with the level of fluency of respondents in Table 91. It can be seen that people in more fluent groups were far more likely to read Gaelic publications. There were, nonetheless, many learners who read, or attempted to read, Gaelic publications despite not being fluent. This suggests that many learners use Gaelic articles, newspapers and magazines as a learning resource.

---

[225] Gaelic columns or pages in local/community newspapers(s), Gaelic column or supplement in other newspaper or magazines: (Scotland) *West Highland Free Press* 79, *Oban Times* 17, *Stornoway Gazette* 13, *Life and Work* (Church of Scotland magazine) Gaelic supplement 12, *Inverness Courier* 11, *Ross-shire Journal* 9, *Am Bràighe* (Canadian Gaelic interest bilingual quarterly newspaper) 8, *Carn* (pan-Celtic/nationalist quarterly magazine) 7, *Scots Independent* (Scottish nationalist monthly newspaper) 6; *Strì* (since defunct bilingual quarterly pan-Celtic nationalist magazine) 5, *Am Bratach* (Sutherland community newspaper) 4, *Free Church Monthly Record* 2, *Catholic Observer* 2, *North Star* 2, *Am Pàipear* (Uist community newspaper) 2, *Westworld* 2, *An Carranach* (Lochcarron local newspaper) 1, *Lochaber News* 1, *Highland news* 1, *Tional* 1, *Strathspey Herald* 1, *Guth Bharraigh* 1. (Rest of UK) *West Highland Free Press* 21, *Oban Times* 6, *Stornoway Gazette* 4, *Am Bratach* (Sutherland community magazine) 3, *Am Bràighe* 1, *Carn* 1, *Tional* 1, *Dusgadh* 1, *Guth Bharraigh* 1, *Crofter* 1. (Rest of World) *Am Bràighe* 10, *West Highland Free Press* 10, *Scottish Banner* 3, *Carn* 2, *Free Church Monthly Record* 1, *Inverness Courier* 1, *Life and Work* 1, *Oban Times* 1, *Scots Independent* 1, *Stornoway Gazette* 1.

[226] Percentages are percentages of those defining themselves as each level of ability in Gaelic who read the publication in question.

Participation in Gaelic-related activities

Two questions were inserted into the questionnaire asking learners which Gaelic language activities they took part in and how often they did so. Results are analysed for Scotland first, followed by other respondents. These questions were aimed at further investigating the use of Gaelic-related services and facilities and the participation of learners in Gaelic-related events.

Composition of these questions presented many difficulties. In the first place, while the questionnaire aimed to find out how much use learners made of Gaelic-related events and facilities, such opportunities to use Gaelic are usually few and far between throughout Scotland. This made it difficult both to select a range of Gaelic-related activities to put on the questionnaire as options and, due to the paucity of such events, to gain meaningful data as to how often respondents took part. This serves to show the weakness of Gaelic in terms of domains of usage.

Table 92: Participation in Gaelic-related events: respondents in Scotland
Question: *Which of the following Gaelic-language activities do you take part in / have you attended or have you taken part in / attended in the past?*

N = 392	regularly		sometimes		seldom		never		not stated	
	N	%	N	%	N	%	N	%	N	%
National Mòd	43	11	47	12	47	12	227	57.9	28	7.1
Local Mòd	42	10.7	52	13.3	38	9.7	231	58.9	29	7.4
Fèis	27	6.9	54	13.8	37	9.4	244	62.2	30	7.7
Gaelic Play	9	2.3	67	17.1	42	10.7	243	62	31	7.9
Gaelic concert / cèilidh	70	17.9	132	33.7	62	15.8	105	26.8	23	5.9
Gaelic church service	17	4.3	43	11	68	17.4	238	60.7	26	6.6
Gaelic meeting / conference	23	5.9	62	15.8	56	14.3	206	52.6	45	11.5
Other Gaelic activity[227]	52	13.3	28	7.1	11	2.8	75	19.1	226	57.7

---

[227] Cèilidhs 3, Choir 6, Cròileagan/Pàrant and Pàiste group (Gaelic pre-school groups) 8, Gaelic animation workshop 1, Gaelic Burns Supper 1, Gaelic classes/courses 17, Gaelic Conversation group 15, Gaelic e-mail conference 1, Gaelic-medium history school-teaching 1, Gaelic poetry readings 2, Gaelic talks 2, meet up with Gaelic speaking friend 2, Speak on Gaelic TV/radio 1, Sradagan (Gaelic youth club) 2, teaching Gaelic to adult learners 6, use Gaelic in workplace 1. Involved with activities of Gaelic group or society Comann Ceilteach 1, An Comunn Gàidhealach branch 3, Comunn nam Pàrant 2, Gaelic language promotional trust 1, Glasgow Gaelic Society 1, Glasgow Skye Association1, Gaelic waulking group 1, Gaelic Walking Club 2, Local Gaelic partnership 1, Taigh na Gàidhlig 1.

Table 93: Frequency of participation in Gaelic-related events: respondents in Scotland
Question: *How often do you do the following (please tick one box for each activity)?*

N = 392	regularly		sometimes		seldom		never		not stated	
	N	%	N	%	N	%	N	%	N	%
Make an effort to go to Gaelic concerts, plays, entertainments when they are put on	79	20.2	130	33.2	71	18.1	83	21.7	29	7.4
Read books in Gaelic	96	24.5	112	28.6	74	18.9	84	21.4	26	6.6
Read internet pages in Gaelic	22	5.6	59	15	33	8.4	246	62.8	32	8.2
Read / write e-mails in Gaelic	23	5.9	30	7.6	37	9.4	272	69.4	30	7.6
Write letters in Gaelic	23	5.9	95	24.2	87	22.2	158	40.3	29	7.4
Take part in campaigns for Gaelic (letter-writing, petition-signing etc)	33	8.4	98	25	70	17.9	159	40.6	32	8.2
Speak Gaelic	142	36.2	131	33.4	75	19.1	26	6.6	18	4.6

Only a minority of respondents indicated that they were regularly involved in many of the Gaelic events or activities suggested in the questionnaire: the National Mòd, local Mòds, Fèisean, attending Gaelic plays, church services, Gaelic-related conferences and meetings or using the internet or email for Gaelic learning.[226] There were, however, significant minorities who did say that they regularly or sometimes took part in the relevant activities and many further learners who said they seldom took part in these activities. More popular were the following, all of which a majority took part in regularly, sometimes or seldom: Gaelic concerts/cèilidhs (67.4% regularly, sometimes or seldom), making an effort to go to Gaelic concerts, plays and entertainments when they are put on (71.5%), reading Gaelic books (72%), taking part in campaigns for Gaelic (51.3%), writing letters in Gaelic (52.3%) and speaking Gaelic (88.7%).

The level of participation in Gaelic-language activities was investigated with relation to the level of fluency of participants. In Tables 94 and 95, the level of participation in Gaelic activities of respondents who have defined themselves as fluent and advanced learners of spoken Gaelic has been charted. As might be imagined, there was a higher level of participation in every single Gaelic activity investigated amongst this group than there was amongst the respondents as a whole. It is likely that fluent and advanced learners make greater use of Gaelic-related activities than less fluent learners as their greater proficiency in Gaelic makes them more able to participate in and enjoy these activities. Greater participation in such activities is also likely to have been a factor in bringing these learners to greater fluency. It may also be the case that fluent/advanced learners often have more awareness of the availability of Gaelic-related activities and services as they are likely to have been involved in the Gaelic 'scene' longer than many less advanced learners.

---

[226] It should be remembered that internet use has greatly expanded since the questionnaire was distributed.

Table 94: Participation in Gaelic-related events: fluent/advanced respondents in Scotland
Question: *Which of the following Gaelic-language activities do you take part in / attended or have you taken part in / attended in the past?*

N = 85	regularly		sometimes		seldom		never		not stated	
	N	%	N	%	N	%	N	%	N	%
National Mòd	13	15.3	17	20	14	16.5	35	41.2	7	7.1
Local Mòd	11	12.9	16	18.8	18	21.2	35	41.2	5	5.9
Fèis	4	4.7	21	24.7	12	14.1	39	45.9	9	10.6
Gaelic Play	5	5.9	28	32.9	15	17.6	30	35.3	7	8.2
Gaelic concert / cèilidh	22	25.9	34	40	16	18.8	9	10.6	4	4.7
Gaelic church service	8	9.4	20	23.5	22	25.9	31	36.5	4	4.7
Gaelic meeting / conference	15	17.6	29	34.1	16	18.8	17	20	2	2.4
Other Gaelic activity	22	25.9	9	10.6	2	2.4	5	5.9	47	55.3

Table 95: Frequency of participation in Gaelic related activities: fluent advanced respondents in Scotland
Question: *How often do you do the following (please tick one box for each activity)?*

N = 85	regularly		sometimes		seldom		never		not stated	
	N	%	N	%	N	%	N	%	N	%
Make an effort to go to Gaelic concerts, plays, entertainments when they are put on	29	34.1	35	41.2	9	10.6	8	9.4	4	4.7
Read books in Gaelic	48	56.5	27	31.8	4	4.7	2	2.4	4	4.7
Read internet pages in Gaelic	8	9.4	19	22.4	11	12.9	41	48.2	6	7.1
Read / write e-mails in Gaelic	14	16.5	10	11.8	12	14.1	43	50.6	6	7.1
Write letters in Gaelic	19	22.4	42	49.4	9	10.6	10	11.8	5	5.9
Take part in campaigns for Gaelic (letter-writing, petition-signing etc)	14	16.5	30	35.3	20	23.5	14	16.5	7	8.2
Speak Gaelic	60	70.6	14	16.5	6	7.1	0	0	5	5.9

The figures suggest that the participation of beginners and intermediate learners tends towards activities which are directly related to the learning process such as reading Gaelic books and speaking Gaelic and to entertainment events such as Gaelic cèilidhs and concerts which do not require fluency in Gaelic to be enjoyed by participants. Other activities such as Gaelic church services or plays are normally too difficult for this group of learners. The figures further suggest that the level of participation in Gaelic affairs increases with the level of fluency, with learners becoming more able to understand and enjoy Gaelic activities and to use Gaelic in a meaningful sense. The level of participation of fluent and advanced Gaelic learners in the activities cited bodes well for RLS and shows that learners reaching this level of fluency tend to become active in many Gaelic activities and thereby contribute to the numbers attending Gaelic plays or services and reading Gaelic books, for example.

Table 96: Participation in Gaelic related events: UK respondents outwith Scotland
Question: *Which of the following Gaelic-language activities do you take part in / have you attended or have you taken part in / attended in the past?*

N = 159	regularly		sometimes		seldom		never		not stated	
	N	%	N	%	N	%	N	%	N	%
National Mòd	5	3.1	11	6.9	8	5	126	79.2	9	5.7
Local Mòd	1	0.6	3	1.9	11	6.9	131	82.4	13	8.2
Fèis	-	-	7	4.4	12	7.6	127	79.9	13	8.2
Gaelic Play	1	0.6	7	4.4	10	6.3	127	79.9	14	8.8
Gaelic concert / cèilidh	12	7.6	36	22.6	30	18.9	71	44.6	10	6.3
Gaelic church service	4	2.5	22	13.8	23	14.5	101	63.5	9	5.7
Gaelic meeting / conference	2	1.3	15	9.4	15	9.4	114	71.7	13	8.2
Other Gaelic activity[229]	10	2.5	14	3.6	11	2.8	37	9.4	320	81.6

Table 97: Frequency of participation in Gaelic related activities: UK respondents outwith Scotland
Question: *How often do you do the following (please tick one box for each activity)?*

N = 159	regularly		sometimes		seldom		never		not stated	
	N	%	N	%	N	%	N	%	N	%
Make an effort to go to Gaelic concerts, plays, entertainments when they are put on	16	10.1	35	22	25	15.7	69	43.4	14	8.8
Read books in Gaelic	37	23.3	45	28.3	32	20.1	40	25.2	5	3.1
Read internet pages in Gaelic	14	8.8	21	13.2	19	12	97	61	8	5
Read / write e-mails in Gaelic	9	5.7	12	7.6	15	9.4	114	71.7	9	5.7
Write letters in Gaelic	12	7.6	38	23.9	37	23.3	65	40.9	7	4.4
Take part in campaigns for Gaelic (letter-writing, petition-signing etc)	3	1.9	26	16.4	27	17	92	57.9	11	6.9
Speak Gaelic	16	10.1	67	42.1	47	29.6	20	12.6	9	5.7

---

[229] Cèilidhs 3, courses 16, choir 4, Gaelic A/B e-mail mailing lists 1, Gaelic Society of London meetings/talks 2, holiday in Gaelic speaking island 1, "promoting the language" 1, regularly meet with another Gaelic learner 1, Runrig concerts 1, listening to Gaelic music 1, song workshops 1, teaching adults 1.

Table 98: Participation in Gaelic related activities: respondents outwith UK
Question: *Which of the following Gaelic-language activities do you take part in / have you attended or have you taken part in / attended in the past?*

N = 89	regularly		sometimes		seldom		never		not stated	
	N	%	N	%	N	%	N	%	N	%
National Mòd	3	3.4	5	5.6	3	3.4	76	85.4	2	2.2
Local Mòd	3	3.4	4	4.5	6	6.7	73	82	3	3.4
Fèis	4	4.5	2	2.2	4	4.5	76	85.3	3	3.4
Gaelic Play	-	-	3	3.4	6	6.7	79	88.8	1	1.1
Gaelic concert / cèilidh	16	18	23	25.8	11	12.4	38	42.7	1	1.1
Gaelic church service	4	4.5	7	7.9	8	8.9	68	76.4	2	2.2
Gaelic meeting / conference	2	2.2	6	6.7	7	7.9	71	79.8	3	3.3
Other Gaelic activity[230]	9	10.1	8	9	4	4.5	30	33.7	38	42.7

Table 99: Rest of world respondents: *How often do you do the following (please tick one box for each activity)?*

N = 89	regularly		sometimes		seldom		never		not stated	
	N	%	N	%	N	%	N	%	N	%
Make an effort to go to Gaelic concerts, plays, entertainments when they are put on	10	11.2	16	18	10	11.2	37	41.6	10	11.2
Read books in Gaelic	28	31.5	24	27	16	18	19	21.4	2	2.2
Read internet pages in Gaelic	14	15.7	22	24.7	10	11.2	41	46.1	2	2.2
Read / write e-mails in Gaelic	7	7.9	12	13.5	10	11.2	56	62.9	4	4.5
Write letters in Gaelic	13	14.6	16	18	22	24.7	36	40.4	2	2.2
Take part in campaigns for Gaelic (letter-writing, petition-signing etc)	2	2.2	15	16.8	11	12.4	57	64	4	4.5
Speak Gaelic	17	19.1	26	29.2	29	32.6	13	14.6	3	3.7

Outside Scotland, the level of involvement in the Gaelic activities mentioned amongst respondents was far lower, reflecting the lack of facilities available outwith Scotland. In activities not restricted by location, however, such as the ability to write Gaelic letters, or to access Gaelic books or the internet, participation was more comparable

---

[230] Celtic festivals 1, cèilidhs 2, classes/courses 8, edit Gaelic newsletter 1, "Gaelic ensemble" 1, Gaelic learners' group 2, Highland Games 2, involved with Gaelic groups 1, An Comunn Gàidhealach Ameireagaidh 2, An Comann Gàidhlig – Auckland NZ 1, "local Gaelic group" 1, university Gaelic society 1.

with the situation in Scotland. This factor suggests that learners outside Scotland do not have less enthusiasm than Scottish learners, but rather have less opportunity to use the language and would probably welcome more such opportunities, an impression which is echoed in the next section. As in Scotland, Gaelic concerts and cèilidhs were popular, as was speaking Gaelic. It is likely that 'speaking Gaelic' outside Scotland is an activity most normally done in the Gaelic class.

Gaelic-related services, facilities, activities desired by learners

Having asked learners about existing facilities for Gaelic learning and use, respondents were further asked: *Are there any Gaelic-related services, facilities or activities that do not exist at present (or do not exist at present in your area) that you would like to take part in? If so, please describe here.*

A great number of comments were received from respondents on this issue; when typed in to the computer database they amounted to some 16 pages of A4 paper. For this reason, comments have been categorised under a number of headings. Respondents in Scotland will be looked at first, followed by those elsewhere.

Availability of suitable Gaelic classes

Altogether, 42 learners mentioned improvements which they would like to see to Gaelic classes in their area. Within this category, the point most often made was the desire to see the availability of Gaelic classes at a suitable level locally. Many respondents did not have a class within easy travelling distance and others found that classes were only available locally at beginners level and not at more advanced levels. Some typical quotations illustrate these points: "better availability of community based evening classes needed: my nearest is Portree and a round trip of 80 miles on a winter evening for an hour class is not practical", "I would welcome community education services classes nearer home", "I want Gaelic classes that exist beyond beginner level. Although there are classes run annually they only cater for beginners".

Other points made by learners included the need for cheaper Gaelic classes ("evening classes by local college too expensive", "I think that cheaper evening classes [...] would enable more non-middle-class people to take up Gaelic) and the need for learners to be given the choice to sit qualifications in Gaelic ("opportunity to sit standard grade, then higher, Gaelic at evening class").

A large number of learners within this category also made comments relating to the format of classes which they wished to see. One learner noted the inconvenience of the lack of Gaelic classes which normally characterises the summer months ("not found any Gaelic learners classes/courses over the summer months in Stornoway – seems to be at least 4 'lost' months even in the Gàidhealtachd heartland!"). Seven learners also stated that they would like to see a full-time or part-time intensive immersion course in their area, with a further six also stating that they would like to see more day or weekend courses as an alternative or companion to evening classes.

Opportunities to use Gaelic outside the classroom

The need for more opportunities to use Gaelic was mentioned frequently. Twenty-seven respondents stated that they would like to see a *Taigh na Gàidhlig* in their area. As discussed in Chapter 3, *Taighean na Gàidhlig* are buildings dedicated to Gaelic activities; a sort of Gaelic community centre. Learners indicated in their answers to this question that they would like to see a Gaelic centre in their area where they could go and use Gaelic at any time on a drop-in basis in order to remedy the lack of opportunities to use Gaelic in day-to-day life. Some typical comments were: "centre for Gaelic speakers to meet on an informal basis and use only Gaelic", "Glasgow where I live, suffers from not having a focus for Gaelic activities.[231] I would certainly welcome and use a *Taigh na Gàidhlig* as an opportunity to converse more in Gaelic" and "àite sam bith far am biodh Gàidhlig ga cleachdadh fad an t-siubhail" ('Any place where Gaelic would be used all the time').

Also coming under this heading were the 27 learners who stated that they would like more opportunities to use Gaelic outwith the classroom, such as Gaelic conversation groups and Gaelic-medium social meetings and events/clubs. Some learners stated for example "I would like to see conversation classes, NOT blackboard based evening classes", "there is a massive need for teaching/recreation of sport and leisure through the medium of Gaelic for fluent speakers and learners". By far the most frequently suggested facility within this category was the Gaelic conversational group/club for learners and fluent speakers. Other possible Gaelic-medium clubs and events suggested were concerts, folk clubs, hill-walking groups, church services and worship groups. Four learners also stated that they would welcome more opportunities to meet with native speakers in a social setting as part of the learning process.

Gaelic Media

Many respondents wished to see changes to the Gaelic media to benefit learners. Thirteen stated that they wished that Radio nan Gaidheal broadcasts could be received in their area or nationally, and seven also noted their dissatisfaction with the unavailability of Gaelic television in southern Scotland.[232] One respondent also stated that s/he felt that a digital Gaelic TV channel would aid the learning process, with a further three learners stating that they would like to see a new radio or TV programme for Gaelic learners. Three respondents wished to see more Gaelic in the newspapers.

Better access to Gaelic books / learning materials

Altogether, eight respondents stated that they would like better access to Gaelic books, videos and learning materials through their local bookshops and libraries. For example, "library facilities – books particularly but videos and tapes would be useful", "local libraries and bookshops do not stock Gaelic books", "would like our local Helensburgh library to have a Gaelic section – to make Gaelic books more available". The ready availability of Gaelic books sales online via outlets such as Comhairle nan Leabhraichean since the survey was conducted has changed this situation greatly.

---

[231] Many respondents living in Greater Glasgow made similar points about the lack of a centre/focus for Gaelic activities in the city despite its large number of Gaelic speakers and reputation as the most Gaelic of Scotland's cities.

[232] As seen in chapter 3, Gaelic broadcasting has since become more accessible via the internet, satellite and Freeview.

Access to any Gaelic provision

For seven learners, the level of Gaelic provision of any type was so limited in their area that they simply stated that they would like to see any Gaelic-related services/facilities/activities in their area. Some examples are: "there is a dearth of Gaelic-related services going on in the area and I would just like to see more opportunities opening up", "rud sam bith" (anything), "yes, I wish there were lots of Gaelic things of any type", "if there were any Gaelic-related activities in my area I would attend", "there are no services at all within the area of Scottish Borders".

Increased use of Gaelic by public bodies

More use of Gaelic in the delivery of public services was suggested by eleven learners. Some made specific suggestions such as increased levels of official public bilingual signage for road signs (six respondents), the availability of bilingual forms and leaflets (two respondents) or the right to use Gaelic when dealing with public bodies (two respondents: "use of Gaelic in banks, shops, police station in dealing with official bodies like courts, crofters commission, crofters union, income tax, medical situation") whereas others made more general points such as "public services in Gaelic (shops, transport etc)", "Gaelic to be a part of most public organisations to a greater or lesser degree", "bilingual services e.g. post office", "I look forward to a time when Gaelic will have as high a profile in public places in Scotland as Welsh has in Wales". Improvements in these fields are now likely as a result of the *Gaelic Language (Scotland) Act 2005*.

Miscellaneous

Nineteen respondents made miscellaneous comments. Four stated that they would like to see improved information services about Gaelic learning or improved publicity regarding Gaelic events/facilities, etc. (e.g.: "The main problem is that generally I do not know what is happening in my local area, as regards Gaelic", "insufficient information and publicity"). Two also stated that they would like to see computer-based learning opportunities for the language, one of these stating that "I would like to see computer based interactive courses developed further but not on the basis of existing courses. Language laboratory type interactive CD-roms, etc. would be useful".

Three respondents stated that Gaelic should be more widely available as a secondary school subject within English-medium education. Other suggestions included: the production of a Gaelic Linguaphone course, Gaelic in-service courses for teachers who want to learn the language, the production of famous films with Gaelic dubbed soundtracks, a holiday homes / B&B scheme where proprietors would speak Gaelic with guests, more efforts to create non-traditional music in Gaelic, the establishment of more backup facilities for families with children in Gaelic-medium education who wish to learn Gaelic and greater efforts by Gaelic groups and public authorities to build a Gaelic community in the Central Belt. Finally, three learners stated that they were fully satisfied with Gaelic provision in their area.

Respondents outwith Scotland

The issue raised most often by learners outwith Scotland was broadcasting, reflecting the isolation often felt by learners outside Scotland. 35 respondents stated that they wished access to Gaelic television or radio by means of satellite, the internet, a digital Gaelic television channel, short wave or medium wave radio or more widespread availability of Gaelic videos. (e.g. "Gaelic radio programmes should be broadcast worldwide", "I would like to be able to watch Gaelic TV and listen to Gaelic Radio", "I would really like to hear Radio nan Gaidheal either over the internet, or over shortwave radio", "it would be enormously helpful to be able to receive radio or TV broadcasts!", "if digital TV means I can pick up Gaelic programmes, I'd feel less cut off and probably make better progress.") Gaelic broadcasting is now more widely available for these groups via to the internet.

34 respondents mentioned classes and courses, mostly noting the total lack of any provision in their area reflecting the limited and piecemeal availability of Gaelic learning classes outside Scotland. 15 respondents also mentioned a need for non-classroom-based opportunities to use Gaelic such as Gaelic conversation groups. Ten learners said that they would like to have access to native speakers and other Gaelic learners in their area. As in Scotland, many respondents also mentioned a wish to have better access to Gaelic materials through local bookshops and libraries (7 respondents, e.g. "library and or bookshop with Gaelic materials within reach – anywhere within London area", "book availability – US outlet for language materials other than 'Teach Yourself Gaelic'".)

14 learners simply stated that they would like any opportunities to learn or to use Gaelic in their area in comments such as "anything in my area!", "I live in Southern California, USA, I would certainly participate in any Gaelic activities", "I would like to see scope for more facilities and contact with other learners in the English Midlands", "there is virtually no medium for Gaelic education in the area where I live – improvement need to be made across the board".

A number of other services/facilities/activities were also suggested. Four respondents stated that they would like to see more Gaelic concerts and more Gaelic choirs. Four also suggested that Scottish companies and public services (some of them operating far beyond the bounds of Scotland) should provide bilingual services which could be used by learners living outside Scotland (e.g. a bilingual telephone operator service, bilingual services in ATM machines and call centres for Scottish Banks, bilingual policy for the Scottish Post Office). Other suggestions were improved distance learning facilities, improved text books and dictionaries, the production of talking books, an internet Gaelic forum, the availability of academic courses in Gaelic in England and the provision of Gaelic-medium education in Northern England.

Interestingly, eight respondents wrote that they would like to see greater institutional support for learners living outside Scotland. Some suggestions included: "I wish there would be an organisation to oversee efforts to help tutors everywhere with materials advice and encouragement outside of Scotland", "I would appreciate some kind of Gaelic learners' organisation in Germany",[233] "a Gaelic learners association for Ireland", "I think once a year there should be someone to come to Australia to talk about Gaelic-related issues", "In NZ we desperately need visits from fluent, educated, native Gaelic speakers, able and willing to teach learners." Related

---

[233] There is now such a group. For further details, see: www.schottisch-gaelisch.de.

suggestions were "I would like to see more development between Irish language and Scottish Gaelic groups", "there should be co-ordination of all Scottish activities in the London area".

Gaelic learners in the Census

A key way in which learners can contribute to RLS is by increasing the numbers of Gaelic speakers. In addition to the direct effect that learners might have on RLS through learning the language, they can also have an indirect effect through contributing to the number of those officially recorded as Gaelic speakers in the Census. The Census figures for Gaelic speakers have very significant implications for language development given that these figures are widely taken to be authoritative by bodies such as the Scottish Executive and are very frequently used in media discussion of Gaelic issues. The number of Gaelic speakers enumerated through the Census has an influence, directly or indirectly, upon official attitudes and policy towards Gaelic and upon public opinion on Gaelic. It is, therefore, to the advantage of RLS efforts that numbers of recorded Gaelic speakers be as high as possible.[234]

As the Census question on Gaelic is based on self-assessment as to whether the respondent is able to speak, read, write or understand Gaelic, an element of subjectivity is involved. Ability to speak, read, write or understand Gaelic might be defined in different ways by different people and there is also the possibility that pro-Gaelic individuals might register themselves as having some ability in Gaelic on the Census, despite having little or none, in order to boost Census figures (MacAulay 1994: 44, Macdonald 1997: 8, 61; MacKinnon 1991a: 179, Rogerson and Gloyer 1995, Thomson 1979: 15, Thomson 1984: 24). This subjectivity of the Census means that despite the paucity of fluent Gaelic learners at present there is still a possibility that learners who are not fluent might record themselves as being Gaelic speakers/learners/writers on the Census. For this reason, two questions about the Census were inserted in the questionnaire.

Respondents were asked firstly whether they had been recorded as being able to speak and/or read and/or write Scottish Gaelic in the 1991 Scottish Census. Those answering affirmatively were asked to specify which of the above they had recorded themselves as being able to do. Respondents were then asked whether they intended to record themselves as being able to speak and/or write and or/understand Gaelic in the next (2001) Scottish Census and, if so, as to which of these abilities they intended to record themselves as having.[235]

Table 100: Gaelic abilities of respondents as returned for the 1991 Census
Question: *Were you recorded in the last Census as being able to speak and/or read and/or write Scottish Gaelic?*

	N	%
Yes	109	27.8
No	210	53.6
Don't know	35	8.9
Not Applicable	31	7.9
Not stated	7	1.8
Total	**392**	**100**

---

[234] For further discussion of Gaelic on the Census, see MacCaluim forthcoming 2007.
[235] A question on the ability to understand spoken Gaelic was also included in the 2001 Census.

Questionnaire Results

Table 101: Gaelic abilities of respondents as recorded in the 1991 Census
Question: *If yes, which of the following were you recorded as being able to do? (please tick as many boxes as apply)*

	N	%
Speak Gaelic	91	83.5
Read Gaelic	93	85.3
Write Gaelic	83	76.1
Not stated	2	1.8
Total	109	100

Altogether, 27.8% of respondents said that they had recorded themselves as being able to read and/or write and/or speak Gaelic. The combination of these abilities was charted in Table 102. It can be seen that the largest single combination was the ability to speak and write Gaelic, which was recorded by almost 70% of respondents, followed by the ability only to speak Gaelic at 12.8% and the ability only to read and write Gaelic at 6.4%.

Table 102: Abilities in Gaelic as recorded in the 1991 Census

	N	%
Speak, read and write	76	69.7
Speak and read only	1	0.9
Speak and write only	0	0
Read and write only	7	6.4
Speak only	14	12.8
Read only	9	8.3
Write only	1	0.9
Not stated	2	1.8
Total	109	100

Those registering themselves as having ability in Gaelic on the Census were analysed by their stated levels of fluency in Gaelic in Table 103. Those recorded as being able to speak Gaelic were tabled in terms of their stated level of fluency in spoken Gaelic, those recorded as being able to read Gaelic in terms of their level of Gaelic reading and so on.

Table 103: Abilities in Gaelic as recorded in the 1991 Census

Ability in Gaelic	Ability recorded on Census					
	Speaking		Reading		Writing	
	N	%	N	%	N	%
Fluent	26	28.6	31	33.3	25	30.1
Advanced	17	18.7	25	26.9	20	24.1
Intermediate	32	35.2	27	29	25	30.1
Basic	15	16.5	10	10.75	13	15.7
Not stated	1	1.1	-	-	-	-
Total	91	100	93	100	83	100

Of those having recorded themselves as being Gaelic speakers, readers or writers in the Census, it can be seen that only minorities were fluent in the field in which they claimed an ability. A significant minority of those recorded in the Census were intermediate and basic learners of Gaelic. This suggests that many Gaelic learners record themselves as being Gaelic speakers/readers/writers despite not being fluent in the language.

The converse was also investigated: fluent Gaelic learners who had not recorded themselves as such on the Census. Those fluent in spoken Gaelic were taken as an example and it was found that 15 of the 41 fluent Gaelic-speaking learners in Scotland had not recorded themselves as being able to speak Gaelic in the last Census. However, the non-appearance in the Census of all but one of these learners could be explained in terms of non-residence in Scotland or not having learnt Gaelic at the time, and all but one stated that they would be recording their ability in 2001. The remaining respondent stated that he had not completed the 1991 Census at all on principle due to the non-production of a Gaelic version of the Census and that he was uncertain as to whether he would participate in the next Census.

Table 104: Gaelic abilities of respondents to be returned in 2001 Census
Question: *Do you intend to be recorded as being able to speak and/or read and/or write and/or understand Scottish Gaelic at the next Census?*

	N	%
Yes	212	54.1
Yes, but only if I am more fluent by then	127	32.4
No	21	5.4
Don't know	25	6.4
Not stated	7	1.8
Total	392	100

Table 105: Communicative skills in Gaelic to be returned in 2001 Census
Question: *If yes, which of the following do you intend to be recorded as being able to do?*

	N	%
Speak Gaelic	190	89.6
Read Gaelic	182	85.85
Write Gaelic	169	79.7
Understand Gaelic	189	89.15
Not stated	3	1.4
Total	212	100

It can be seen from Table 104 that a majority of respondents stated that they intended to record themselves as being able to speak and/or read and/or write and/or understand Gaelic in the 2001 Census. This figure was far higher than that registered for learners recorded in the 1991 Census, reflecting the fact that all the respondents in question were both resident in Scotland and interested in Gaelic at the time of completing the questionnaire. A further 32.4% said that they intended to be recorded, but only if they were more fluent by then. Only 5.4% stated that they did not intend to be recorded as having an ability in Gaelic in the Census, with 6.4% being undecided on the matter. Once again, these figures indicate that a far larger percentage of the respondents than those fluent in the language intended to be recorded on the Census. Of those intending to be recorded, by far the largest number intended to be recorded as being able to speak, read, write and understand Gaelic.

Table 106: Abilities in Gaelic to be returned in 2001 Census

	N	%
Speak, read, write and understand	155	73.1
Speak only	9	4.2
Speak and read only	1	0.5
Speak and understand only	12	5.7
Read, write and understand only	6	2.8
Speak, read, understand only	8	3.8
Understand only	6	2.8
Speak, read, write only	5	2.4
Read and understand only	2	0.9
Read only	2	0.9
Read and write only	3	1.4
Other combinations	0	0
Not stated	3	1.4
Total	**212**	**100**

It is interesting to speculate as to why so many respondents who were not fluent or advanced in the language have recorded or intend to record an ability in Gaelic on the Census. One possible reason is that respondents considered themselves to be able to speak/read/write/understand Gaelic on the basis of their limited knowledge of Gaelic. Another is the wish to maximise the Census results for Gaelic. The fact that 40% of respondents in Scotland identified with the identity of *Gaelic speaker* elsewhere in the questionnaire (11% identifying *very much* and 29% *on the whole*) suggests that both tendencies are at play: the figure is larger than the percentage of those fluent or near-fluent in Gaelic but smaller than that of those intending to record themselves as having an ability in Gaelic in the 2001 Census.

Membership of Gaelic-related organisations:

Learners were asked what Gaelic-related organisations they belonged to. In Scotland, 67.9% of respondents were members of CLI. Other Gaelic organisations of which there were many members in Scotland were *An Comunn Gàidhealach*, the Gaelic cultural body which organises the Mòd, of which 20.2% were members, and *A' Chiste Leabhraichean*, the Gaelic book club, of which 15.8% were members. Almost 20% of respondents were also involved in a local Gaelic society. Many respondents also belonged to other societies. Around 80% of respondents were members of at least one Gaelic organisation and just under half (47.18%) of respondents in Scotland were members of at least two. There was also a high level and relatively similar distribution of membership of Gaelic societies outwith Scotland, as can be seen in Tables 109–112.

Table 107: Gaelic related organisations: respondents in Scotland
Question: *Are you a member of any of the following Gaelic-related organisations?*

Group	N	%
A' Chiste Leabhraichean	62	15.8
An Comunn Gàidhealach	79	20.2
Celtic League	20	5.1
Celtic Congress	15	3.8
Comann an Luchd-Ionnsachaidh	266	67.9
Comann nam Pàrant	22	5.6
Comhairle nan Sgoiltean Àraich	26	6.6
Comunn na Gàidhlig	23	5.9
Gaelic Society of Inverness	17	4.3
Gaelic choir	32	8.2
Gaelic drama group	1	0.3
Local Gaelic learners' group	76	19.4
University Gaelic society	34	8.7
Other Gaelic-related group[236]	40	10.2

Table 108: Numbers of organisations of which Scottish respondents are members

	0	1	2	3	4	5	6	7+
N	80	127	85	51	24	16	6	3
%	20.4	32.4	21.68	13	6.1	4.1	1.5	0.8

Total = 392

Table 109: Gaelic-related organisations: respondents in rest of UK:
Question: *Are you a member of any of the following Gaelic-related organisations?*

Group	N	%
A' Chiste Leabhraichean	12	7.6
An Comunn Gàidhealach	34	21.4
Celtic League	4	2.5
Celtic Congress	2	1.3
Comann an Luchd-Ionnsachaidh	128	80.5
Comann nam Pàrant	0	0
Comhairle nan Sgoiltean Àraich	4	2.5

---

[236] (Scotland) Celtic Film and TV Association/Festival 1, Ceòl is Gàire – small local Gaelic social group 1, Coimhearsnachd Ghàidhlig Dhùn Èideann 1, An Comunn Gaidhealach Ameireagaidh 1, An Comunn Gàidhealach Kilmarnock 1, Comann Eachdraidh Sgìre Raoird 1, Comunn Luaidh Bhàideanach 1, Cothrom Còmhraidh – local Gaelic conversation group 1, Gaelic e-mail lists 3, Glasgow Family Learning Group 1, Glasgow Gaelic Society 2, Gaelic in the Borders 2, "Gaelic self-help evening class" 1, Gaelic Society of London 1, Gaelic Society of Perth 1, Gaelic walking club 1, Kilmarnock Cròileagan 1, Lewis and Harris Gaelic Learners Group 1, Local Fèis 3, local Gaelic conversation groups 1, local Sradagan 2, local Gaelic partnership 1, Lochaber Gaelic Development Group 1, Moray Gaelic Choir 1, Stornoway Gaelic Lunch Club 1, Taic – local Gaelic group 1, Scottish Gaelic Texts Society 1, Taigh na Gàidhlig 4, Urras Brosnachaidh na Gàidhlig (Gaelic Promotional Trust) 1, "Weekly meeting of Gaelic speakers" 1.

Table 110: Numbers of organisations of which respondents in UK outwith Scotland are members

No reply	0	1	2	3	4	5	6+
N	1	15	77	40	17	5	3	1
%	0.6	9.4	48.4	25.2	10.7	3.14	1.9	0.6

Total = 159

Table 111: Gaelic-related organisations: respondents outwith UK
Question: *Are you a member of any of the following Gaelic-related organisations?*

Group	N	%
A' Chiste Leabhraichean	7	7.9
An Comunn Gàidhealach	13	14.6
Celtic League	5	5.6
Celtic Congress	4	4.5
Comann an Luchd-Ionnsachaidh	61	68.5
Comann nam Pàrant	0	0
Comhairle nan Sgoiltean Àraich	2	2.2
Comunn na Gàidhlig	7	7.9
Gaelic Society of Inverness	2	2.2
Gaelic choir	3	3.4
Gaelic drama group	0	0
Local Gaelic learners' group	10	11.2
University Gaelic society	8	8
Other Gaelic-related group[237]	23	25.8

Table 112: Numbers of organisations of which respondents outwith UK are members

	0	1	2	3	4	5+
N	18	36	14	9	9	3
%	20.2	40.4	15.7	10.1	10.1	3.4

Total = 89

---

[237] (Rest of world) An Comunn Gàidhealach Ameireagaidh 8, An Comunn Gàidhealach Victoria 3, Bulawayo and Harare Caledonian Societies 1, Comunn na Gàidhlig Canterbury 1, Gaelic Society of New Zealand 2, Gaelic Society of Toronto 1, Glengarry Highland Society (Ontario) 1, Scottish Heritage Society of Western Australia 1, University of Illinois Scottish Gaelic Society 1.

Section 4: Gaelic in the Family

Respondents were asked a series of questions relating to Gaelic in their households/families in order to ascertain whether other members of respondents' households/families were Gaelic speakers.

Table 113: Household size: respondents in Scotland
Question: *How many people are there in your household?*

	1	2	3	4	5	6+	Not stated
N	48	135	64	61	29	13	42
%	12.2	34.4	16.33	15.6	7.4	3.3	10.7

Total = 392

Table 114: Gaelic spoken in the home: respondents in Scotland
Question: *Can anybody else living in your household speak Gaelic?*

	N	%
Yes	90	23
No	212	54.1
Live alone	48	12.2
Not Stated	42	10.7
Total	**392**	**100**

Table 115: Speakers of Gaelic at home: respondents in Scotland
Question: *If yes, please give details.*

Households containing at least one person with some knowledge of Gaelic = 90

Households where all members have some knowledge of Gaelic (excluding 1 member households) = 29

Households where, excluding the respondent, all members are fluent Gaelic speakers (excluding 1 member households) = 12

Households in which all members are fluent Gaelic speakers (excluding 1 member households) = 8

Households containing at least one fluent speaker (excluding 1 member households)= 36

Households where respondent's partner is a fluent speaker = 16

It can be seen from Table 114 that 23% of the respondents in Scotland lived in households where at least one other person had some knowledge of Gaelic. This is a rather high level and ties in with the fact that having Gaelic-speaking relatives was frequently cited in the questionnaire as a reason for learning Gaelic. Knowledge of Gaelic in the household was investigated in more detail in Table 115; it can be seen that of the 90 households in which at least one person had a knowledge of Gaelic, 36 or 9.1% of the total households contained a fluent speaker, with all members of the household other than the respondent being fluent in twelve of these. In 16 cases, the respondents' partner was a fluent speaker. Of the 41 respondents in Scotland who were fluent in spoken Gaelic, eight lived in households where all other members were fluent Gaelic speakers with a further three using Gaelic with their children although their partner was not a Gaelic speaker. A further 12 fluent learners lived in one-person households.

Respondents were then asked if they had any children. Those who did have children were asked to state their children's ages and whether they had attended or would be attending Gaelic-medium education (GME). Those who had not taken advantage of GME for their children were asked to specify their reasons for not doing so.

Table 116: Children: respondents in Scottish
Question: *Do you have any children?*

	N	%
Yes	198	50.5
No	187	47.7
Not Stated	7	1.8
Total	392	100

In all 50.5% of respondents stated that they had children. 37 (9.4%) had children of pre-school age and of these, 70.3% stated that their children either were attending or would in the future attend a Gaelic playgroup or nursery school. Of the eight who answered 'no' to this question, most stated that they would have liked a Gaelic-medium education for their children but that it was not available in their area.

Table 117: Uptake of Gaelic-medium pre-school education: respondents in Scottish
Question: *If you have any children of pre-school age, are they currently attending, or will they attend a Gaelic playgroup (Cròileagan) or Gaelic nursery school?*

	N	%
Yes	26	70.3
No	8	21.6
Don't know	3	8.1
Total	37	100

Of those answering *No*, the reasons were as follows:

Reason why child(ren) did not attend Gaelic-medium unit	N
I did not want my children to be educated through the medium of Gaelic	0
I would have liked a Gaelic-medium education for my child, but it was not available in my area	6
I was not aware of the availability of Gaelic-medium education in my area at the time	0
I was not interested in Gaelic at the time when I decided upon my child's education	0
Other[238]	2
Not stated	0

---

[238] Other: child lives in England due to separation of parents 1, "I was interested but my partner wasn't and I was a bit shaky. I spoke Gaelic only to my eldest child until she was 2.5 but stopped because my commitment was not enough to overcome lack of support" 1.

Of those answering *Don't know*, the reasons were as follows:

Reason for stating don't know	N
Unsure as to whether my wife would be prepared	1
I have not considered the issue yet	1
I don't know whether it is available	1

67 respondents had children of school age (17.1% of respondents) and of this total, 30 or 44.7% were attending Gaelic-medium units at school. As with the figures for nursery education, this is a very significant figure given that only a very small percentage of the Scottish population as a whole utilise Gaelic-medium education (around 2000 pupils altogether at the time of the survey). It is even more significant when it is remembered that GME is not available in many areas of Scotland and has only become available in many areas relatively recently, so that not all respondents had the option of GME for their children. These latter factors can be seen from the fact that over half of those who did not choose GME for their children stated that they would have liked to have done so but that it was not available in their area. For this reason, it is likely that the uptake of GME amongst similar groups of learners to the present respondents will increase in future.

Table 118: Uptake of Gaelic-medium education: respondents with children of school age
Question: *If you have any children of school age, are they attending a Gaelic medium unit at school?*

	N	%
Yes	30	44.7
No	37	55.2
Total	67	100

Of those answering *no*, the reasons were as follows:

Reason why child(ren) did not attend Gaelic medium unit	N	%
I did not want my children to be educated through the medium of Gaelic	0	0
I would have liked a Gaelic-medium education for my child, but it was not available in my area	20	54.1
I was not aware of the availability of Gaelic-medium education in my area at the time	5	13.5
I was not interested in Gaelic at the time when I decided upon my child's education	6	16.2
Other[239]	6	16.2
Not stated	0	0
Total	37	100

---

[239] Separated: children not living with me, partner not in favour of GME: 2, the children were not interested: 2, moved from England when children were too old to enter GME: 1.

The same question was also asked of respondents who had children who had left school: 134 respondents altogether. Of these, 2 had children who had been educated through the medium of Gaelic. This small figure reflects the fact that GME only began in 1985, with the first handfuls of GM pupils from the first two initially small Gaelic units only reaching school-leaving age in the late 1990s. While few respondents' children had been educated through Gaelic, 35 respondents said that they would have liked a Gaelic-medium education for their children but that it was not available in their area at the time.

It is also significant that 33 respondents stated that they were not interested in Gaelic at the time when they were making decisions regarding their children's education. This underscores the fact that adult Gaelic learners often begin learning Gaelic in later life, particularly while middle-aged, meaning that a large proportion of learners will have raised children by the time that they become interested in learning Gaelic. This means not only that few learners learn the language before meeting a partner and entering parenthood, so as to assist intergenerational transmission of the language, but also that many learners typically become interested in the language too late to ensure intergenerational donation of the language through choosing Gaelic-medium education. These factors strengthen the argument made above that the top-heavy age range of learners is a matter of concern and that more attention needs to be paid to attracting younger learners and providing them with opportunities to become fluent in Gaelic.

Table 119: Uptake of Gaelic-medium education: respondents with children who have left school
Question: *If you have any children who have left school, did they attend a Gaelic-medium unit at school?*

	N	%
Yes	2	1.5
No	132	98.5
Total	**134**	**100**

If you answered *No*, which of the following best describes the reason for your choice for your child's education:

Reason why child(ren) did not attend Gaelic medium unit	N	%
I did not want my children to be educated through the medium of Gaelic	2	1.5
I would have liked a Gaelic-medium education for my child, but it was not available in my area[240]	35	26
I was not aware of the availability of Gaelic-medium education in my area at the time	9	6.7
I was not interested in Gaelic at the time when I decided upon my child's education	33	24.6
Other[241]	35	26.1
Not stated	20	14.9
Total	**134**	**100**

Respondents who did not have children were asked if they were likely to have children at some point in the future, and if so, if they would like their children to be educated through the medium of Gaelic if facilities were available in their area. 83 or 83.4% of those in this category said that they would, this being 21.2% of the Scottish sample as a whole.

Table 120: Possible future uptake of Gaelic-medium education: respondents in Scotland
Question: *If you do not have children at present, but are likely to at some point in the future, would you like them to be educated through the medium of Gaelic if facilities were available in your area?*

	N	%
Yes	83	83.8
No	1	1
Don't know	15	15.2
Total	99	100

The questions regarding GME revealed a high level of support for this form of education, with large percentages of parents with pre-school or school-age children stating that they had chosen or would be choosing GME for their children and with a large majority of potential future parents saying that they too would choose GME for their children if it were available in their area. This is a hopeful sign for RLS, showing that many Gaelic learners ensure that their children become fluent in the language, even if many never become fluent themselves. Even when it is taken into account that many people stated elsewhere in the questionnaire that having children in GME was an influence in leading them to learn Gaelic, there can still be no doubt that the converse is also a significant tendency.

Less hopeful is the fact that a significant proportion of learners do not become involved with the language until ages at which they may already have met non-Gaelic speaking partners, become parents or have missed the opportunity of choosing GME for their children. For these reasons, the picture in general for actual Gaelic use within the home for Gaelic learners is not encouraging.[242]

---

[240] 1 family noted that they had 2 Gaelic-speaking sons, but that they had been unable to go to GMU as not available.

[241] Lived outside Scotland 5, was not available at the time 23, family moved around with Armed Forces 2, "Not relevant at time. Would not wish to push it on them", "limited choice of school, husband would never have agreed", "question did not arise in Kircudbright in the 60s".

[242] The picture with regard to Gaelic use within the family amongst the small number of fluent Gaelic learners who responded was far more encouraging.

Section 5: Opinions on Gaelic

Table 121: Definition of the term *Gael*: all respondents: all respondents
Question: *There has been some discussion of the meaning of the word* Gael *in recent times. Which of the following is closest to your own understanding of the word* Gael?

Definition	Scotland N	%	UK N	%	World N	%
A native Gaelic speaker	89	22.7	31	19.5	19	21.35
A native Gaelic speaker from the Highlands or Islands	79	20.15	21	13.2	6	6.7
A Highlander or Islander regardless of whether or not s/he can speak Gaelic	92	23.5	41	25.8	13	14.6
Anyone whose people where Gaelic speaking Highlanders or Islanders	59	15.05	47	29.6	20	22.5
Anyone who can speak Gaelic	26	6.6	7	4.4	13	14.6
Other[243]	31	7.9	8	5	11	12.4
Don't know	3	0.8	-	-	2	2.25
Not Stated	13	3.3	4	2.5	5	5.6
Total	392	100	159	100	89	100

---

[243] Scotland comments: Definition of Gael: "a Highlander or Islander regardless of whether or not s/he can speak Gaelic but has a commitment to learning some and has most other elements of a Gaelic cultural background", "a Gaelic speaker aware of Highland culture", "a native Gaelic speaker plus other who are fluent in the language and also identify themselves with the culture of the Highlands and Islands", "up to 1 remove – anyone whose people were Gaelic speaking Highlanders or Islanders", "a Gael is more than a Gaelic speaker", "a native Highlander or Islander", "anyone who can speak Irish, Scottish or Manx Gaelic", "don't know – I don't use the word", "the term is no longer relevant as it reflects a period in history", "anyone whose people come from the Gàidhealtachd or Ireland including Ulster", "anyone whose people were Gaelic speakers", "anyone who was born in the Highlands and Islands", anyone with Celtic ancestry 2, Scottish, Irish or Manx person 3, "any Scots or Irish person: all Scots/Irish once spoke Gaelic", "anyone who has a deep love of Scotland", "anyone familiar with Gaelic culture/tradition", "I think these definitions need public debate and re-negotiation and redefinition". 2 respondents ticked more than one box in the questionnaire. Rest of UK comments: anybody whose people were Gaelic speaking Highlanders or Islanders and who can speak Gaelic: 2, "someone who in their heart has affinity with Gaelic language and culture", "anyone whose heart is Gaelic", "someone who is either a native Gaelic speaker or a Highlander or Islander regardless of whether or not s/he can speak Gaelic", "a native of the Gàidhealtachd", "I'm told it is from inside you". Rest of world comments: "someone who can speak Gaelic/be of Celtic descent", "anyone with Celtic roots in Alba, Éire", "anyone who can speak Gaelic or whose people were Gaelic speakers", "Person from Ireland, Scotland or Isle of Man", "anyone who uses it on a personal level", "a native speaker, a highlander or especially an islander", only historic, no application nowadays: 2, "Irish people/Scottish people", "all descendants of Gaelic speakers of native origin", "Celtic (speaker, culture)", "anyone with Scottish/Irish roots with Gaelic/Irish".

Gaelic learners were asked to choose the definition of the term *Gael* closest to their understanding of the term from a multiple choice table. It can be seen that there was no consensus as to the meaning of the word, with different respondents putting different weight on the possible ethnic and linguistic elements of the term. This lack of agreement was emphasised by the large numbers of respondents who did not choose any of the definitions given in the questionnaire and who added a definition of their own. While many definitions were based on those suggested in the questionnaire, others defined *Gael* as referring to all Scots, or all Scots, Irish and Manx or to all speakers of any of the three Gaelic languages. Some definitions included neither an ethnic nor a linguistic element, being based rather on affinity with Gaelic culture. Some other respondents said that they felt that the term now meant little. This issue is discussed further in chapter 4, the Social Identity of Gaelic Learners.

Attitude Statements

Learners were asked to give their views on 32 statements relating to the language. Responses were given on a five-point Likert-type scale, some of the questions being posed positively and some negatively in mixed order. The results have been recorded in full in Tables 127–129.

Gaelic as a national and as a regional language

A series of the questions included in the opinions section of the questionnaire related to learners' views on Gaelic as a national and as a Highland language. This was in order to investigate whether respondents tended to view Gaelic in a national sense as being *a* national language or as *the* national language and as a language which should promoted throughout Scotland, or to see Gaelic mainly as a language which is only important to, or which should only be promoted in, the Highlands and Islands.

Table 122: Opinions on Gaelic as a national language: respondents in Scotland

	Agree Strongly	Agree	Neither agree nor disagree	Disagree	Disagree Strongly	Not Stated
	%	%	%	%	%	%
Gaelic is one of Scotland's national languages	80.6	16.8	1.3	0.3	-	1
To really understand Scottish culture, you must know Gaelic	21.9	38.5	20.9	15.3	1.8	1.5
Gaelic is important for Scotland as a whole	52	38.5	5.9	1.5	0.3	1.8
Gaelic is only important to the Highlands and Islands	0.5	2.6	5.4	60.2	29.1	2.3
Gaelic is Scotland's national language	18.9	23.5	26.5	23.7	4.1	3.3
Gaelic should not be encouraged throughout Scotland	0.3	2.3	3.8	26	65.1	2.3

The results suggest that respondents tended to view Gaelic as a language which is of importance to Scotland nationally and which should be promoted throughout Scotland. The learners overwhelmingly agreed with the statements that Gaelic is one of Scotland's national languages, with 97.4% of the sample agreeing and 80.6% agreeing strongly. For the more controversial statement that 'Gaelic is Scotland's national language', the views of respondents were less united, with a relatively even split between those who agreed strongly (18.9%), agreed (23.5%), neither agreed nor disagreed (26.5%) or disagreed (23.7%). Having said this, however, the percentage agreeing with the statement (42.4%) was much higher than might be expected amongst the population in general, and few people disagreed strongly.

Less controversial was the statement that *Gaelic is important for Scotland as a whole* with 90.5% agreeing (52% agreeing strongly, 38.5% agreeing) and less than 2% disagreeing. Almost 90% of respondents disagreed with a statement suggesting that Gaelic was not important for Scotland was asked (*Gaelic is only important to the Highlands and Islands*), with only 3.1% agreeing. Over 90% of respondents disagreed with the statement that 'Gaelic should not be encouraged throughout Scotland', most of them strongly, with less than 3% agreeing. One further statement relating to the relationship between Gaelic and Scotland was *To really understand Scottish culture, you must know Gaelic*. Over 60% of respondents agreed with this proposition, though most of these 'agreed' rather than 'agreed strongly' and significant numbers either disagreed (15.3%) or neither agreed nor disagreed.

The results of these questions for the respondents outside Scotland showed very similar trends to those resident in Scotland, suggesting that respondents outwith Scotland also tend to view Gaelic as a language of national importance which should be promoted nationally.

Table 123: Opinions on Gaelic development: respondents in Scotland

	Agree Strongly	Agree	Neither agree nor disagree	Disagree	Disagree Strongly	Not Stated
	%	%	%	%	%	%
Gaelic should be one of the languages officially used by the Scottish Parliament	50.8	30.1	13	3.8	0.5	1.8
Too much money is spent on Gaelic	-	-	5.4	32.9	60	1.8
In order to work in the public sector in Gaelic areas, one should speak Gaelic	28.6	42.4	16.3	9.7	1.5	1.5
Gaelic is only important at a personal level	0.8	4.3	8.7	45.9	38	8.7
Gaelic should be given official status	61	31.9	3.8	1.3	0.5	1.5
Gaelic does not need any special encouragement	0.5	1	3.3	38.3	55.6	1.3
Official bodies should do more to encourage Gaelic in public affairs	44.1	43.4	9.7	0.3	0.3	2.3
People should be allowed to use Gaelic in courts of law	41.8	37	14.3	4.6	0.8	1.5
Companies should be offered tax breaks in order to offer bilingual services	17.1	34.7	36.5	7.6	1.3	2.8
Councils should be legally obliged to provide Gaelic-medium education where demand exists	53.1	37	4.8	2.6	0.3	2.3
Bilingual signs are a waste of money	1.8	2	5.1	40	49.7	1.3
Knowledge of Gaelic is good for people's job prospects	13.5	46.7	34.2	3.3	0.3	2
Children in any part of Scotland should be able to learn Gaelic if they or their parents want them to	55.1	38.8	3.3	0.8	0.3	1.8

Opinions on Gaelic Development

Learners were asked their views on a range of questions relating to language policies, language development and similar matters (Table 123). The responses to these questions reveal a high level of support amongst the respondents for Gaelic and for a range of Gaelic development policies.

As it is conceivable that some learners might have a personal interest in Gaelic without being interested in or supportive of the well-being or development of the language, two questions were asked to investigate whether learners were in favour of the promotion of Gaelic in general. One attitude statement declared 'Gaelic does not need any special encouragement' and another 'Gaelic is only important at a personal level'. A large majority of learners disagreed with both of these statements, 93.9% with the former and 83.9% with the latter, with few learners agreeing: 1.5% and 5.1% respectively. On a similar theme, the questionnaire sought views on the statement 'too much money is spent on Gaelic'. Overall, 92.9% of respondents disagreed and not a single respondent agreed.

A series of the statements related to specific suggestions for promoting Gaelic such as official status, bilingual signage, the right to Gaelic education and parliamentary use of Gaelic. The responses revealed a high level of support for various policies to support the language. Large majorities of respondents agreed that Gaelic should be officially used by the Scottish Parliament (80.9%), that Gaelic should be given official status (92.9%), that official bodies should do more to encourage Gaelic in public affairs (87.5%), that people should be allowed to use Gaelic in courts of law (78.8%), that councils should be legally obliged to provide Gaelic-medium education where demand exists (90.1%) and that children in any part of Scotland should be able to learn Gaelic if they or their parents wanted them to (93.9%). In none of these cases did more than 5% disagree with the statements. For the statement that bilingual signs are a waste of money, 89.7% disagreed and only 3.8% agreed.[244] 71% of respondents agreed with the statement that "in order to work in the public sector in Gaelic areas, one should speak Gaelic", though for this statement, there was a higher level of disagreement than with the other questions on development policies, with 11.2% disagreeing in total. The statement that "companies should be offered tax breaks in order to offer bilingual services" was supported by 51.8% of respondents and rejected by 8.9%, with a large proportion (36.5%) answering that they neither agreed or disagreed, this latter tendency possibly reflecting the fact that such a policy has not been suggested by Gaelic organisations up to that point.[245]

Gaelic learners outside Scotland showed a similarly high level of support for pro-RLS policies in general and for a range of specific policies to those living within Scotland.

It should be noted that it was difficult to compare the views of Gaelic learners from the Gaelic Learners' Survey with the public as a whole or with native speakers of Gaelic, as very little research has been done on this issue. National public opinion polls on Gaelic issues were conducted in 1981 and 2003 (MacKinnon 1981, BBC 2003). Views of native speakers on some Gaelic issues were investigated by MacKinnon in

---

[244] Several respondents who answered that bilingual signs are a waste of money stated that signs should be monolingual in Gaelic alone in Gaelic speaking areas.

[245] A number of respondents disagreeing stated that they felt that companies should face tax penalties for *not* providing bilingual services rather than receiving tax breaks *for* providing them.

the Euromosaic Survey and, more recently, views of residents of the Western Isles were analysed by the Western Isles Language Planning Project (MacKinnon 1998b, Western Isles Language Planning Project 2005). While these contained some useful questions on attitudes to the language, however, more detailed and comprehensive studies are needed for both academic and language planning purposes (MacKinnon 1997b: 4, 1998b: 8, 1998c: 2).

Opinions on Linguistic Issues

Four questions were asked on linguistic issues relating to Gaelic. The first of these related to the perception of learners as to the differences between Gaelic dialects, an issue which is often the focus of discussion by Gaelic learners. The remainder of the questions related to the idea that Gaelic should become more standardised for learners. It is a suggestion which is occasionally made by learners, paralleling the debate on standard Irish in Ireland and on Cymraeg Byw (a standardised form of Welsh) in Wales.

Table 124: Opinions on linguistic issues: respondents in Scotland

	Agree Strongly	Agree	Neither agree nor disagree	Disagree	Disagree Strongly	Not Stated
	%	%	%	%	%	%
There are great differences between Gaelic dialects	8.2	32.1	30.6	21.7	2.3	5.1
Spoken Gaelic needs to become more standardised with less localised variation	3.6	13.3	29.1	38.8	13.8	1.5
Gaelic learners should learn a standardised variety of Gaelic	7.6	22.4	28.1	27.8	7.6	6.4
Learners should learn Gaelic dialects	9.4	36.7	38.5	12	1.3	2

There were mixed views on the statement that *there are great differences between Gaelic dialects*, with large numbers (30.6%) neither agreeing nor disagreeing and with around a quarter disagreeing (24%). The largest single grouping, however, agreed that there were great differences between Gaelic dialects (40.3%). Relatively similar results emerged for respondents outside Scotland. This result is rather surprising on one hand given that there is, as Morgan has pointed out, "no major dialect issue in Scots Gaelic" amongst the surviving dialects, which are all easily mutually intelligible, and given that the degree of variation between Gaelic dialects is far less than that between the dialects of the Irish and Welsh languages (Morgan 2000:130, MacInnes 1992:120, McLeod 2001:23). On the other hand, these figures are perhaps unsurprising, given the commonly held belief amongst many non-Gaelic speakers and many native speakers that there are great dialectal differences in Gaelic which can hinder communication, a belief which is, arguably, not primarily based upon linguistic differences.

As Morgan has said about this belief, "any problem is one of laziness on the part of the speakers or of local prejudice" (Morgan 2000:130). MacInnes has pointed out that "there is some debate about mutual intelligibility of dialects [...]. Mutual comprehension, of course, involves individual skills and confidence" (MacInnes 1992:120). Some of the factors that bear upon the individual's skills and confidence in the language are level of competency in Gaelic, the frequency with which the language is used, the range of people with whom it is used, the range of domains within which it is used and the ability or otherwise to read Gaelic. These factors are at least as important as actual linguistic differences in determining the perceptions of native speakers on issues of mutual comprehension of dialects. It is to be hoped that future attempts to publicise and promote the learning of Gaelic as recommended elsewhere in this study will put emphasis on exploding the damaging misconception that Gaelic is very difficult to learn for linguistic (as opposed to other) reasons and that difference of dialect leads to communication problems between Gaelic speakers and difficulties for learners.

On the issue of standardisation, it can be seen that there was no clear consensus among respondents. For the questions *spoken Gaelic needs to become more standardised with less localised variation*, *Gaelic learners should learn a standard variety of Gaelic* and *Gaelic learners should learn Gaelic dialects*, there was a lack of polarisation of views, with large percentages of respondents neither agreeing nor disagreeing (around or more than 30% in all cases) and with most of those agreeing or disagreeing not doing so strongly. In the case of the questions directly addressing standardisation, more learners took a view suggesting that they did not favour standardisation of Gaelic than took pro-standardising views. With regard to the related question of whether learners should learn Gaelic dialects, more respondents (46.1%) agreed than disagreed (13.3%). It seems from the results of the questions relating to the standardisation of the language that this issue is not one about which most learners have strong feelings, nor perhaps one to which they have given much thought.

Outside Scotland a similar pattern emerged, with a lack of polarisation of opinions and with a high level of "neither agree nor disagree" responses and with similar general patterns of views emerging for each of the questions.

Learning Gaelic

Table 125: Opinions on Gaelic: respondents in Scotland

	Agree Strongly	Agree	Neither agree nor disagree	Disagree	Disagree Strongly	Not Stated
	%	%	%	%	%	%
On the whole, native Gaelic speakers do not want other people to learn Gaelic	3.6	13	35.2	32.7	14	1.5
It is artificial to learn Gaelic	1.3	2	5.1	40.8	49	1.8
Learning Gaelic is a hobby for me	5.6	36.5	14.8	27.8	11	4.3

Three statements were included in the questionnaire about learning Gaelic: *It is artificial to learn Gaelic* (this being a frequently heard criticism of Gaelic learning) and *Learning Gaelic is a hobby for me*, this question being to investigate whether learners viewed Gaelic learning as a pastime or as more than this. The third of these questions was *On the whole, native speakers do not want people to learn Gaelic*, a statement which reflects a charge frequently levelled by learners against native speakers.

A large majority disagreed, mainly strongly, with the idea that it is artificial to learn Gaelic (89.8% Scotland, 88.6% UK, 86.5% world). On the question of Gaelic learning being a hobby, 42.1% of respondents in Scotland agreed that Gaelic was a hobby for them as compared with 38.8% who did not consider Gaelic to be a hobby. Outside Scotland, respondents were more likely to view Gaelic learning as a hobby: in the remainder of the UK, 60.3% agreed and 25.2% disagreed with the statement, with the figures for the rest of the world being 52.8% agreeing and 33.7% disagreeing.

On the question as to whether *On the whole, native speakers do not want people to learn Gaelic*, a significant minority of 16.6% of respondents in Scotland agreed, with 35.2% neither agreeing nor disagreeing and 46.7% disagreeing. Outside Scotland, the figures were: 13.3% agree, 39% disagree and 45.3% neither agree nor disagree for the rest of the UK, with the corresponding figures for the rest of the world being 7.9%, 47.2% and 44.9%.

Miscellaneous Questions

Table 126: Opinions on Gaelic: respondents in Scotland

	Agree Strongly	Agree	Neither agree nor disagree	Disagree	Disagree Strongly	Not Stated
	%	%	%	%	%	%
To keep their true identity, the Highlands and Islands need their Gaelic speakers	63.3	28.1	4.3	2	-	4.3
In a globalising world, Gaelic helps to give me a sense of cultural continuity	32.4	46.2	16.1	1.5	1	2.8
Languages are more than a means of communication	59.7	35	3.8	-	0.5	1
Knowledge of Gaelic is good for people's job prospects	13.5	46.7	34.2	3.3	0.3	2
Gaelic can only be saved if Gaelic speaking communities continue to exist in the Islands	29.3	38.3	13.5	14	1.8	3.1
Gaelic is a dying language	4.3	15	19.6	39.5	19.1	2.3
In an impersonal world, Gaelic helps to give me a sense of community	26.3	43.4	22.4	4.8	0.5	22.4

The statement that *To keep their true identity, the Highlands and Islands need their Gaelic speakers* met with very strong agreement among learners (91.4% Scotland, 94.3% UK, 93.2% world), with very few disagreeing and none disagreeing strongly. The level of support for the statement was very similar to that found in MacKinnon's 1994–5 Euromosaic study of fluent Gaelic speakers (MacKinnon 1998: 3).

A majority of learners also agreed with the statements that *In a globalising world, Gaelic helps to give me a sense of cultural continuity* (78.6% Scotland, 68.5% UK, 75.3% world) and that *In an impersonal world, Gaelic helps to give me a sense of community* (69.7% Scotland, 57.3% UK, 70.5% world). The statement that *Languages are more than a means of communication* met with even more support, with 94.7% of respondents in Scotland and in the rest of the UK and almost 99% of respondents elsewhere agreeing. Most of those agreeing agreed strongly with the statement.

For the statement that *Knowledge of Gaelic is good for people's job prospects*, 60.2% in Scotland agreed, most agreeing rather than agreeing strongly. Outside Scotland 45.3% in the rest of the UK and 45% in the rest of the world agreed, with over 40% answering that they neither agreed nor disagreed, this presumably reflecting the lack of Gaelic-related jobs outwith Scotland and perhaps also a lack of awareness of the Gaelic-related job opportunities available in Scotland.

Learners were asked their views on the statement that *Gaelic can only be saved if Gaelic-speaking communities continue to exist in the Islands*, a question which is of considerable importance given the advanced stage which Gaelic to English language shift has reached in the Hebrides. This question was also of interest given that most of the respondents neither lived in nor hailed from the Gaelic-speaking islands. From the results of the questionnaire, it can be seen that respondents did feel that the continued existence of traditional Gaelic-speaking communities was of crucial importance, as 67.6% of Scottish respondents agreed with the statement. 15.8% disagreed. The figures were 72.3% and 10.1% in the rest of the UK and 70.8% and 10.1% in the rest of the world.

Table 127: Opinions on Gaelic: respondents in Scotland

N=392	Agree Strongly	Agree	Neither agree nor disagree	Disagree	Disagree Strongly	Not Stated
	%	%	%	%	%	%
1. To keep their true identity, the Highlands and Islands need their Gaelic speakers	63.3	28.1	4.3	2	-	4.3
2. Gaelic should be one of the languages officially used by the Scottish Parliament	50.8	30.1	13	3.8	0.5	1.8
3. Gaelic is one of Scotland's national languages	80.6	16.8	1.3	0.3	-	1

N=392	Agree Strongly %	Agree %	Neither agree nor disagree %	Disagree %	Disagree Strongly %	Not Stated %
4. Too much money is spent on Gaelic	-	-	5.4	32.9	60	1.8
5. In order to work in the public sector in Gaelic areas, one should speak Gaelic	28.6	42.4	16.3	9.7	1.5	1.5
6. Gaelic is only important at a personal level	0.8	4.3	8.7	45.9	38	8.7
7. To really understand Scottish culture, you must know Gaelic	21.9	38.5	20.9	15.3	1.8	1.5
8. Gaelic should be given official status	61	31.9	3.8	1.3	0.5	1.5
9. Gaelic does not need any special encouragement	0.5	1	3.3	38.3	55.6	1.3
10. In a globalising world, Gaelic helps to give me a sense of cultural continuity	32.4	46.2	16.1	1.5	1	2.8
11. Official bodies should do more to encourage Gaelic in public affairs	44.1	43.4	9.7	0.3	0.3	2.3
12. Gaelic is important for Scotland as a whole	52	38.5	5.9	1.5	0.3	1.8
13. Languages are more than a means of communication	59.7	35	3.8	-	0.5	1
14. People should be allowed to use Gaelic in courts of law	41.8	37	14.3	4.6	0.8	1.5
15. On the whole, native Gaelic speakers do not want other people to learn Gaelic	3.6	13	35.2	32.7	14	1.5
16. There are great differences between Gaelic dialects	8.2	32.1	30.6	21.7	2.3	5.1
17. Companies should be offered tax breaks in order to offer bilingual services	17.1	34.7	36.5	7.6	1.3	2.8
18. Gaelic is only important to the Highlands and Islands	0.5	2.6	5.4	60.2	29.1	2.3
19. Spoken Gaelic needs to become more standardised with less localised variation	3.6	13.3	29.1	38.8	13.8	1.5

Questionnaire Results

	Agree Strongly	Agree	Neither agree nor disagree	Disagree	Disagree Strongly	Not Stated
	%	%	%	%	%	%
20. Gaelic is Scotland's national language	18.9	23.5	26.5	23.7	4.1	3.3
21. Councils should be legally obliged to provide Gaelic-medium education where demand exists	53.1	37	4.8	2.6	0.3	2.3
22. Gaelic learners should learn a standardised variety of Gaelic	7.6	22.4	28.1	27.8	7.6	6.4
23. It is artificial to learn Gaelic	1.3	2	5.1	40.8	49	1.8
24. Learning Gaelic is a hobby for me	5.6	36.5	14.8	27.8	11	4.3
25. Bilingual signs are a waste of money	1.8	2	5.1	40	49.7	1.3
26. Knowledge of Gaelic is good for people's job prospects	13.5	46.7	34.2	3.3	0.3	2
27. Gaelic can only be saved if Gaelic speaking communities continue to exist in the Islands	29.3	38.3	13.5	14	1.8	3.1
28. Gaelic is a dying language	4.3	15	19.6	39.5	19.1	2.3
29. Gaelic should not be encouraged throughout Scotland	0.3	2.3	3.8	26	65.1	2.3
30. Learners should learn Gaelic dialects	9.4	36.7	38.5	12	1..3	2
31. Children in any part of Scotland should be able to learn Gaelic if they or their parents want them to	55.1	38.8	3.3	0.8	0.3	1.8
32. In an impersonal world, Gaelic helps to give me a sense of community	26.3	43.4	22.4	4.8	0.5	22.4

Table 128: Opinions on Gaelic issues: respondents in UK outwith Scotland

N=159	Agree Strongly %	Agree %	Neither agree nor disagree %	Disagree %	Disagree Strongly %	Not Stated %
1. To keep their true identity, the Highlands and Islands need their Gaelic speakers	69.8	24.5	3.1	0.6	-	3.1
2. Gaelic should be one of the languages officially used by the Scottish Parliament	55.4	34.6	6.9	1.3	-	1.9
3. Gaelic is one of Scotland's national languages	80.5	17	1.3	0.6	-	0.6
4. Too much money is spent on Gaelic	1.3	0.6	10.1	32.7	52.8	2.5
5. In order to work in the public sector in Gaelic areas, one should speak Gaelic	24.5	42.8	17	12	1.9	1.9
6. Gaelic is only important at a personal level	1.9	3.1	8.8	51.6	32.7	1.9
7. To really understand Scottish culture, you must know Gaelic	19.5	37.7	22	18.2	0.6	1.9
8. Gaelic should be given official status	68.6	23.3	4.4	0.6	0.6	2.5
9. Gaelic does not need any special encouragement	1.3	-	3.1	38.4	55.4	1.9
10. In a globalising world, Gaelic helps to give me a sense of cultural continuity	28.3	40.2	25.8	1.3	1.3	3.1
11. Official bodies should do more to encourage Gaelic in public affairs	45.3	42.8	8.2	1.9	-	1.9
12. Gaelic is important for Scotland as a whole	52.8	40.2	5	1.3	-	0.6
13. Languages are more than a means of communication	64.8	30.2	1.3	1.3	-	2.5
14. People should be allowed to use Gaelic in courts of law	47.2	34	11.3	3.8	1.3	2.5
15. On the whole, native Gaelic speakers do not want other people to learn Gaelic	1.3	12	45.3	27	12	2.5
16. There are great differences between Gaelic dialects	6.3	39.6	34.6	15.1	1.3	3.1

Questionnaire Results

	Agree Strongly %	Agree %	Neither agree nor disagree %	Disagree %	Disagree Strongly %	Not Stated %
17. Companies should be offered tax breaks in order to offer bilingual services	16.4	40.2	32.7	6.3	0.6	3.8
18. Gaelic is only important to the Highlands and Islands	1.3	1.9	6.9	67.9	20.1	6.9
19. Spoken Gaelic needs to become more standardised with less localised variation	2.5	18.9	30.8	35.8	10.1	1.9
20. Gaelic is Scotland's national language	18.2	22.6	27	25	4.4	2.5
21. Councils should be legally obliged to provide Gaelic-medium education where demand exists	40.9	49.7	5.7	0.6	-	3.1
22. Gaelic learners should learn a standardised variety of Gaelic	6.3	34.6	28.3	23.3	5	2.5
23. It is artificial to learn Gaelic	-	2.5	5	40.2	48.4	3.8
24. Learning Gaelic is a hobby for me	20.1	40.2	11.3	17	8.2	3.1
25. Bilingual signs are a waste of money	2.5	1.3	4.4	40.2	49.1	2.5
26. Knowledge of Gaelic is good for people's job prospects	8.2	37.1	44.6	5.7	1.3	3.1
27. Gaelic can only be saved if Gaelic speaking communities continue to exist in the Islands	39.6	32.7	15.1	8.2	1.9	2.5
28. Gaelic is a dying language	3.1	18.2	20.8	35.8	20.1	1.9
29. Gaelic should not be encouraged throughout Scotland	1.8	1.3	3.8	32.7	57.9	2.5
30. Learners should learn Gaelic dialects	8.2	32.1	44	13.8	-	1.9
31. Children in any part of Scotland should be able to learn Gaelic if they or their parents want them to	53.5	40.2	2.5	1.9	-	1.9
32. In an impersonal world, Gaelic helps to give me a sense of community	20.8	36.5	36.5	1.9	0.6	3.8

Table 129: Opinions on Gaelic issues: respondents outwith UK

N=89	Agree Strongly %	Agree %	Neither agree nor disagree %	Disagree %	Disagree Strongly %	Not Stated %
1. To keep their true identity, the Highlands and Islands need their Gaelic speakers	68.5	24.7	4.5	2.2	-	-
2. Gaelic should be one of the languages officially used by the Scottish Parliament	53.9	34.8	9	-	2.2	-
3. Gaelic is one of Scotland's national languages	80.9	14.6	3.4	1.1	-	-
4. Too much money is spent on Gaelic	-	-	19.1	22.5	56.2	2.2
5. In order to work in the public sector in Gaelic areas, one should speak Gaelic	38.2	41.6	15.7	2.2	2.5	-
6. Gaelic is only important at a personal level	-	3.4	8.9	43.8	43.8	-
7. To really understand Scottish culture, you must know Gaelic	31.5	41.6	15.7	10.1	1.1	-
8. Gaelic should be given official status	61.8	33.7	3.4	-	-	1.1
9. Gaelic does not need any special encouragement	-	-	5.6	39.3	55.1	-
10. In a globalising world, Gaelic helps to give me a sense of cultural continuity	39.3	36	19.1	1.1	-	4.5
11. Official bodies should do more to encourage Gaelic in public affairs	49.4	37.1	10.1	2.2	1.1	-
12. Gaelic is important for Scotland as a whole	59.6	27	10.1	1.1	2.2	-
13. Languages are more than a means of communication	86.5	12.4	1.1	-	-	-
14. People should be allowed to use Gaelic in courts of law	48.3	41.6	9	1.1	-	-
15. On the whole, native Gaelic speakers do not want other people to learn Gaelic	3.4	4.5	44.9	27	20.2	-
16. There are great differences between Gaelic dialects	4.5	29.2	37.1	23.6	1.1	4.5

	Agree Strongly %	Agree %	Neither agree nor disagree %	Disagree %	Disagree Strongly %	Not Stated %
17. Companies should be offered tax breaks in order to offer bilingual services	20.2	36	36	3.4	2.2	2.2
18. Gaelic is only important to the Highlands and Islands	-	3.4	7.9	56.2	31.5	1.1
19. Spoken Gaelic needs to become more standardised with less localised variation	2.2	18	28.1	34.8	13.5	3.4
20. Gaelic is Scotland's national language	29.2	27	24.7	12.4	4.5	2.2
21. Councils should be legally obliged to provide Gaelic-medium education where demand exists	52.8	33.7	9	3.4	-	1.1
22. Gaelic learners should learn a standardised variety of Gaelic	6.7	38.2	1.1	23.6	5.6	1.1
23. It is artificial to learn Gaelic	3.4	3.4	4.5	33.7	52.8	2.2
24. Learning Gaelic is a hobby for me	14.6	38.2	11.2	19.1	14.6	2.2
25. Bilingual signs are a waste of money	1.1	1.1	4.5	30.7	60.7	1.1
26. Knowledge of Gaelic is good for people's job prospects	37.1	7.9	43.8	4.5	1.1	5.6
27. Gaelic can only be saved if Gaelic speaking communities continue to exist in the Islands	42.7	28.1	18	9	1.1	1.1
28. Gaelic is a dying language	3.4	11.2	25.8	41.6	16.8	1.1
29. Gaelic should not be encouraged throughout Scotland	1.1	3.4	2.2	19.1	71.9	2.2
30. Learners should learn Gaelic dialects	13.5	28.1	44.9	11.2	1.1	1.1
31. Children in any part of Scotland should be able to learn Gaelic if they or their parents want them to	61.8	37.1	-	-	-	1.1
32. In an impersonal world, Gaelic helps to give me a sense of community	36	34.8	16.8	5.6	2.2	4.5

Learners were also asked their views on the statement that *Gaelic is a dying language*. In Scotland, 58.6% disagreed with this statement, with most disagreeing rather than disagreeing strongly. A significant minority of 19.3% agreed with the statement, however. The figures for the remainder of the UK and the remainder of the world were 55.9% and 21.3% and 58.4% and 14.6% respectively. It should be noted, however, that respondents to the Gaelic Learners' Survey were less optimistic on this subject than the fluent Gaelic speakers of MacKinnon's survey, 70% of whom disagreed that Gaelic was a dying language (1998b: 4).

How Difficult is Gaelic?

Learners were asked if they felt Gaelic to be difficult to learn, and if so, for what reason. This question was asked to see whether respondents shared the perception which is commonly encountered amongst the general public that Gaelic is a particularly difficult language to learn due to its linguistic structure. This idea has been challenged by many commentators (Blacklaw 1978, Morgan 1992, MacNeil and Beaton 1994: 54). MacNeil and Beaton have suggested that while Gaelic might be more difficult linguistically for English learners to learn than languages such as French, Spanish, Italian, Dutch and German, it is at around the same level of difficulty for English speakers to learn as Danish, Norwegian, Portuguese and Romanian: languages not normally considered to by English speakers to be very difficult to learn (MacNeil and Beaton 1994). The question was also included in order to investigate what difficulties faced learners in acquiring the language.

Table 130: Opinions about difficulty of learning Gaelic: all respondents
Question: *Some people believe that Gaelic is a particularly difficult language to learn, others do not. Do you think that Gaelic is a difficult language to learn?*

	Scotland		UK		World	
	N	%	N	%	N	%
Yes	249	63.7	100	62.9	45	50.6
No	110	28.1	42	26.4	37	41.6
Don't know	16	4.1	10	6.3	1	1.1
Not Stated	16	4.1	7	4.4	6	6.7
Total	392	100	159	100	89	100

It can be seen from Table 130 that despite there being much evidence to suggest that Gaelic is not as difficult linguistically to learn as commonly perceived, most learners nonetheless felt Gaelic to be a difficult language to learn, with a majority of those answering in this way stating that the language was linguistically difficult. There were however, significant minorities who did not feel the language to be difficult or who did not consider the language to be difficult for linguistic reasons.

Table 131: Reasons for difficulty of learning Gaelic: all respondents
Question: *If you felt Gaelic to be difficult to learn, why do / did you feel Gaelic to be difficult?*

	Scotland		UK		World	
	N	%	N	%	N	%
a) Linguistically, I feel that Gaelic is a difficult language to learn (e.g. word order, spelling, pronunciation)	199	79.9%	75	75%	24	53.3%
b) There is nowhere where I can go where Gaelic is spoken all the time by everybody	177	71.1%	95	95%	42	93%
c) Learning materials, facilities and support for Gaelic are poorer than those for most other languages	110	44%	42	42%	29	64.4%
d) I find it difficult to learn languages	64	25.7%	27	27%	8	17.8%
e) There are no circumstances in which I have to use Gaelic and cannot use English	166	66.6%	68	68%	32	71.1%
f) Other	47	18.9%	16	16%	14	31.1%
	Total = 249		Total = 100		Total = 45	

While an argument can be made that Gaelic is not particularly difficult to learn for linguistic reasons, however, there can be no doubt that there are many non-linguistic factors which can make minority languages such as Gaelic more difficult to learn than other languages. These reasons are reflected in Table 131, where a majority of the respondents express the view that learning is made difficult partly by the lack of a place where Gaelic is spoken all the time by everybody and by the lack of circumstances in which only Gaelic can be used. A large number of respondents (44% in Scotland, 42% in the rest of the UK and 64.4% in the rest of the world) also stated that they felt that the quality of learning materials, facilities and support for Gaelic to be a factor making the language difficult to learn. Generally learners who felt the language to be difficult felt that it was difficult for more than one reason.

Many comments were made about the difficulty or otherwise of Gaelic. Of those who stated that *other* factors were important in leading to Gaelic being difficult for them to learn, the most common were personal circumstances, isolation and the sometimes tense relationship between the learner and native speaker of Gaelic. Under the first category come such reasons as old age, a lack of funds (e.g. "I don't have unlimited funds to access all Gaelic materials e.g. courses, internet, books, associations") and a lack of time, each of which was raised by several respondents.

Isolation was mentioned by sixteen respondents. Many learners mentioned a difficulty in finding other Gaelic learners or native speakers to practice with and several learners outside the UK mentioned the lack of any infrastructure for Gaelic learning or Gaelic-speaking opportunities in their country. Some typical comments were "I don't know anyone who speaks Gaelic", "I live in the wrong country", "all languages are difficult to learn outside the area where spoken in that it just takes much longer".

Thirteen questionnaires said that native Gaelic speakers made it difficult to learn the language. Comments included "many native speakers are either shy or negative about communication with learners", "Some native speakers tend to be impatient with struggling learners", "There are a lot of negative attitudes towards Gaelic from native speaking Gaels which put up psychological barriers to speaking Gaelic", "Lack of encouragement or even hostility from native speakers who do not understand people wanting to learn "their" language", "Gaelic speakers are intolerant of learners. Think their own dialect and accent are correct and others wrong".

Section 6: Comments

In the final section of the questionnaire a blank sheet of paper was provided for comments. The following instructions were given: *I would be grateful for any additional comments which you might want to make on any of the matters raised in this questionnaire: (e.g. about learning Gaelic, the current state of and future prospects for the language, the way forward for Gaelic etc. Please continue overleaf if necessary).*

A large number of comments were received in this section on a variety of issues. Due to their large volume, comments have been categorised into a range of different headings. The comments for all respondents regardless of place of residence are analysed together. It should be noted that the comments received were, in general, of a very high quality, with respondents typically showing a sophisticated understanding of Gaelic issues which suggested that those choosing to make comments had spent much time considering such topics. Subjects raised in the comments section of the questionnaire covered a wide range of Gaelic-related subjects and were by no means restricted to Gaelic learning. This suggests once again that learners tend to be concerned with the well-being of the language in general and that their interest in Gaelic is not confined to an interest in learning the language alone.

Native Speakers and Learners

One of the themes most frequently raised in the comments section was that of the relationship between native speakers and learners of Gaelic. Forty-six comments were made on this area. These comments were almost entirely critical of native speakers and their treatment of learners. The main points made were that some native speakers were unwilling to speak the language to learners or were against the learning of Gaelic. Only one learner used the comments section to refute these commonly heard charges against native speakers. Fourteen further comments were made regarding the sometimes uneasy relationship between native speakers and their language which many respondents felt was a factor in leading to language shift. Some of these respondents felt that learners could help reverse some of the ambiguous attitudes of native speakers. Two learners with children in Gaelic-medium education further argued that a rethinking of the term "native speaker" was necessary due to the growth in the number of children who have become fluent in Gaelic through Gaelic-medium education. Comments about native speakers have been reproduced in full as Appendix 2 due to their relevance to the discussion of the social identity of Gaelic learners elsewhere in this study.

The Learning Process

Unsurprisingly, many comments were made on the process of learning Gaelic. These mainly related to current weaknesses in the infrastructure for Gaelic learning and often echoed comments already seen in this chapter in the context of learners' views on Gaelic-related services, facilities and activities.

The quality of Gaelic learning materials was one issue raised, with a respondent noting that "although there are good modern materials like *Speaking Our Language*, a number of the text books on sale are 70 and more years old and only go to reinforce the idea that Gaelic is old-fashioned, a thing of the past". It was also stated by three learners that there are more and better materials for the beginner than there are for learners at later stages. Similar comments were also made by two learners in relation to Gaelic evening classes, as fewer are available at intermediate level than at beginner level. The sometimes poor quality of Gaelic tuition was also mentioned seven times by respondents, who noted that tutors often have no training in language tuition.

Ten learners felt that the expense of learning Gaelic held back their progress in the language (e.g. "*Speaking Our Language* materials unnecessarily expensive", "evening classes by local college too expensive", "cost, especially of Speaking our Language is a problem", "it is an expensive hobby over a long period of time", "another thing which makes learning Gaelic difficult is that I don't have unlimited funds to access all Gaelic material e.g. courses, internet, books, associations").

Raised by another sixteen learners was the observation that work and family commitments made it difficult to find the time to learn Gaelic or to attend intensive or residential courses (e.g. "working full-time, having home etc to see to plus other interests such as teaching in Sunday School I don't give nearly as much time as I should to learning Gaelic", "because of work commitments, I can't go to immersion/summer courses nor attend school classes as an adult", "Alas, I have not much spare time to learn regularly (too busy a job)", "being in full-time employment, with a young family, I'm finding it difficult to study unfortunately!", "up at 5.00 in the morning and home at 6.00 at night things to do when I get home. Tea and then a shower. By the time I settle down at night it is usually about 8.00 p.m. Then you are tired. It is hard to focus on your notes from evening classes", "as a Gaelic learner for several years, my difficulty has been to progress beyond the basic conversational/comprehension level to reach some higher level of fluency. I believe that this can only be achieved through periods of intense Gaelic immersion e.g. Sabhal Mòr Ostaig, but my own circumstances prevent this. I fear I will remain in the category of the 'perpetual beginner'!", "I have to do a great deal of work on various issues against the clock", "I do not feel I can afford to leave full-time employment to do a course at college – no matter how tempting", "I would like to do an immersion course, but I have a family to support and no guarantee of a job at the end".

Many suggestions were put forward as to ways in which the learning process could be improved. The creation of better learning resources was suggested by many. Eight respondents stated the need for new Gaelic dictionaries and a comprehensive Gaelic grammar for learners. One respondent suggested an increased range of Gaelic 'talking books' and another suggested a parallel-text Gaelic English bible.[246] Another suggestion, put forward by three respondents, was that Linguaphone should produce a Gaelic course. That more Gaelic programmes should be made available on video was also mentioned by 3 learners, with one saying that scripts should be available alongside videos and another saying that popular films/videos should be dubbed into Gaelic for the benefit of learners.

The production of computer-based learning materials was suggested twice, with one respondent suggesting improved CD-rom learners' courses and another a Gaelic spell-checker, thesaurus and other computer lexical products. Two learners commented on Gaelic columns as an aid for learners, with one saying that there should be more light-hearted material in Gaelic in the newspapers and another specifically suggesting a Gaelic column in the *Scots Magazine*. A related suggestion was that there should be a Gaelic comic for adults.

---

[246] A new parallel-text New Testament has since been produced (Comann-Bhioball na h-Alba 2002).

Many comments related to structures for learning. Views received on this subject were once again similar in nature to those seen earlier in this chapter during the discussion of the learners' comments on Gaelic services, facilities and activities. The need for more immersion courses and for more flexible intensive learning courses was suggested several times, for example, as was the need for more classes at the intermediate/advanced level. The reform of university Celtic/Gaelic courses was also suggested. Three respondents argued that more emphasis should be placed in the universities on teaching modern spoken Gaelic. One stated "I have looked at various university Celtic Studies prospectuses. They seem to offer a Gaelic version of my German/French degree in 1971 – a thorough knowledge of middle high German poetry etc. [...] Perhaps the time has come to forget Modern Welsh or Ancient Irish as options, and to look at practical options of Gaelic!"

The need for a teacher-training programme for tutors of adult learners was also suggested four times. One learner said that "natives do not necessarily make the best teachers. Learning as a child and learning as an adult are entirely different experiences and natives need to be taught how to teach their own language" and another noted that "tutors should perhaps be trained in such [immersion] technologies or have chance to witness these technologies of teaching totally in the language through visiting other countries or institutions which make these a specialisation."

The extension of the availability of Gaelic broadcasting was another infrastructural matter which was frequently raised. In addition to the comments already seen earlier in this chapter, three learners called in this section for a national, all-day Radio nan Gaidheal service and for a Gaelic television channel, while another called for the continuation of Gaelic programming on English-medium television channels after the establishment of the proposed Gaelic television channel in order to publicise the language and increase numbers of learners.

Mentioned even more frequently was the need for opportunities to use the language outwith the classroom setting such as through a *Taigh na Gàidhlig* or similar setting or through recreational activities. Some examples included: "learners need a bit of opportunity to use the language in a light hearted way as a supplement to study" and "a Gaelic centre in the Glasgow area where natives and fluent learners could meet and speak Gaelic." Other suggestions were also made as to how opportunities could be created for learners to use the language. Four respondents suggested a holiday scheme whereby learners would stay with Gaelic-speaking families who would speak Gaelic with them. The possibility of university halls of residence for Gaelic speakers was put forward by one Gaelic learner. On a much smaller scale but still important in terms of facilitating the use of Gaelic was the suggestion, made twice, that there should be a *Fàinne* ('ring') scheme like that in Ireland and Mann whereby Gaelic learners can wear badges to show that they have an ability in the language.

The more ambitious suggestion of the construction of a Gaelic-speaking settlement something along the lines of the Belfast Shaws Road Gaeltacht (Maguire 1991) was put forward by three respondents. One expressed the idea as follows: " 'a Gaelic New Town'. How would this work? A series of small towns situated within commuting distance of large cities, e.g. in Perthshire, Stirlingshire, Argyll with a small local economy based on a shop, B&B, teachers etc. The rest of the people commuting for work. Gaelic must be the language of the community." Another respondent stated "I would like to see some sort of long term project set up as an immersion community somewhere in Scotland, preferably in the Highlands or Skye where people could live, work (& earn a living) and could stay a year or two or as long as they liked, somewhere with schools, workshops and Gaelic media." Similarly, two learners suggested: "domains need to be created where Gaelic will be the primary language to give learners and native speakers the opportunity to speak Gaelic and to encourage them to pass it on to their children" , "there has to be some real socio-economic use for, and preferably advantage in using the language after the leaning process or there isn't too much point".

Gaelic Development Suggestions

A large number of suggestions about ways to develop Gaelic were made in this section of the questionnaire: when entered into the computer, these took up seventeen pages of text. Many of the suggestions related to the level of government and public sector support for Gaelic. Nine respondents stated that they felt that Gaelic should have official status and a further expressed the view that they felt that the Scottish Parliament, which was just about to open at the time of questionnaire distribution, should play a important role in RLS. In addition to specific proposals relating to the Parliament and the legal status of Gaelic three learners simply advocated more funding and support for Gaelic by the Government.

Some of the comments on this issue included: " 's e cothrom math a tha ann am Pàrlamaid na h-Alba. Bu chòir tiotal sa Ghàidhlig a bhith air gach roinn 's gach dreuchd agus headed paper le Gàidhlig a bharrachd air Beurla",[247] "It must be made 'official' in the new Scottish Parliament", "new Parliament should induce a new attitude and funding", "I think for Gaelic to survive it must have legal status. It should be the same as the Welsh act", "the question of official status needs to be addressed, specifically as it will need to be prominent in the Scottish Parliament". The suggestion of a Gaelic development board similar to the Welsh Language Board was also made by two respondents. The need of a language corpus planning authority to advise on terminology extension and acceptable measures for pronunciation and grammatical regulation and reform was also mentioned once. Since the survey, Gaelic has been granted a measure of official status through the *Gaelic Language (Scotland) Act 2005*. The Scottish Parliament also makes provision for the language.

Proposals suggested for the development of Gaelic were not confined to central government but also included local government and other public bodies. The provision of bilingual services was seen to be important by many respondents. Altogether eleven comments came within this category. Suggestions included greater use of Gaelic by public bodies in general (6 mentions), by banks (1 mention), the Post Office (1 mention), local authorities (3 mentions), official forms and leaflets (3 mentions), courts, tribunals and children's hearings (1 mention).

Some suggestions made included: "in order to halt the decline, Gaelic must be made the working language of Gaelic speaking areas, in education, administration and offices and English pushed back otherwise the decline won't stop", "for the language to grow, all that is needed is use. This has to come 'from the top'. People and committees within Scottish Office, local councils to give people the confidence to use the language in public situations", "use of Gaelic in banks, shops, police station, in dealing with official bodies (e.g. courts, crofters commission, crofters union, income tax, medical situations)", "awareness of the language is vital for its growth, more public organisations using it is one possible action", "I think that the public need to be

---

[247] "The Scottish Parliament is a good opportunity. Each department and post should have a Gaelic name and their headed paper should be in Gaelic as well as English."

informed about the Gaelic language and culture in a living context. My research has shown that too many people believe that Gaelic is dead/dying and I believe that this is due to a lack of Gaelic in the public service sector".

It can be seen that increasing publicity and raising the awareness of the existence of Gaelic was a key justification given for many of the above suggestions. This was also the case for increased Gaelic road-signage, which was suggested by nine respondents. One respondent also suggested Gaelic airport signs and another railway and shop signs. One learner commented: "all visible signs of Gaelic are to be welcomed, whether on official documents as part of a bilingual policy on road signs, shops etc".

The suggestion seen here that more efforts should be made to publicise Gaelic and to bring it to the attention of non-Gaelic-speakers was a topic very frequently raised, being raised twenty-four times altogether. The main points made were that it was important that Gaelic should have a higher profile and that accurate information about the language should be more widely disseminated amongst the general public, and indeed amongst Gaelic speakers, to increase interest in the language and to dispel commonly held misconceptions and prejudices surrounding the language. A representative selection of these comments can be seen in Table 132.

Table 132: Views on the need of publicity for Gaelic:

There are generations of Scots who have never heard nor seen a word of Gaelic. With the assembly to look forward to in the year 2000, this would be the perfect time to raise awareness of the language.
Scottish Gaelic has an identity problem – I was / am still surprised how many organisations such as colleges and people, even with Scottish ancestors, assume that Gaelic (Irish) and Gàidhlig are one and the same language.
I would like to see a big advertising program in Highlands and Islands first promoting Gaelic e.g. a billboard of a famous Gael stating I can speak Gaelic…can you? I believe that this will have an impact.
I do think that there could be a resurgence of youngsters learning the language with no background of Gaelic with well-targeted education and advertising.
There is a need to 'educate' the rest of the population as to why and how Gàidhlig is relevant to Scotland in this day and age and not just for historical reasons.
Place-name evidence demonstrates that Gaelic was spoken over all of what is now Scotland (except Shetland, Orkney, and parts of the Borders), This should be made more widely known to show the relevance of Gaelic to all Scots.
More awareness of the importance of Gaelic for general public and non-speakers.
The level of 'Gaelic awareness' needs to be raised; it needs to be felt present in everyday life, as well to raise the attention of non-natives as for natives to boost the social status of Gaelic.
More publicity of the fact that Gaelic is a national language.
I think that the public need to be informed about the Gaelic language and culture in a living context. I also found that people were not against Gaelic, on the whole, but were happy to let it get on with itself as it was not part of their life. I think that education is the way forward, to correct such misconceptions.

> There is bias from non-Gaelic speakers, who are under the impression that Gaelic is overfunded, this hardens their resolve and makes it harder for Gaelic to obtain sufficient funds. Education and publicity are needed to overcome this.
>
> Too little is done to enthuse and encourage Gaelic speakers to use the language as a matter of principle, specially with the kids.
>
> Publicise the importance of bilingualism as a skill: I think Gaelic, like other languages, should be regarded as important as I believe that the ability to speak ANY other language, apart from your own, is a useful skill and helps in many other areas.
>
> If we do not spread the word, it [Gaelic] will become a 'dead' language.

The idea that more publicity for Gaelic was important to RLS also came through strongly in the 40 comments made about Gaelic in the schools. Eight of these comments were suggestions that some accurate information about the history and the present situation of Gaelic should be taught to pupils in all Scottish schools. Some also suggested that some basic Gaelic should be taught. As stated elsewhere, such subjects are normally not taught at all in most Scottish schools. Views on this matter can be seen in Table 133.

Table 133: Views on the need to teach about Gaelic in Schools

> As a minimum, all Scottish primary children should have an understanding of Gaelic and its place in Scottish history. They should be able to read and pronounce Gaelic placements on a map. This level of Gaelic should be compulsory at primary – there can be no other country in Europe, possibly the world, where 98% of the population cannot read or understand or pronounce place-names on their own!
>
> I believe that Gaelic could and should be given a higher profile in all Scottish schools by means of song, music and poetry, drawing attention to and explaining meaning of family and place-names. Giving children some background in Gaelic literature and history.
>
> I would support an awareness and a positive consideration of the status of Gaelic in all the schools in the early years. I believe that to achieve this it will be necessary to introduce Gaelic (basic) as a subject at all Scottish teacher training colleges and to include the subject as part of the teachers Graduation certificate.
>
> Every schoolchild should grow up with knowledge of some Gaelic to help it survive.
>
> Every school in Scotland should feature Gaelic in its curriculum in an appropriate form.
>
> Hopefully one day Gaelic will be taught in all primary and secondary schools all over Scotland.
>
> Push for more Gaelic instruction in secondary schools – at an interest level / simple conversation – short courses (taster types).
>
> I guess when it comes down to it, the decision to learn Gaelic is a personal one but I still think it should be encouraged more in the Scottish educational system.

Ten learners made the point that Gaelic should be more widely available as an subject for learners both at primary and at secondary levels (e.g. "I think that the OPTION to learn Gaelic should be open to everyone", "more availability of learning Gaelic in schools", "the current state of the language in non-Gaelic medium schools but in Gaelic speaking areas needs desperately sorted. Visiting Gaelic teachers to give children a flavour of language is essential and immediately attainable").

A number of other comments were made on Gaelic in the education system. There was wide support for Gaelic-medium education (GME). Five learners registered general support (e.g. "as a former teacher I fully support the provision of Gaelic-medium education at all levels within the state system"), two said that they would like to see the availability of GME in their area and a number of others made more detailed points. Five learners said that there should be more governmental support with a legal underpinning for GM provision and a right to GME, e.g. "Gaelic-medium education needs to be more secure with more secure foundations to encourage people without a Gaelic background to send their children to it. Everyone fears a GM school being closed through lack of government support and having to send their children to English schools".

Six respondents argued for increased GM provision in the secondary school where provision is currently limited (e.g. "it is important that secondary education continues the good work started in the primary school", "proper Gaelic medium in the secondary school needed"). One respondent also suggested that GME should increasingly be provided through all-Gaelic schools rather than Gaelic units and another suggested that GME should be compulsory in schools in the Comhairle nan Eilean Siar council area.

Four further comments were made about Gaelic in the schools. One person stated that a Gaelic After-School-Club scheme for learners should be established and another suggested that the teacher training system should allow non-Gaelic-speaking teachers to learn the language as part of their training. Two suggested that it was important that GME was supported by opportunities to use the language outside the school as education on its own is insufficient for RLS purposes.

The need for what might be termed a more inclusive and modern approach to Gaelic was suggested by 22 respondents. These comments made suggestions such as that Gaelic should be given a more modern image and that the importance of learners to the future of Gaelic be recognised. These comments are recorded in full below in Table 134.

Table 134: Views on the need for a more inclusive and modern approach to Gaelic

I feel that learners have an extremely important part to play in determining the manner in which the language develops particularly within Scotland.

An inclusive attitude on the part of its [Gaelic's] supporters, i.e. let everyone join in without being mocked or looked down upon.

Gaelic has a future. However it will have to evolve and grow.

Gaelic is dying despite our efforts, because it is too narrowly based. Virtually everything in Gaelic harks back to times past; *Cothrom* is full of adverts urging readers to trace their Celtic roots – but what about those of us who are not Celts (and proud of it!)? There has to be a wider appeal. If Gaelic is to have a future in the modern work then it has to look to that future: this obsession with the past is the linguistic equivalent of the man with the red flag walking in front of the car.

The language needs 'learners' and for the good of the language we need to be accepted by the majority.

I think Gaelic radio has to start thinking about how to attract young people, with some modern music, otherwise young people will just turn off the radio.

In order to remain a living language its diversity and new growth among urban young populations must be encouraged.

I don't think Gaelic can be exclusive.

The young should also not be ignored, interactive PC media, which is widely used by young people, should be considered a matter of priority. Packaging for them should be modern and not concerned with 'sheep, peat and fish'.

I feel that the link between Gaelic and traditional subjects is excessive. When one learns a language – say Spanish or Italian – the learner is not plunged into the equivalents of crofting, moors, fiddle songs and 1745. [...] Languages are means to travel the world .. Gaelic seems to lead only to the Islands. [...] When you listen to a Basque radio station, of course you get a taste of the Basque background, but you get also, and in a generous proportion, the same kinds of debates, subjects and music that you would in wider, more powerful languages. This is good for the language and the growth of a standard audience – not just an audience of learners and lovers of local music.

Gaelic is too insular, and relies too much on seemingly 'old-fashioned' and isolated communities in the islands. I would like to see Scotland a truly bilingual country in a European setting.

I want Gàidhlig to survive as a vibrant, modern language which people feel free to use whenever they want, to express the lives they live.

The whole decline of Gaelic is about Gaels being convinced they were inferior to English speakers. Gaelic's fortunes will rise as the older generation dies and take their stupid ideas with them to the grave. Many old-time Gaelic speakers are convinced Gaelic should and will die, and the fact that they are Gaelic-speakers appears to give their ideas credibility.

Table 134(continued): Views on the need for a more inclusive and modern approach to Gaelic

From my point of view I see the biggest threat to the future prospects for the language as being the tendency to 'fossilise' it. Any successful modern language must not hide in a corner and try and fend off all outside influences – to grow and expand it must absorb more from other language (as English has done) and turn this to its own advantage. I do get the impression that its modern development is being constrained by groups that would like to keep it in a strait-jacket.

The way forward for Gaelic is to get over the last 300 years and grow up. In attitude it is adolescent and isolationist and will kill itself, if allowed, with no outside help. Gaelic is, and will be, valid, but attitudes need to change.

I know MANY people (from non-Gaelic background) who are interested in, or are learning, Gaelic. The future of the language, in that sense, is good. But the native speakers need (and should) find more opportunities to interact with those learners so that those learners feel themselves as USERS of the language and not just learners – then the language will really be secure.

Associations like the Lewis and Harris which I've gone to seem to be following a formula used years ago. Life has moved on and the personnel should be aware that left in their hands the language will die.

They kept Latin alive for 1,000 years after the last speaker died, no one really knows what it originally sounded like and yet kids all over the world are being tortured with it. Maybe Gaelic ought to go the opposite route; make it fun! Try and get them to want to learn it!

Kids and teens in Northern Germany use so many English words in everyday conversation today, that they almost blur the lines (Germlish?) Why do they do that? Because most of the music they listen to, most of the movies they see and even most of the food they eat is American. They wear Michael Jordan shirts never having seen him play, except maybe in one of those fake all-stars v Europe things. What's the point? Children are the future, so give them comic books, fun shows and music in Gaelic and they'll love it. 100-year old textbooks in stuffy classrooms are strictly for (some) adults.

The most important things for Scots to lead ordinary, modern life in the Scottish language, until Gaelic is modernised and recognised this will not happened. It is the property of all Scotland.

As an English person committed to Scotland, and staying in Scotland, learning Gaelic seems a wholly appropriate way of getting closer to Scotland. It also seems to me that if the language is to survive, it must not become a "ghetto" tongue, merely a badge of identity for surviving Gaels, but must seek to propagate itself like other European languages.

With the native speakers dispersed, the future will depend increasingly on the zeal of non-native speakers.

Gaelic must be strengthened in the islands but in the long term has to be in common usage in the mainland 'Gàidhealtachd' towns – Oban, Fort William, Inverness.

Complementary to the view that there should be a more inclusive approach to Gaelic was the opinion that there should be closer links between Gaelic and other minority languages and that lessons should be learned from their experiences. Manx, Irish and Welsh were mentioned four times each in this context, with Breton and Hebrew being mentioned once and with minority languages in general being mentioned six times. (e.g. "the co-operation between Europe's 'minorities' should be developed to share experience, ideas and avoid making the same mistakes over and over", "the preservation of Gaelic is part of the general scenario in preserving other minority languages. The more ways that ideas and suggestions can be shared between these groups e.g. through conferences and networks, the better."). On a similar note, ten respondents stated that the Scots language should be developed alongside Gaelic (e.g. "more should be done to promote Lowlands Scots. While much is now doing to promote Gaelic, Scots is still relatively neglected", "I love Gaelic and wish to see the language flourish, but I'm also keen that our other traditional tongue doesn't disappear").

Several other Gaelic development suggestions were made. Tourism was mentioned twice by learners who felt that more should be done to promote tourism through Gaelic and Gaelic through tourism. Also suggested twice was the importance of taking measures to encourage newcomers to Gaelic-speaking areas to learn Gaelic: "Somehow we much change the climate so that people who move into the area to live see it as incumbent upon themselves to learn Gaelic", "I feel quite strongly about the need for intensive courses and encouragement for non-Gaelic speakers in Gaelic communities. It is harder to organise such courses in rural areas, but if people don't learn Gaelic quickly then they will be too used to speaking English with their neighbours to effect a changeover". Along similar lines, four learners suggested that Gaelic agencies should put more emphasis upon promoting Gaelic in the home: in maintaining and re-establishing intergenerational transmission.

Interestingly, the suggestion that Gaelic groups should do more to use Gaelic themselves was mentioned five times (e.g. "certain institutions project themselves as operating through the medium of Gaelic which is not the case. Some examples: Lèirsinn, Cànan, BBC's Gaelic department (TV). It is has to be said that Sabhal Mòr Ostaig has a growing linguistic problem which is not being tackled properly. To summarise: window dressing and lip service are of no use to anyone serious about saving the language", "I would like to see Gaelic groups be forced to use Gaelic", "when even Gaelic promotional bodies conduct their business in English, what point is there in learning it?", "while the slogan of An Comunn is 'Ar Cànain 's ar Ceòl', no effort is made to promote the language in the National Mòd with the result that most learners don't attend what should be regarded as the annual gathering for all interested in the language").

On the question of where Gaelic should be developed, 14 of the 17 pertinent comments stated that the language should be promoted and developed throughout Scotland and 3 took an opposing view, arguing that development efforts should be concentrated mainly or exclusively on Gaelic-speaking island communities.

The final issue relating to Gaelic development raised in the comments section of the questionnaire was to what extent if any RLS efforts should involve compulsion. Seven comments were made on this subject, of which six warned against using too much compulsion and with four of these specifically using the example of Ireland as an argument against undue compulsion in Gaelic promotion. Only one learner did advocate compulsion, putting forward the rather uncommon view that Gaelic should replace English in Scotland and that all school pupils in Scotland should be taught through the medium of Gaelic.

The Future of Gaelic

The future prospect for Gaelic was a subject frequently touched upon by respondents. Many comments (12) were positive and up-beat about the future of Gaelic, some typical examples being "I expect Gaelic to thrive and grow and to become established as part of Scotland's culture in the next century", "Gaelic is thriving at the moment", "I think that the future of Gaelic is very good and the prospects are much more encouraging than even 5 or 10 years ago". A further seven respondents stated or suggested that they were not certain as to what the future would hold for Gaelic (e.g. "as to future prospects, so much depends on money and education", "I shall be interested to see whether Gaelic exists in a century's time", "I think Gaelic faces an uncertain future, as it stands, I think Gaelic is a dying language [...] however there is an apparently large interest in learning Gaelic gathering momentum and it will be interesting to see how things develop".)

Five comments were more pessimistic about the future of Gaelic, e.g. "at present I do not feel that Gaelic is receiving the backing it requires in order to stabilise its position in Scotland", "I'm afraid that my view about the ultimate fate of Gaelic is not optimistic", "the current state of Gaelic is dire with the number of speakers according to the best estimates decreasing by over 1000 per year, and the breakdown of the use of Gaelic within the family in the Western Isles. Its future prospects are death as a community language. [...] There is no way forward for Gaelic because so few people in Scotland care about it, and so many are hostile to it. There is no will, from central government down to community councils to do anything meaningful to keep the language alive. A great proportion of the small resources that are available for Gaelic are frittered away on useless displacement activities like Mòds and Fèisean. The only future of Gaelic is to become the hobby of a few enthusiasts like Cornish and Manx are now".

Standardisation of Gaelic

25 comments were made in the questionnaires about the standardisation of Gaelic. Of those commenting, few advocated radical standardisation of the language (3 respondents – e.g. "We must standardise the pronunciation of the language.") or rejected any further standardisation (2 respondents– e.g. "I do not believe in teaching standardised Gaelic."). Rather, all of the remaining respondents who commented advocated moderate standardisation of the language (in terms of vocabulary, grammar and spelling) as taught to learners, at least in the initial stages of learning, and/or the standardisation of high-register Gaelic as used for official purposes such as news broadcasting. Most of those comments also wished to preserve dialects (e.g. "I think it is necessary to move towards a standard form of the language for official status, literary language and for learners, but I don't think the dialects should be denigrated [...] as they are vibrant, evolved forms of modern Gaelic. They should be encouraged within their communities to survive." "I think that teaching should largely be of standardised Gaelic, but along with that dialects should not be positively discouraged, even in early stages, and could be positively encouraged in later stages to everyone's benefit."

Gaelic "more than a means of communication"

In the questionnaire, learners were asked their views on the following three statements:

- *Languages are more than a means of communication, in a globalising world.*
- *Gaelic helps give me a sense of cultural continuity in an impersonal world.*
- *Gaelic helps to give me a sense of community.*

Eleven comments making points similar to these were made in the comments section of the questionnaire. Examples of these are given in Table 135.

Table 135: Gaelic *more than a means of communication*

I have found out more about myself by learning the language.
Gaelic is the language that represents not only magnificent art, music, but spirituality and a way of thinking that must be cherished and nourished.
I have a growing respect for Gaelic oral tradition and am increasingly fed-up with English / European values, literature (shallow, selfish, neurotic, anti-spiritual).
I got involved in the Gaelic movement as a student; the revival helped me to understand cultural process.
I would like to emphasise the importance of Gaelic not being simply an alternative method of every-day communication. There are special insights which only particular languages can give.
Learning Gaelic gives me a strong feeling of identity especially as my family has strong connections with the islands. I feel part of a special community that non-Gaelic speakers can't comprehend and I feel proud that I'm learning Gaelic although I realise I may never become fluent.

The implications of the Gaelic Learners' Survey findings for RLS

Having looked at the results of the Gaelic Learners' Survey in detail, the main findings will now be summarised with particular reference to their significance for RLS. The results will be investigated in terms of the six headings used above: social background, learning Gaelic, using Gaelic, Gaelic in the family, opinions on Gaelic and comments. Unless stated otherwise, comments made in this section will refer to respondents resident in Scotland.

The first section of the questionnaire looked at the personal details of the learners. In terms of their social background, respondents tended to differ significantly from the Scottish population as a whole in many respects. Respondents tended to be educated to a higher level than the population in general and to be disproportionately drawn from the professional and managerial classes. Politically, respondents tended to be on the centre, or more often, on the left of centre, and also showed very high levels of support for political nationalism. Similarly, the survey showed a high level of identification with the Scottish identity and a low level of identification with the British identity. The respondents also differed from wider society in terms of their tendency towards a high level of knowledge of languages and the survey further suggested an uneven gender balance amongst Gaelic learners.

In all of these respects, the survey findings have tended to follow trends seen in previous studies of Gaelic learners (CnaG/CLI 1992, MacCaluim 1995, Pringle 1985, MacNeil and MacDonald 1997). While the respondents in this study and in the previous Gaelic learners' studies referred to are clearly not representative of the general population in many respects, and while it is obviously desirable that Gaelic learners reflect as broad a cross-section of society as possible, it can be argued nonetheless that none of these findings are a matter of great concern for RLS at the present time.

Of much more concern with regard to RLS is the age of the sample. Most respondents were middle-aged or older, with few learners falling into the strategically important 16–25 age group. This is, of course, the very age group where people tend to choose college or university courses and make decisions as to their future career. It is also in the twenties and thirties that people tend to meet partners and to start a family. The under-representation of younger people amongst respondents, therefore, has negative implications for such areas as the uptake of intensive Gaelic courses, Gaelic employment opportunities and Gaelic-medium education, and, crucially, for the intergenerational transmission of Gaelic. The results of previous surveys of Gaelic learning have also suggested that the under-representation of younger people amongst learners is typical of the national Gaelic learning situation (CnaG/CLI 1992, MacCaluim 1995, MacNeil and MacDonald 1997).

A more encouraging finding relating to the social background of learners was that a majority of learners neither resided in the Highlands or came from the Highlands and that only a minority of learners had Gaelic-speaking parents or grandparents. This shows that the appeal of Gaelic is not confined to those with such backgrounds, who form only a small minority of the Scottish population.

The second section of the questionnaire investigated the learning of Gaelic, looking both at progress in learning Gaelic and at motivation for learning. This section showed that respondents had, on average, spent a long time learning but that pace and extent of progress in learning the language tended to be slow and limited with there also being a high drop-out-rate amongst learners. While a large majority of learners aimed for full fluency and literacy in the language, less than half of respondents expected to reach their desired level of fluency. Progress in learning Gaelic tended to be even more limited amongst learners outside Scotland. This is all worrying reading from the point of view of RLS and also mirrors findings of earlier surveys of Gaelic learning (MacNeil and MacDonald 1997, Wells 1997).

Several infrastructural weaknesses were identified by respondents as reasons for this lack of progress, the most commonly mentioned being a lack of Gaelic classes/courses in many areas of Scotland, a lack of provision for learners at the post-beginner stage, a lack of intensive Gaelic courses, a lack of flexible Gaelic courses for those unable to attend conventional Gaelic classes and a lack of informal opportunities to use Gaelic outside the classroom.

More positive for RLS was the section relating to motivation for learning. While learners typically had a range of reasons for learning Gaelic, the desire to keep Gaelic alive was the most widely quoted by respondents as being important to their decision to take up the language, with over 90% stating that this factor had been important to their decision to learn. This suggests that respondents tend to see learning Gaelic as being part of the broader language maintenance effort and not merely as a personal interest. As motivation is considered to be a very important influence on successful outcome in language learning (MacNeil and Beaton 1994) it is encouraging for RLS purposes that learners' decisions to learn tended to be influenced by strong integrative/expressive/idealistic motivations related to areas such as national and personal identity. Positive attitudes towards the target language are also understood to predispose learners towards more effective learning (MacNeil and Beaton 1994: 19) and it can be seen both from the reasons for learning given by the respondents and from the responses to the attitude statements in the questionnaire discussed below that respondents to the survey had very positive attitudes towards the language.

Also relatively hopeful for RLS was the third section of the questionnaire which investigated the extent to which learners took advantage of Gaelic-related activities, services and facilities. While this area was somewhat difficult to investigate given the very small number and range of Gaelic activities, services and facilities in existence, learners did show an encouraging level of uptake of the formal opportunities to use Gaelic which are on offer. Large majorities of learners regularly listened to Radio nan Gaidheal, watched Gaelic television and regularly read at least one Gaelic publication other than the Gaelic learners' magazine *Cothrom*, for example. Smaller but significant numbers of learners also took part in other Gaelic-related activities such as concerts, plays, church services and Gaelic-related conferences and meetings and it is likely that these figures would have been higher if such activities were more widely available. The level of uptake of Gaelic events, activities and facilities was higher amongst advanced and fluent learners.

This section suggested, therefore, that learners are providing a market for Gaelic-related services, activities and facilities and that the more fluent they become, the more likely they are to use these. Also positive for RLS is the fact that a large number of the learners (fluent or otherwise) have recorded themselves as being Gaelic speakers on the Census, thus adding to the official numbers of Gaelic speakers.

A mixed picture for RLS emerged from the findings of section four of the questionnaire which investigated Gaelic in the family. Learners tended to be isolated, with few (36) living in households in which there was a fluent Gaelic speaker and with even fewer living in households in which all other members were fluent Gaelic speakers (12). For the majority of respondents, therefore, reaching fluency in Gaelic would not enable significant use of the language within the family.

This section also investigated whether or not respondents chose Gaelic-medium education for their offspring. This produced results which were more promising from the RLS viewpoint. It was seen that a number of respondents with pre-school and school-aged children were educating their children through the medium of Gaelic. 70% of the 37 respondents with pre-school age children and 45% of the 67 respondents with school-age children said that their children attended Gaelic-medium education. In addition, a large majority of 84% of the 99 non-parents who expected to have children in future said that they would choose Gaelic-medium education were it available in their area.

Once again, however, this section showed the importance of attracting learners at as early an age as possible. The single largest section of respondents (134 in total) were those with grown-up children and many had become interested in Gaelic only after deciding upon their children's education. Of those who had not educated or were not educating their children though the medium of Gaelic, around half stated either that they were not aware of the availability of GME in their area at the time their children started school or that they were not interested in Gaelic at the time. This suggests that the uptake of GME would be higher if more learners were attracted at an earlier age.

Section five of the questionnaire investigated learners' opinions on Gaelic through attitude statements. The results demonstrated that respondents tended to hold very pro-Gaelic attitudes. Learners completing the questionnaire mainly felt that Gaelic needed official encouragement and favoured strong measures to promote the language such as official status for the language and a legal right to GME. The very high levels of support for strong language development measures amongst the respondents can only be helpful to RLS. Also likely to aid RLS is the fact that respondents tended to view Gaelic as a language of importance to Scotland as a whole and as one which should be promoted nationally. The final section of the questionnaire in which learners were invited to make comments on any Gaelic-related matters was also positive with regard to RLS. The findings in this section showed that respondents tended to have a high level of knowledge of Gaelic issues and to have given them considerable thought.

Conclusion

Having summarised the findings of the Gaelic Learners' Survey, some overall conclusions can now be drawn. The first of these is that learners frequently bring many qualities to Gaelic which can contribute to RLS efforts. These include, amongst other things, enthusiasm for the language, knowledge of Gaelic issues, pro-Gaelic views and the provision of a market for Gaelic-related goods and services.

The second main conclusion is that this potential of Gaelic learners to act as a force for RLS is not being fulfilled at present, as very few Gaelic learners ever reach fluency. There can be little doubt that the main reason for the failure of learners to reach fluency is the inadequacy of the Gaelic learning infrastructure, which, as Comann na Gàidhlig have pointed out, is: "fragmented, lacks co-ordination and needs a more structured approach" (CnaG/CLI 1992: 65). The slow and limited progress made by most learners in Gaelic lends weight to the argument made in chapter 3 that significant changes are needed to the Gaelic learning infrastructure in order to ensure that more learners become fluent.

The final main conclusion arising from the Gaelic Learners' Survey is that the age of Gaelic learners is a matter for particular concern. As has been shown in this survey and in previous surveys of Gaelic learners, there are far too few learners in the strategically important under-30 group. While intensive courses at Sabhal Mòr Ostaig and other venues have begun to bring more younger learners to fluency, learners remain overwhelmingly middle-aged. For Gaelic learning to be translated into intergenerational transmission or donation, it is very important that learners be attracted at a young age. In this respect, the findings of the survey strengthen the argument made in chapter 3 that a range of measures need to be taken to attract more and younger Gaelic learners.

6: Conclusion

> Chan e *optional extras* a th' annainn tuilleadh.[248] (Peadar Morgan, on the position of learners in the Gaelic community, *Aithris na Maidne*, BBC Radio nan Gaidheal, 27.07.01).

It was noted in the introduction to this study that Gaelic learners are a large and growing force within the Gaelic speech community. It was further argued that learners have a central position to play in the Gaelic community and in RLS efforts given the very weak position of Gaelic and rapidly declining number of native Gaelic speakers. This study has investigated the experience of learning of Gaelic in the present day, with particular reference to the position of learners in RLS.

Chapter 3, "The Gaelic Learning Infrastructure", described the current facilities available for Gaelic learning and assessed their effectiveness in attracting Gaelic learners and in bringing them to fluency. It was seen that the Gaelic learning infrastructure is fragmented, has many significant gaps in provision and lacks any overall strategic co-ordination. Particularly serious gaps in provision include the absence of any tutor training structure and a lack of intensive courses and of flexible learning opportunities. The result of the fundamental flaws identified in the Gaelic learning infrastructure is quite simply that very few Gaelic learners, both as an absolute number and as a percentage of all Gaelic learners, reach fluency in the language.

In comparing the Gaelic learning infrastructure of 2006 with that of 1992 as described in the *Feumalachdan Luchd Ionnsachaidh* report (CnaG/CLI 1992), it was seen that very little progress has been made over the past decade in addressing the structural weaknesses identified above. While some minor improvements have been made to the facilities available for learners, the only developments of real significance in the past decade have been the establishment and expansion in Gaelic immersion courses and other full-time courses and the development of the flexible learning Gaelic Access Course. Extremely valuable though these courses are, however, they are still small in number and thus have not been sufficient to bring more than a few dozen, or at best, a few hundred learners to fluency in the language.

Chapter 4, "The Social Identity of Gaelic Learners", investigated the relationship between Gaelic learners and native speakers and between learners and non-speakers of Gaelic. This chapter also looked at the issue of the social identity of Gaelic learners on the larger scale, investigating the question of what position Gaelic learners occupy within the Gaelic community and the practical implications of this.

It was seen that the Gaelic learner occupies a somewhat anomalous position. By being neither a native speaker nor a non-speaker of Gaelic, the learner challenges conventional perceptions of Gaelic whereby Gaelic is believed either to be spoken natively by people from a particular background or not to be spoken at all. As a result of this, the position of the Gaelic learner has both advantages and disadvantages.

One advantage for the individual learner is that learning the language creates an opportunity to gain an understanding both of the views of the Gaelic and non-Gaelic communities as regards the language and as regards each other. This is of advantage to RLS as is the fact that the Gaelic learner can bring new experiences and perceptions

---

[248] "We are no longer optional extras".

to the language and act, for native speakers and learners alike, as a consciousness raiser.

It was also seen that the position of the Gaelic learner contains some disadvantages such as the charge of "artificiality" sometimes made against learners by speakers and non-speakers of Gaelic and the ambiguous semi-detached relationship which learners may feel they have with the Gaelic community. The relationship between Gaelic learners and native speakers can sometimes, though by no means always, be an uneasy one due to the different backgrounds and perceptions of these two groups.

When magnified from an individual scale to the national scale, it was seen that the issue of the position of the Gaelic learner was one with great importance for Gaelic development. Regardless of the qualities which learners may bring to RLS efforts, how much of a role Gaelic learners will actually be able to play in reversing language shift in practice depends to a great extent on the nature of Gaelic policies drawn up by government and by Gaelic organisations. The nature of these policies depends in turn upon social identity issues such as how the Gaelic community is defined by policy makers and on how much Gaelic learners (and by extension the areas in which they mainly live) are seen to belong to or be relevant to this community.

Quite simply, if Gaelic learners (and by extension the areas in which they mainly live) are not considered to be a part – an important part – of the Gaelic community, it is unlikely that the needs and aspirations of Gaelic learners and the importance of Gaelic learners to reversing language shift will be taken into account in policy making. In such circumstances, it would be highly unlikely that policies necessary to deliver the significant numbers of fluent Gaelic learners necessary for RLS purposes would be introduced.

Chapter 5, "The Gaelic Learners' Survey", described and discussed the findings of a large-scale study of Gaelic learners investigating the social background of learners, their motivation, the impact of learners on regenerating the language, the views of learners with regard to the language and related questions. This chapter strengthened many of the arguments made in chapter three, showing both that respondents had mainly made slow and limited progress with the language and also evidencing a high level of dissatisfaction with current learning facilities. Material in the survey also supported the contents of chapter four, further illustrating the ambiguity of the term 'Gael' and showing that learners often had an uneasy relationship with native speakers of the language. It was also, seen, however, that learners often bring characteristics to Gaelic which can contribute to RLS efforts. These include, amongst other things, enthusiasm for the language, knowledge of Gaelic issues, pro-Gaelic views and the provision of a market for Gaelic-related goods and services.

With regard to motivation, while respondents typically had a range of reasons for learning, the desire to keep Gaelic alive was quoted by over 90% as a motivating factor. This suggests that respondents tend to see learning Gaelic as being part of the broader language maintenance effort and not merely as a personal interest. Other motives frequently cited by learners were an interest in Gaelic culture and national, local and personal identity. As motivation is considered to be a very important influence on successful outcome in language learning it is encouraging for RLS purposes that learners' decisions to learn tended to be influenced by strong integrative/expressive/idealistic motivations such as these.

Through the survey and through written comments, it was seen that respondents tended to hold very pro-Gaelic attitudes, favouring strong measures to promote the language such as official status for the language and a legal right to Gaelic-medium education. Through written comments in questionnaires, it was also seen that respondents tended to have a relatively high level of knowledge of Gaelic issues.

Such factors are likely to be of value to RLS as is the fact that respondents tended to view Gaelic as a language of importance to Scotland as a whole and as one which should be promoted nationally. On a similar note, survey results suggested that the appeal of Gaelic is not confined to those coming from or living in Highland or Gaelic speaking areas or to those having close family connections with the language. Most respondents neither lived in nor had been raised in the Highlands nor had any Gaelic-speaking parents or grandparents.

Also hopeful for RLS was the extent to which learners took advantage of Gaelic-related activities, services and facilities. Respondents showed an encouraging level of uptake of the formal opportunities to use Gaelic which are on offer, few those these are. The level of uptake increased in line with the level of fluency of respondents.

In terms of the social background of Gaelic learners, it was seen that respondents tended to differ from the Scottish population as a whole in many respects. For example, the learners tended to be educated to a higher level, to have a higher level of knowledge of languages, to be disproportionately in managerial and professional employment, and to be politically more left-wing and politically more nationalist that the population in general. The survey further showed a high level of identification with the Scottish identity and low level with the British identity. Results also suggested an uneven gender balance amongst Gaelic learners, though findings on this matter were less conclusive.

While respondents in the survey varied from the general population in many respects, and while it is desirable that learners reflect as broad a cross-section of society as possible, it can be argued nonetheless that these findings are not a matter of great concern for RLS at present. More worrying was the limited progress made by learners in Gaelic as referred to above and the high average age of learners.

Most respondents were middle-aged and older, with very few learners falling into the strategically important under-30 age group. This high average age of learners has negative implications for intergenerational transmission, for uptake of Gaelic-medium education and for a number of other areas crucial in ensuring RLS.

In short, chapter five found that while learners frequently bring qualities to Gaelic which can contribute to RLS efforts, the potential of learners to act as a force for RLS is not being fulfilled due to the fact that very few learners reach fluency in the language at present, largely as a result of the inadequacy of the Gaelic learning infrastructure. In this respect the findings of the survey corroborate the findings of earlier studies, suggesting that this picture is typical of the national Gaelic learning scene. The advanced average age of learners is also a matter for great concern.

Discussion

At the beginning of the twenty-first century, Gaelic finds itself in a very weak position. Language shift from Gaelic to English has reached a very advanced stage. This can be seen in terms of the declining numbers of Gaelic speakers, the low level of intergenerational transmission of the language, the increasingly elderly age profile of the speech community and the weakening of Gaelic as a community language (GROS 2005; MacKinnon 1997b, 1998a, 1998c, 1998d, 1999, Western Isles Language

Planning Project 2005). The numbers of children in Gaelic-medium education are still far from being able to compensate numerically for the number of Gaelic speakers dying each year (MacKinnon 1998c: 1, 1998d: 1; 2003) and it is far from certain in any case that Gaelic-medium education alone will lead to any significant degree of intergenerational transmission of the language given the generally very weak position of the language in the family and community (Fishman 1991: chapter 13, 2001: 15, McLeod 2002a: 285).[249]

For these reasons adult learners, and particularly young adult learners, must necessarily play a central role in the Gaelic community if any significant progress is to be made towards the goal of reversing language shift. Significant numbers of fluent adult learners of Gaelic are necessary to increase levels of intergenerational transmission of Gaelic, to reverse the decline of numbers in speakers, to add to the consumers and providers of Gaelic-related goods and services, to add to the number of those lobbying for the language and to overcome the difficulty in filling Gaelic-related jobs.

In addition to these objective factors, it has also been seen during the course of this study that learners can also aid RLS through more subjective qualities. Learners can expand the level of social diversity and the skills and experience base represented within the language community, for example, and often bring new viewpoints and enthusiasm to the language.

In investigating the experience of learning Gaelic in modern Scotland, this study has looked at whether learners have been able to become a central part of the Gaelic community and of RLS efforts. The findings of this study suggest that learners do not currently occupy such a central position and are, in fact, largely on the periphery both of the existing community of Gaelic speakers and even on the periphery of efforts to promote increased and more sustainable use of the language.

Gaelic learners are peripheral to the Gaelic speech community in terms of numbers. Largely as a result of the current infrastructure for learning Gaelic, very few Gaelic learners reach fluency at present. Census data suggests that around 700 new Gaelic speakers would have to be created each year to sustain numbers of Gaelic speakers at their current level. While no detailed research has yet been carried out into the number of fluent Gaelic learners, there can be no doubt that fewer than 700 learners are reaching fluency each year. In fact, the experience of the present author would suggest that there are fewer than 700 fluent learners of the language *in total*. Rather than significantly adding to the number of Gaelic speakers, learners form a small minority within Scotland's small minority of Gaelic speakers.

This situation could be undoubtedly be changed relatively quickly by determined government and Gaelic agency policy to ensure an effective infrastructure for Gaelic learning. That no such action has been taken to date reflects another conclusion of this study: that the Gaelic learning infrastructure is on the periphery of Gaelic development efforts. To date, Gaelic development policy and discourse has centred almost exclusively upon Gaelic-medium school education, Gaelic broadcasting and, to a lesser extent, on economic development. Gaelic learners have not formed a significant part of either Gaelic development policy or debate. This reflects the fact that Gaelic development efforts in Scotland do not tend to be based upon strategic planning or upon RLS theory (McLeod 2002a).

---

[249] For current statistics for the number of children in Gaelic-medium education, see http://www.cnag.org.uk/stats.

This study also found that even those learners reaching fluency in the language may still be on the periphery of the Gaelic community in many respects. The social position of the fluent Gaelic learner in relation to the community of native Gaelic speakers is in general an ambiguous and somewhat semi-detached one, with many learners finding it difficult to gain acceptance as Gaelic speakers.

In addition to its implications for the individual Gaelic learners, it has also been seen that the issue of the position which learners occupy within the Gaelic community has significant implications for RLS. Gaelic-related policy-making depends, whether consciously or unconsciously, on the view which policy-makers hold as to the nature of the Gaelic community.

Gaelic has tended in recent times to be spoken almost exclusively by people raised as native speakers in traditional Gaelic communities, principally in the Western Isles, and who tend to view the language as being closely tied to the lifestyle and culture of these islands. This perception of Gaelic is also very common amongst non-speakers of Gaelic. For these reasons, there has been a tendency for language policy and discourse to be based on a definition, whether conscious or unconscious, of the Gaelic community as a largely island-based community of native Gaelic speakers. Such a definition no longer fits the demography of Gaelic in present-day Scotland or the needs of RLS and has the practical effect of peripheralising Gaelic learners, the Gaelic learning infrastructure and Lowland Scotland in Gaelic development policies.[250]

The remaining community of traditional Gaelic speakers from the Highlands and Islands could be said to be on the periphery of Scotland in many senses. Numbering fewer than 60,000 members and constituting less than 1.5% of the Scottish population, this group is peripheral both in terms of numbers and of geography. The remaining geographical Gaelic communities, situated in the Inner and Outer Hebrides, are peripheral in that a large physical distance separates them from the Scottish power centres of the cities and Central Belt. While a majority of Gaelic speakers live outside the remaining Gaelic-speaking communities and are resident in areas of Scotland where Gaelic is not the community language, these Gaelic speakers are also peripheral in that they generally form a small minority of the population in the areas where they live.

In addition to the demography of the language, the language itself is also rather peripheral to Scottish life. Gaelic is not a major issue in mainstream Scottish politics or in the media and it is rarely seen or heard by most Scots. It would be fair to say that most people in Scotland are ignorant as to even the most basic information about the history and present situation of the language (McLeod 2001a: 6, McLeod 2001c: 96, A. Gillies 2000, Ó Maolalaigh 2000). It would also be fair to say that the connection between Gaelic and Scottish national identity tends to be weak, or even non-existent, in the mind of most Scots (McLeod 2001c: 91).

This study has seen that adult learners of Gaelic learners have a great potential to contribute to reversing language shift and by doing so to ensure that Gaelic becomes less peripheral to mainstream Scottish life in future. It has also been seen, however, that this potential is not being fulfilled at present. Rather than being able to play a central role in the Gaelic community, learners are at present on the periphery of this already peripheral group.

---

[250] For further discussion of the policy implications of the geographical distribution of the modern Gaelic community, see also MacCaluim, forthcoming 2007; MacCaluim and McLeod 2001.

Deficiencies in the Gaelic learning infrastructure mean that learners are not becoming fluent in sufficient numbers to have a significant impact on language revitalisation efforts. Learners are also peripheral to Gaelic development policy-making and strategy, neither of which reflect the importance to RLS of attracting and bringing increasing numbers of learners to fluency or the implications of this. At present, Gaelic learners could be said to be the Cinderella sector of the Gaelic world, being, as MacLennan has argued: "a largely ignored mass, it has to be said, under-financed and suffering from a complete dearth of provision which taxes their undoubted commitment to the very limit" (MacLennan 1996: 16).

As Morgan has argued above, Gaelic learners are no longer an "optional extra" for the Gaelic community. For language shift to be reversed in Scotland, it is essential that far larger numbers of Gaelic learners reach fluency and that learners move from the periphery to the centre of policy decisions on future Gaelic development. Reports to the Scottish Executive by the Taskforce on the Public Funding of Gaelic (2000) and the Ministerial Advisory Group on Gaelic (2002) recommended a reorganisation of the Gaelic development infrastructure through the establishment of a new Gaelic development board with a language planning approach. As a result of these, Bòrd na Gàidhlig, the Gaelic language board has been founded. This new organisation and the language planning approach upon which it is based offer an opportunity for the recognition of the significance and value of Gaelic learners. It can only be hoped that this opportunity will be taken to place Gaelic learners at the very heart of reversing language shift.

References

Allardyce, Jason 1996. 'Gaelic TV Channel Preferred', *The Scotsman,* 12 October, p. 4.
An Gàidheal Ùr 2002a. 'Tuilleadh phrògraman rèidio Gàidhlig', *An Gàidheal Ur,* An Cèitean 2002.
An Gàidheal Ùr 2002b. 'Ionad Gàidhlig Ghlaschu a' feitheamh ri co-dhùnadh', *An Gàidheal Ùr,* An Cèitean 2002.
Anderson, Benedict 1983. *Imagined Communities: Reflections on the Origin and Spread of Nationalism,* London: Verso.
Azkue, Jokin and Perales, Josu 2005. 'The Teaching of Basque to Adults', *International Journal of the Sociology of Language,* 174: 73–83.
Bagguley, Paul 1992. 'Social Change, the Middle Class and the Emergence of 'New Social Movements': A Critical Analysis', *Sociological Review,* 40, 26–47.
Bagguley, Paul 1995. 'Protest, Poverty and Power: A Case Study of the Anti-Poll Tax Movement', *Sociological Review,* 43: 693–719.
Bagguley, Paul 1997. 'Review article: Beyond political sociology? Developments in the sociology of social movements', *Sociological Review,* 45: 147–161.
BBC 1979. *Can Seo – a BBC Television course for beginners in Gaelic,* London: BBC.
BBC 1998. *BBC Digital – The Adventure Starts Here,* London: BBC.
BBC 2003. *Attitudes To The Gaelic Language* – an opinion survey by Market Research UK for the BBC, September 2003.
Beardsworth, Alan and Kial, Teresa 1992. 'The Vegetarian Option: Varieties, Conversations, Motives and Careers', *Sociological Review,* 40: 253–93.
Bentahila, Abdelali and Davies, Eirlys, 1993. 'Language Revival: Restoration or Transformation?', *Journal of Multilingual and Multicultural Development,* 14: 355–74.
Berresford Ellis, Peter 1993. *Celtic Dawn: Celtic survival in the modern world,* London: Constable.
Black, Andrew 2002. 'Minister's Gaelic action plan gets frosty reception', *The Press and Journal,* 15 June.
Black, Ronald 1992. *Cothrom Ionnsachaidh: A Chance to Learn – Scottish Gaelic Grammar and Exercises,* Edinburgh: University of Edinburgh Department of Celtic.
Black, Ronald 1999. *An Tuil – Anthology of 20th Century Scottish Gaelic Verse,* Edinburgh: Polygon.
Black, Ronald, Gillies, William and Ó Maolalaigh, Roibeard 1999. *Celtic Connections: Proceedings of the Tenth International Congress of Celtic Studies: Volume One: Language, Literature, History, Culture,* East Linton: Tuckwell Press.
Blacklaw, Bill 1978. *Bun-Chùrsa Gàidhlig – Scottish Gaelic, A Progressive Course,* Glasgow University Department of Celtic.
Blackie, John Stuart 1876. *The Language and Literature of the Scottish Highlands,* Edinburgh: Edmonston and Douglas.
Blackie, John Stuart 1882. *Altavona: Fact and Fiction from my Life in the Highlands,* Edinburgh: David Douglas.
Blackie, John Stuart 1910. *Notes of a Life,* Edinburgh: William Blackwood and Sons.
Bòrd na Gàidhlig 2004. *Aithisg Bhliadhnail / Annual Report 2003–4,* Inverness: Bòrd na Gàidhlig.
Bòrd na Gàidhlig 2005. *Aithisg Bhliadhnail / Annual Report 2004–5,* Inverness: Bòrd na Gàidhlig.

Bottomore, Tom 1954. 'Social Stratification in Voluntary Organisations' in *Social Mobility in Britain,* ed. by D. V. Glass, London: Routledge.
Bowie, Fiona 1993. 'Wales from Within: Conflicting Interpretations of Welsh Identity', in *Inside European Identities: Ethnography in Western Europe,* ed. by Sharon MacDonald, Oxford: Berg, 167–93.
Brown, Callum G. 1997. *Religion and Society in Scotland Since 1707,* Edinburgh: Edinburgh University Press.
Buchanan, Dougal and RLS Ltd. 1998. *Gaelic–English/English–Gaelic Dictionary,* New Lanark: Lomond Books.
Buchanan, Dougal and RLS Ltd. 2004. *Gaelic–English/English–Gaelic Dictionary,* New Lanark: Geddes and Grosset.
Byrne, Michel 2002. *Gràmar na Gàidhlig,* Cearsiadar: Stòrlann Nàiseanta na Gàidhlig and Stornoway: Acair.
Caimbeul, Maoilios 2006. *Gràmar na Gàidhlig: leabhar-teagaisg le earrannan leughaidh, eacarsaich is freagairtean,* Isle of Lewis: Stòrlann Nàiseanta na Gàidhlig.
Caimbeul, Tormod 2000. 'The Politics of Gaelic Development in Scotland', in *Aithne na nGael – Gaelic Identities,* ed. by Gordon McCoy with Maolcholaim Scott, Belfast: Institute of Irish Studies / ULTACH Trust, 53–66.
Campbell, Angus Peter 1999. 'Cò Mi agus Cò Às? / Who am I and From Whence?', *Cothrom* 19: 10–12.
Campbell, John Lorne 1945. *Gaelic in Scottish Education and Life: Past, Present and Future,* Edinburgh: Saltire Society.
Campbell, Kenna 1983. 'Gaelic' in *Minority Languages in Central Scotland,* ed. by J.D. McClure, 11–14. Aberdeen: Association for Scottish Literary Studies.
Chapman, Malcolm 1978. *The Gaelic Vision in Scottish Culture,* London: Croon Helm.
Chapman, Malcolm 1993. *The Celts: The Construction of a Myth,* London: St Martin's Press.
Comann-Bhioball na h-Alba 2002. *Tiomnadh Nuadh ar Tighearna agus ar Slanaighir Iosa Criosd / The New Testament of our Lord and our Saviour Jesus Christ,* Edinburgh: Comann-Bhioball na h-Alba.
Comann an Luchd-Ionnsachaidh 1984. *Cuairt Litir Ionnsachaidh,* 1.
Comann an Luchd-Ionnsachaidh 1984. *Cuairt Litir Ionnsachaidh,* 3.
Comann an Luchd-Ionnsachaidh 1985. *Cuairt Litir Ionnsachaidh,* 4.
Comann an Luchd-Ionnsachaidh 1987. *Cuairlitir ChLI / CLI Newsletter,* December.
Comann an Luchd-Ionnsachaidh 1994. *Cuairtlitir ChLI / CLI Newsletter,* June.
Comann an Luchd-Ionnsachaidh 1994. *Cuairtlitir ChLI / CLI Newsletter,* September.
Comann an Luchd-Ionnsachaidh 1995. *Cothrom,* 4, Samhradh 1995.
Comataidh Craolaidh Gàidhlig 1997. *Gaelic Broadcasting: New Dimensions for a New Millennium – Draft Discussion Paper.*
Comataidh Craolaidh Gàidhlig 1998. *Aithisg Bhliadhnail agus Cunntasan / Annual Report and Accounts 1997–8.*
Comataidh Telebhisean Gàidhlig 1993. *Aithisg Bhliadhnail agus Cunntasan / Annual Report and Accounts 1992–3.*
Comataidh Telebhisean Gàidhlig 1994. *Aithisg Bhliadhnail agus Cunntasan / Annual Report and Accounts 1993–4.*
Comataidh Telebhisean Gàidhlig 1995. *Aithisg Bhliadhnail agus Cunntasan / Annual Report and Accounts 1994–5.*
Comataidh Telebhisean Gàidhlig 1996. *Aithisg Bhliadhnail agus Cunntasan / Annual Report and Accounts 1995–6.*

Comataidh Telebhisean Gàidhlig 1997. *Aithisg Bhliadhnail agus Cunntasan / Annual Report and Accounts 1996–7.*
Comhairle nan Eilean Siar 2006. *Gaelic Policy Implementation: Pilot Phase – Education Provision Consultation Document – February 2006,* Stornoway: Comhairle nan Eilean Siar.
Comhluadar and Foras na Gaeilge 2001. *Ag tógáil clainne le Gaeilge-treoirleabhar do thuismitheoirí / Speaking Irish at home – a guide for parents,* Dublin: Comhluadar and Foras na Gaeilge.
Comunn na Gàidhlig and Comann an Luchd-Ionnsachaidh 1992. *Feumalachdan Luchd-Ionnsachaidh – Rannsachadh Nàiseanta / Provision for Gaelic Learners' – a National Survey,* Inverness: Comunn na Gàidhlig.
Comunn na Gàidhlig 1995. *Thig a Theagasg,* [Gaelic teacher training promotional pack], Inverness: Comunn na Gàidhlig.
Comunn na Gàidhlig 1997a. *Securing the Future for Gaelic,* Inverness: Comunn na Gàidhlig.
Comunn na Gàidhlig 1997b. *Inbhe Thèarainte dhan Ghàidhlig: Secure Status for Gaelic,* Inverness: Comunn na Gàidhlig.
Comunn na Gàidhlig 1997c. *Innleachd airson Adhartais: Poileasaidh Nàiseanta airson Foghlaim Gàidhlig / Framework for Growth: A National Policy for Gaelic Education,* Inverness: Comunn na Gàidhlig.
Comunn na Gàidhlig 1997d. *Fios is Freagairt – Information for parents in Gaelic education,* Inverness: Comunn na Gàidhlig.
Comunn na Gàidhlig 1998. *Còmhdhail 98 Annual Congress: Bho linn gu linn – Gaelic's New Millennium,* Inverness: Comunn na Gàidhlig.
Comunn na Gàidhlig 1999a. *Inbhe Thèarainte dhan Ghàidhlig – Dreach Iùl airson Achd Gàidhlig / Secure Status for Gaelic – Draft Brief for a Gaelic Language Act.*
Comunn na Gàidhlig 1999b. *Gàidhlig PLC: Plana Leasachaidh Gàidhlig / A Development Plan for Gaelic,* Inverness: Comunn na Gàidhlig.
Comunn na Gàidhlig 2000. *Bith Beò ann an Gàidhlig: Gaelic Career Opportunities,* Inverness: Comunn na Gàidhlig.
Comunn na Gàidhlig, Gaelic Educational Trust, Glasgow City Council, Glasgow Development Agency 2000. *Glasgow Gaelic Centre – Summary Report.*
Cormack, Art 2000. Lecture to annual Gaelic Congress, Nairn, 8 September.
Cormack, Mike 1994. 'Programming for Cultural Defence: The Expansion of Gaelic Television', *Scottish Affairs,* 6: 114–39.
Cormack, Mike 1995. 'The Use of Gaelic in Scottish Newspapers', *Journal of Multilingual and Multicultural Development,* 16: 269-80.
Cormack, Mike 2006. 'The media, language maintenance and Gaelic', in *Revitalising Gaelic in Scotland: Policy, Planning and Public Discourse,* ed. by Wilson McLeod, Edinburgh: Dunedin Academic Press, 211–19.
Cotgrove, Stephen and Duff, Andrew 1980. 'Environmentalism, Middle Class Radicalism and Politics', *Sociological Review,* 28: 333–51.
Cox, Richard A.V. 1991. *Brìgh nam Facal: Faclair Ùr don Bhun-sgoil,* Glasgow University Department of Celtic.
Cox, Richard A.V. 1998. 'Tokenism in Gaelic', *Scottish Language,* 17: 70–5.
Davies, Alan 2003. *The Native Speaker, Myth and Reality*, Clevedon, Multilingual Matters.
Davies, Janet 1993. *The Welsh Language,* Cardiff: The University of Wales Press.

Department of Transport and Industry / Department of Culture Media and Sport 2002. *Draft Communications Bill – A New Future for Communications,* London: DTI/DCMI.
Dieckhoff, Henry Cyril 1992. *A Pronouncing Dictionary of Scottish Gaelic,* Glasgow: Gairm.
Dòmhnallach, Aonghas 2006. 'Nuair a Chaidh Sinn Uil' Air Bòrd Innt", *Press and Journal,* 4 February.
Dorian, Nancy C. 1970. 'A Substitute Name System in the Scottish Highlands', *American Anthropoligist,* 72: 303–319.
Dorian, Nancy C. 1979. 'Traditions End: A Threatened Language and Culture', *Philological Quarterly,* 58.
Dorian, Nancy C. 1980. 'Linguistic Lag as an Ethnic Marker', *Language in Society,* 9: 33–41.
Dorian, Nancy C. 1981. 'The Valuation of Gaelic by Different Mother-Tongue Groups Resident; in The Highlands', *Scottish Gaelic Studies,* 13: 169–82.
Dorian, Nancy C. 1987. 'The Value of Language Maintenance Efforts Which are Unlikely to Succeed', *International Journal of the Sociology of Language,* 68, 57–67.
Dunbar, Robert 2000. 'Legal and Institutional Aspects of Gaelic Development', in *Aithne na nGael – Gaelic Identities,* ed. by Gordon McCoy with Maolcholaim Scott, Belfast: Institute of Irish Studies / ULTACH Trust, 67–87.
Dunbar, Robert 2006. 'Gaelic in Scotland: The Legal and Institutional Framework', in *Revitalising Gaelic in Scotland: Policy, Planning and Public Discourse,* ed. by Wilson McLeod, Edinburgh: Dunedin Academic Press, 1–23.
Dunn, Catherine M. and Robertson, A. G. B. 1989. 'Gaelic in Education', in *Gaelic and Scotland,* ed. by William Gillies, Edinburgh: Edinburgh University Press, 44–55.
Dwelly, Edward 1911. *The Illustrated Gaelic–English Dictionary,* 1994 edition, Glasgow: Gairm.
Ferguson, Calum n.d. *Sàth: the Gaelic Teaching Course,* Glasgow: Gaelfonn Recordings.
Fishman, Joshua A. (ed.) 1985. *The Rise and Fall of the Ethnic Revival: Perspectives on Language and Ethnicity,* Berlin: Mouton.
Fishman, Joshua A. 1991. *Reversing Language Shift – Theoretical and Empirical Foundations of Assistance to Threatened Languages,* Clevedon: Multilingual Matters.
Fishman, Joshua A. (ed.) 2001. *Can Threatened Languages be Saved?,* Clevedon: Multilingual Matters.
Forster, Peter G. 1982. *The Esperanto Movement,* The Hague: Mouton.
Fraser, Anne 1989. *Gaelic Primary Education: A Study of the Development of Gaelic Bilingual Education in Urban Contexts',* unpublished Ph.D thesis, University of Glasgow.
Fraser, Neil 1998. *A Review of Aspects of Gaelic Broadcasting,* Edinburgh: Scottish Office Education and Industry Department, Arts and Cultural Heritage Division.
Gaelic Broadcasting Taskforce 2000. *Gaelic Television: A Dedicated Channel,* Edinburgh: The Scottish Executive.
Gaelic Media Service 2006. News release: *New Digital Service gets the go ahead*.
Gaelic Medium Teachers' Action Group 2005. *The report of the Gaelic Medium Teachers' Action Group,* Edinburgh: The Scottish Executive.

Gàidhlig '96 1997. *Gàidhlig '96 Project Manager's Report from 4 March to 15 December 1996.*
Gàidhlig '97 1997. *Gaelic Matters – A Week of Activities as Part of Gàidhlig '97.*
Galloway, John 1994. 'The Gaelic Job Market', in *Studies in Scots and Gaelic, Proceedings of the Third International Conference on the Languages of Scotland,* ed. by Alexander Fenton and Donald A. MacDonald, Edinburgh: Canongate 138–48.
Galloway, John 1995a. *The Role of Employment in Gaelic Language Maintenance and Development,* unpublished PhD thesis, University of Edinburgh.
Galloway, John 1995b. *Estimation of the Number and Distribution of Adult Learners of Gaelic: Final Report,* Inverness: Comunn na Gàidhlig.
Gawne, Philip 1999. *Survey of Manx Speakers and Learners: Preliminary Findings,* Manx National Heritage and Manx Heritage Foundation.
General Register Office for Scotland 1994. *1991 Census/Cunntas-Sluaigh 1991, Gaelic Language / A 'Ghàidhlig, Scotland/Alba.* Edinburgh: HMSO.
General Register Office for Scotland 2005. *Scotland's Census 2001: Gaelic Report,* Edinburgh, GRO(S).
Gillies, Anne Lorne 2000. 'Creating Culture', in *Aithne na nGael – Gaelic Identities,* ed. by Gordon McCoy with Maolcholaim Scott, Belfast: Institute of Irish Studies / ULTACH Trust, 96–104.
Gillies, William 1987. 'Scottish Gaelic – The Present Situation', in *Third International Conference on Minority Languages: Celtic Papers,* ed. by Donncha Ó hAodha, Anders Ahlqvist and Gearóid MacEoin, Clevedon: Multilingual Matters, 27–45.
Gillies, William 1989a. 'A Century of Gaelic Scholarship', in *Gaelic and Scotland,* ed. by William Gillies, Edinburgh: Edinburgh University Press, 3–21.
Gillies, William 1989b. 'The Future of Scottish Gaelic Studies', in *Gaelic and Scotland,* ed. by William Gillies, Edinburgh: Edinburgh University Press, 22–43.
Gillies, William 1994 'A Gaelic Thesaurus', in *Studies in Scots and Gaelic: Proceedings of the Third International Conference on the Languages of Scotland,* ed. by Alexander Fenton and Donald A MacDonald, Edinburgh: Canongate, 149–62.
Glaser, Konstanze 2004. 'Ethno-Cultural continuity through language: The case of Scots Gaelic', in *Communicating Cultures,* ed. by Ullrich Kockel and Máiréad Nic Craith, Münster: Lit Verlag, 176–97.
Glaser, Konstanze 2006. 'Reimagining the Gaelic community: ethnicity, hybridity, politics and communication', in *Revitalising Gaelic in Scotland: Policy, Planning and Public Discourse,* ed. by Wilson McLeod, Edinburgh: Dunedin Academic Press, 169-184.
Glaser, Konstanze, Forthcoming 2007. *Minority Languages and Cultural Diversity in Europe: Gaelic and Sorbian Perspectives,* Clevedon: Multilingual Matters,
Grampian Television 1994. *Viewers Choice – Television in the North of Scotland.*
Grampian Television 1994. *Attitudes to Gaelic Television in North Scotland.*
Grampian Television 1997. *The Root of the Story – Opinions of Gaelic Speaking Viewers in North Scotland.*
Grampian Television 1996. *Viewers Choice – Television in the North of Scotland.*
Grin, Francois, and Vaillancourt, Francois 1999. *The Cost-Effectiveness Evaluation of Minority Language Policies: Case studies on Wales, Ireland and the Basque Country,* Flesburg, Germany: European Centre for Minority Issues.

Hanham, H. J. 1969. *Scottish Nationalism*, London: Faber and Faber.
The Herald 1999. 'Gaelic Lecture "not electioneering"', *The Herald*, 24 August.
Hicks, Davyth and Stiùbhart, Domhnall Uilleam 2000. 'Wilson MacLeòid: aiseirigh gun phlana', *The Scotsman*, 28 April.
Hindley, Reg 1990. *The Death of the Irish Language: A Qualified Obituary*, London: Routledge.
Hindley, Reg 1993. 'Lessons from Irish Experience: Some Dangers of Gaelic Language "Revival" Policies and Methods', paper presented at *FASGNAG II: Second Conference on Research and Studies on the Maintenance of Gaelic*, Sabhal Mòr Ostaig, 24–26 March.
Hirner, Ute 1997. *Language Death and Revival: A Sociolinguistic Investigation of Cornish and Welsh*, unpublished MA thesis, Department of English, Graz University.
HMIE 2005. *Improving Achievement in Gaelic – HMIE Improvement Series* [available online at www.hmie.gov.uk/documents/publication/iage.htm].
Hornberger N.H and King K. A. 2001. 'Reversing Quechua Language Shift in South America', in *Can Threatened Languages be Saved?*, ed. by Joshua A. Fishman. Clevedon: Multilingual Matters, 166–94.
Hunter, Janet 1995. *Report on the Survey of Gaelic and Gaelic-related Courses in the University of Aberdeen*, Aberdeen University Department of Celtic.
Hutchinson, Roger 1995. *A Waxing Moon: The Modern Gaelic Revival*, Edinburgh: Mainstream Publishing.
Jones, Noragh 1989. 'Blod and the Brush Salesman', *Planet* 76: 9–13.
Johnstone, Richard 1994. *The Impact of Current Developments to Support the Gaelic Language – Review of Research*, Stirling: Scottish CILT.
Kabel, Lars 2000. 'Irish Language Enthusiasts and Native Speakers: an Uneasy Relationship', *in Aithne na nGael – Gaelic Identities*, ed. by Gordon McCoy with Maolcholaim Scott, Belfast: Institute of Irish Studies / ULTACH Trust, 133–8.
Kennedy, Howard Angus 1895. *Professor Blackie: His Sayings and Doings*, London: James Clark and Co.
Lang, Alison 2006. 'Cruthachadh is cleachdadh: ceistean air planadh cànain agus na h-ealain Ghàidhlig', in *Revitalising Gaelic in Scotland: Policy, Planning and Public Discourse*, ed. by Wilson McLeod, Edinburgh: Dunedin Academic Press, 199-240.
Lang, Alison and McLeod, Wilson, 2005. 'Gaelic Culture for sale: language dynamics in the marketing of Gaelic music', paper presented at the Fourth Mercator International Symposium, Aberystwyth, 26–28 October (available at: http://www.aber.ac.uk/~merwww/english/events/mercSym2005papers.htm)
Learning and Teaching Scotland 2002. *Education for Citizenship in Scotland: A Paper for Development*, Dundee: Learning Teaching Scotland.
Leyland, Janet 1996. 'Irish Language Learners in North-West England', in *Watching One's Tongue: Issues in Language Planning*, ed. by Máiréad Nic Craith, Liverpool: Liverpool University Press, 145–75.
Lìon 1999. Proposed Consultancy Study on Gaelic Learning Infrastructure.
Lloyd, David 1995. 'Wales, Welsh-L, and the Internet', *Planet* 116, 77–80.
Lloyd Humphreys, Humphrey 1992. 'The Breton Language', in *The Celtic Connection*, ed. by Glanville Price, Gerrards Cross: Colin Smythe, 245–275.
Lo Bianco, Joseph 1991. *Language and Literacy Policy in Scotland*, Stirling: Scottish CILT.

McAllister Groves, Julian 1992. 'Learning to Feel: The Neglected Sociology of Social Movements', *Sociological Review*, 43: 435–461.
MacAlpine, Neil 1971. *Pronouncing Gaelic–English Dictionary*, Glasgow: Gairm.
MacAulay, Donald 1994. 'Canons, Myths and Cannon Fodder', *Scotlands*, 1: 35–54.
MacBain, Alexander 1982. *An Etymological Dictionary of the Gaelic Language*, Glasgow: Gairm.
MacCaluim, Alasdair 1995. 'Cò tha ag Ionnsachadh na Gàidhlig agus Carson? Who Learns Scottish Gaelic and Why', unpublished M.A dissertation, University of Glasgow.
MacCaluim, Alasdair 1998a. Review of *Reimagining Culture: Histories, Identities and the Gaelic Renaissance* by Sharon MacDonald, *Cothrom*, 16: 52–4.
MacCaluim, Alasdair 1998b. 'Nach cuir thu air an teilidh – tha mi 'g iarraidh rudeigin a leughadh' *The Scotsman*, 25 November, p. 15.
MacCaluim, Alasdair 2001. Review of *Aithne na nGael / Gaelic Identities* ed. by McCoy with Maolcholaim Scott', *Cothrom*, 27: 52–6.
MacCaluim, Alasdair 2002. *Periphery of the Periphery? Adult Learners of Scottish Gaelic and Reversal of Language Shift*, unpublished PhD thesis, University of Edinburgh.
MacCaluim, Alasdair 2006. 'Air iomall an iomaill? Luchd-Ionnsachaidh na Gàidhlig ann an ath-thilleadh gluasad cànain', in *Revitalising Gaelic in Scotland: Policy, Planning and Public Discourse*, ed. by Wilson McLeod, Edinburgh: Dunedin Academic Press, 185–97.
MacCaluim, Alasdair forthcoming 2007. '"More than Interesting": Gàidhlig anns a' Bhaile Mhòr', in *Gàidhealtachdan Ùra: Leasachadh na Gàidhlig anns a' Bhaile Mhòr*, ed. by Wilson McLeod, Edinburgh: Celtic and Scottish Studies, University of Edinburgh.
MacCaluim, Alasdair with McLeod, Wilson 2001. *Revitalising Gaelic? A Critical Analysis of the Taskforce on Public Funding of Gaelic*, Edinburgh: Celtic and Scottish Studies, University of Edinburgh, published online at: http://www.arts.ed.ac.uk/celtic/poileasaidh/
McCoy, Gordon 1997. *Protestants and the Irish Language in Northern Ireland*, unpublished PhD thesis, Queen's University Belfast.
McCrone, David 1992. *Understanding Scotland: The Sociology of a Stateless Nation*, London: Routledge.
MacDonald, Lorraine 1999. 'Language Culture and Identity', *Dalriada, the Journal of Celtic Culture, Heritage and Traditions*, 14: 26-30.
Macdonald, J.A. 1976. *Gàidhlig Bheò*, Cambridge: National Extension College, Cambridge.
McDonald, Maryon 1989. *We are not French! Language, Culture and Identity in Brittany*, London: Routledge.
MacDonald, Rhoda 1993. 'Renaissance v Preservation', *Media Education Journal*, 14: 11–13.
Macdonald, Sharon 1997. *Reimagining Culture: Histories, Identities and the Gaelic Renaissance*, Oxford: Berg.
Macdonald, Sharon 1999. 'The Gaelic Renaissance and Scotland's Identities', *Scottish Affairs*, 26: 100–18.
McEwan-Fujita, Emily 1997. 'From "The rude speech of barbarous people" to "Scotland's Celtic Legacy": Ideologies of Revival and Revitalisation in Gaelic–English Contact', *Chicago Linguistics Society 33: Papers from the Panels*, 75–83.

McEwan-Fujita, Emily 1998. *Scottish Gaelic and the Politics of Ethnicity in Contemporary Scotland,* unpublished M.A thesis, Department of Anthropology, University of Chicago.
MacIlleathain, Ruaraidh 1997. 'Eil an t-àm ann air son Pàrlamaid do na Gàidhil?', *The Scotsman,* 20 June.
MacIlleathain, Ruaraidh 2000. 'Gun ach lethcheud mile Gaidheal air fhàgail?', *The Scotsman,* 11 May.
MacIlleathain, Ruairidh 2005. *Leabhar nan Litrichean: Litir do Luchd-Ionnsachaidh 1–200 as broadcast on BBC Radio nan Gàidheal,* Inverness: Clì Gàidhlig.
MacIlleathain, Ruairidh 2006. *Ceum air cheum: leabhran taice do Luchd-stiùiridh Chlasaichean Còmhraidh Gàidhlig / Handbook for Tutors of Gaelic Conversation Classes,* Stornoway: Stòrlann Nàiseanta na Gàidhlig.
MacIlleChiar, Iain 1985. 'Adult Education: The Language Issue – Repressed or Exorcised', in *Gaelic – Looking to the Future,* ed. by John Hulbert, Dundee: Andrew Fletcher Society, 41–5.
MacIlleChiar, Iain 1985. 'Gaelic Medium Schools – Why? and When?' in *Gaelic – Looking to the Future,* ed. by John Hulbert, Dundee: Andrew Fletcher Society, 28–33.
MacInnes, John 1989. 'The Gaelic Perception of the Lowlands', in *Gaelic and Scotland* ed. by William Gillies, Edinburgh: Edinburgh University Press, 89–100.
MacInnes, John 1992. The Scottish Gaelic Language', in *The Celtic Connection,* ed. by Glanville Price, Gerrards Cross: Colin Smythe, 101–30.
MacIver, Margaret 2001. *Gaelic Medium Secondary Provision Throughout Scotland: the Present Position,* paper to Gaelic Secondary Provision Seminar, East Ayrshire Council, 5 September.
McKay, Girvan 1974. *English–Gaelic Key to Dwelly's Illustrated Gaelic-English Dictionary,* Glasgow: Gairm.
McKee, Vincent 1994. 'Politics of the Gaelic Language in Northern Ireland and the Scottish Hebrides: A Focus for Contrast, Part one – Historical Overview', *South Bank University Politics Division Occasional Papers 3, Questions of Ideology,* 34–48.
McKee, Vincent 1997. *Gaelic Nations: Politics of the Gaelic Language in Scotland and Northern Ireland in the 20th Century,* London: Bluestack Press.
Mackechnie, John 1962. *Gaelic without Groans,* Edinburgh: Oliver and Boyd.
MacKinnon, Kenneth 1972a. *Language Education and Social Processes in a Gaelic Community* London: Routledge and Kegan Paul.
MacKinnon, Kenneth 1972b. 'Education and Social Control: The Case of Gaelic Scotland', *Scottish Education Studies,* 4: 125–37.
MacKinnon, Kenneth, 1974. *The Lion's Tongue,* Inverness: Club Leabhar.
MacKinnon, Kenneth 1981. *Scottish Opinion on Gaelic,* Hatfield: Hatfield Polytechnic.
MacKinnon, Kenneth 1984. 'Power at the Periphery: The Language Dimension – and the Case of Gaelic Scotland', *Journal of Multilingual and Multicultural Development,* 5: 491–510.
MacKinnon, Kenneth 1985. 'Gaelic in the Census: A Tenacious Survival', in *Gaelic – Looking to the Future,* ed. by John Hulbert, Dundee: Andrew Fletcher Society, 11–21.
MacKinnon, Kenneth 1988. 'A Century on the Census', in *Gaelic and Scots in Harmony – Proceedings of the Second International Conference on the Languages of Scotland,* ed. by Derick S. Thomson, Glasgow: Glasgow University Department of Celtic, 163–83.

MacKinnon, Kenneth 1991a. *Gaelic – A Past and Future Prospect*, Edinburgh: Saltire Society.
MacKinnon, Kenneth 1991b. 'The Gaelic Speech Community', in *Multilingualism in the British Isles The Older Mother Tongues and Europe*, ed. by Safder Allandina and Viv Edwards, London: Longman, ch. 3.
MacKinnon, Kenneth 1997a. 'Gaelic as an Endangered Language – Problems and Prospects', paper presented to the workshop in Endangered Languages: Steps in Language Rescue, University of York, 26–27 July.
MacKinnon, Kenneth 1997b. 'Minority Languages in an Integrating Europe: Prospects for Viability and Maintenance', in *Language Minorities and Minority Languages in a Changing Europe, Proceedings of Sixth International Conference on Minority Languages, Gdansk 1–5 July 1996*, ed. by B. Synak and T. Wicherkiewicz, Gdansk: Wydawníctwo Uníwerstetu Gdanskíego, 93–108.
MacKinnon, Kenneth 1998a. 'Identity, Attitudes and Support for Gaelic Policies: Gaelic Speakers in the Euromosaic Survey 1994–95', paper presented to British Sociological Association Scottish Conference: Scotland's Boundaries and Identities in the New Millennium (available at www.sgrud.org.uk/anfy/gaelic_articles/euromosiac_identity_belf.htm)
MacKinnon, Kenneth 1998b. 'Celtic Language-Groups and their Millennium: Social and Demographic Perspectives', paper presented to the New Directions in Celtic Studies Conference, Institute of Cornish Studies, Truro, 13–14 November.
MacKinnon, Kenneth 1998c. 'Learning Gaelic in the New Millennium', paper presented to the Lìon Gaelic Learners' Conference, 4 December.
MacKinnon, Kenneth 1998d. 'Gaelic in Family, Work and Community Domains: Euromosaic Project 1994–95', *Scottish Language*, 17: 55–69 (available on the Internet at http://www.sgrud.org.uk/anfy/celtic/language_use.htm).
MacKinnon, Kenneth 1999. 'Can the Heartlands Hold? Prospects of post-modern speech communities in the Celtic Homelands', paper presented to the 11 International Congress of Celtic Studies, University College Cork, 25–31 July, (available at http://www.sgrud.org.uk/anfy/gaelic_articles/ 11_celt_cong.htm).
MacKinnon, Kenneth 2000. 'Neighbours in Persistence – Prospects for Gaelic Maintenance in a Globalising English World', in *Aithne na nGael – Gaelic Identities*, ed. by Gordon McCoy with Maolcholaim Scott, Belfast: Institute of Irish Studies / ULTACH Trust, 144–55.
MacKinnon, Kenneth 2003. *Bòrd Gàidhlig na h-Alba: New Thinking for a Fresh Start?*, seminar paper presented to Edinburgh Department of Celtic and Scottish Studies, 05.03.03 (available at http://www.arts.ed.ac.uk /celtic/poileasaidh/newthinking/index.html)
MacKinnon, Kenneth 2006a. 'The Western Isles Language Plan: Gaelic–English language shift 1972–2001', in *Revitalising Gaelic in Scotland: Policy, Planning and Public Discourse*, ed. by Wilson McLeod, Edinburgh: Dunedin Academic Press, 49–61.
MacKinnon, Kenneth 2006b. 'Migration, Family and Education in Gaelic Policy Perspective', paper presented to a Language Planning and Policy Seminar, University of Edinburgh, 8 March. (Available at www.sgrud.org.uk)
MacKinnon, Roderick 1971. *Teach Yourself Gaelic*, Sevenoaks, Kent: Hodder and Stoughton.

MacLennan, Malcolm 1979. *A Pronouncing and Etymological Dictionary of the Gaelic Language: Gaelic-English, English–Gaelic,* Stornoway: Acair / Aberdeen: Aberdeen University Press.

MacLennan, Hugh Dan 1996. '1995 Confcrence on Gaelic Learners / Co-Labhairt an Luchd-Ionnsachaidh '95', *Cothrom* 6: 16–17.

MacLeod, John 1996. 'Mu thèid a' Ghàidhlig a chuir gu bas, chan aithnich Gaidheil an latha a-màireach na h-ealain san cultur aca fhèin (if Gaelic is lost, tomorrow's Highlanders will be strangers to their own art and culture)', *Daily Mail,* 13 September.

MacLeod, Catherine 2005. 'Anger as Gaelic time cut in digital TV deal', *The Herald*, 2 November.

MacLeod, Donald 1995. 'Footnotes', *West Highland Free Press,* 6 October.

MacLeod, Donald 1998. 'Footnotes', *West Highland Free Press,* 2 July.

MacLeod, Donald 1999. 'Footnotes', *West Highland Free Press,* 26 June.

MacLeod, Donald 2002. 'Footnotes', *West Highland Free Press,* 8 March.

McLeod, Wilson 1996. *Official Status for Gaelic: Prospects and Problems,* unpublished M.Sc thesis, Edinburgh University.

McLeod, Wilson 1997. 'Official Status for Gaelic: Prospects and Problems', *Scottish Affairs,* 21: 95–118.

McLeod, Wilson 1998a. *Computer-Assisted Learning for Gaelic: Towards a Common Teaching Core,* Edinburgh: Board of Celtic Studies (Scotland).

McLeod, Wilson 1998b. 'Scotland's Languages in Scotland's Parliament', *Scottish Affairs,* 24: 68–82.

McLeod, Wilson 1998c. 'Autochthonous language communities and the Race Relations Act', in 1998 *Web Journal of Current Legal Issues,* no. 1 (available at http://webicli.ncl.ac.uk/1998/issue1/mcleodl.html).

McLeod, Wilson 2000. 'A' Dealbh Linn Ùr dhan Ghàidhlig / Planning a Future for Gaelic', *Cothrom,* 24: 15–6.

McLeod, Wilson 2001a. 'Gaelic in the New Scotland: Politics, Rhetoric, and Public Discourse', *Journal on Ethnopolitic and Minority Issues* (July 2001), (available at http://www.ecmi.de/jeniie/download/JEMIE02MacLeodlO-07-01.pdf)

McLeod, Wilson 2001b. *The State of the 'Gaelic Economy': A Research Report.* Edinburgh: Department of Celtic and Scottish Studies, University of Edinburgh (available at http://www.arts.ed.ac.uk/celtic/poileasaidh/ GAELJOBSREP3.htm)

McLeod, Wilson 2001c. 'A ' Ghàidhlig anns an 21mh Linn: Sùil air Adhart', *Léachtaí Cholm Cille*, 31, 90–109.

McLeod, Wilson 2002a. 'Gaelic in Scotland: A "Renaissance" Without Planning', in *Hizkuntza Biziberritzeko Saoiak / Experiencias de Inversión del Cambio Lingüístico / Récupération de la Perte Linguistique / Reversing Language Shift*, Vitoria-Gasteiz: Eusko Jaurlaritzaren Argitalpen, Zerbitzu Nagusia/Servicio Central de Publicaciones del Gobierno Vasco, 279–95.

McLeod, Wilson 2002b. 'Language Planning as Regional Development: The Growth of the Gaelic Economy', *Scottish Affairs,* 38: 51–72.

McLeod, Wilson 2003a. 'Àireamhan Ùra is Dùbhlain Ùra: sùil air cor na Gàidhlig', *Gath*, 1: 7–10.

McLeod, Wilson 2003b. 'Gàidhlig agus an Eaconamaidh: Nàdar nan Deasbadan ann an Alba An-Diugh', in *Towards Our Goals in Broadcasting, the Press, the Performing Arts and the Economy: Minority Languages in Northern Ireland, the Republic of Ireland, and Scotland*, ed. by John M. Kirk and Dónall P. Ó Baoill, Belfast: Cló Ollscoil na Banríona, 238–44.

McLeod, Wilson 2004. 'Lessons from Gaelic-Medium Higher Education in Scotland', in *Ollscolaíocht Ghaeilge: Dúshláin agus Léargais – Páipéir Chomhdhála / University Education in Irish: Challenges and Perspectives – Conference Papers*, ed. by Caoilfhionn Nic Pháidín and Donla uí Bhraonáin, Dublin: FIONTAR, Dublin City University, 43–51.

McLeod, Wilson 2005. *Gàidhlig ann an Dùn Èideann: Cleachdadh agus Beachdan / Gaelic in Edinburgh: Usage and Attitudes*, Edinburgh: Celtic and Scottish Studies, University of Edinburgh.

McLeod, Wilson 2006a. 'Leasachadh solarachadh sheirbhisean poblach tro mheadhan na Gàidhlig:duilgheadasan idè-eòlach agus pragtaigeach', in *Revitalising Gaelic in Scotland: Policy, Planning and Public Discourse*, ed. by Wilson McLeod, Edinburgh: Dunedin Academic Press, 25–47.

McLeod, Wilson 2006b. 'Securing the Status of Gaelic? Implementing the *Gaelic Language (Scotland) Act 2005*', *Scottish Affairs*, 57: 19–38.

MacLeòid, Murchadh 1999. 'Mì-rùn nan Gaidheal – am bheil a leithid ann?', *The Scotsman,* 13 January.

MacLeòid, Murchadh 2006a. 'Chan fhaigh sinn bàs: Chan eil, chan eil, chan eil', *Scotland on Sunday,* 12 March.

MacLeòid, Murchadh 2006b. 'An sianail Gàidhlig: cnap-starradh eile air falbh', *Scotland on Sunday,* 7 May.

MacNeil, Morag M. and Beaton N. 1994. *Immersion Teaching and Language Learning: Meeting the Needs of the Gaelic Economy,* Isle of Skye: Sabhal Mòr Ostaig, Lèirsinn.

MacNeil, Morag M. and MacDonald, Brian K. 1997. *Gaelic Television Programmes as a Resource for Language Learning,* Isle of Skye: Lèirsinn and Comataidh Craolaidh Gàidhlig.

Mac Pàdraig, Mìcheil Rob 1998. 'Despairing of Native Speakers', *Cothrom* 16: 14–15.

MacSween, Annie 1990. *Abair,* Stornoway: Acair and Comunn na Gàidhlig.

Maguire, Gabrielle 1987. 'Language Revival in an Urban Neo-Gaeltacht', in *Third International Conference on Minority Languages: Celtic Papers,* ed. by Donncha Ó hAodha, Anders Ahlqvist and Gearóid MacEoin, Clevedon: Multilingual Matters, 73–88.

Maguire, Gabrielle 1990. *Our Own Language – An Irish Initiative,* Clevedon: Multilingual Matters.

Malcolm, Ian 1997. 'Living with Irish', in *The Irish Language in Northern Ireland,* ed. by Aodán Mac Póilin, Belfast: ULTACH Trust, 7-31.

Martin, Iain 1996. 'Study Dashes Hopes of a Gaelic Revival', *The Sunday Times,* 11 August, p. 7.

Mark, Colin 2004. *The Gaelic–English Dictionary – Am Faclair Gàidhlig–Beurla,* London: Routledge.

Maté, Iain 1996. *Scots Language. A Report on the Scots Language Research carried out by the General Register Office for Scotland in 1996,* Edinburgh General Register Office (Scotland).

Ministerial Advisory Group on Gaelic 2002. *A Fresh Start – Report by Ministerial Advisory Group on Gaelic / Cothrom Ùr don Ghàidhlig – Aithisg le Buidheann Comhairleachaidh an Riaghaltais air Gàidhlig,* Inverness: Ministerial Advisory Group on Gaelic.

Ministerial Action Group on Languages 2000. *Citizens of a Multilingual World,* Edinburgh: Scottish Executive.

Moffat, Alistair 1995. *Dreams and Deconstructions / Dòchas agus Dì-chruthachadh: The Sabhal Mòr Lecture 1995,* Glasgow: Sabhal Mòr Ostaig and Scottish Television.
Montgomery, Mary 1989. *A Study of the Attitudes Towards Learning Gaelic Among Adult Learners of the Language in Glasgow,* unpublished dissertation undertaken as part-fulfilment of the Diploma of Adult Education, University Glasgow Department of Adult and Continuing Education.
Morgan, Peadar 1992. 'A' Tumadh anns a' Ghàidhlig', *Carn,* 77: 2.
Morgan, Peadar 1997. 'San dol Seachad', *Cothrom* 11: 9.
Morgan, Peadar 2000. 'The Gael is Dead; Long Live the Gaelic – The Changing Relationship Between Native and Learner Gaelic Users', in *Aithne na nGael – Gaelic Identities,* ed. by Gordon McCoy with Maolcholaim Scott, Belfast: Institute of Irish Studies / ULTACH Trust, 126–33.
Neill, Uilleam 1997a. 'Gàidhlig ann no Às (1)', *Gairm,* air. 179: 248–51.
Neill, Uilleam 1997b. 'Gàidhlig thall 's a bhos', *Gairm,* air. 181: 48–53.
Neill, Uilleam 1997c. 'Chan eil Càil gun Chànan / Naught without the Lingo', *Cothrom,* 11: 12–13.
Neill, Uilleam 1997d. 'Language is what makes a Gael', *Scotsman,* 3 February.
Neill, Uilleam 1998. 'Gàidhealtachd Bheag Eile', *Gairm,* air 182: 156–9.
Newton, Michael 1997. *Gaelic in Scottish History and Culture,* Belfast: An Clochán.
Newton, Michael 2000. *A Handbook of the Scottish Gaelic World.* Dublin: Four Courts Press.
NicCoinnich, Màiri A. 1998. 'Gillean tha cur an cùil ri 'cànan nan caileag", *The Scotsman,* 2 June.
NicAoidh, Magaidh 2006. 'Pròiseact Plana Cànain nan Eilean Siar', in *Revitalising Gaelic in Scotland: Policy, Planning and Public Discourse,* ed. by Wilson McLeod, Edinburgh: Dunedin Academic Press, 72–86.
NicDhòmhnaill, Joan forthcoming 2007. 'Taigh na Gàidhlig: a' strì airson Ionad Gàidhlig ann an Dùn Èideann', in *Gàidhealtachdan Ùra: Leasachadh na Gàidhlig anns a' Bhaile Mhòr,* ed. by Wilson McLeod, Edinburgh: Celtic and Scottish Studies, University of Edinburgh.
NicFhionghuin, Donalda 2001. 'Caochladh Cànain is Coimhearsnachd, Caochladh Chothrom / Changing Communities and Language, Different Opportunities', *Cothrom,* serialised in issues 31–34. (Also available at www.cli.org.uk)
Nicholson, Rangi 1997. 'Marketing the Maori Language', in *Teaching Indigenous Languages,* ed. by Jon Reyhner, Flagstaff, AZ: Northern Arizona University, 206–13.
Nuffield Languages Inquiry 2000. *Languages: the Next Generation – The final report and recommendations of the Nuffield Languages Inquiry,* London: The Nuffield Foundation.
Ó Baoill, C. 1991. *Gaelic is Fun: A new course in Gaelic for the Beginner,* Stornoway: Acair.
O' Cornell, Helen and Richardson, Bill 1995. 'Adults Learning Languages', *Teangeolas,* 34: 20–23.
Ó Maolalaigh, Roibeard 2000. 'Leighis na Cànain a Bruidhinn gun Teagamh / The Remedy for the Language is in its Speaking Without a Doubt'; *Cothrom,* serialised in issues 27–30. (Also available at www.cli.org.uk)
Ó Maolalaigh, Roibeard and MacAonghais, Iain 1996. *Scottish Gaelic in Three Months,* Woodbridge, Suffolk: Hugo.

Ó Riagáin, Pádraig 2001. 'Irish Language Production and Reproduction', in *Can Threatened Languages be Saved?*, ed. by Joshua A. Fishman. Clevedon: Multilingual Matters, 195–214.

Ofcom 2005. News Release: *Ofcom Agrees Terms for a Gaelic Digital Channel.* (Available at: http://www.ofcom.org.uk/media/news/2005/11/nr_20051101)

Office of Population Censuses and Surveys 1990. *Standard Occupation Classification* volume 1, London: HMSO.

Office of Population Censuses and Surveys 1990. *Standard Occupation Classification* volume 2, London: HMSO.

Office of Population Censuses and Surveys 1991. *Standard Occupation Classification* volume 3, London: HMSO.

Oliver, James 2005. 'Scottish Gaelic Identities: Contexts and Contingencies', *Scottish Affairs,* 51, 1–24. (Available at http://www.scottishaffairs.org/onlinepub/sa/oliver_sa51_spr05.html)

Oliver, James 2006. 'Where is Gaelic? Revitalisation, Language, Culture and Identity', in *Revitalising Gaelic in Scotland: Policy, Planning and Public Discourse,* ed. by Wilson McLeod, Edinburgh: Dunedin Academic Press, 155–68.

Osborn, Andrew 2001. 'UK at Bottom of class in foreign languages', *The Guardian,* 20 February.

Owen, Robert C. 1993. *The Modern Gaelic–English Dictionary / Am Faclair Ùr Gàidhlig-Beurla,* Glasgow: Gairm.

Parkin, Frank 1968. *Middle Class Radicals,* Manchester.University Press.

Paterson, John M. 1952. *Gaelic Made Easy* (Book 1), Glasgow: Gaelic League of Scotland.

Paterson, John M. 1953. *Gaelic Made Easy* (Book 2), Glasgow: Gaelic League of Scotland.

Paterson, John M. 1958. *Gaelic Made Easy* (Book 3), Glasgow: Gaelic League of Scotland.

Paterson, John M. 1960. *Gaelic Made Easy* (Book 4), Glasgow: Gaelic League of Scotland.

Paterson, John M. 1964. *The Gaels Have a Word for it: A Modern Gaelic Vocabulary,* Glasgow: Gaelic League of Scotland.

Pedersen, Roy 2000. 'The Gaelic Economy', in *New Directions in Celtic Studies,* ed. by Amy Hale and Philip Payton, Exeter: University of Exeter Press, 152–66.

Powell, R. and Smith R. 2003. *Evaluation of the National Welsh for Adults Programme – Final Report,* National Foundation for Educational Research. (Available at www.elwa.ac.uk)

Press, J. Ian 1994. 'Breton Speakers in Brittany, France and Europe: constraints on a search for an identity', in *The Changing Voices of Europe,* ed. by M.M. Parry, W.V. Davies and R.A.M. Temple, Cardiff: University of Wales Press.

Pringle, Janis 1985. *An Analysis of Factors Influencing the Motivation of Adults Learning Gaelic in Scotland Today,* unpublished dissertation submitted as part of a Postgraduate Diploma in Linguistics, Polytechnic of Central London.

Pritchard, Rosalind M.O. 1990. 'Language Policy in Northern Ireland', *Teangeolas,* 27: 26–35.

Pritchard Newcombe, L. and Newcombe, Robert G. 2001. 'Adult Language Learning: The Effect of Background, Motivation and Practice on Perseverance', *International Journal of Bilingual Education and Bilingualism,* 4: 332–53.

Pritchard Newcombe, L. 2002. 'Snakes and Ladders', *Planet* 151: 86–92
Renton, R.W. and MacDonald, J.A. 1979. *Abair! Faclair: Gàidhlig-Beurla/Beurla-Gàidhlig / Gaelic-English, English–Gaelic dictionary,* Glasgow: Gairm.
Rhind, Màiri 1998. 'Buidhe do na Gaidhil ann an Inbhir Pheofharain', *The Scotsman,* 2 June.
Robasdan, Boyd 2006. 'Foghlam Gàidhlig: bho linn gu linn', in *Revitalising Gaelic in Scotland: Policy, Planning and Public Discourse,* ed. by Wilson McLeod, Edinburgh: Dunedin Academic Press, 87-117. [See also Roberston, Boyd]
Robertson, Boyd 1999. 'Gaelic Education', in *Scottish Education,* ed. by T.G.K Bryce and W.M Humes, Edinburgh: Edinburgh University Press, 244–255.
Robertson, Boyd 2001a. *Gaelic Immersion Courses – Report on Gaelic Immersion Course Provision in Scotland,* Glasgow: Scottish Qualifications Authority.
Robertson, Boyd 2001b. *The Gaelic language in education in the United Kingdom,* Leeuwarden: Mercator Education (also available at http://www.mercator-education.org (under "Regional Dossiers")).
Robertson, Boyd 2002. *Àireamhan Sgoilearan ann am Foghlam Gàidhlig / Pupils Numbers in Gaelic Education 2001–02,* Glasgow: University of Strathclyde Education.
Robertson, Boyd 2003. *Àireamhan Sgoilearan ann am Foghlam Gàidhlig / Pupils Numbers in Gaelic Education 2002–03,* Glasgow: University of Strathclyde Education.
Robertson, Boyd 2004. *Àireamhan Sgoilearan ann am Foghlam Gàidhlig / Pupils Numbers in Gaelic Education 2003–04,* Glasgow: University of Strathclyde Education.
Robertson, Boyd 2005. *Àireamhan Sgoilearan ann am Foghlam Gàidhlig / Pupils Numbers in Gaelic Education 2004–05,* Glasgow: University of Strathclyde Education.
Robertson, Boyd 2006. *Àireamhan Sgoilearan ann am Foghlam Gàidhlig / Pupils Numbers in Gaelic Education 2005–06,* Glasgow: University of Strathclyde Education.
Rogerson, Robert J. and Gloyer, Amanda 1995. 'Gaelic Cultural Revival or Language Decline?', *Scottish Geographical Magazine,* 111: 46–53.
Sabhal Mòr Ostaig 1993. *An Stòr-Dàta Briathrachais Gàidhlig / The Gaelic Terminology Database,* Isle of Skye: Clò Ostaig.
Rothach, Gillian 2006. 'Reimagining the Gaelic community: ethnicity, hybridity, politics and communication', in *Revitalising Gaelic in Scotland: Policy, Planning and Public Discourse,* ed. by Wilson McLeod, Edinburgh: Dunedin Academic Press, 221–237.
Scottish Consultative Council on the Curriculum 1997. *Scottish History in the Curriculum,* Dundee: SCCC.
Scottish Consultative Council on the Curriculum 1999. *The School Curriculum and the Culture of Scotland – A Discussion and Consultation,* Dundee: SCCC.
Scottish Executive 2001. *Citizens of a Multilingual World: Scottish Executive Response,* Edinburgh: Scottish Executive.
Scottish Funding Council 2006. *Consultative Seminar on Gaelic education: Summary of Gaelic education provision in Scotland* (paper presented to the Consultative Seminar on Gaelic Education, Edinburgh, 1 December).
Scottish Office Education Department (SOED) 1994. *Provision for Gaelic Education in Scotland: A Report by HM Inspectors of Schools,* Edinburgh: SOED.

Scottish Parliament, Scottish Executive and Comunn na Gàidhlig 2001. *Faclair na Pàrlamaid / Dictionary of Terms,* Edinburgh: The Scottish Parliament.

Scottish Parliament Information Centre 2002. *Gaelic Language (Scotland) Bill / Bile Cànan na Gàidhlig (Alba)*, SPICe Briefing 02/137, (11 December) (available at www.scottish.parliament.uk/business/research/pdf_res_brief/sb02–137.pdf and www.scottish.parliament.uk/business/research/pdf_res_brief/sb02–137g.pdf)

Scottish Parliament Information Centre 2004. *Gaelic Language (Scotland) Bill / Bile na Gàidhlig (Alba)*, SPICe Briefing 04/81, (12 November) (available at www.scottish.parliament.uk/business/research/briefings-04/sb04–81.pdf and www.scottish.parliament.uk/business/research/briefings-04/ sb04–81g.pdf)

Sheppard, Fergus 2006. 'Gaelic TV Channel gets £16.8M go-ahead', *The Scotsman*, 29 August.

Skogen, Ketil 1996. 'Young Environmentalists: Post-Modern Identities or Middle-class Culture?', *The Sociological Review*, 44: 452–73.

Sproull, Alan, and Brian Ashcroft 1993. *The Economics of Gaelic Language Development: A Research Report for Highlands and Islands Enterprise and the Gaelic Television Committee with Comunn na Gàidhlig*, Glasgow: Glasgow Caledonian University.

Sproull, Alan and Chalmers, Douglas 1998. *The Demand for Gaelic Artistic and Products and Services: Patterns and Impacts*, Glasgow: Glasgow Caledonian University.

Smith, John A. 1968. 'The Position of Gaelic and Gaelic Culture in Education', in *The Future of the Highlands,* ed. by Derick S. Thomson, London: Routledge and Kegan Paul.

Stockdale, Aileen, Bryan MacGregor and Gillian Munro 2003. *Migration, Gaelic-medium Education and Language Use*. Sleat, Isle of Skye: Ionad Nàiseanta na h-Imrich, Sabhal Mòr Ostaig (available at http://www.ini.smo.uhi.ac.uk/projects/migrationandGME.htm)

Stoddart, Anne M. 1895. *John Stuart Blackie: A Biography,* 2 vols, Edinburgh and London: William Blackwood and Sons.

Stornoway Gazette 1995. 'Gaelic TV takes on language decline', *Stornoway Gazette*, 28 August.

Thomas, Ned 1971. *The Welsh Extremist,* Talybont: Y Lolfa.

Taskforce on the Public Funding of Gaelic 2000. *Ag Ath-Bheothachadh Gàidhlig Neamhnuid Nàiseanta: Aithisg bho Buidheann-Gnìomh Maoineachadh na Gàidhlig / Revitalising Gaelic – a National Asset: Report by the Taskforce on Public Funding of Gaelic,* Edinburgh: The Scottish Executive.

Thompson, F.G. 1972. 'Gaelic in Politics', *Transactions of the Gaelic Society of Inverness*, XLVII: 67–100.

Thompson, F. G. 1985. 'How Strong the Horsehair', in *Gaelic – Looking to the Future,* ed. by John Hulbert, Dundee: Andrew Flecher Society, 1–11.

Thompson, F. G. 1992. 'Gaelic Dictionaries and Their Makers', *Transactions of the Gaelic Society of Inverness,* vol LVII: 51–69.

Thompson, F.G. 1992. *History of An Comunn Gàidhealach – The First Hundred (1891–1991),* Inverness: An Comunn Gàidhealach.

Thomson, Derick S. 1968. 'The Role of the Writer in a Minority Culture', *Transactions of the Gaelic Society of Inverness,* XLIV: 256–71.

Thomson, Derick S. (ed.) 1976. *Gàidhlig ann an Albainn / Gaelic in Scotland: A Blueprint for Official and Private Initiatives*, Glasgow: Gairm.

Thomson, Derick S. 1979. 'Gaelic: Its Range of Uses', in *Languages of Scotland,* ed. by A.J Aitken and Tom McArthur, Edinburgh: Chambers, 14–25.
Thomson, Derick S. 1980. 'Gaelic in Scotland: Assessment and Prognosis', in *Minority Languages Today,* ed. by E. Haugen *et al.*, Edinburgh: Edinburgh University Press, 10–20.
Thomson, Derick S. 1981. *The New English–Gaelic Dictionary,* Glasgow: Gairm.
Thomson, Derick S. (ed.). 1983. *The Companion to Gaelic Scotland,* 1994 edition, Glasgow: Gairm.
Thomson, Derick S. 1984. *Why Gaelic Matters,* Edinburgh: The Saltire Society and An Comunn Gàidhealach.
Thomson, Derick S. 1994. 'Attitudes to Linguistic Change in Gaelic Scotland', in *The Changing Voices of Europe,* ed. by M.M. Parry, W.V. Davies and R.A.M. Temple, Cardiff: University of Wales Press, 227–35.
Times Higher Educational Supplement, 1996. *Gaelic Revival Myth Scotched by Student,* 12 January.
Trosset, Carol S. 1986. 'The Social Identity of Welsh Learners', *Language in Society,* 15: 165–191.
Tuckett, Alan and Cara, Sue 1999. *Tongue-tied but trying?: A NIACE survey on the languages adults speak in Great Britain,* Leicester: National Institute of Adult Continuing Education (England and Wales).
Watson, Angus 2001. *The Essential Gaelic-English Dictionary – a Dictionary for Students and Learners of Scottish Gaelic,* Edinburgh: Birlinn.
Watson, Angus 2005. *The Essential English–Gaelic Dictionary – A Dictionary for Learners of Scottish Gaelic,* Edinburgh: Birlinn.
Watson, Ridseard 1998. 'Dà sheòrsa Gàidhlig ann 's gun ghin air a' bhocsa', *The Scotsman,* 8 August.
Western Isles Language Planning Project 2005. *Research and Outcome of Phase 1 of the Project – Final Report.* Stornoway: Western Isles Language Project.
West Highland Free Press 1995. 'Working group to look at Gaelic Broadcasting', 6 October.
West Highland Free Press 1996. 'New survey shows shift of opinion in favour of single Gaelic TV channel', 8 March.
West Highland Free Press 2002. '"No" to £44 for Gaelic TV channel', 10 May.
Wells, Gordon 1993. 'A Placement Test in Gaelic Reading Skills for Adult Learners Development Administration and Analysis', Paper presented to Fasgnag II: The Second Conference on Research and Studies into the Maintenance of Gaelic, Sabhal Mòr Ostaig, 24–27 March.
Wells, Gordon 1996a. 'Convener's Message', *Comann an Luchd-Ionnsachaidh Annual Report 1996–96,* 1.
Wells, Gordon 1996b. 'Working with the Gaelic Learners' Association; a case study of learner-led initiatives in Heritage Language Teaching', *Language Issues,* 1: 6–7.
Wells, Gordon 1997. 'The Validity of Language Learners' Self-reports of Proficiency: A Study of Scottish Gaelic', *Language Issues,* 9: 23–24.
Welsh Language Board 2006. *Welsh Language Use Survey,* Cardiff: Welsh Language Board.
Williams, Glyn 1992. *Sociolinguistics: A Sociological Critique*, London: Routledge.
Williams, Tim 1999a. 'What's Gaelic for Dead Loss', *The Scotsman,* 18 March.
Williams, Tim 1999b. 'Barbarous Brogues no More', *The Scotsman,* 3 June.
Wilson, Brian 1995. 'Brian Wilson Writes', *West Highland Free Press,* 14 July.

Withers, Charles W.J. 1984. *Gaelic in Scotland, 1698–1981: The Geographical History of a Language*. Edinburgh: John Donald.
Withers, Charles W.J. 1988. *Gaelic Scotland: The transformation of a culture region*, London: Routledge.
Withers, Charles W.J. 1992. 'The historical creation of the Scottish Highlands' in *The Manufacture of Scottish History* ed. by I. Donnachie and C. Whatley, Edinburgh: Edinburgh University Press / Polygon, 143–156
Wmffre, Iwan. 2004. 'Learners, native speakers and the authenticity of language', in *Communicating Cultures*, ed. by Ullrich Kockel and Máiréad Nic Craith, Münster: Lit Verlag, 149–75.
Wright, Sue 2000. *Community and Communication: The Role of Language in Nation State Building and European Integration*, Clevedon: Multilingual Matters.
Zall, Carol 1999. 'Cabadaich a' neartachadh na Gàidhlig', *The Scotsman,* 17 March.

Appendix 1: The Gaelic Learners' Survey

PART 1: Personal Details

1. Are you: Male   Female

2. What age are you?

3. What is your usual place of residence? (Which village/town/city? Which country if outwith Scotland?)

4. Where were you brought up? (Which village/town/city. Which country if outwith Scotland.)

5. To what level are you qualified?

No Formal Qualifications		Teaching / Nursing Qualification	
Basic Vocational / Scotvec		First Degree	
O Grades / Standard Grades / O Levels or Equivalent		Postgraduate Certificate / Professional Diploma	
Higher / A Levels or Equivalent		Higher Degree	
ONC / OND		Other	
HNC / HND / Dip He or Equivalent			

If OTHER, please state

6. At the moment, which of the following best describes your position as regards work?

Employed Full-Time		In Full-Time Education	
Employed Part-Time		On a Government Training or Employment Scheme	
Unemployed		Looking after House Full-Time	
Armed Forces		Retired	
Permanently Sick or Disabled		Other	

If OTHER, please specify

7. If you are presently working, what is your occupation? (Please be as detailed as possible, e.g. what is your job title? If you are a civil servant, what grade, if a teacher, what type of school? etc.)

8. If you are currently retired or unemployed, what is your most recent occupation? (Please be as detailed as possible). If you look after the house full time, what is your partner's occupation?

9. Which political party do you feel closest to:

Conservative		Scottish National Party	
Labour		Other Party	
Liberal Democrat		Wouldn't Vote	
Scottish Green Party		Don't Know	

If OTHER PARTY, please state

10. On a left-right political spectrum where would you place yourself?
(Please circle one number.) (0 = hard left, 5 = absolute centre, and 10 = far right)

    0   1   2   3   4   5   6   7   8   9   10

11. If you live in Scotland, which of these national identity categories best describes you:

Scottish not British	
More Scottish than British	
Equally Scottish and British	
More British than Scottish	
British not Scottish	
Other	

If OTHER, please specify

12. If you live outside Scotland, what is your nationality?

13. How much do you feel yourself to be each of the following identities (please tick one box for each of the suggested identities)

	Yes, Very Much So	Yes, On The Whole	No/Not Really
Gael			
Gaelic speaker			
Highlander			
Islander			
Local identity (please specify)			
Scottish			
British			
European			
Celt			
Other			

If specifying a LOCAL IDENTITY or OTHER, please state:

Appendix 1

14. Do you know or are you learning any languages other than Gaelic and English? (If so. please state language(s) and whether you are a native speaker or a learner. If a learner, please give some idea of fluency, e.g. Swedish, learner, advanced.

15. Apart from Gaelic groups, are you – or have you been – a member of any interest or pressure groups (e.g. CND, RSPB, a local tenants' group, etc.)? (Please write down as many as you can remember.)

16. Do you regard yourself as belonging to any particular religion?

    Yes   No

    If NO, please move on to question 17.

    If YES, which denomination or religious group are you connected with?

    Are you a full member?   Yes   No

    Apart from special occasions such as funerals and baptisms, how often do you attend religious services or meetings?

Once a month	
Several times a month	
At least once a month	
Several times a year	
At least once a year	
Less often than once a year	

17. Do or did either of your parents speak Gaelic?

    Yes   No   Don't Know

    If YES, which one(s)?

18. Do or did any of your grandparents speak Gaelic?

    Yes   No   Don't Know

    If YES, which one(s) (e.g. grandmother on father's side)?

Part 2: Learning Gaelic

1. Are you currently learning Gaelic?   Yes   No

   If NO, please indicate which of the following best describes you (Please tick one box only.)

I made an attempt or attempts at learning Gaelic but am no longer doing so.
I have been learning Gaelic on and off but am not learning at the moment
I have learnt Gaelic to fluency.
Other (Please specify).

2. What level of ability in Gaelic would you say you have at present in terms of Speaking understanding, reading and writing? Please tick the appropriate box for each.

	Fluent	Advanced	Intermediate	Basic
Speaking				
Understanding				
Reading				
Writing				

3. If you are not already fluent in Gaelic, how fluent do you wish to become? (Please tick one box only.)

I would like enough Gaelic to understand simple sentences / conversations.
I would like to learn enough Gaelic to help me with a hobby or interest.
I would like to become fluent in reading and writing Gaelic.
I would like to become fluent in speaking Gaelic.
I would like to become fluent in speaking, reading and writing Gaelic.
Other (please state).

4. Do you expect ever to reach the level of fluency that you have indicated above?

5. Do you have any formal qualifications in Gaelic (e.g. O Grade, Standard Grade, Higher, Scotvec, University course, or other)?

6. For how many years, roughly, have you been learning Gaelic?

Appendix 1

7. Please rate the importance of each of the following to your decision to learn Gaelic by ticking the appropriate boxes.

Reason	Very Important	Quite Important	Not Important At All / Not Applicable
(a) I would be able to enjoy Gaelic music better.			
(b) I would be able to understand Gaelic TV.			
(c) I would be able to understand Gaelic literature.			
(d) I would be helping to keep Gaelic alive.			
(e) I live in a Gaelic speaking area.			
(f) Adult members of my family can/could speak Gaelic.			
(g) Gaelic would be useful for my hobbies or interests (e.g. place-names, tracing ancestry).			
(h) Gaelic would be useful in present/future employment.			
(i) As a Scot / someone living in Scotland, I feel that I should speak Gaelic.			
(j) As a Highlander/Islander /someone living in the Highlands and Islands I feel I should speak Gaelic.			
(k) Gaelic would help me get closer to my roots.			
(l) I did not feel like a complete Scot without a knowledge of Gaelic.			
(m) My children are in Gaelic-medium education.			
(n) I have Gaelic speaking friends.			
(o) I am interested in languages.			
(p) I want to live in the Highlands / in Scotland.			
(q) I like to visit the Highlands/Islands.			
(r) Other Reasons.			

If you indicated that another reason or other reasons were important, please write them here:

If you stated that hobbies or interests were important in your decision to learn Gaelic, please list them here:

8. Which of the reasons (a-r) mentioned in question 12 (above) was the most important to your decision to learn Gaelic? (Please write down only one reason.)

9. How important on a scale of 0–10 would you say that the following were to your decision to learn Gaelic? (Please tick one number for each reason. 0 = not important at all, 10 = very important indeed.)

	0	1	2	3	4	5	6	7	8	9	10
(a) Patriotic, nationalistic or national identity reasons											
(b) Highlands and Islands identity reasons											
(c) Cultural reasons (e.g. music, literature)											
(d) Career or economic reasons											
(e) Immediate family reasons											
(f) Community reasons											
(g) Family background/roots reasons											

10. What have been your main ways of learning Gaelic? (e.g. evening classes, summer courses, distance learning, using a published Gaelic course at home, going to live in a Gaelic community, full time college/university course, etc.)

11. If you would like to a make any comments on why or how you are learning Gaelic or related matters, please write them here:

Appendix 1

Part 3: Using Gaelic

1. Can you receive Radio nan Gaidheal (the Gaelic radio station) where you live?

    Yes   No   Don't Know

    If YES, how many hours of Gaelic radio do you listen to on the average day, if any?

None	2–4
up to 1	4–6
1–2	6+

2. Can you receive Gaelic television where you live?

    Yes   No

    If YES, how many of the Gaelic television programmes do you usually watch in an average week, if any? (Please tick one box only.)

All of them	a few
most of them	I watch Gaelic TV very occasionally
about half	I don't usually watch any Gaelic programmes

    On average, how many hours per week of Gaelic TV do you watch per week all told?

3. Do you regularly read any of the following? (Please tick yes or no for each publication.)

Publication	Yes	No
Gairm		
Cothrom		
An Gàidheal Ùr		
The Scotsman Friday Gaelic column		
The Scotsman Wednesday Gaelic page		
Press and Journal (Highland Edition) Gaelic column		
Gaelic columns or pages in local/community newspapers (please specify)		
Gaelic column or supplement in other newspaper/magazine (Please specify.)		

4. Which of the following Gaelic-language activities do you take part in/attend or have you taken part in/attended in the past? (Please tick one box for each activity.)

	Regularly	Sometimes	Seldom	Never
National Mòd				
Local Mòd				
Fèis				
Gaelic play				
Gaelic concert/cèilidh				
Gaelic church service				
Gaelic meeting /conference				
Other Gaelic activity				

If OTHER Gaelic activity, please state:

5. How often do you do the following? (Please tick one box for each activity.)

	Regularly	Sometimes	Seldom	Never
make an effort to go to Gaelic concerts, plays and entertainments when they are put on				
read books in Gaelic				
read internet pages in Gaelic				
read/write e-mails in Gaelic				
write letters in Gaelic				
take part in campaigns for Gaelic (letter writing, petition signing etc.)				
speak Gaelic				

6. Are there any Gaelic related services, facilities or activities that do not exist at present (or do not exist at present in your area) that you would like to use or take part in? If so, please describe here:

7. Were you recorded in the last Census as being able to speak and/or read and/or write Scottish Gaelic?

Yes   No   Don't Know   Not Applicable

If YES, which of the following were you recorded as being able to do? (Please tick as many boxes as apply.)

Speak Gaelic   Read Gaelic   Write Gaelic

Appendix 1

8. Do you intend to be recorded as being able to speak and/or read and/or write and/or understand Scottish Gaelic at the next Census? (Please tick as many boxes as apply.)

Speak Gaelic	
Read Gaelic	
Write Gaelic	
Understand Gaelic	

If YES, which of the following do you intended to be recorded as being able to do? (Please tick as many boxes as apply.)

9. Are you a member of any of the following Gaelic related organisations:

A' Chiste Leabhraichean (Book Club)		Comunn na Gàidhlig	
An Comunn Gàidhealach		Gaelic Society of Inverness	
Celtic League		Gaelic Choir	
Celtic Congress		Gaelic Drama Group	
Comann an Luchd-Ionnsachaidh		Local Gaelic Learners' Group	
Comann nam Pàrant		University Celtic Society	
Comhairle nan Sgoiltean Àraich		Other Gaelic Related Group	

If you are a member of a Gaelic related organisation or organisations not mentioned above, please name:

10. Out of all the people with whom you use Gaelic, how many would you say were native speakers and how many learners? (Please tick one box only.)

All/almost all are native speakers	
Most are native speakers	
Equal number of native speakers and learners	
Most are learners	
All/almost all are learners	

PART 4: Gaelic In Your Family

1. Do you have any children?   YES   NO

   If so, what are their ages?

   If you have no children, please move on to question 5.

2. If you have any children of pre-school age, are they currently attending, or will they; a Gaelic playgroup (Cròileagan) or Gaelic nursery school?

   Yes   No   Don't Know

   If you answered NO, please indicate why by ticking one of the following boxes:

I do not want my child(ren) to be educated through the medium of Gaelic.	
I would have liked a Gaelic-medium education for my child(ren), but it is not/was not available in my area.	
I was not aware of the availability of Gaelic-medium education in my area at the time when I decided upon my child's/children's education.	
I was not interested in Gaelic at the time when I decided upon my child's/children's education.	
Other (please state).	

   If you answered DON'T KNOW, please indicate why by ticking one of the following box

I am unsure whether or not my I want my child(ren) to be educated through the medium of Gaelic.	
I don't know if there is a Gaelic playgroup or nursery school in my area.	
I have not considered the issue yet.	
Other (please state).	

3. If you have any children of school age, are they attending a Gaelic-medium unit at school?

   YES   NO

   If you answered NO, please indicate why by ticking one of the following boxes:

I did not want my children to be educated through the medium of Gaelic.	
I would have liked a Gaelic-medium education for my child(ren), but it is not/was not available in my area.	
I was not aware of the availability of Gaelic-medium education in my area at the time when I decided upon my child's/children's education.	
I was not interested in Gaelic at the time when I decided upon my child's/children's education.	
Other (please state).	

Appendix 1

4. If you have any children who have left school, did they attend a Gaelic-medium unit at school?

    YES   NO

    If you answered NO, which of the following best describes the reason for your choice for your child's education:

I did not want my children to be educated through the medium of Gaelic.	
I would have liked a Gaelic-medium education for my child, but it was not available in my area.	
I was not aware of the availability of Gaelic-medium education in my area at the tone.	
I was not interested in Gaelic at the time when I decided upon my child's education.	
Other (please state).	

5. If you do not have children at present, but are likely to at some point in the future, would you like them to be educated through the medium of Gaelic if facilities were available in your area?

    Yes   No   Don't Know   Not Applicable

    If you would like to make any further comments regarding Gaelic in your family or Gaelic-medium education, please write them here.

6. How many people are there in your household?

7. Can anybody else living in your household speak Gaelic?
    If YES, who (e.g. partner, daughter, mother, father in law)?

    For each Gaelic speaker, please write N next to their name if they are a native speaker, L if they are currently learning and FL if they are a fluent learner (e.g. partner N, mother FL).

PART 5: Opinions On Gaelic

1. There has been some discussion of the meaning of the word *Gael* in recent times. Which of the following is closest to your own understanding of the word "Gael"? (Please tick one box only.)

A native Gaelic speaker	
A native Gaelic speaker from the Highlands or Islands	
A Highlander or Islander regardless or whether or not s/he can speak Gaelic	
Anyone whose people were Gaelic speaking Highlanders or Islanders	
Anyone who can speak Gaelic	
Other (Please specify)	

2. Do you agree or disagree with the following statements about Gaelic? (Please tick one box for each statement.)

	agree strongly	agree	neither agree nor disagree	disagree	disagree strongly
1. To keep their true identity, the Highlands and Islands need their Gaelic speakers.					
2. Gaelic should be one of the languages officially used by the Scottish Parliament.					
3. Gaelic is one of Scotland's national languages.					
4. Too much money is spent on Gaelic.					
5. In order to work in the public sector in Gaelic areas, one should speak Gaelic.					
6. Gaelic is only important at a personal level.					
7. To really understand Scottish culture, you must know Gaelic.					
8. Gaelic should be given official status.					
9. Gaelic does not need any special encouragement.					
10. In a globalising world, Gaelic helps to give me a sense of cultural continuity.					
11. Official bodies should do more to encourage Gaelic in public affairs.					
12. Gaelic is important for Scotland as a whole.					
13. Languages are more than a means of communication.					
14. People should be allowed to use Gaelic in courts of law.					

Appendix 1

Question 2 (cont'd)	agree strongly	agree	neither agree nor disagree	disagree	disagree strongly
15. On the whole, native Gaelic speakers do not want other people to learn Gaelic.					
16. There are great differences between the Gaelic dialects.					
17. Companies should be offered tax breaks in order to offer bilingual services.					
18. Gaelic is only important to the Highlands and Islands.					
19. Spoken Gaelic needs to become more standardised with less localised variation.					
20. Gaelic is Scotland's national language.					
21. Councils should be legally obliged to provide Gaelic-medium education where demand exists.					
22. Gaelic learners should learn a standardised variety of Gaelic.					
23. It is artificial to learn Gaelic.					
24. Learning Gaelic is a hobby for me.					
25. Bilingual signs are a waste of money.					
26. Knowledge of Gaelic is good for people's job prospects.					
27. Gaelic can only be saved if Gaelic speaking communities continue to exist in the Islands.					
28. Gaelic is a dying language.					
29. Gaelic should not be encouraged throughout Scotland.					
30. Learners should learn Gaelic dialects.					
31. Children in any part of Scotland should be able to learn Gaelic if they or their parents want them to.					
32. In an impersonal world, Gaelic helps to give me a sense of community.					

3. Some people believe that Gaelic is a particularly difficult language to learn, others do not. Do you think that Gaelic is a difficult language to learn?

Yes   No   Don't Know

If YES, why do/did you find Gaelic difficult? (Please tick as many boxes as apply.)

a) Linguistically, I feel that Gaelic is a difficult language to learn (e.g. word order, spelling, pronunciation).
b) There is nowhere where I can go where Gaelic is spoken all the time by everybody.
c) Learning materials, facilities and support for Gaelic are poorer than those for most other languages.
d) I find it difficult to learn languages.
e) There are no circumstances in which I have to use Gaelic and cannot use English.
f) Other (Please state).

Appendix 1 265

PART 6: Comments

I would be grateful for any additional comments which you might want to make on any of the matters raised in this questionnaire e.g. about learning Gaelic, the current state and future prospects for the language, the way forward for Gaelic etc. (Please continue overleaf if necessary.)

*THANK YOU VERY MUCH
FOR THE TIME AND TROUBLE
WHICH YOU HAVE TAKEN
TO FILL IN THIS QUESTIONNAIRE.*

Appendix 2: Learners' Views on Native Speakers
(Gathered from the Gaelic Learners' Survey responses)

The Behaviour of Native Speakers towards Learners

"I feel there is very much a 'learner' v 'native speaker' divide and have encountered many native speakers who tend to belittle the efforts of learners."

"The few local native Gaelic speakers here can't read and write easily and feel inferior and do not want to encourage learners – so we make no progress."

"In my experience native Gaelic speakers seem very unwilling (or too impatient) to converse in Gaelic with learners, and help them to improve. As this is a personal matter I doubt if any improvement can be effected by institutions."

"Having met some negative native speakers, it would appear that keeping the more positive majority 'on side' is essential if the regional diversity is to be maintained."

"Some native speakers tend to be impatient with struggling learners."

"I would like to see more enthusiasm shown by native speakers as they do tend unfortunately to be rather reluctant to converse at an appropriate basic level of learners."

"There is often an attitude that no matter how fluent, a 'learner' is inferior to a native speaker."

"In my experience, native speakers do not want learners to learn Gaelic".

"Too many [native speakers] reply in English when you speak to them in Gaelic – this is often humiliating."

"The greatest problem continues to be the difficulty of sustaining conversation with native speakers, many of whom felt that learners will ask (as they often do) awkward and unanswerable questions. In addition, many have a seemingly unalterable mindset – speak Gaelic to native Gaelic speakers, English to native English speakers – which makes it difficult to sustain a conversation in halting Gaelic, no matter how good the intentions."

"I cannot understand why native Gaelic speakers I have met are not supportive in maintaining their language and helping learners. I would like to see much more praise and media coverage of those who do."

"I feel people who are lucky enough to have Gaelic as their first language sometimes don't 'understand' Gaelic learners desire to learn and some even adopt a 'why should we help' attitude. Surely to continue with the language we should all pull together. Others, of course are more than pleased to help."

"Discouragement by some native speakers of Gaelic learners."

"One of the biggest problems for learners is the attitude of certain speakers of Gaelic (who claim to be 'native', although their ability to write the language and their understanding and familiarity with its written form is often minimal) who will belittle any attempt to learn the language; the frightening thing is that some of these people are (fairly senior) schoolteachers in the Highlands. It is not a common attitude, but a small number of repeated posts to various internet newsgroups have managed to destroy the morale of a large number of learners."

"I have experienced animosity from native speakers. The local Gaelic learners' group have organised many activities and have never had anybody from the local native speaking community. This is very detrimental to the overall situation locally, creating a Them and Us situation."

On native speakers attitudes to learners

"Experience in Skye – landlady hostile – as I was English no doubt – ignorance here."

"Attitude of some native speakers to learners is a difficulty for learners."

"Negative attitudes towards Gaelic from native speaking Gaels which put up psychological barriers to speaking Gaelic."

"Fluent speakers are often, but not always, impatient. Non-Gaelic speakers, especially young people, have the attitude that it's not the in thing to do and that its not worth bothering about. The young people who are fluent speakers completely refuse to speak Gaelic outside the home. Those who aren't fluent generally understand the language but have no interest in taking it further. Occasionally I come across a patient native speaker who will have a short conversation with me, but to be honest, tha mi air mo shàrachadh."

"I have asked myself why I am bothering with this language many times. Not having been brought up in the Highlands, I don't understand all the taboos associated with this language. All I know is that my father didn't speak his native language to me and, being brought up in Glasgow I didn't have the option to study Gaelic, even to O' Grade. These things made me angry and upset as a young adult, especially the fact that the only time I heard Gaelic was when adult family members wanted to exclude me from their conversation. Gaelic has probably been spoken in my family for hundreds of years and I feel upset and guilty that it has stopped in my generation, even though I had no choice about learning it as a child. When I hear Gaelic, it often makes me want to cry. It sounds very right, but it's still something I'm excluded from. I'm still on the wrong side of the language barrier, and it feels like many native speakers are dismissive of my very broken Gaelic. There seem to be few paths across this language barrier for adult learners but I hope I'll find a way. I achieved near fluency in French by living and working in French speaking communities for six months and having to speak it. However, I realise that learning Gaelic is not so simple. English is always an option. I am good at language and I know that if I HAD to speak Gaelic for six months, I would achieve near fluency. At the same time, I know I can't spend six months in a Gaelic speaking environment."

Perhaps the fact that I had no opportunities in Gaelic and have had to struggle to regain what I wasn't given has made me value the language. The only young people who will speak Gaelic with me are other learners. I find that sad and discouraging, except that the other learners are very enthusiastic.

I wish I understood the psychology of this language and why people are so reluctant to speak it – including my own father. I also wish I understood why English, my only native language, seems inadequate and cold. I sometimes find myself hating English because it has taken away the language I should have had. I know I shouldn't feel this way, but I think I have to become a fluent Gaelic speaker, if only to achieve a reconciliation with the English language. I firmly believe that language goes deeper than simple communication. There is something of a national character and soul in it. I know that when I began to become fluent in French, I felt freer to express my feelings and emotions than I did in English. Maybe I want to learn Gaelic because I feel that English isn't adequate to express my identity and my character. I hope your research helps to untangle some of the native speaker / learner issues. To be honest, I don't have the courage, or insensitivity (?) to speak Gaelic to people no matter what. If my attempts to murder the Gaelic language in conversation are met with annoyance or impatience, I desist. Maybe I am a coward because even if a sympathetic Gaelic speaker is around, I find it hard to speak Gaelic to them if other people are overhearing who:

(a) don't speak or understand Gaelic and resent it being spoken in case Gaelic speakers are using the language to exclude them;

(b) are fluent speakers who are liable to laugh at my attempts to speak their language;

(c) are young people who understand and / or speak Gaelic and seem to resent my attempts to learn Gaelic. I'm not sure why but they seem to see it as uncool and something which doesn't fit into everyday life. As a person who is still young, I find it hard not to be influenced by the attitudes of other young Gaels."

"Native speakers do not allow for lack of dialects in learners."

On whether native speakers want learners to learn Gaelic

"Some do, some don't. Probably about 50 / 50."

"Not all native speakers are helpful."

"Why oh why are native Gaelic speakers so loathe to speak to us (non-Gaelic speakers) on their 'mother tongue'. I went to a Cèilidh where a fair amount were Gaelic speakers yet no one spoke to me in Gaelic."

"Native speakers do not encourage learners enough."

"Gael/non-Gael relationship: I feel as a non-Gael, I would be intruding at concerts etc. organised by native Gaels and would not feel welcome. I agree with Mìcheal MacPhàdraig [article in *Cothrom* 16] that native speakers are not helpful to learners – some are positively obstructive – others just too keen to revert to English."

"I think some native Gaelic speakers are against learners especially non-Scottish learners. I feel as long as the language is growing then why worry about who is speaking it?"

"I find I can sometimes feel intimidated by native speakers when speaking Gaelic. Sometimes they also mock you and you end up thinking why bother if no-one is going to take you seriously."

"When I first came to live here I enquired about Gaelic classes, none were available then and that hasn't changed in 20 years. I had more confidence in my ability to learn the language then as local native speakers tend to laugh at mistakes rather than encourage and correct."

"On the question about native speakers and whether or not they want others to learn, I have noted that the 'academic' Gaelic speakers are less encouraging of Sasennachs (almost snobbish against outsiders)."

"I've been told that 'you can never learn Gaelic from a book' – by a native speaker. Native speakers absorbed it naturally in daily life with family, school, work, church etc."

"Gaelic needs an inclusive attitude on the part of its supporters, i.e. let everyone join in without being mocked or looked down upon."

"In my time on the island I have met many wonderful people who have helped my Gaelic by taking the time to speak to me. The locals are very supportive, of course I have met people, some of them locals, who do not think Gaelic is worth saving. Thankfully, I think these are the minority."

On native speakers and whether they want learners to learn

"Some don't – because they see it as a [handwriting indecipherable] but many are very pleased to encourage learners. Gaelic is a difficult language to learn because many people shift to English when they meet learners."

"The requirement for perfect pronunciation by native speakers does intimidate learners. English speakers have no difficulty with French natives speaking English with French vowel sounds."

"Traditionally Gaels have been courageous, outgoing and hospitable. If our language is to flourish we must welcome learners from other cultures, not sneer at them. I have introduced Germans, French, Italians, Malayans and Chinese to Gaelic songs. Am I to dampen their enthusiasm? How many from Stornoway are faultless in these foreign languages? Let us not become so timid and narrow minded that we cannot welcome new friends. They really will not steal the language."

"I recently spent two weeks on Barra to practice Gaelic. I had a hard time to persuade people to speak Gaelic in front of me. They thought it was 'rude'."

"Learners should be encouraged not discouraged."

"The people who have Gaelic need to be more understanding to people who are struggling to learn the language, and not to leave them out in the cold!"

"One of my big questions is – who amongst the many Gaelic organisations genuinely want to welcome learners into their rather tight-knit worlds?"

"Attitudes to people learning Gaelic: positive and negative from Gaelic and non-Gaelic speakers. I've had really stinging comments from both plus being laughed at in the face. Not a nice experience. But on the whole, people are very positive and helpful, especially Gaelic speakers who are prepared to commit time to help."

"Even the older folk talk to me in English when I try to practice Gaelic with them. It's as if they think it's wrong not to use English."

"Will my own people stop switching to English or avoiding teaching / talking to their children in Gaelic? The attitude that it's the language of the underclass, something to be hidden and lost, seems to run deep, and English, as the global *lingua franca* (there's an irony) is all pervasive."

"It is difficult to learn Gaelic by going to live in a Gaelic community as everybody speaks English to outsiders / incomes. I feel quite strongly about the need for intensive courses and encouragement for non-Gaelic speakers in Gaelic communities. It is harder to organise such courses in rural areas, but if people don't learn Gaelic quickly then they will be too used to speaking English with their neighbours to effect a changeover."

"What's all this stuff about native speakers not being helpful to learners? In almost seven years I have not one instance of this. Sure native speakers must get bored with yet another 'Kim er a tha oo' pronounced as I spell it – with the chance of a reply being understood close to zero!"

The Role of Native Speakers in the Decline of Gaelic

"The whole decline of Gaelic is about Gaels being convinced they were inferior to English speakers. Gaelic's fortunes will rise as the older generation dies and take their stupid ideas with them to the grave. Many old-time Gaelic speakers are convinced Gaelic should and will die, and the fact that they are Gaelic-speakers appears to give their ideas credibility. From my point of view I see the biggest threat to the future prospects for the language as being the tendency to 'fossilise' it. Any successful modern language must not hide in a corner and try and fend off all outside influences – to grow and expand it must absorb more from other language (as English has done) and turn this to its own advantage. I do get the impression that its modern development is being constrained by groups that would like to keep it in a strait jacket."

"The most serious problem Gaelic has is the internalised evaluation of Gaelic amongst native speakers which induces them to fail to pass their language on. Learners have an important role to play in showing native speakers who suffer from a poor image of their own language that it is valuable and worth taking seriously."

"I find some 'native' Gaels' attitude to their own culture and language very fatalistic and depressing in terms of its future survival. Some Gaelic speakers appear to find their political allegiances a stumbling block to support and development of the language."

"Gaelic will only thrive as a language when native-speakers use the language within the family situation and where there are ample educational opportunities to continue the learning processes within the education system. If Gaelic is given official status it is to be hoped that native speakers will be less diffident in using their language and pass it on to others – learners. There are of course, notable exceptions to this."

"I won't be here to see it but with the strong encouragement I have had from learners who have become fluent, and with children learning a standard Gaelic, also with the present generation of 'defeated' native Gaelic speakers dying out, I expect Gaelic to thrive and grow and to become established as part of Scotland's culture in the next century."

"I have a relation in Wester Ross who knows Gaelic. His mother speaks it with her sister, when they are alone, he is 40 years old and was working with somebody from Stornoway who kept saying to him in Gaelic 'why don't you speak to me in Gaelic? What future then, for the language is someone who has lived there all their life and still doesn't use it, but would rather use English."

"I have been learning Gaelic for under a year now, and I am enjoying it very much. To me, the fact that I can learn it all the way out in Australia with no native speakers to help suggests that it can and should be learnt by people where it is actually spoken. I think it is terrible that people in Scotland (particularly the Highland and Islands) don't teach the language to their children, and it would be a tragedy if the language died out because of this reason. I think to be bilingual is not only important for holding onto your heritage. I find it exciting to learn such an ancient and fascinating languages, so I can't understand why native Scots could not want to learn it!"

"Gaelic will live and die with the commitment and its attitude of its speakers."

"For many people, Gaelic is a burden of sadness and loss which they can't seem either to bear or put down."

"The Gaels have a reticence which does not naturally lead to expansion."

"I feel that it will be GME [Gaelic-medium education] that will be the saviour of Gàidhlig because these kids will not have the 'historical baggage' of the older generation."

"I find the attitude that Gaelic identity is determined by being a native Gael worrying. If Gaelic is only for native speakers – this will eventually execute the language. I believe we 'Gaidheil Ùra' will protect the Gaelic way of life along with the help of native Gaelic speakers."

"Though I have strong family links to Lewis and spend one week in four there, I still learn more Gaelic from classes etc. than from the people around me. Other people always speak to me in English as a matter of politeness and apologise if they inadvertently skip back into Gaelic. They regard my attempts to speak Gaelic as embarrassing and unnecessary and always answer in English. At the same time they are astonished and mystified by the fact that I read Gaelic books and write to them in Gaelic while I am away. People of my own age deny hotly speaking Gaelic at all, though I remember them well when we were younger and they knew no English. It is a matter of not wishing to be considered backward and unfashionable. By and large they consider the 'Gaelic Revival' as ridiculous and don't see it as relating to them. I believe that they love the language and hold it in great respect and have a wide and deep knowledge of its song and poetry, but they are so used to it being a closed world that they don't really believe it possible to learn except at your mother's knee and if you haven't done that it is pointless to try."

"Many of the younger native speakers don't give a damn about Gaelic. While some of them mature to realise the worth of the language, many do not. As this group is the future of the language, it doesn't look good. As far as employment is concerned, learners have less chance than natives. A lot of importance is placed on accent and as few learners sound like natives they are discriminated against."

The Changing Definition of 'Native Speaker'

"Gaelic-medium education has been a tremendous success, my daughter in p5 is a fluent speaker and the children seem to have a rounder education. Not being a native speaker and having my children in GME [Gaelic-medium education], has led a lot of native speakers to say my children will only be learners and not native speakers. I find this quite annoying, my daughter going into p5 is fluent in all aspects of Gaelic, her teacher thought we only spoke Gaelic at home, but others brand her as a learner. These children are speaking Gaelic for 6 hours a day possibly four more than if they were native speakers going to mainstream schools. There also seems confusion as to which exams whey will sit, having seen the new Higher Still in Gaelic, for learners, I would expect children in P6 to cope with this. Surely some new category must be given to children in GMU [Gaelic-medium units], although not native Gaels, they are surely native speakers, being taught by natives from Pàrant is Pàisde, Cròileagan and GMU."

"Tha clann co-ionnan ri Native Speakers – tha seo a' leantainn air foghlam tro mheadhan na Gàidhlig, le taic o thelebhisean, o leabhraichean, o Rèidio nan Gàidheal agus a chionn 's gu bheil iad ga cleachdadh gu ìre aig an taigh."

Non-Gaelic Speakers in Gaelic-speaking Areas

"As an 'incomer' interested in learning Gaelic, I find people pleased but surprised (and sometimes embarrassed at their own lack of the language) and all this in a village which had many Gaelic speakers just one generation ago. Somehow we much change the climate so that people who move into the area to live see it as incumbent upon themselves to learn Gaelic. The Welsh have shown that it can be done. Of course, it could become threatening but I am certainly not in favour of – 'settler watch' mentality – I was born in England after all – however, it needn't be and after many years of Gaelic persecution perhaps it is time for a more 'in your face' approach."

Index

A
Abair Thusa 44
ability in Gaelic
  of grandparents 149t
  of respondents 152t–3t, 157t, 185t–8t
adult learners 1–2
  consortium 72–3
  defined 6
  in employment 4
  roles within GIDS 10–11
age of respondents 115t, 116t
An Comunn Gaidhealach 71
An Cùrsa Inntrigidh (Gaelic Access Course) 36
artificiality of Gaelic 87, 94, 96, 230

B
BBC Alba 50, 52
BBC Radio nan Gaidheal 13, 16, 49–51, 172t, 216
Board of Celtic Studies (Scotland) 31
books
  for courses 38–9
  as informal learning resource 46–7, 174t–5t
Bòrd na Gàidhlig 18–19, 28, 59, 70–1, 72, 74, 106
broadcasting 16, 17, 18
  as learning resource 47–51, 172t, 173t, 216
Broadcasting Act (1990) 61
Brown, Gordon, M.P., on saving Gaelic 1

C
CALL (Computer Assisted Language Learning) 31
Carnan 87
Census (1991) 185t–6t
Census (2001) 187t–8t
children of respondents 192t
Citizens of a Multilingual World 58
CLDRG (Community Learning and Development Review Group for Gaelic) 64, 66–7, 69, 72
CLI 64–6, 68, 70, 71, 72, 73, 108–10
  members by residence 119t, 120t
  members as learners of Gaelic 151t–2t
  sex of membership 113t
Clì Gàidhlig *see* CLI
Columba Initiative 71
Comhairle nan Eilean Siar 3, 13
Computer Assisted Language Learning 31
Comunn na Gàidhlig 1, 13, 15, 18, 43, 56–7
  strategic planning 71, 73
  target for secondary education 35

courses
   books 38–9
   deficiencies 37–9
   distance learning 36
   evening *see* evening classes
   intensive–full time 25–8, 74, 81, 215, 229
   open learning 36
   secondary school 32–5, 220
   summer 25, 42, 81
   university 29–32, 216
   weekend 25, 42

D
dictionaries 39–42
digital television 48, 62
discussion of RLS 231–4

E
economic position of respondents 125t
evening classes 22–5
   advances 23
   drop–out rate 24
   problems 22–4
   time–scale for proficiency 24

F
family–home–neighbourhood–community 7–8
Feumalachdan Luchd–Ionnsachaidh 20–1, 34, 36, 37, 39, 42, 46, 47, 68, 71, 229
Fishman, J. A.
   Can Endangered Languages be Saved? 3–4
   Graded Intergenerational Disruption Scale *see* GIDS
   theory of *Reversing Language Shift* 7–19
fluency target of respondents 153t–4t
funding for courses 70–1, 73

G
Gael, meaning of 98–103, 196t–7
Gaelic
   formal qualifications of respondents 155t
   learning *see* learning
   more than a means of communication 225t
   national or Highland language 14, 94
   need for new approach 221t
   need to teach in schools about 219t
   official status 200, 217
   in primary school 56–9
   problems with learning infrastructure 20–1, 229, 233
   promotion of 53–5, 200
   publicity for 54–5, 218t–219
   repondents' opinions 197t, 199t, 201t–4t, 207t, 209t, 211t

Index 275

secondary school subject 32–5, 33t
standardisation of 202, 224
Gaelic Access Course (*An Cùrsa Inntrigidh*) 36
Gaelic arts and culture 16–17
Gaelic broadcasting 16, 17, 18, 47–51, 172t, 173t, 216
Gaelic community, attitude towards learners 76–107
Gaelic in the Community (*Gàidhlig sa Choimhearsnachd*) 15
Gaelic development agencies 1, 13, 74
  lack of planning and research 14–15
Gaelic dialects 224
Gaelic economy, use of term 17
Gaelic houses 44, 216
Gaelic Language for Primary Schools (GLPS) pilot programme 57–8
Gaelic Language (Scotland) Act (2005) 18–19, 35, 54, 57, 72, 217
Gaelic learners
  distribution by country of residence 117t
  organisations 64
  students per year 32t
  see also learners
Gaelic Learners' Survey 33–4
  conclusion 228
  implications of findings 225–8
  methodology 108–11
  questionnaire format 252–66
  relevance to present day 111
  results *see* GLS, Comments; GLS, Gaelic in the Family; GLS, Learning Gaelic; GLS, Opinions on Gaelic; GLS, Respondents' Social Background; GLS, Using Gaelic
Gaelic native speakers *see* native speakers
Gaelic night clubs 45
Gaelic publications read by respondents 174t–5t
Gaelic related events, participation by respondents 176t–80t
Gaelic related organisations, respondents as members 189t–90t
Gaelic and Related Studies programme 28
Gaelic revivalists 86–7, 91
Gaelic sector, use of term 17
Gaelic speakers
  by age group 2–4
  community issues 84–92
  within family 3–4
  at home 191t
  by locality 2–4
Gaelic–medium education
  uptake 192t–5t
  viewed as a vacuum 15
Gàidhlig sa Choimhearsnachd 15
General Register Office for Scotland (GROS) 1, 2
GIDS (Graded Intergenerational Disruption Scale for Threatened Languages) 7
  explained 8–12, 9t
  relating to Gaelic 10–13

GLPS (Gaelic Language for Primary Schools) pilot programme 57–8
GLS, Comments 214–28
  future of Gaelic 224
  Gaelic development suggestions 217–20
  Gaelic more than means of communication 225t
  the learning process 214–17
  modern approach to learning 221t–3
  native speakers and learners 214
  need of publicity for Gaelic 218t–9
  need to teach Gaelic in schools 219t–20
  standardisation of Gaelic 224
GLS, Gaelic in the Family 191–5, 227–8
  children 192t–4t
  middle–school education 193t–5t
  pre–school education 192t
GLS, Learning Gaelic 151–71, 229–30
  level of competency 151t–3t, 226–7
  level of fluency 153t–5
  methods 171
  motivation 158t–170t
  qualifications 155t
  time spent 155t–7t
GLS, Opinions on Gaelic 196–213, 228
  development of Gaelic 199t–201
  difficulty of Gaelic 211t–13
  learning of Gaelic 202t–11
  linguistic issues 201t–2
  as national, regional language 197t–8
GLS, Respondents' Social Background 112–50, 225–6
  age 115t–16, 228
  education 122t–4t
  geographical location 116–17t
  grandparents' Gaelic speaking ability 148t–9t
  knowledge of languages 142–4t
  membership of interest groups 144–6
  national identity 134t–5t
  other identities 136t–40
  outside UK identities 140t–2
  place of residence within Scotland 118–120t
  place of upbringing 117t–18t
  politics 129t–34t
  religion 147t–8t
  residence in Highlands and Lowlands 120–2t
  sex 112t–15
  social class 126t–9
  socio–economic status 124t–5t
GLS, Using Gaelic 172–90, 227
  access to any Gaelic provision 183
  availability of suitable classes 181

Index

    better access to books, learning materials 182
    broadcasting and media 172t–5t
    desired services, facilities, activities 181
    Gaelic learners in *Census* 185t–8t
    Gaelic media 182
    increased use by public bodies 183
    membership of Gaelic–related organisations 188–90t
    opportunities outside classroom 181–2
    other uses 183
    participation in Gaelic–related activities 176t–81
    respondents outwith Scotland 184–5
Graded Intergenerational Disruption Scale for Threatened Languages *see* GIDS
GROS 1, 2

H
hobbies of respondents 160t

I
identification of respondents
    with Gael 137t–8t
    with Gaelic speaker 138t
    with Highlands 139t
    with Islands 139t
identity, retention of own 203t–4
identity of respondents 134t–6t, 140t–1t
immersion courses 25–8, 31, 74, 81, 110, 215, 229
interests of respondents 160t
Internet, learning resource 51–3

L
language ability of respondents 143t–4t
language shift, Gaelic to English 2–4
learners
    defined 76–8
    and native speakers 78–92
    and non–Gaelic speakers 92–6
    social identity 76–107
    views about native speakers 78–81, 267–73
    ways to attract 53–5, 75
    zeal for Gaelic issues 84–5
learning
    distance 36
    flexible 36
    informal 42–7
    infrastructure weaknesses 68–74
    Internet 51–3
    open 36
    as a process 97–104
    radio 49–51, 64, 172t

reading and writing 46–7
reasons for 161t, 163t–4t
respondents' difficulties 211t–12t
respondents' motivation 158t, 165t, 167t–70t
respondents' timescale 156t
self–help groups 43–5
social groups 43–5
teaching materials 37–9, 215
television 47–9, 59–64, 173t
to professional levels 31f
Likert–type five–point scale 197
links to other minority languages 223
Lìon 64, 67–8, 72, 73
location of respondents in UK 117t

M
Machair 60, 61
Ministerial Advisory Group on Gaelic, (2002) 2
Modern Language for Primary Schools (MLPS) initiative 57
motivation of respondents for learning Gaelic 158t, 165t, 167t–70t

N
national resource centre, recommendation for 39
native speakers 76–92
  appropriate use of Gaelic 89–90
  defined 76–8
  fall in numbers 1
  learners' views on 267–73
new Gael 101–2, 103
newspapers, informal learning resource 46, 174t–5t

P
political preference of respondents 129t–133t
Postgraduate Certificate of Education, teaching English to adults 69
primary school Gaelic 56–9
Provision for Gaelic Learners in Scotland (*Feumalachdan Luchd–Ionnsachaidh*) (1992)
  20–1, 34, 36, 37, 39, 42, 46, 47, 68, 71, 229
public funding, negative aspects 17–18
publicity for Gaelic 54–5, 218t–219

Q
qualification level of respondents 122t–4t
Questionnaire 112–228
  format 252–66
  results *see* GLS, Comments; GLS, Gaelic in the Family; GLS, Learning Gaelic;
    GLS, Opinions on Gaelic; GLS, Respondents' Social Background; GLS, Using
    Gaelic

R
radio
  for attracting learners 64
  as learning resource 49–51, 64

Radio nan Gàidheal 13, 16, 49–51, 172t, 216
religious affiliation of respondents 147t–8t
Reversing Language Shift *see* RLS
RLS
  basic principles 7–8
  discussion of 231–4
  Fishman's theory 7–19
  Gaelic learners summary 2–4
  relating to Gaelic 12–13
  Scottish initiatives 13–19

S
Scots 223
Scottish Qualifications Authority (SQA) 26
Secure Status for Gaelic 35
sex of respondents 112t
signage, use of Gaelic 53–4, 200, 218
social class of respondents by occupation 126t–7t
socio-economic status of respondents 124t, 125t
Speaking Our Language 1, 60, 61, 214–15
SQA (Scottish Qualifications Authority) 26
standardisation of Gaelic 202, 224
Stòrlann Nàiseanta na Gàidhlig 39, 70
strategic planning for learners 71–2
  solutions to problems 72–4

T
teaching materials 37–9
television 16, 17, 18
  for attracting learners 59–64
  as learning resource 47–9, 59–64
Telford College, Edinburgh 36
tourism to promote Gaelic 223
tutor training and support 68–70, 74, 81, 216

U
UHIMI (University for the Highlands and Islands Millennium Institute) 28, 30, 36
Ulpan system 70
university courses 29–32
upbringing of respondents by place 117t, 118t, 121t, 122t

W
websites, Gaelic–related 52–3
Welsh for Adults consortia 72
Welsh learners 83–5, 92–5, 98, 104